X

A PEACE DENIED

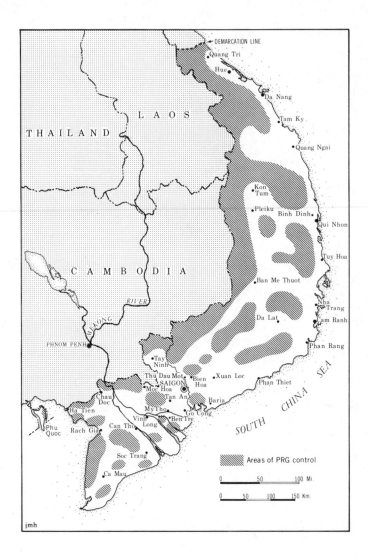

The PRG zone of control late 1972–early 1973. Adapted from the *Vietnam Courier* (Hanoi), February 1973.

A PEACE DENIED

The United States,
Vietnam, and
the Paris Agreement

Gareth Porter

INDIANA UNIVERSITY PRESS
Bloomington & London

Published in Canada by Fitzhenry & Whiteside Limited,
Don Mills, Ontario
Manufactured in the United States of America

Library of Congress Cataloging in Publication Data
Porter, Gareth, 1942-
A peace denied: the United States, Vietnam, and
the Paris agreement.
Includes bibliographical references and index.
1. Vietnamese Conflict, 1961-   --Peace.
2. Vietnamese Conflict, 1961-   --United States.
I. Title.
DS559.7.P67   1975   959.704'31   75-3890
ISBN 0-253-16160-6   1 2 3 4 5 79 78 77 76 75

CONTENTS

PREFACE

When the Paris Agreement on Vietnam was signed on January 25, 1973, most Americans hoped that it would not only bring home the last American troops and American prisoners of war but also put an end to the bloodshed and begin the process of healing the deep wounds of the Vietnam War. In the two years that followed, those hopes gave way to despair and cynicism over continuing fighting. Moreover, instead of ending its political and military involvement in Indochina, the United States continued to provide billions of dollars each year to support the wars in Vietnam and Cambodia up to the time of its sudden withdrawal in the spring of 1975.

During the period following the Paris Agreement, the question of war and peace was still very much in the hands of the United States, as it had been for a quarter of a century. And although the agreement had supposedly been the basis of US policy since January 1973, there seems to be little understanding of that agreement—how it came to be negotiated and why it did not bring peace to Vietnam. The terms of the agreement itself remain obscure, and even more important, the underlying political interests of the parties to the agreement which determined how—or whether—they would be implemented have tended more and more to recede from public understanding.

The purpose of this book, then, is to provide a coherent explanation of the failure of diplomacy to bring peace to Vietnam. The public dialogue on American policy in Vietnam since early 1973 has suffered from three circumstances: first, it has been divorced from the whole political-diplomatic history of the conflict —the basic continuity of policies in Hanoi, Saigon, and Washington over the past two decades on the question of a negotiated settlement of the Vietnam conflict. Certain common characteristics of the Geneva Agreement of 1954 and the Paris Agreement of 1973,

I believe, help to answer the question "Why did the peace agreement fail to bring peace to Vietnam?"

Second, certain critical facts about the negotiation of the Paris Agreement and then the negotiations over its implementation have not been publicized up to now, either because they were not made public by either party to the negotiations or because they were poorly reported. The result is that the public understanding of the relationship of the Nixon administration on one hand, and the Democratic Republic of Vietnam (North Vietnam) on the other, to the final agreement has been confused and distorted. It makes a great deal of difference to one's interpretation of the breakdown of the agreement whether one believes that it resulted from North Vietnam's being dragged, against its will, back to the negotiating table in January 1973, or whether, on the contrary, one sees it as the result of the exhaustion of the Nixon administration's resistance to North Vietnamese terms.

Third, the press, guided by a concept of "balanced" reporting which was more political than journalistic, assiduously avoided analysis of the responsibility for the failure of the agreement to bring peace. Reporters invariably contented themselves with formulas holding both sides to have violated the agreement, without examining the interests of the parties in relation to the agreement's provisions. This was in part because of a lack of understanding of the political dynamics of the situation but more importantly a result of pressures from editors not to appear too critical of US policy.

In order to fill in the major gaps in the existing public record, from June to November 1974 I interviewed a number of US officials who participated in the Paris negotiations, as well as American and Canadian officials involved in the negotiations within the International Commission for Control and Supervision and the Joint Military Commission established by the Paris Agreement. Much of the information on the negotiations and implementation of the agreement comes from these officials, who consented to be interviewed on condition that their names would not be used. I have not cited these interviews but have treated them journalistically. In addition, in December 1974 and January 1975 I was able to have several interviews in Hanoi with a member of the Central Committee of the Lao Dong Party, Hoang Tung, all of which were on the record. Those interviews are cited in the notes.

In order to put the Paris Agreement in proper perspective, I have also written an extensive analysis of the political, military, and diplomatic strategies of the United States and of the Lao Dong Party leadership since the inception of the struggle. Here again, public understanding of the policy of the Vietnamese revolutionaries has suffered over the years from inadequate attention to evidence from published and internal Vietnamese Communist documents. The historian of the Vietnam conflict is indebted to the works of George McT. Kahin and John W. Lewis, and Jeffrey Race, for their contributions toward constructing a more balanced political, military, and diplomatic history of the origins of the war by using documents from the other side. I have tried to present a more comprehensive interpretation of the Lao Dong Party's policy by drawing on both published documents and the captured documents now available in the collections assembled by Jeffrey Race and Douglas Pike. These collections were consulted at the Center for Research Libraries, in Chicago, and Cornell University's Wasson Collection, respectively.

The first three chapters on the background of North Vietnamese and US military and diplomatic strategies draw upon the research which I carried out intermittently between 1967 and 1973. During a visit to South Vietnam from June to August 1968 I was able to obtain documentation from reports of interrogations of Party cadres captured during the Tet Offensive. I also spent all of 1971 in South Vietnam researching the impact of Western imperialism on Vietnamese society.

During the research and writing of this book, I was a doctoral candidate in the Southeast Asia Program at Cornell University as well as Co-Director of the Indochina Resource Center, Washington, D. C. Without the support of my advisor, Professor George McT. Kahin, as well as that of Fred Branfman, Co-Director of the Indochina Resource Center, this book would not have been possible.

I wish to thank David Marr for reading the complete manuscript and offering helpful comments for revision, and John Spragens, Jr. and George McT. Kahin for reading parts of the manuscript and offering their comments. All of the interpretations are, of course, the sole responsibility of the author.

G.P.

ABBREVIATIONS

AID   Agency for International Development
ARVN   Army of the Republic of Vietnam (South)
CIA   Central Intelligence Agency (US)
COSVN   Central Office for South Vietnam (Lao Dong Party)
DRV   Democratic Republic of Vietnam (North)
DMZ   Demilitarized Zone
GVN   Government of Vietnam (South)
ICC   International Control Commission (1954–1972)
ICCS   International Commission of Supervision and Control
               (1973–)
JMC   Joint Military Commission
MACV   Military Assistance Command, Vietnam
NLF, NLFSV   National Liberation Front (South)
PF   Popular Forces (ARVN)
PLAF   People's Liberation Armed Forces (South)
PRG   Provisional Revolutionary Government of the Repub-
               lic of South Vietnam
RF   Regional Forces (ARVN)
RVN   Republic of Vietnam (South)
SAM   Surface-to-air missile
SEADAG   Southeast Asia Development Advisory Group
USIS   United States Information Service
USSAG   United States Support Activities Group (Thailand)

A PEACE DENIED

1: Negotiating Peace: The View from Hanoi

For nearly twenty-five of the past thirty years, Vietnamese revolutionaries were carrying on armed struggle. Yet they never resorted to arms without having first tried to negotiate with their foreign foes to find a peaceful solution which would permit the Vietnamese people to determine their own future. From the perspective of the Vietnamese, therefore, the warfare which plagued their country for all those years was brought by foreign powers—first the French and later the Americans—who tried to impose an alien political regime on Vietnam by force.

Even after entering into armed struggle, moreover, the leaders of the Lao Dong Party, far from being committed by doctrine or habit to resolving the conflict by military means, displayed a remarkable sophistication and flexibility in their diplomacy. The Vietnamese Communist leaders were uncompromising idealists in regard to the objectives of the revolution, but they also were utterly realistic and pragmatic when it came to war and peace. They knew that the defeat of foreign powers and their client governments would not come quickly or all at once but would have to be achieved in phases, by pushing their foes back one step at a time.

For Vietnam, a small, poor, underdeveloped nation, protracted resistance to the French and the Americans involved extremely high costs in human and material resources. And its leaders knew that the resistance could not end in the complete military defeat of the foreign power. The DRV—the Democratic Republic of Vietnam (North) thus had to accept negotiations and compromise with its foreign enemies as a fact of life and an integral part of the struggle. It needed periods of peace in which to consolidate political, economic, and military strength.

The Vietnamese leaders always believed that there was a time to negotiate and compromise as well as a time to move decisively in military and political struggle. And they held firmly to the view that every major advance in the revolution had to come when the objective conditions were right, and neither sooner nor later than that. At times, negotiations or diplomatic initiatives served the defensive purpose of trying to fend off or delay military confrontation in order to gain time and build up strength. At other times, in coordination with a military offensive, they were aimed at bringing an end to the war and forcing the French or Americans to make major political concessions. In both 1954 and 1972, negotiations were aimed at accomplishing both of these goals, signalling the end of armed struggle and the beginning of a phase of the struggle which would rely first of all on political rather than military means to defeat a foreign-sponsored government.

The willingness of the DRV to compromise in its diplomacy was also related to its desire to maximize political support in South Vietnam for the goal of replacing the Saigon regime with a more broadly based government. From 1954 on, the North Vietnamese leaders offered many substantial political concessions to those who did not share their goal of a socialist revolution in Vietnam, in order to win their support for an end to US military involvement and acceptance of a legitimate role for the revolutionary left in South Vietnamese political life.

The Party's attitude toward negotiations with the United States during the second Vietnam war was clearly shaped by the experiences of 1946 and 1954, when agreements with France were openly violated by the Western powers in spite of the willingness of the DRV to abide by them. The fate of these agreements underscored a general principle which was already part of the Party's operational code: that a foreign power which was determined to impose its will on Vietnam would carry out an agreement only to the extent that it was compelled to by the strength of the forces arrayed against it in the world, and, especially, in Vietnam itself. But although the Vietnamese leaders could never rely on diplomatic agreements alone to remove the influence of foreign powers from their country, they knew that they could never achieve the goal of complete independence without such an agreement. And their diplomacy therefore reflected the belief that a negotiated political settlement which brought about the retreat of imperialist military power and reaffirmed the right of the Vietnamese people to self-determination was in the interest of the revolution.

1. From the March 6 Accord to the Geneva Agreement

The first experience of the Vietnamese revolutionaries in negotiations with the French came only seven months after the DRV declared its independence from France in September 1945. The French government, having reached an agreement with the Chinese under which the latter would withdraw their troops from Tonkin, was preparing to introduce French troops into that region. The Ho Chi Minh government, unable to get any support from the United States against French ambitions to reoccupy Indochina, and facing the worst famine in contemporary Vietnamese history, desperately needed time to consolidate its economic and military position. So the DRV negotiated with France the March 6, 1946 accord, which recognized Vietnam as a "free state within the French Union" and allowed France to introduce 15,000 troops into Tonkin. These troops were to be withdrawn, however, at a rate of 3,000 per year beginning the following year. A referendum in Cochinchina was to determine whether that part of Vietnam, previously a full-fledged French colony rather than a protectorate like Annam and Tonkin, would become part of a reunified Vietnam.[1]

Vietnam's first peace agreement was an ambiguous compromise which satisfied no one, and the young Vietnamese government had to use all of its prestige with its people to maintain popular support for the agreement. But the conditions were not yet favorable for armed resistance, not only because the DRV was isolated internationally, but also because the revolution had not yet established a strong political base in many areas of the North and because the economy and defense of the DRV were still too weak. As one of Ho Chi Minh's top aides, Vo Nguyen Giap, explained to a large crowd in Hanoi on March 7, 1946, "we have above all negotiated to protect and reinforce our political, military and economic position. Our country is a free country, and all our freedoms are in our hands. We have all the power and all the time [we need] to organize our interior administration, to reinforce our military means, to develop our economy and to raise the standard of living of the people." Giap went on to point to the example of other nations which had been "able to surmount difficulties by knowing how to wait for an occasion more favorable to their progress." [2]

But the French, who were intent on reestablishing full control over Vietnam, began to violate the March 6 accord as soon as it was signed. French forces in Cochinchina carried out "police operations" against Viet Minh forces; they established new military enclaves in territory controlled by the Vietnamese at the time of the agreement, created a puppet Cochinchinese government, and equivocated on the referendum in Cochinchina on reunification with the rest of Vietnam.[3] The DRV negotiated almost continuously throughout the spring and summer with a recalcitrant France, knowing already that an all-out resistance to the French would come sooner than they had wanted it. The war began before the end of 1946, but not before the DRV had gained precious time through the negotiations to prepare for their military and political struggle.[4]

The second compromise settlement agreed to by the DRV, the Geneva Agreement of 1954, is crucial to an understanding of the DRV attitude toward negotiations with the United States during the second Indochina war. For the terms of the settlement established the fundamental framework of its policy toward the South for the next two decades. On one hand, the Communist leadership accepted a temporary division of the country into two zones and conceded control over the South to the French and their client regime. But on the other hand, they demanded—and obtained—French acquiescence to the principle that Vietnam was one country and could not be divided against her will. Moreover, they succeeded in getting a specific commitment to nationwide elections to reunify the two zones within two years. The negotiating behavior of the DRV at Geneva demonstrated its flexibility regarding the timing of the overthrow of the political residue of colonialism and the final reunification of the country, as well as its absolute inflexibility on the fundamental principle of the unity of Vietnam. Both aspects of the DRV negotiating behavior would be evident in its negotiating policy during the second war.

The Geneva Conference began at a time when France had just sustained its heaviest military defeat in the course of the eight-year war with the Viet Minh, and when the French government was under pressure at home to end the war quickly. The Viet Minh already dominated three-fourths of Vietnam and were in the process of expanding their political control in the heavily populated Red River Delta.[5] The balance of forces within Vietnam had swung so sharply toward the Viet Minh that an agreement which reflected that balance would have involved an early election and the quick withdrawal of foreign military forces. But US threats of military intervention had introduced a new factor which the Vietnamese leaders had to take into account. Beginning with Secretary of State John Foster Dulles's statement of March 29, 1954 calling for "united action" against the Viet Minh in Indochina, it appeared that there was a serious possibility that the United States might send ground troops or planes to Indochina. Such an intervention would mean that the war would not only be prolonged but also changed dramatically with the appearance of a new and far more powerful military force on the side of the French.

The Soviet Union and China were both eager to avoid this prospect, since their foreign policies were concerned with avoiding military confrontation with the United States and emphasized the possibility of peaceful resolution of East-West issues. Neither socialist power could look with equanimity on a failure by the Geneva Conference to negotiate a settlement which would prolong the war and could precipitate US military intervention in Indochina. The Soviets were making policy in Indochina, moreover, with an eye to the future of the European Defense Community, which they hoped the Mendes-France government would oppose if it survived the Geneva Conference.[6] It seems clear, therefore, that Soviets and Chinese were both urging moderation on the DRV at Geneva.

But the DRV leaders themselves had reason to want a quick end to the war even at the cost of concessions going beyond what was warranted by the political-military position of the French Union forces in Vietnam. They did not want to fight the United States as well as France, regardless of the degree of Soviet and Chinese military and diplomatic support. And the leaders of the DRV had to take into account the high cost of the nearly nine years of war to the millions of poor peasants who had supported and carried on the anti-French resistance. The mobilization of some 300,000 men into the Vietnam People's Army, in addition to the government and Party cadres and hundreds of thousands of civilians who served as part-time porters, demanded increased resources while at the same time disrupting production.[7] Both taxes and inflation were high, and the standard of living, already at a subsistence level for most Vietnamese, necessarily declined still further.[8]

The Vietnamese were acutely conscious of the adverse effect that indefinite prolongation of the war would have on a population which had been asked to make sacrifices in rice and in blood for so many years. The people needed a respite from war, and the DRV needed a period of consolidation, in which it could begin to carry out the social and economic tasks which had been so long deferred: the completion of land reform, increasing agricultural production, and establishing an industrial base for a socialist economy.

Editorials in the Party and Army newspapers, in April and May 1954, reflected the urgency with which the Party and government viewed the negotiation of a peace agreement and their alarm at the threat to such an agreement posed by US policy. As early as the first week in April, *Nhan Dan* (The People), the official organ of the Lao Dong Party, drew attention to the "warmongering plots of the American imperialists" and declared that peace-loving peoples were "determined to push the movement to demand the resolution of all international conflicts by means of peaceful negotiations." [9] *Quan Doi Nhan Dan* (People's Army) noted in an April 20 editorial that the United States had "tried by every means to prevent the peaceful solution of the Indochina problem" and said that the US agreement to go to the Geneva Conference was "an important success for us and the peace-loving peoples of the entire world." [10] The importance which the Vietnamese leadership placed on nailing down a settlement at Geneva was underlined in the April 23 issue of *Nhan Dan*, entitled "Ending the Indochina War Is an Urgent Demand." [11] A few days later, the same newspaper discussed the American attempt to prevent a settlement and specifically mentioned that the United States had "displayed its hydrogen bomb threat. . . ." [12]

The Soviet Union and China were instrumental in persuading

the DRV delegation to make two concessions which were quite generous to the French. First, the DRV agreed to draw the demarcation line between the two zones of control at the seventeenth parallel, thus giving up control over the Viet Minh strongholds in Quang Nam and Quang Ngai. And second, it agreed to put off the elections for reunifying the country for two years rather than the six months which they were first demanding.[13] Both of these concessions were made in the interests of breaking deadlocks and wrapping up the final settlement, but the Vietnamese may very well have felt that with stronger backing from their socialist friends they might have struck a better bargain.

But the most important element of the final settlement, which represented a compromise with far-reaching implications, was the decision by the DRV delegation to propose a division of Vietnamese territory into two temporary administrative zones. The alternative to this "two zones" arrangement was a "leopard spot" truce, with military regroupment zones scattered about the country. The French delegation had, in fact, suggested such a plan after consultation with its Vietnamese clients.[14] After carefully considering the advantages and disadvantages of each alternative, the DRV delegation chose a single demarcation line.

There were two major reasons for this choice. First, a "partition by enclaves" would have left the French-supported administration in control of the important cities, seaports, airports, and communications routes in both North and South Vietnam. By dividing the country into two zones, on the other hand, the DRV gained, in the words of one Viet Minh policy document, "more than half the population, a capital, a port, airfields, an airspace, a maritime zone, strategic communications routes, large cities, mines and economic opportunities." [15]

Only with these resources could the DRV consolidate its gains from the resistance in order to develop economically, politically, and militarily. As Ho Chi Minh explained in a speech to the Sixth Plenum of the Central Committee on July 15, 1954, "We must have an exceedingly large area [where we would have] enough means for building, consolidating, and developing our forces for the purpose of influencing other regions, and thereby bringing about reunification." [16]

Second, a "leopard-spot" arrangement, which the Party con-

ceded would have offered the revolutionary forces "bases which
could be used as springboards to attack the enemy" at a later
time,[17] would also have represented a dangerously unstable cease-
fire. The DRV leaders wished to avoid the possibility of provoca-
tions and incidents which the Diem government and its French and
American patrons could use in order to start the war anew.[18]

What the DRV decision for a single demarcation line meant,
then, was that the Party had already determined that a period of
peaceful development was more important than the possibility of
early reunification at the risk of renewed war throughout Vietnam.
The revolutionary movement in the South would not turn again to
armed struggle for an extended period of time, whether or not the
French and the Americans faithfully implemented the agreement's
provision for nationwide elections in 1956. Instead the Party would
rely on political struggle in the South in order to deal with the
problem of foreign imperialist domination.

The basic decision to concentrate on rebuilding the North
would shape the DRV's policy toward the South for the next two
decades, making possible an active and flexible diplomacy which
would seek a political compromise in the South falling far short of
immediate Communist control and immediate reunification. But
this did not mean that the Communist leadership accepted the
partition of the country into two ideologically hostile states, as part
of a deal between the United States and the Soviet Union. For the
DRV delegation, despite its willingness to compromise on setting a
date for the election and on the drawing of the military demarcation line, had steadfastly refused to compromise on the principle
that Vietnam was one country, which could not be divided against
the will of its people, and that the people would determine who
would rule a reunited Vietnam in elections which would be carried
out by a given date. The French, under pressure from Dulles,
attempted as late as July 16—four days before the signing[19]—to
resist the setting of a date for elections, but the Viet Minh were
adamant and refused to sign the cease-fire agreement in the absence
of such a provision.[20] Thus the cease-fire agreement recognized
explicitly that the demarcation line between the two zones was a
"provisional military demarcation line," and the final declaration
of the conference added that this line "should not in any way be
interpreted as constituting a political or territorial boundary." [21]

Equally important was the final declaration stating that "general elections shall be held in July 1956 under the supervision of an international commission composed of representatives of the Member States of the International Supervisory Commission. . . ."[22]

It has been suggested by some Western observers that the DRV delegates knew in advance that there would never be an election as called for in the agreement, because of a great-power understanding, and were thus resigned to the permanent partition of the country. But the behavior of both the DRV and the Viet Minh political apparatus in the South belies this argument. The Lien Viet (United National Front) organization, which was the broad political front that supported the DRV during the war against the French, made preparations for the election its first priority for 1955, and Party workers in the South were reported by Western sources to be hard at work propagandizing for the Viet Minh in the expected electoral contest.[23]

The Vietnamese thought that they had reason to believe that France would carry out its side of the agreement. After all, the Mendes-France government had come to power on the promise of a peace settlement in spite of American objections. It did not seem committed, therefore, to American plans to prevent the peaceful resolution of the Indochina conflict. The Party's analysis of French politics saw a cleavage within the French ruling class between the Laniel and Bidault governments, which were "partisans of war," and the Mendes-France government and its supporters, who were "partisans of peace."[24] The assumption of the DRV leaders at the time of Geneva that the Mendes-France government would not fall into line with US policy was revealed at a cadre conference following the Party's Seventh Central Committee Plenum in June 1955, in which it was admitted that there had been a mistake in seeing only the "contradictions" among the French, the United States, and Diem and not their fundamental agreement.[25]

Although it seems clear that the DRV government did have hopes that there would be elections in 1956, the evidence also suggests that the Vietnamese leaders were not so imprudent as to base all of their planning on that assumption. They knew, for example, that the United States would attempt to prevent the agreement from being carried out, by diplomatic and political means. And the American refusal to endorse the final declaration, with its commitment to an election within two years, reinforced the already existing suspicions of American intentions toward the agreement. As one DRV official later recalled, "The fact that Bedell Smith made a separate statement at Geneva was a warning." [26] The first few months after Geneva confirmed the worst fears of the Vietnamese leadership about the Americans, and showed that the French would not resist American pressures to build up the Diem regime as an anti-Communist bastion and evade the Geneva elections. By late October the radio station of the Viet Minh was warning its followers in the South that the Geneva Agreement was already running into grave difficulties. "Our struggle will certainly be difficult and complicated," it declared.[27] A week later, the former Chairman of the Southern Resistance Committee reminded Southerners that Uncle Ho had "announced a long-term struggle." [28]

2. *Diplomacy to "Maintain Peace": 1955 to 1960*

Although the DRV continued to press its demand for a consultative conference with the Diem government to arrange for free elections under the inspection of delegations from India, Canada, and Poland, Diem's refusal to negotiate over elections and the failure of the French—or the Soviets—to do anything about it were clear by mid-1955. But the frustration of their hopes for a peaceful reunification through elections did not change the basic decision which had already been made by the Party leadership in the North: whatever the difficulties in the South, the North needed peace above all else. As the Political Bureau of the Party reported to the August 1955 plenum of the Central Committee, "Under whatever circumstances, the North must be consolidated and taken to socialism." [29]

While ruling out a return to armed struggle in the South, the Vietnamese leaders believed that there was a good possibility that the revolution would triumph in South Vietnam without the intervention of the Vietnam People's Army or even a guerrilla war. The Party viewed the Diem regime as rent by serious internal contradictions and as lacking any solid base of popular support. To the extent that it served American interests in prolonging the division of the country and pursuing a policy of force rather than of reconciliation, in this view, it would alienate many of those in the government and the army who were opposed to Communism but tired of war and civil strife. "The fondest aspiration of the Southern people is to maintain peace and achieve national reunification," said a high-level Party directive on revolutionary strategy in the South in 1956. "The revolutionary movement in the South must be able to mobilize and move to success on the basis of raising the flag of peace, in harmony with popular feelings." [30] The document ordered the Party apparatus in the South to carry out a peaceful political struggle in support of the Geneva Agreement and to avoid precipitating an armed conflict. It tried to reassure Party members and sympathizers in the South that the revolution "can develop according to a peaceful line," despite the efforts by Diem and the United States to destroy the Viet Minh–Lao Dong Party organization. [31]

This new strategy in the South, forbidding for an indeterminate period any use of armed force, even in reprisal against local Saigon government officials who were repressing former resistants and Party members, [32] came close to asserting the possibility of overthrowing the Diem regime without any armed struggle, even though that regime was using "fascist violence." It urged the revolutionaries to "exploit the enemy's internal contradictions" in order to win over officials within the Diem administration, while it was strengthening the revolution's political base of workers and peasants. [33] Moreover, the new line required that the objective of the struggle in the South be the replacement of the Diem regime with a "national democratic" government, which would be nonsocialist in character. The Party, it said, had to form a "democratic alliance" with conservative political elements who were amenable to normal relations with the North. [34] As early as January 1956, non-Communist opposition politicians in the South reported that they were being quietly encouraged by the Viet Minh to topple Diem on the understanding that different regimes in the two zones could peacefully coexist and that reunification could be postponed "for as long as ten years." The only condition for such coexistence, according to these politicians, was the removal from South Vietnam of American military influence. [35] The Party newspaper *Nhan Dan* even gave prominent and favorable coverage to the views of the former pro-French premier Tran Van Huu, who was calling for a "social democratic regime" in Saigon which would establish normal economic and cultural relations between the two zones.[36]

The public diplomatic stance of the DRV toward the South was also attuned to the objective of producing a moderate reconciliatory regime rather than a revolutionary upheaval. The main feature of this conciliatory diplomatic stance, aimed at exploiting divisions within the Diem administration and the urban middle class in the South, was a series of proposals for normalization of relations between the two zones. While continuing to propose a consultative conference to discuss general elections for reunification of the country, the DRV began in 1956 to deemphasize immediate reunification in favor of a long-term process of normalizing relations in the economic and cultural fields.[37] This was seen as an intermediary phase which would "pave the way for contacts between the two sides leading to a consultative conference to discuss the question of the unification of the country through free national elections." [38] These proposals were made not only in speeches and diplomatic notes but also, during 1957, in personal diplomatic contacts between representatives of the two governments in Rangoon, Burma.[39]

In an attempt to remind its Southern compatriots of the traditional economic complementarity of the two zones, Hanoi offered to sell coal, cement, fabrics, handicraft products, fine art products, and paint to the South, and to buy in return rubber, coconut oil, sugar, coffee, *nuoc mam,* cinnamon, coconut fiber, hemp, and rice.[40] North Vietnam had always been a rice deficit area, while the South was a rice exporting area. The restoration of the traditional transfer of rice from Cochinchina to Tonkin would therefore have served the economic interests of both zones, while avoiding a reorientation of trade patterns which would increase the difficulty of eventual reunification.

But the DRV's diplomacy of normalization and its peaceful line in the South were both frustrated by the Diem government's policy of attempting to destroy any potential opposition to the regime. After the government moved in to occupy former Viet Minh areas, it launched a program of "anti-Communist denunciation" involving mass arrests, "people's courts," and frequent executions.[41] Tens of thousands were imprisoned and an unknown number executed in the Diemist terror.[42]

The peaceful line ordered by the Central Committee in the North was clearly unpopular with Party members and resistance veterans who were under the gun in the South. According to a Party Cadre's account of the Party's difficulties during this period, by 1958, "the majority of the Party members and cadres felt that it was necessary to launch immediately an armed struggle in order to preserve the movement and protect the forces." [43]

Until 1959, demands from the South for approval to use armed force were answered by a reaffirmation of the peaceful line of struggle from the Central Committee.[44] Although most Party members in the South faithfully followed this line, they could not understand how they could succeed in carrying on a political struggle without being able to defend themselves.[45]

By early 1959, when the Fifteenth Conference of the Central Committee was held, the Party leadership realized that the situation in the South had reached a critical stage, because the entire Party organization there was in danger of being wiped out.[46] Le Duan himself later told a cadre conference that by 1959 Party branches in the South had been up to 70 or 80 percent destroyed.[47] In this desperate situation the Central Committee, meeting in January 1959, authorized the limited use of armed force in the South to preserve the Party structure and to permit the development of a political struggle movement.[48]

But this decision did not mean that Hanoi approved the seizure of power in the South by military means. It was at pains to point out the limits on the use of armed force. As the Party's theoretical journal in the South emphasized, in explaining the new revolutionary line, "Armed struggle at present is not guerrilla warfare, nor is it long-term warfare, fighting to liberate zones and to establish a government as at the time of the resistance. Armed struggle at present is the whole people arming to defend themselves and to propagandize." [49]

"We had found an alternative so that there was little possibility of US armed intervention," said Central Committee member Hoang Tung in a later interview. "Out of a concern to avoid the possibility of armed intervention, we held that the liberation of South Vietnam was a direct obligation of South Vietnam. . . . We could have declared the 17th parallel no longer valid, because the French recognized the Vietnamese nation as one and the Geneva

Agreement recognized the reunification of Vietnam as a must." But in order to avoid any "provocation" to the United States, he recalled, the Party decided to adhere to the Geneva framework completely in the process of overthrowing the client regime in Saigon.[50] This was the meaning of Party Secretary Le Duan's remark in April 1960 that "in the present conjuncture . . . we can and must guide and restrict within the South the solving of the contradiction between imperialism and colonies in our country." [51]

While Party leaders in Hanoi had viewed the new line as limiting the use of armed force strictly to defense of the Party branches, those who actually carried it out in the South tended to view it as an authorization for ridding themselves of the local government apparatus which had been hunting them down and for seizing power openly in the countryside. Party leaders were unhappy with this development, which they feared could provoke a response by the United States and Diem and lead to a new war. The Regional Party Committee for the South, evaluating the first few months of implementation of the new line, complained that local Party organs were "getting into rash adventures," which were "destroying the legal status of the population." [52] Specifically the report mentioned such actions as "dissolving local administrative machinery, guiding people to tear up their ID cards, pushing them to commit provocative actions such as taking over posts, setting fire to village offices, cutting down trees, digging up roads, setting up obstacles. . . ."

Such activities, appropriate to a period of guerrilla warfare or general uprising, were "provocative" at a time when the leadership was determined to avoid a new war, and in particular a military intervention by the United States. The time had not yet come to "wipe out the enemy's government machinery," the circular warned. The Party could only "chip it and damage it." Armed activities were to be used only to "oppose terrorism," as an auxiliary to the political struggle.

But regardless of the determination of the Party leaders in the North to contain the struggle in order to carry on the rebuilding of North Vietnam, powerful forces had been unleashed in the South which could not be kept within the modest and defensive boundaries of the Party's line. A non-Party participant in the revolutionary movement later recalled in an interview with a US-financed research team that the Southerners were "ready for rebellion." They were, he said, "like a mound of straw ready to be ignited." [53] A sudden surge of revolutionary armed activity in late 1959 and 1960 shook the Diem apparatus to its roots. By the end of 1960, the revolutionaries claimed to control some 2,500 hamlets and to be administering two-thirds of them directly.[54]

Another result of violent change in the balance of power in the countryside, however, was a major step-up in the military operations of the Diem regime. Vietnam Press, the Saigon government's news agency, referred to several "mopping up operations" each month in 1960.[55] The Liberation Press Agency claimed that ARVN (Army of the Republic of Vietnam [South]) carried out twenty large-scale raids on revolutionary strongholds during 1960 involving forces of regimental or division strength.[56]

In order to deal with this escalation of violence, the Party once more had to adjust its policy in the South. At the Third Party Congress in September 1960 the Party recognized the necessity to develop regular military forces with which to counter Saigon's regular army. This shift in policy was reflected in the creation of a People's Liberation Armed Forces (PLAF) command in early 1961, and the rapid increase in military forces from only about 5,000 at the end of 1960 to more than 25,000 a year later.[57]

But even as it was recognizing the reality of an armed struggle in the South, which it had hoped at least to delay, Hanoi still insisted that the level of the struggle and its goals had to be subordinated to the interest of the revolution as a whole in a peaceful North Vietnam. As the language of the resolution of the Third Party Congress indicated, the Party leadership was determined to prevent the conflict from spreading to the North. The task of socialist construction in the North, the resolution said, was "the most decisive task for the development of the whole Vietnamese revolution [and] for the cause of national reunification." The resolution also reminded its followers in the South that the revolutionary struggle had the objective of overthrowing the Diem regime but also of "frustrating the attempts of the US-Diem clique to rekindle war." [58] This meant that the United States should not be given a pretext for an attack on North Vietnam. As one Hanoi broadcast to the South said, "Our Southern compatriots are always yearning for peace and are eager to find a way to liberate themselves with the least damage possible." [59] Hoang Tung described the Party's strategy in this period as "trying to win a special war by means of local uprisings and small-scale battles to make the Saigon administration disintegrate part by part . . . to make striking at the center unnecessary." [60]

The very creation of the National Liberation Front (NLF) in South Vietnam in December 1960 appears to have been aimed not at prosecuting an armed struggle for the overthrow of Diem, but at winning over a segment of the Diem administration and the urban political strata and ultimately precipitating a change of government in Saigon.

Significantly, the NLF was quite different in both form and function from its predecessors, the Viet Minh and the Lien Viet of the resistance period. It did not claim to be either a government or a political front in support of a government; rather it was created as a political front which openly invited those within the Saigon government and Saigon political circles who wished to end the war to negotiate with it on the formation of a new government. It was not until many months after its creation, in fact, that the National Liberation Front even developed organs at provincial, district, and village levels, suggesting that it may have been originally conceived primarily as a means of facilitating political contact and compromise with urban political elements who could overthrow Diem rather than as the political and administrative organ of an armed struggle.[61]

The record of DRV policy toward the South thus shows that even after the outbreak of fighting in late 1959 and early 1960, the Vietnamese leaders much preferred a *modus vivendi* with more conservative elements to an armed struggle, which they feared would bring a growing US military role and very possibly an attack on the North. The image of the Vietnamese Communists as infatuated by doctrines of violence and armed struggle, which became so popular in the United States during the war, could hardly have been further from the truth. With a set of priorities which ruled out war as a means of reunification, the DRV attempted to rely on a diplomacy of peaceful coexistence and normalization between the two zones and of compromise between revolutionary and anti-Communist elements in the South. And even when diplomacy gave way to armed struggle, the quest for a compromise political settlement continued.

3. *The Laotian Model and the Diplomacy of Neutralization*

The Geneva Agreement on Laos in July 1962 provided an opportunity for the DRV and NLF to open a diplomatic offensive on behalf of a political solution to the Vietnam war. For the first time since the Americans had replaced the French as the sponsors of the Saigon regime, the Vietnamese revolutionaries were interested in probing American willingness to negotiate. The Laotian solution had obvious relevance to the prospects for a settlement in Vietnam: on one hand, the Laotian tripartite coalition regime, whose neutrality toward the cold war power blocs was guaranteed both by internal agreement and by the great powers, provided a concrete example to skeptical South Vietnamese that a coalition government between Communist and anti-Communist elements was possible; on the other hand, the active participation of the United States in reaching the Laotian agreement seemed to suggest that the Americans were capable of diplomatic flexibility in situations where their political and military position was relatively weak.[62] The settlement was hailed by the DRV and NLF leaders, therefore, as evidence that a similar arrangement was possible for Vietnam.[63]

On July 20, 1962 the NLF issued a "four-point manifesto" which called for an "international agreement" to be signed by the great powers, to guarantee the "sovereignty, independence, territorial integrity and neutrality" of South Vietnam.[64] It also proposed the formation of a "neutral area," to include South Vietnam, Cambodia, and Laos as fully sovereign states. Even more important, the NLF statement modified its previous call for the overthrow of the Diem regime and brought its position into line with the Laotian model of a settlement. It asked that "concerned parties" stop the war and that a coalition government be formed, including representatives of "all political parties, cliques, groups of all political tendencies, social strata, members of all religions," thus including Diem and his followers. That government would then organize free elections for a new National Assembly, while pledging to keep itself free of all military blocs.

In effect, the DRV and NLF were now prepared to accept a South Vietnam whose independence and neutrality were guaranteed by the great powers in return for a guarantee of a political role for the NLF and the end of US military presence in the South. As long as the possibility of eventual reunification was not foreclosed and the United States was not in a position to dictate the political complexion of the South, the Communist leaders were willing to accept very far-reaching compromises in the sharing of political power.

The hope that the Kennedy administration would be willing to concede a political role for the Front and withdraw from South Vietnam as part of a "neutralization" agreement was frustrated by the administration's determination to resolve the problem by applying its counterinsurgency techniques. Although there was no response from Washington to its initiative, the DRV did not abandon its diplomatic efforts on behalf of a peace settlement. It turned increasingly to the French government and the influential Vietnamese exile community in France, which included many political figures of the French era. Tran Van Huu, former Prime Minister under Bao Dai, who led a small neutralist group in Paris called the Comité pour la Paix et la Rénovation du Sud-Vietnam, was approached by the DRV in Geneva in August 1962 and asked to use his influence with the French government to convince it that a neutralist solution for Vietnam was desirable and feasible. They asked Huu himself to take on the role played by Souvanna Phouma in Laos, leading the neutralist segment of a coalition government.[65] The DRV gave him formal assurances that the question of reunification could wait "fifteen or twenty years." [66]

In the spring of 1963 the problem of negotiating peace in Vietnam was suddenly transformed when President Ngo Dinh Diem and his brother Nhu came to the conclusion that the Americans represented a greater potential threat to Vietnam in general, and their own regime in particular, than the Communists. Embittered by what they perceived as American arrogance, suspicious of American motives, and confident of the success of their strategic hamlet program, they considered US military personnel both a political liability and a potential threat to the authority of the regime. Nhu announced in May 1963 that he wanted half of the 12,000 to 13,000 American military men to leave the country.[67]

At about the same time, Diem and Nhu decided to explore the possibility of a peaceful settlement with Hanoi. Nhu confided to a former Vietnamese premier that he intended to find a *modus vivendi* with "the men of Dien Bien Phu." [68] Diem and Nhu summoned Mieczyslaw Maneli, head of the Polish delegation to the International Control Commission, and asked him to sound out Hanoi on terms for a cease-fire, through French Ambassador Roger Lalouette.[69]

The Party leadership in Hanoi responded to this approach by Diem by making a new, more generous offer of a negotiated settlement, under which US forces would be removed and a cease-fire arranged. In the spring and summer, both Ho Chi Minh and Pham Van Dong discussed with Maneli a plan under which a coalition government, including NLF representatives, would be formed which would develop normal postal, economic, and cultural relations with North Vietnam but would remain separate for some years. After much prodding by Maneli, the North Vietnamese finally agreed that Diem could head such a coalition.[70]

The contacts between Diem and the North through the Polish intermediary thus resulted in agreement on some basic principles of a peace settlement. In September Diem and Nhu decided to reach a definitive agreement. Tran Van Dinh, then an RVN diplomat in the Embassy in Washington who had dealt with DRV representatives on behalf of Diem as Ambassador to Rangoon in 1957–58, was chosen to complete the negotiations with the North Vietnamese in New Delhi in November. According to Dinh, in late September President Diem told him, in a three-hour interview filled with bitterness against the Americans, that there was already agreement on a cease-fire, the departure of all US forces, and the acceptance of NLF representatives into his government and an election—possibly within a year—in which the Communists could participate.[71] Before Dinh reached New Delhi as Minister Plenipotentiary, however, Diem and Nhu were dead—and the peace plan with them.

Taking advantage of the fluidity of the political situation in Saigon in the wake of the coup, the Front approached the new military junta with a plan for a peace settlement. Through various intermediaries, including the Vietnamese neutralists in Paris, who were personally close to leading figures in the new regime, such as

Chief of State General Duong Van Minh, the DRV and NLF renewed their offer to negotiate a cease-fire in return for the formation of a broader government with a neutralist policy, to include the NLF.[72] At the same time, another offer of a neutralist solution was communicated to the United States through UN Secretary U Thant.[73] The State Department again vetoed any neutralist arrangement on the ground that the military regime was far too feeble to hold its own in any political competition with the Front.

As the Saigon government's political and military position declined during 1964, the threat of a military confrontation between the United States and the Vietnamese revolutionaries, North and South, was posed more sharply than ever before. In December 1963 the Party Central Committee had held its Ninth Plenum and had passed a resolution calling for a step-up in the war effort to "rapidly strengthen our military forces in order to create a basic change in the balance of forces between the enemy and us in South Vietnam." But the resolution also made it clear that the Party was still eager to avoid an escalation of the war which would result in its spreading to North Vietnam. "Because of the necessity to contain the enemy in the special war and confine this war within South Vietnam, the participation in the war by North and South Vietnam is different," the document said.[74] The DRV was determined not to offer the United States an excuse to attack the North or send troops to the South by intervening in the South in force. As Premier Pham Van Dong told Canadian diplomat J. Blair Seaborn in mid-1964, "The DRV will not enter the war . . . we shall not provoke the U. S." [75]

The DRV apparently hoped that the military setbacks sustained by Saigon would put pressure on the United States to consider negotiations as an alternative to escalation. Throughout 1964, as the NLF stepped up its recruitment and its military attacks, spokesmen for the Front and North Vietnam confided to foreign diplomats and journalists, as well as to foreign Communist delegations, that they did not seek a military victory in the South but desired a political settlement. A North Vietnamese diplomat told a French journalist in April 1964 that it was militarily impossible for the Front to seize power in Saigon.[76] And Lao Dong Party leaders explained to a French Communist Party delegation that they were willing to accept the political separation of North and South Vietnam for an indefinite period, as long as the South was free of American interference and the two halves of the country could at least enjoy normal commercial relations and freedom of movement for civilians.[77]

Clearly, this willingness to accept an independent and neutralized South Vietnam for many years was in part a means of sweetening for the United States the bitter pill of withdrawing its military presence and allowing South Vietnam to go its own way. But, as the Vietnamese frequently explained to foreigners, there were even more fundamental reasons for Hanoi and the Front to view the problem of reunification as one to be solved only over a good many years. The impact of more than eighty years of colonial rule and of nearly a decade of American hegemony in the South had given the two zones very different social and economic structures. By 1964 North Vietnam had undergone a socialist transformation in the agricultural field as well as in industry and handicrafts. The South, of course, had an economy which encouraged the accumulation of wealth by private capitalists and a society which had become undisciplined, if not anarchic.

The long and unbroken period of economic and political dependence on foreign powers had produced a wealthy and educated middle and upper class in the South which feared the revolutionary change which they thought would result from immediate reunification. The political unity which existed in the North after the regroupment of 1954–55, as the Vietnamese leaders admitted, was not matched in the South. The North Vietnamese, according to a French Communist delegation which visited the country in 1965, "recognized frankly the reservations which a large fraction of South Vietnamese people have with regard to Communism and their rejection of Hanoi's leadership." [78] Once the Americans were finally gone from the South, Vietnam would need the talents of those managers, entrepreneurs, technicians, and intellectuals who were hostile to Communism. And in order to have their cooperation, the Front's Secretary General Huynh Tan Phat said in 1965, their demands for all the individual freedoms found in a bourgeois democracy would have to be respected.[79]

Consistent with their Marxist-Leninist ideology, the Vietnamese Party leaders did not believe that the "objective conditions" for a socialist revolution existed in South Vietnam. The South would have to go through a period of social and political change, once the Americans departed, in order to bring those conditions about. In the meantime, why should the Party be eager to take on the unnecessarily difficult and hazardous task of trying to impose socialism on a society which was not yet ready for it? The Lao Dong Party's support for an autonomous, nonsocialist South as part of a negotiated settlement was thus in accord not only with its immediate interest in building a viable socialist economy in the North and protecting it from American attack, but also with its ideological tenets.

July and August 1964 brought yet another diplomatic offensive by the DRV in favor of a negotiated settlement, supported now by France, the Soviet Union, and U Thant. On July 16 the DRV representative in Paris, Mai Van Bo, supported the convening of a new Geneva Conference on Indochina. Within a few days both U Thant and President de Gaulle had made similar proposals for a new conference, primarily aimed at resolving the Vietnam conflict. And on July 25 the Soviet government called upon the participants in the Geneva Conference on Laos to reconvene.[80] This Soviet initiative met with a prompt and positive response from Hanoi, which urged the reconvening of the conference "as rapidly as possible . . . to preserve the independence, peace and neutrality of Laos and to preserve the peace of Indo-China and Southeast Asia." [81] Then, following the Gulf of Tonkin incident and the American bombing raids against the North, Hanoi undertook two more diplomatic initiatives: first, it asked the Co-Chairmen of the 1954 Geneva Conference once again to convene the conference; at the same time, it communicated to U Thant its willingness to meet privately with US representatives.[82]

But the United States once again closed the door, both publicly and privately, as it had done in 1962 and 1963, on any possibility of negotiations or an international conference to deal with the Vietnam problem. And by the end of 1964, Hanoi faced mounting evidence that the United States would carry the war to the North before it would agree to a political settlement. As the possibilities for diplomacy seemed to be reduced to zero, events also seemed to open up the prospect for a quick military victory in the South. The morale and effectiveness of ARVN continued their downward spiral, as defeat and desertions seriously weakened Saigon's regional and popular forces.[83] It must have appeared to the leaders in Hanoi that a concerted drive to destroy ARVN main force units could cause a military collapse in a relatively short period of time—perhaps before the United States could intervene with its own troops in the South.

Equally important in the changing North Vietnamese perspective on the struggle in the South was an event which appeared to the rest of the world to bear no relationship to the Vietnam conflict: the replacement of Khrushchev by the team of Brezhnev and Kosygin in the Soviet Union. Khrushchev, whose policy of détente with the United States and lukewarm attitude toward support of revolutionary movements in the third world had been one of the central issues in the widening dispute with China, had apparently had little enthusiasm for the war in the South, and presumably opposed any push for military victory regardless of the refusal of the Americans to engage in a negotiated settlement. Hanoi had been openly critical of the Soviet policy of détente and placed most of the blame for disunity in the socialist bloc on Khrushchev. A Party reorientation document dated March 1965 went so far as to call Khrushchev a "traitor who distorted revolutionary ideals." [84] The Vietnamese leaders knew that in any military confrontation with the United States they could not count on strong Soviet backing.

But after Khrushchev's ouster, the new Soviet leaders adopted a much firmer policy in support of the DRV and NLF. Three weeks after the collective leadership took charge in Moscow, DRV Prime Minister Pham Van Dong visited Moscow on the occasion of the annual celebration of the October revolution. The results of his talks with Soviet leaders appear to have been significantly increased economic and military aid [85] to the DRV and a new understanding on strategy regarding the war in the South. Moscow and Hanoi would continue to press for a negotiated settlement, but if the United States refused, the Soviet Union would support an offensive aimed at bringing about the military collapse of ARVN and deter the United States at least from invading North Vietnam. Late in 1964, according to the Pentagon's account, Soviet Foreign Minister Gromyko assured the DRV that the Soviet Union would support it against aggressive actions against the North by the United States.[86]

The crucial importance of the turn in Soviet policy in

permitting the North Vietnamese to plan for a military push in the South was underlined by Party Secretary Le Duan in an address to Party cadres in July 1965. "The attitude of the Soviet party today regarding strengthening the socialist camp as well as regarding the national liberation movement in general and Vietnam in particular is different from that of Khrushchev before," he said. The Soviet comrades, he added, "agree completely with our path. . . ." [87]

The decision to go for an all-out military campaign in the South, therefore, must be understood in the context of the "opportune moment" *(thoi co)*. From the very beginning of the Communist movement in Vietnam, when Ho taught a course in Canton on revolutionary theory to the first recruits of the Vietnam Revolutionary Youth League, he emphasized the importance of learning to assess the "balance of forces," not only within Vietnam but in the world outside as well. "Because they do not understand the world situation, do not know how to assess the balance of forces and lack tactics," Ho had told his disciples, "people often act when conditions are not ripe and inversely they do not act when they should." [88] It was the conjunction of favorable conditions in Vietnam and abroad that triggered the decision to launch the August Revolution in 1945, and again, to go over to the counter-offensive against the French in 1951.[89]

The DRV had tried to compromise on the South in order to strengthen the North while waiting for the situation either in the South or within the socialist bloc to change in their favor. After the start of the armed struggle in 1960, the situation in the South ripened, but the unity of the socialist camp had been disrupted by Khrushchev's détente policies. By late 1964, the international situation and the situation in Vietnam had come into convergence, presenting, in the view of the Vietnamese leaders, the "opportune moment" for a decisive move forward. They feared that to let the occasion pass would risk losing the momentum built up in the South, and perhaps the strong support of the Soviets as well.

As noted earlier, the DRV had for many years deliberately pursued a policy of avoiding any provocation of an American attack on the North, in order to preserve its hard-won economic gains as well as to avoid the massive destruction and loss of life which they knew would accompany such strikes. They had hoped, moreover, for either an internally generated political change in the

South or a decision by the United States to negotiate a political settlement. By the end of 1964, however, the DRV was prepared to send some combat units from the North into battle in the South if necessary in order to inflict a decisive defeat on the Saigon forces. This decision was not taken lightly. Clearly the Party would have held back its own combat units from the South if it had felt that it would be permitted to defeat ARVN with Southern troops alone, without large-scale destruction of the North.

But the multiple warnings which the United States had conveyed to the DRV throughout 1964 did not appear to leave open that option. For these warnings had made no distinction between a military threat to Saigon by Southern revolutionary forces alone and one in which troops from the North were engaged. As the Defense Department account of the period points out, the United States had carried out an "essential psychological campaign" to convince Hanoi that it was considering escalating the war if the war in the South was not called off. This campaign included "hints and warnings that the United States might escalate the war with countermeasures against North Vietnam, such as guerrilla raids, air attacks, naval blockade, or even land invasion." [90] On June 18, 1964, before the Gulf of Tonkin incident, the United States had dispatched J. Blair Seaborn, the Canadian delegate to the International Control Commission, to Hanoi with the message that it intended to "see the [South Vietnam government's] writ run throughout SVN [South Vietnam]," and that "U.S. patience was running thin." Seaborn also warned that if the conflict should escalate, "the greatest devastation would of course result for the DRV itself." [91]

The American air strikes against the North in reprisal for alleged attacks by North Vietnamese PT boats on US destroyers in the Gulf of Tonkin indicated to the DRV that the United States was prepared to bomb the North, whether or not the Vietnam People's Army entered the South. Premier Pham Van Dong, in another meeting with Seaborn on August 13, declared that the United States had found it "necessary to carry the war to the North in order to find a way out of the impasse . . . in the South," and said he anticipated further attacks. He repeated that the North had "tried to avoid serious trouble; but it becomes more difficult now because the war has been carried to our territory. . . ." [92] On

September 29 US Assistant Secretary of State William Bundy, in a speech in Japan, declared that "expansion of the war outside South Vietnam" could be "forced upon us by the increased external pressures of the Communists, including a rising scale of infiltration." In a background briefing with American newsmen, Bundy revealed that there were already contingency plans for bombing staging bases in Laos and North Vietnam.[93] Meanwhile, the United States was accelerating the construction of major airbases in Thailand and South Vietnam, establishing stockpiles of bombs, and carrying out such provocative actions as maritime raids by Saigon's forces against the North Vietnamese coast and US destroyer patrols close to the coast in the Gulf of Tonkin.[94]

Far from miscalculating about the American response to a Liberation Army offensive in the South, therefore, the DRV was fully expecting air attacks on the North, probably a commitment of US combat troops in the South, and possibly even an invasion of the North by US and Saigon forces. An internal Party document issued on January 2, 1965 as part of a "reorientation campaign" suggested that the Americans might "increase attacks and destruction of the North," intervene in Laos and Cambodia, launch a "full scale war with the more direct participation of U.S. troops and troops from U.S. client states," or "broaden the war to the whole country," meaning an invasion of the North.[95] The DRV was prepared to meet an invasion of the North by calling on the Chinese for assistance if necessary. "At that point," declared Le Duan, in a mid-1965 address, "we would not be fighting the U.S. alone; there would also be our whole camp, and especially China. Striking into North Vietnam means that the U.S. has the intention of fighting with China, because North Vietnam and China are two socialist countries linked extremely tightly to each other." [96]

The very high probability that the United States would broaden the war into North Vietnam in order to save Saigon from military defeat—*whether or not military units from the North were involved in the South*—gave the DRV no incentive for holding back its own main force units from the South; on the contrary it would be in their interest to conclude the destruction of ARVN as quickly as possible, before the United States could carry out a major military build-up in the South. These were probably the considerations underlying the decision in late 1964 to send three regiments of the

Vietnam People's Army, some 4,500 men, into the South. As long as the United States kept the door closed to a diplomatic settlement, there was no way to end the war except by dealing a shattering blow to ARVN. The "opportune moment" for such an offensive had arrived, and not even the threat of US intervention and devastation of the North could defeat that decision.

4.   Fighting for a "Stalemate"

One of the likely US responses to the progressive disintegration of the Saigon army, as noted above, was to launch a "full-scale war" with American troops and those from client states in Asia and the Pacific. It was no surprise to the DRV leaders, therefore, when the United States began in 1965 a major build-up of combat troops and air power in Vietnam. But the Vietnamese leaders saw the Americanization of the war in the South merely as opening up a new phase of the conflict. Although they were realistic enough to know that the Americans could not be physically driven into the sea, they also felt confident that the Americans could not gain control of the situation militarily or politically. And failing that, they reasoned, the United States would have to give up its original ambitions and agree to a compromise such as they had been offering.

So the DRV decision on an all-out military effort in the South did not change its willingness to agree to a diplomatic settlement, although the *emphasis* of DRV policy shifted toward its determination to resist the American onslaught until its principles for a settlement were recognized. After the United States began bombing North Vietnam on a daily basis and sent combat troops to South Vietnam, the DRV refused to come to the conference table for "unconditional discussions," but issued instead its "four points" of April 8, 1965, as the basis for a negotiated solution:

1. Recognition of the basic national rights of the Vietnamese people: peace, independence, sovereignty, unity, and territorial integrity. According to the Geneva agreement, the US government must withdraw from South Vietnam US troops, military personnel, and weapons of all kinds, dismantle all US military bases there, and cancel its military alliance with South Vietnam. It must end its policy of intervention and aggression in South Vietnam. According to the

Geneva agreements, the US government must stop its acts of war against North Vietnam and completely cease all encroachments on the territory and sovereignty of the DRV.

2. Pending the peaceful reunification of Vietnam, while Vietnam is still temporarily divided into two zones the military provisions of the 1954 Geneva agreements on Vietnam must be strictly respected. The two zones must refrain from entering into any military alliance with foreign countries and there must be no foreign military bases, troops, or military personnel in their respective territories.

3. The internal affairs of South Vietnam must be settled by the South Vietnamese people themselves in accordance with the program of the NLFSV without any foreign interference.

4. The peaceful reunification of Vietnam is to be settled by the Vietnamese people in both zones, without any foreign interference.[97]

Hanoi's terms for a settlement thus left considerable room for negotiation as to the character of a transitional government and a new political process. The reference to the National Liberation Front's program in the third point, to which the Americans immediately raised objections, did not foreclose such negotiations at all but merely stated the demand that the existing government give way to one which would be more broadly representative of the various social and political forces in South Vietnam. The program actually stated that the Saigon regime had been imposed by the United States, and demanded that it be replaced by a government "composed of representatives of all social classes, of all nationalities, of the various political parties, of all religions." It also called for a new constitution, elections for a new national assembly, and the institution of democratic liberties.[98] There was nothing in the NLF program, nor in the four points demanding a regime controlled by the NLF, which ruled out free choice by election of a new government.

But while the document left wide latitude for negotiations on the modalities of transition to a postwar political system, it also made clear what it would not concede. Two of the principles were direct challenges to American policy in Vietnam: the principle that the Saigon regime did not represent the political will of the South Vietnamese people and would not be permitted to rule; and the principle that Vietnam was one country and could not be divided against the will of the people. "There are matters which are negotiable and those which are not," said a DRV official in July 1965. "For us Vietnamese the unity of our country is no more a matter for negotiation than our independence. It is not possible to accept a discussion of the basis of the partition of Vietnam." [99]

This was another expression of the sharp distinction which the DRV had made at Geneva in 1954 and would continue to make during the long years of diplomatic maneuvering between the modalities of bringing about a transitional regime and the fundamental principles for which they were fighting. For the armed struggle which the NLF was carrying on with DRV support was conceived not as a bid for power by the Communist Party or the Front or a socialist ideology, but a struggle against the imposition of an anti-Communist regime in the South and the partition of the country by the United States. It was, in fact, precisely because the objectives of the struggle were defined in terms of national independence rather than in terms of power for a particular party or group that the diplomacy of the DRV would be able to make tactical concessions in negotiations with the United States.

Such considerations shaped the attitude of the DRV toward American offers of "unconditional discussions" and for "mutual deescalation," as much as practical considerations. Although the DRV could have seized upon the American offer to open talks and use them as a propaganda forum for its own position, it refused, fearing that it would have lent some legitimacy to the American military intervention at a time when the United States was not yet ready to negotiate seriously. The DRV always insisted that its diplomatic stance reflect the moral distinction between the two sides, which was central to the meaning of their struggle: the Americans were aggressors—foreigners with no legitimate basis for their presence in Vietnam—while the DRV and the NLF were engaged in a fight for national independence and unity. Thus the DRV continued to insist that it would not come to the conference table while the bombing of its territory continued, even though it softened its original position that the four points had to be accepted by the United States as the basis for a settlement before talks could begin.

Similarly the DRV was never willing to commit itself publicly to any "reciprocal action" in return for an end to the bombing. To accept a limitation on its own actions in the South in return for a halt to the bombing would imply that the two actions were equally illegitimate, and this the DRV could not accept. As Vietnamese officials often pointed out, the DRV could not offer any matching military concession for a bomb halt, since it was not conducting any similar military activity against US territory.

The DRV refusal to offer any concession in return for a bombing halt was also based on the Party leadership's conviction that the United States was not seriously interested in negotiating a settlement and was manipulating its "peace efforts" to placate US public opinion and to cover its escalation of the war. This conviction was reinforced as the United States continued to increase its troop strength in South Vietnam, escalated the air war against the North, and publicly declared its refusal to withdraw its troops until the insurgency was brought under control. The timing of a new round of bombing of Hanoi in December 1966 to coincide with the beginning of a scheduled meeting between the US and DRV representatives in Warsaw was undoubtedly taken as another signal of American disinterest in substantive negotiations. "The American imperialists' familiar trick is to couple the intensification of their aggressive war with a ballyhoo about their 'will for peace,' " declared General Vo Nguyen Giap in a January 1966 article.[100] The DRV did not want, by participating in public talks with the United States, to help give the impression that the United States was trying to bring about a peace settlement.

Moreover, the Vietnamese had the distinct impression by mid-1967 that the Americans were planning to turn up the pressure against the North in the hope that the DRV would agree to American demands. Pham Van Dong told two French intermediaries in July 1967 that his government believed the Americans were still determined to achieve a military victory. "U. S. power is enormous and the U. S. government wants to win the war . . . ," he said. He expected that the attacks on the North would increase still further, and the DRV government had already made provision against attacks on the network of dikes which prevented flooding in the Red River Delta.[101]

So the DRV was determined to avoid any move which might be seen by the United States as a sign of weakness and which would thus encourage the advocates of victory through bombing the North. After interviewing Pham Van Dong in September 1967, American journalist David Schoenbrun was told by the DRV Foreign Ministry official Ngo Dien that he should not begin his story by referring to the DRV's terms for peace but rather with Dong's expression of "determination to resist American aggression." The story Schoenbrun had written, Dien complained, made it "look as though the Prime Minister put his major emphasis on peace talks and took the initiative to tell you his peace terms." This was not correct, the official said. "He placed his major emphasis on our refusal to be pressured or beaten down by bombing." Schoenbrun noted that, at a time when the bombing was being escalated, Hanoi was "fiercely determined not to give the slightest sign that they could be pressured into talks." [102]

From early 1965 until 1968, then, the DRV's diplomatic stance remained virtually frozen by its perception of the United States as aiming at military victory. Thus the United States would be ready to negotiate a compromise settlement, the Party leaders reasoned, only when it became convinced that such a victory was no longer possible. Their strategy for the war in the South was thus aimed at compelling the Americans to admit that they could not win. In order to defeat the Americans, they believed, it would not be necessary to achieve a conventional military victory over US forces, or even necessarily to win a single decisive battle. It was only necessary to prevent the Americans from succeeding in their aims of destroying the main force units of the People's Liberation Armed Forces and pacifying the countryside. By frustrating the American strategy, they could bring about a situation of stalemate, which to the Vietnamese meant failure and defeat for the Americans. In order to avoid a "stalemated situation" [103] the Americans had to both destroy the PLAF and capture the population of the countryside, which was largely in the hands of the Front. If they did not succeed in these tasks within a relatively short period of time, they would be defeated.[104]

As Giap and his colleagues compared the war against the Americans with the war against the French, they believed the Vietnamese resistance held an infinitely stronger position in relation to the Americans than it had in the early stages of the first war. The PLAF was already in an "offensive" when the first

American combat troops arrived. Indeed, the Americans had been forced to send their own troops to "rescue" the Saigon government because the revolutionary forces were on the verge of winning militarily in 1965, and the population was already mobilized to resist the Americans from the start.[105] So the struggle would not have to recapitulate the "defensive" and "equilibrium" phases of the resistance war against France. While the Party still adhered to the principle of "protracted war" and set no time-table for how long it would take to force the Americans to leave Vietnam, its leaders also thought that it would be possible to defeat the Americans in a "relatively short period of time"—only a few years instead of the eight or nine years required to force the French to negotiate an agreement.[106]

From this analysis had emerged a military strategy of "continuous offensives," with maximum military pressure on both the Americans and the Saigon army in order to compel the United States to admit that it was stalemated and could not win a military victory.[107] When the Americans finally recognized their real situation, the Party leaders believed, it would mark the beginning of the last stage of the war: the "stage of fighting while negotiating." The United States would then indicate that it was interested in serious negotiations. General Nguyen Van Vinh, an alternate member of the Central Committee, explained in a speech to Party leaders in the South in April 1966 that the fighting would continue "until the emergence of a situation where both sides are fighting indecisively. Then a situation where fighting and negotiations are conducted simultaneously may emerge." During the phase of fighting while negotiating, according to Vinh, the two sides would be struggling to determine the final terms of the settlement. The revolutionary forces would then have to "fight to win great victories with which to compel the enemy to accept our conditions," he said. The war would finally end with the negotiation and signing of an agreement which would reflect the superior strategic position of the NLF.[108]

The immediate strategic problem for the Lao Dong Party, therefore, was to transform a situation which was, in General Vinh's words, "not yet ripe for negotiations" into one which was. By mid-1967 the Americans had not yet been able to alter the basic strategic advantage which the NLF had held more than two years earlier when they were on the verge of complete victory. But the Americans were not yet ready to acknowledge their quandary. As one of the leading Communist military commentators, Truong Son, wrote in June 1967, the United States and Saigon had "not yet sustained very serious defeats" but they had also "not yet been able to reach any strategic objectives." And while the United States was still strong militarily, it had been "driven into a political, strategic and tactical crisis," because its expectation of a quick military victory over the NLF had been shattered. Despite "repeated defeats," however, the United States, "because they are stubborn and because they have large forces, still hope to secure a military solution and decisive victories on the battlefield. . . ." [109]

In other words, the Americans had been frustrated but were not yet out of strategic options. In order to hasten the stage when the United States would have to recognize a strategic stalemate, therefore, the Liberation Army had not only to maintain the initiative, but to try to push the struggle to an even higher level. The time was judged ripe for the most important campaign of the war, the first "General Offensive and Uprising" against the American forces and the Saigon regime. As early as December 1965 the Party Central Committee had considered that the Liberation Army was "in preparation for a general offensive and uprising which will take place when the opportunity avails itself and the situation ripens." [110] The offensive planned for the winter and spring of 1968 would be aimed at a political and military breakthrough, a "forward leap" such as was referred to by Truong Son when he said in a 1966 article that the development of a war "usually has forward leaps that we must take advantage of to step up the process and results of war." [111] It would be known to the rest of the world as the "Tet Offensive."

2: Negotiating Peace: The View from Washington

From the time it first became involved in the Vietnam conflict on the side of the French, the United States regarded it as a problem to be settled by force rather than by diplomacy and negotiations. The possibility of negotiations was not merely ignored by US policymakers but deliberately rejected. One searches in vain through the record of American policy in Vietnam for evidence of willingness to accept any outcome but the elimination of the Viet Minh and their successors as a political force. A political compromise which might have avoided or brought an end to the bloodshed was ruled out every time the opportunity presented itself. Instead the United States always chose to crush the revolutionaries by unilateral force.

The spurning of negotiations in dealing with the Democratic Republic of Vietnam and the National Liberation Front can only be understood in terms of three characteristics of the Vietnamese conflict and the American role in it: first, the fact that the Communist-led movement for independence was from the beginning the dominant political force throughout Vietnam; the fact that the United States, as the greatest military power on earth, could not believe that a small, underdeveloped state could resist the weight of American resources and military power; and the fact that the United States chose to make Vietnam a test of its ability to suppress a "national liberation movement" in order to discourage revolutionary movements elsewhere in the world.

One of the recurrent themes in American policy toward Vietnam was that the political strength of the revolutionary opposition and the weakness of the client state constituted an unfavorable balance of power which demanded French and American intervention. The Viet Minh, and later the National Liberation Front, were able to mobilize powerful popular support for the goals of agrarian revolution and complete independence from foreign domination, thus threatening to overwhelm the succession of governments dependent on American protection. In order to avoid the collapse of the American-sponsored political faction in the South, the United States had to insist that the Saigon regime maintain complete control over the political process and that it have a free hand to call upon the United States to intervene with whatever military force might be necessary. And that meant that any political solution involving an opening up of the political process and the withdrawal of US military involvement and commitment had to be avoided.

A second theme in American policy was the persistent overconfidence of American officials in their ability to bring the insurgents under control by force once the Viet Minh army had been evacuated from South Vietnam under the terms of the Geneva Agreement of 1954. From 1955 to 1963 the military weakness of the former Viet Minh resistants and the significant commitment of US resources to the repressive effort contributed to the assumption that military force and police controls would be sufficient to solve the problem of Communist-led resistance to Saigon's authority. When the US counterinsurgency effort collapsed in 1964 optimism regarding a military victory turned on the overwhelming power which the United States could bring to bear both in the South and against the DRV. The American refusal to concede that the political strength and determination of the Vietnamese revolutionaries ruled out a unilaterally imposed solution delayed until very late in the war the decision by the United States to bargain seriously with its foes.

Had Vietnam been treated by American officials as one of dozens of underdeveloped countries emerging from colonialism and determined to take their own path—some of which would be bound to take a socialist route to development—the above considerations need not have prevented a diplomatic accommodation on Vietnam. After all, the United States decided to accept a Communist regime in Cuba and was prepared to deal on a diplomatic level with a number of Eastern European socialist regimes. But the makers of American foreign policy chose to make Vietnam a "test case," regarding it as an opportunity to prove that a Communist revolutionary movement could be defeated by American tutelage, support, protection, and, if necessary, American military forces. General Maxwell Taylor, formerly US Ambassador in Saigon and an important adviser to Presidents Kennedy and Johnson, testified to Congress in February 1966, "We intend to show that the 'war of liberation' . . . is costly, dangerous and doomed to failure." [1] The refusal to countenance any compromise on Vietnam was thus a reflection of a broader effort to prevent revolutionary change in the third world, which the United States perceived as a threat to its version of international stability.

All of these considerations—the political strength of the Vietnamese revolution, America's confidence that it could bring about a solution by force, and the desire to show in Vietnam how a "national liberation movement" could be defeated—combined to rule out negotiations on Vietnam until military force had succeeded in destroying the insurgents or bringing them under control—or until the failure of military force compelled the United States to accept compromise. It was, in fact, only deepening discouragement over the prospects for a military solution and popular pressures for an end to the war that finally made diplomatic negotiations a serious instrument of American policy in Vietnam.

1.   Subverting the Geneva Agreement

By 1952 the French war against the Viet Minh had long since bogged down, the Viet Minh forces had continued to strengthen themselves as the fighting was protracted, and the puppet Bao Dai regime had failed to rally any significant support from the ranks of the resistance. The French failure to win a decisive victory on the battlefield raised the question of a diplomatic arrangement to end the war. But the United States vetoed any exploration of a political settlement, which it felt certain would involve a withdrawal of French troops from Indochina and therefore the demise of the Bao Dai regime. A 1952 National Security Council policy statement on Indochina contained an annex warning against any diplomatic settlement which would end in the departure of French forces from

Indochina. "Because of the weakness of the native governments, the dubious attitudes of the population even in areas under French control, and the certainty of continued communist pressure," the document asserted, "it is highly probable that any settlement based on a withdrawal of French forces would be tantamount to handing over Indochina to communism." It concluded that American policy should "continue to oppose any negotiated settlement with the Viet Minh." [2]

The issue of negotiating peace in Vietnam became acute for US policymakers in 1954 when France indicated its willingness to negotiate an end to the war. The United States' response was to dissociate itself from French policy and leave itself free to take independent action in Vietnam. A memorandum from the National Security Council in March 1954 recommended that, if "despite all U. S. efforts to the contrary," the French decided on a negotiated settlement which would permit the Viet Minh to gain uncontested control over large areas of Vietnam, the United States should "decline to associate itself with such a settlement and should pursue directly with the governments of the Associated States and with other allies (notably the U. K.), ways and means of continuing the struggle against the Viet Minh in Indochina with participation of the French." [3]

Although the United States was unable to intervene in the war militarily both because of Congressional opposition and because of British reluctance, it kept up pressure on the French not to agree to any settlement which would "risk the loss of the retained area to Communist control." This was obviously a reference to any provision for an election for a new government for all of Vietnam.[4] When the Geneva Agreement was finally completed, the United States refused to endorse the final declaration, thus maintaining a free hand to intervene in South Vietnam in whatever way it might find necessary in order to keep all of Vietnam from falling under Communist control.[5]

The United States was prepared to accept DRV administrative control of all the territory north of the seventeenth parallel, but it would not give its guarantee to an agreement providing for nationwide elections to be held within two years under the supervision of the International Control Commission. American officials were virtually certain that such elections would be won overwhelmingly by the Viet Minh. The Joint Chiefs of Staff had advised the Secretary of Defense in March 1954 that "current intelligence leads the Joint Chiefs of Staff to believe that a settlement based upon free elections would be attended by almost certain loss of the Associated States (Vietnam, Laos, and Cambodia) to Communist control." [6] And the Central Intelligence Agency gave its estimate right after the agreement that "if the scheduled national elections are held in July 1956, and if the Viet Minh does not prejudice its political prospects, the Viet Minh will almost certainly win." [7]

Secretary of State Dulles hoped to frustrate the electoral provision by demanding in advance such stringent safeguards for free choice that no Communist government would agree to them, but he was warned by intelligence analysts that the "Nationalist appeal in Viet-Nam is so closely identified with Ho Chi Minh and the Viet-Minh movement that, even in areas outside Communist control, candidates and issues connected with 'nationalism' and supported by the Viet Minh would probably be supported by the majority of the people." As a result, they warned, the Viet Minh might be "so confident of success that they would be willing to permit 'free' elections under international supervision albeit continuing to utilize all the standard communist processes and tactics in an attempt to assure the outcome they would desire." [8] In the end, the Eisenhower administration advised Diem to "go through the motions" of negotiating on free elections but to refuse to make an agreement on the ground the elections could not be truly free as long as there was a Communist regime in the North.[9] When Diem refused even to consult with the DRV on arranging the preconditions for free elections, arguing that he was not bound by the agreement, Dulles immediately supported his position.[10] It was American political support, backed by the implicit threat to intervene if there was any renewal of fighting, which, in the words of a later memorandum from Secretary of Defense McNamara to President Johnson, "enabled Diem to refuse to go through with the 1954 provision calling for nationwide 'free' elections in 1956." [11]

Even before the United States and Diem successfully evaded the Geneva elections, they had begun a military and police offensive against all those who were believed to be active supporters of the Viet Minh. At a time when the Viet Minh were still actively preparing for the 1956 elections, Diem's armed forces and police, advised by American CIA personnel,[12] began to hunt down suspected Communist and Viet Minh cadres and sympathizers in an effort to completely destroy the political apparatus whose very existence threatened the regime. The United States encouraged Diem to try to wipe out the Communist organization, on the assumption, as a CIA estimate put it, that "Diem's success in by-passing the July 1956 election date without evoking large scale Communist military reaction will reassure many Vietnamese and encourage them to cooperate with GVN [Government of Vietnam] programs to expose and root out Communists." [13]

This campaign of physical repression, whose consequences were analyzed in the previous chapter, was an open violation of Article 14(c) of the Geneva Agreement, prohibiting reprisals or discrimination against those who had collaborated with either side.[14] What was even more important, however, was that it signified an American effort to resolve the issue of Vietnam's political future by force rather than by a Vietnamese expression of political choice. By substituting force for a political process, the United States was claiming the power to determine unilaterally by whom South Vietnam would be governed.[15]

Once the supremacy of "security" considerations was accepted, American officials could view the division of Vietnam into North and South as part of the same pattern of cold war politics which had divided Germany and Korea into Communist and anti-Communist zones—a pattern which, they argued, had to be maintained intact in order to avoid upsetting the cold war balance of power. American cold war policy insisted that ideological dividing lines, regardless of their moral or legal status, become permanent cold war lines by virtue of the need for "stability."

The American view of Vietnam as another exercise in cold war politics overlooked the basic facts which made any attempt to resolve the issue by force a dangerous policy: the roots of the revolutionary movement in the South were too deep and too broad to be completely destroyed. The Viet Minh movement still represented millions of South Vietnamese who had been deprived of any expression of political will by the cancellation of the 1956 elections. The political demands of these South Vietnamese who had fought for the Viet Minh or supported it—not to mention the nearly 100,000 Viet Minh troops who had regrouped temporarily in the North under the terms of the agreement in anticipation of the elections—could be postponed but not resolved by physical repression against the Communists.

The policy of keeping Vietnam divided and ignoring the Geneva political provisions was encouraged by the passive attitude of the Soviet Union toward the Vietnam issue. The USSR had the dual role of being, with Britain, Co-Chairman of the Geneva Conference, as well as the main source of military and economic support for the DRV. So it had the power to create a diplomatic crisis over the issue of the implementation of the Geneva elections. But the Soviet leaders, preoccupied with European issues which were more vital to their interests, and reluctant to push the United States too hard in an area where their own influence was limited, failed to press the issue strongly with the United States and Britain. According to former State Department official Paul M. Kattenburg, who was following the diplomatic aspect of Indochinese affairs at the time, "It may be conservatively estimated that more than a dozen formal communications flowed from the Democratic Republic of Vietnam (DRV) in Hanoi to the Soviet Geneva Co-Chairman between mid-1954 and late 1955 requesting him and the British Co-Chairman to bring about the inter-zonal (North–South) consultations called for in the 1954 accords. . . ." But the notes went unanswered, according to Kattenburg, "because of an apparent lack of interest in the question in Moscow." [16] Finally, in early 1956, the DRV prevailed upon the Soviet government to call for a new Geneva Conference, but a meeting between Soviet and British representatives in April produced a noncommittal statement emphasizing the maintenance of the cease-fire more than the holding of elections.[17]

The Soviet Union's unwillingness to make the failure of the United States, France, and Saigon on the promised nationwide elections a major East-West issue thus permitted the provisional demarcation line at the seventeenth parallel to harden in the minds of American officials into a permanent political boundary between states belonging to two different cold war blocs. This did not mean, however, that the Vietnamese, North or South, accepted the division of Vietnam on American terms or the Saigon government as an expression of South Vietnamese political will. By 1960 the former Viet Minh and their supporters were taking up arms once again against the Diem government. By its attempt to destroy the Viet Minh political apparatus, the United States had made the second Vietnam war inevitable.

2. *The Kennedy Administration: Diplomacy vs. Counterinsurgency*

The Kennedy administration, faced with a renewed armed struggle in the South in 1961, responded by defining Vietnam as a test of its ability to deal with revolutionary movements around the world by applying its newly developed "counterinsurgency" warfare techniques.[18]

Without claiming that a monolithic world Communist organization existed or that the Vietnamese Communists were not independent of Moscow and Peking, the Kennedy administration succeeded in establishing an intellectual structure which would rationalize US intervention to prevent the success of any armed revolt. It defined revolutionary movements as inherently "aggressive" and without internal motivation. Insurgents were described in ways which implied that they could not have had either popular support or a justification for armed struggle. Thus President Kennedy himself, in a major address on the subject of "wars of liberation," referred only to "agitators," "subversives," "saboteurs," and "insurrectionists." [19] According to the Kennedy administration's theorist, Walt W. Rostow, there was no relationship between popular dissatisfaction and the success of a revolutionary movement. The appearance of a revolutionary movement, Rostow argued, was not a result of genuine grievances but of "aggression" from outside.[20]

The administration's counterinsurgency theory thus aimed at justifying US counterinsurgency programs and ultimately American intervention anywhere in the world, but particularly in South Vietnam. It attempted to gloss over the history of the Vietnam conflict and the moral and political difficulties confronted by "counterinsurgency" in the Vietnamese setting by the doctrinaire assertion that revolutionary movements with a Communist component were *inherently* illegitimate. Armed with this rationale, the Kennedy administration threw itself into a new phase of US policy in Vietnam. Having adopted an ambitious "counterinsurgency plan" for South Vietnam, the administration set out to test its techniques for repressing an indigenous revolutionary movement. The main elements of the administration's strategy for South Vietnam, as outlined by one of its chief architects, Assistant Secretary of State Roger Hilsman, were those of colonial powers for pacifying dissidence in their overseas possessions: forcible relocation of whole villages, stringent population controls, the development of an efficient police apparatus, and the establishment by the military forces of an "iron grid of security" throughout the country.[21]

Since the Kennedy administration regarded Vietnam as a "police problem"—a matter to be resolved unilaterally by the United States and its client government—it failed to see in the armed struggle of the National Liberation Front a problem calling for international diplomacy. For unlike the Laotian situation, over which the Kennedy administration had already lost control in early 1961, the insurgency in Vietnam still seemed "manageable." At the Vienna meeting between Kennedy and Khrushchev in June 1961, Kennedy pressed Khrushchev over a compromise Laotian settlement but, significantly, he indicated no interest in a diplomatic arrangement on Vietnam.[22] It appears, in fact, that the administration looked upon the Laotian settlement of July 1962 as one means of taking the pressure off South Vietnam and thus bringing the insurgency there under control.[23]

Committed to resolving the problem within the framework of its "counterinsurgency" plan, the United States apparently gave no thought to a diplomatic arrangement which could have taken the three states of South Vietnam, Laos, and Cambodia out of the sphere of cold war politics by constituting a "neutral zone." What made such a neutral zone a realistic prospect was not simply that the National Liberation Front of South Vietnam was proposing it, but that it also had the strong support of the People's Republic of China. Contrary to the image which the Kennedy and Johnson administrations attempted to portray of a China bent on proving the effectiveness of armed struggle in Vietnam, the Chinese had never called for armed struggle; on the contrary, their statements always urged diplomacy and political struggle—such as urban demonstrations—as the appropriate means for resolving the problems in the South.[24] Peking had made it clear almost as soon as the struggle began in 1960 that its aim would be a diplomatic settlement based on the Geneva accords, not an armed seizure of power in the South. As one high Chinese official said in obvious reference to Vietnam in mid-1960, "The struggle of the masses and diplomatic negotiations must be closely coordinated. The struggle of the masses provides diplomatic negotiations with the strongest backing." [25]

A careful analysis of Chinese policy toward Indochina indicates, in fact, that the Chinese were interested less in revolutionary change in Southeast Asia than in a peaceful rear at a time when their attention was directed primarily at threats from Japan, Korea, and Taiwan. What they were most concerned about was avoiding an increased US military presence and pressure in Southeast Asia. In September 1960, just as the North Vietnamese were authorizing the building up of a revolutionary army in the South for the first time, Premier Chou En-lai, speaking at a DRV embassy reception, restated China's long-standing desire "to see this region bordering on China become an area of peace." With regard to Vietnam Chou said this meant support for "strict observance of the Geneva Accords" and for "peaceful reunification of Vietnam." [26]

China was still far from playing up an armed struggle in South Vietnam as a model for liberation movements when the United States established the Military Assistance Command Vietnam (MACV) in February 1962. But this US move, which indicated a growing direct American military role in South Vietnam, led Peking to upgrade the struggle in South Vietnam as necessary in order to deny the United States a military victory over a revolutionary movement. "If this new war scheme of US imperialism should succeed in Southern Viet-Nam," Chinese Foreign Minister Chen Yi stated, "not only all peoples striving for freedom will suffer, but the danger of wars of bigger scale will be greatly increased." [27]

As China stepped up its political support for the NLF in 1962, however, it also pushed for a diplomatic alternative to a military confrontation between US military power and the liberation movement in Vietnam. In June 1962, as the settlement of the Laotian conflict moved toward an international conference to guarantee its "neutralization" through a tripartite coalition government, China publicly called for a similar neutralization agreement for South Vietnam. Chen Yi observed that the Laotian agreement showed that "acute and complicated international disputes can be settled through negotiation" and said China "ardently hopes that the peaceful settlement of the Laotian question will be a new starting point in the relaxation of tension." He called for an end to US "armed intervention" in Vietnam and "peaceful consultations in accordance with the 1954 Geneva Agreements." [28] In September 1962 the Chinese press and political organizations endorsed the NLF proposal for a Laotian-type agreement in Vietnam and an international agreement to guarantee South Vietnam's neutrality and her participation in a neutral zone with Cambodia and Laos.[29]

Such a diplomatic arrangement guaranteeing against great-power interference in South Vietnam would have been advantageous to the United States, of course, only if the internal balance of power in the South was already favorable to the Diem regime. But American officials recognized that the power of the NLF was solidly based on the Southern population, and that it was Diem's lack of popular support which had made the increased US military presence necessary. Explaining why the United States could not agree to the neutralization of South Vietnam, Kennedy aide Theodore Sorenson has written, "South Vietnam was too weak to stand alone; and any attempt to neutralize the nation in 1961 . . . at a time when the Communists had the upper hand and were the most forcible element in the South as well as in the North, would have left the South Vietnamese defenseless against externally supported Communist domination." [30] The Kennedy administration continued to increase its military presence in South Vietnam from 1,400 men at the end of 1961 to about 15,500 men by the end of 1963, and increased its air power there in 1962 and again in 1963.[31]

In a real sense, therefore, it was Kennedy and not Mao who chose to make Vietnam a "test case," preferring to establish the American willingness and ability to defeat a "national liberation movement" by its counterinsurgency techniques. The Kennedy administration's opposition to a negotiated settlement which would involve the withdrawal of US military advisers also extended to the policy of the Diem regime. As the tensions between the United States and President Diem's family mounted during 1963, the possibility began to emerge that Ngo Dinh Nhu, President Diem's shrewd and unpredictable brother, would attempt to negotiate a cease-fire and political settlement with the Communists. The Kennedy administration quickly began to suspect such a maneuver. "Sometime after the Buddhist crisis, Diem was asked point blank about whether Nhu had or intended to have contacts with the North," recalls Michael Forrestal of Kennedy's National Security Council Staff, "and Diem gave a very equivocal answer." [32] By mid-August, according to Roger Hilsman, there were "repeated intelligence reports that Nhu had some notion . . . that he could negotiate an end to the war and that he had been attempting to set up a secret channel of communications with Hanoi." [33]

By the end of August Ambassador Henry Cabot Lodge and Secretary of State Rusk reportedly feared that Diem would turn immediately to Hanoi for help if the United States tried to pressure him into purging his brother Nhu.[34] It was in this atmosphere of growing suspicion in Washington of the intentions of Diem and Nhu that French President Charles de Gaulle on August 29, 1963 issued a statement appearing to offer French assistance to any effort by the two Vietnams to reunify the country and end the war. As always, the statement was couched in the most lofty and ambiguous terms, but the fact that it addressed the Vietnamese people and "all of Vietnam" suggested to the United States that the General was encouraging an immediate settlement of the war between North and South Vietnam. It pledged support for efforts toward "independence" as well as "peace and unity." [35]

The Kennedy administration was openly hostile to this suggestion that France was ready to help in bringing about some kind of "neutralization" in Vietnam. French Ambassador Hervé Alphand was summoned to the State Department for an hour-long interview with Secretary Rusk, who demanded clarification of the statement. (Alphand explained the goals of reunification and peace as long-term in character.[36]) The day after de Gaulle's statement, on August 30, Hilsman wrote a memorandum for Rusk urging that, if Diem and Nhu asked for support from France in an effort to bring about the "neutralization" of Vietnam, "We should point out publicly that Vietnam cannot be effectively neutralized unless the Communists are removed from control of North Vietnam." The memo also proposed that the United States publicize any evidence of moves by Diem and Nhu to negotiate with the North in order to justify later countermoves against them. It further noted that a

coalition which permitted any Communist participation in the
government "would be the avenue to a Communist takeover in
view of the relative strength of the two principals in the coalition." [37]

Three weeks later, after an interview with Nhu, columnist
Joseph Alsop reported that Nhu had told him the French were
working closely with the North Vietnamese to promote a negotiated
settlement of the war, but that he, Nhu, was having nothing to do
with it.[38] The State Department clearly remained unconvinced of
Nhu's innocence; when asked for a comment, the Department's
spokesman read a carefully worded statement: "It would not
appear to be in the interests of the South Vietnamese, of ourselves,
or of the other Free World nations, to consider negotiating away
what has been accomplished by the courage and heavy expense in
life and effort of the Vietnamese." [39] The United States was thus
coming very close to saying publicly that such negotiations were
being contemplated by Saigon and issuing a scarcely veiled warning
to Diem and Nhu that the United States would not tolerate it.

By October 2, when Secretary McNamara and General Taylor
reported to the President on their mission to Saigon, they, too, were
expressing concern about Nhu's apparent interest in negotiating a
settlement. A "disturbing feature" of Nhu's thinking, the report
said, was his "flirtation with the idea of negotiating with North
Vietnam, whether or not he is serious in this at present." This
flirtation not only disturbed "responsible Vietnamese," wrote
McNamara and Taylor, but "suggests a possible basic incompati-
bility with US objectives." [40]

It is not clear what significance Washington's fear of a
negotiated settlement between Diem and the Communists had in
the ultimate decision to encourage a coup d'état against the regime,
as there were other US complaints about the regime's policies. But
it is clear that Washington not only was unwilling to entertain a
diplomatic settlement of the war itself, but was prepared to exercise
a veto power over any such arrangement by encouraging the
military to seize power. Once a coup against Diem and Nhu was
under way, Hilsman's memo noted, "We can point to the obvious
refusal of South Vietnam to accept a Diem-Communist coalition." [41]

3. *The Johnson Administration Pursues Military Victory*

As the threat to the Saigon regime from the National Liberation Front grew increasingly serious during 1964, international
pressures for a negotiated political solution increased accordingly.
But the Johnson administration was determined to resist any such
pressures for a diplomatic solution on the same grounds as the
Kennedy administration had used to reject negotiations in 1962
and 1963. Secretary of Defense McNamara's memorandum to
President Johnson on March 16, 1964 shows that US officials
considered any American military withdrawal tantamount to the
collapse of the Saigon regime. Discussing de Gaulle's proposal for
the neutralization of South Vietnam, McNamara wrote that it
clearly implied the withdrawal of "all external military assistance
and specifically total US withdrawal." The United States had to
explicitly reject any solution based on such a self-limitation,
McNamara said, because "only the US presence held the South
together under far more favorable circumstances. . . ." Even
discussing the possibility of an American withdrawal as part of a
political settlement, he warned, would "undermine any chance of
keeping a non-Communist government in South Vietnam. . . ." [42]

Similarly the Johnson administration rejected all calls for an
international conference to settle the Vietnamese conflict. Only a
day after de Gaulle called for a summit meeting to agree on the
evacuation of all foreign forces from Indochina and a guarantee of
the neutrality of *all* Indochina, President Johnson declared, in a
statement which might have been written by John Foster Dulles a
decade earlier about the original Geneva Conference, "We do not
believe in conferences called to ratify terror. . . ." [43] The following
day, the Pentagon announced an increase in US military personnel
in South Vietnam from 16,000 to 20,000.[44] "After, *but only after,* we
have established a clear pattern of pressure," wrote William P.
Bundy, in an August 11, 1964 draft policy paper, "we could accept
a conference broadened to include the Viet-Nam issue." [45]

By late 1964 the US security apparatus was already planning
for direct US military pressures on North Vietnam. A high-level
National Security Council Working Group, formed to draft policy
options for the President, offered two alternative strategies for
bombing the North: either rapid escalation or a more deliberate,

carefully graduated campaign.[46] A meeting of President Johnson's principal national security advisers in late November leaned toward the initiation of gradually escalated bombing attacks against North Vietnam "soon." [47]

The main reason for the consensus within the administration in favor of such bombing attacks on the DRV was not that it was expected to force the DRV to end its support for the NLF in the South—for there was widespread agreement that it probably would not—but that it was necessary to head off the tendency within South Vietnam toward a peace settlement with the NLF and Hanoi. A draft paper written by William Bundy, the Working Group's chairman, on November 7, 1964, pointed out that, if the United States continued the existing policy or even added reprisal bombings in response to specific Communist attacks in the South, it would "accept the risk that South Vietnamese elements would themselves open negotiations with the Liberation Front or with Hanoi directed probably to ceasefire and a coalition government that would admit the Liberation Front." [48] Even limited "reprisal bombings" of the North, Bundy wrote in another memo, would probably not prevent further deterioration of morale, which could lead to "a new government committed to a ceasefire and a negotiated end of the war on almost any terms." [49]

Bundy noted that the United States "would probably have the capability to install and protect a GVN subservient to US wishes," averting the threat of such a peace settlement. But by that time, he wrote, "the situation might have deteriorated to such an extent that there would be less nation-wide support for this government." His conclusion was that even stronger military moves would be necessary in order to "hold morale" in Saigon.[50]

In a paper prepared for Secretary Rusk's meeting with the President on January 6, 1965, Bundy and two other top State Department officials noted that the disintegration in Saigon was proceeding "more rapidly than we had anticipated in November" and forecast a "government of key groups starting to negotiate covertly with the Liberation Front or Hanoi. . . ." The memo urged "stronger action," including both "an early occasion for reprisal action" against the DRV and the introduction of some US ground troops into Northern South Vietnam. These moves, it said, might not "bring about a more effective government," but would have a "stiffening effect on the Saigon political situation"—presumably meaning that it would halt any moves toward negotiation with the Communists.[51]

The primary preoccupation of policymakers in the period from November 1964 to February 1965 was thus the avoidance of any negotiations by Vietnamese among themselves to end the war. Although it was admitted that the American public probably would not react strongly to such an outcome and that an "eventually unified Communist Vietnam would reassert its traditional hostility to Communist China," these officials were unable to accept such a resolution of the conflict by the Vietnamese themselves. For, as William Bundy wrote in November, "In key parts of the rest of Asia, notably Thailand, our present posture . . . appears weak." [52] In order to avoid the appearance of "weakness" to Asian clients, they felt the need to do *something* to show that the United States would not passively acquiesce in the defeat of its policy.

When the NLF attacked Camp Holloway at Pleiku on February 7, 1965, it was the "reprisal opportunity" which the Johnson administration had been waiting for. In fact, when the attack took place, McGeorge Bundy, Johnson's national security adviser, had already decided, after three days in South Vietnam, to recommend a policy of "sustained reprisal," primarily as a "stimulant" to the Saigon government to prosecute the war. He expressed the fear that the value of the "stimulant" would decline over time, urging that the United States "take full advantage" of the new policy to change the "whole US-GVN relationship" and obtain greater leverage over Saigon politics and policy.[53]

Since the primary point of the bombing was to prevent any tendency toward accommodation between Saigon and the NLF, the Vietnamese authorities were not even consulted on the decision. General Nguyen Khanh, chairman of the governing military council, was summoned to Pleiku on February 7 and informed by Bundy and Westmoreland that they had decided to recommend to Johnson the sustained reprisals policy.[54]

While United States was planning its air attacks against the DRV it was also rebuffing an offer by the North Vietnamese to meet in secret with American representatives. The offer, conveyed to US Ambassador Adlai Stevenson through U Thant, was formally rejected at the end of January 1965, after four months' delay.

Stevenson explained to Thant that the United States would not meet in secret with Hanoi because it would demoralize the Saigon government if the talks were discovered.*

As the bombing campaign against North Vietnam began, Washington again openly rejected an opportunity to move toward a negotiated settlement. Soviet Premier Kosygin, on a visit to Hanoi, declared on February 7, the day of the first reprisal bombing, that the Soviet government supported the convocation of a "new international conference on Indochina with a view to the peaceful settlement of the questions which have arisen there." [55] The US response to Kosygin's initiative was Secretary Rusk's remark on February 25 that the DRV would have to "indicate a willingness to end its aggression" before the United States would consider negotiations.[56]

The term "negotiations," as commonly used in diplomatic parlance, implies that two or more parties are engaged in a process of bargaining in which each makes concessions. In order to avoid that implication, the administration created a distinction between "negotiations" and "discussions." In President Johnson's April 7, 1965 address at the Johns Hopkins University he offered "unconditional discussions" over Vietnam, a phrase which suggested to an unwary public that the United States was ready to resolve the conflict by other than military means.[57] The distinction between the two terms was pointed out in a briefing by a US official for certain selected journalists, who were told that only "discussions" and not "negotiations" were unconditional.[58] The administration's negative attitude toward "negotiations" was further underlined by Ambassador Lodge's comment a few weeks later that "negotiations would be disastrous." [59]

The central issue of the war from the beginning was the demand for a political voice by former Viet Minh supporters and

---

* This admission came only after a round of diplomatic fencing between the State Department and U Thant, who refused to believe the official US argument that the indications from its own channel were that Hanoi was not interested in secret talks with the United States. Thant demanded to know what the source of information was, and when told it was the Canadian ICC delegate, checked with the Canadian government to find out whether or not this was true. He was informed by Ottawa that the Canadian delegate in Hanoi was not in a position to know whether or not Hanoi desired negotiations with the United States. (David Kraslow and Stuart H. Loory, *The Secret Search for Peace in Vietnam* [New York: Random House, 1968], pp. 98–101; Chester Cooper, *The Lost Crusade* [New York: Dodd, Mead, 1970], pp. 327–328.)

others who opposed the Saigon government. If there was to be any negotiated settlement, it would have to involve a sharing of political power with the NLF, at least until there was a free election in which the dissidents could compete. But the Johnson administration made it clear that it would not even consider elections in which the NLF could participate. At a press conference on February 25, 1965 Secretary Rusk was asked whether the United States would agree to free elections in South Vietnam, under international supervision, if infiltration from the North stopped. Rusk refused to commit the United States to such elections, insisting instead that the "pacification of the country" would be "easy" once the "external aggression" was stopped.[60]

In December 1965 Rusk said that the "Viet Cong" could participate in elections if they would "lay down their arms" and "accept amnesty." [61] When Rusk testified before the Senate Foreign Relations Committee in February 1966, he was asked by Chairman Fulbright whether it was not the United States position that "there is no possibility of any participation by the National Liberation Front [in elections]" and that, therefore, the NLF had "no alternative but to fight on?" Rusk replied frankly, "They do have an alternative . . . of quitting, of stopping being an agent of Hanoi and receiving men and arms from the north for the purpose of taking over South Vietnam." [62] These statements robbed the endorsement by the United States of the principle of "free elections" in South Vietnam of any value.[63]

In fact, the administration had decided before its direct military intervention of 1965 began that there could be no political settlement and no free elections until *after* the United States had destroyed the NLF militarily and pacified the countryside. French scholar Philippe Devillers recalled later that William Bundy had explained to him in August 1965 that "in his opinion there was no chance of a political settlement for at least two or three years, during which time, he said, we shall have rebuilt the social structure of the countryside, the peasants will be so disgusted with the Vietcong, that they will denounce them, and Saigon will be able to wipe them out completely, or to bring them under strict control." Only then, Bundy said, could there be "free elections," after which what remained of the revolutionary left could be dealt with by negotiations.[64]

But the Johnson administration, which was eager to show that it was ready to make peace, tried to deemphasize the political issues which were central to the conflict and focus public attention on military issues. In order to shift attention from political to military problems the United States offered "reciprocity"—an American bombing halt in return for a deescalation by the other side of the ground war in the South.

Despite differences of opinion within the administration over the effectiveness of bombing as a means of forcing North Vietnam to accept American demands to abandon the war in the South, there was general agreement that the bombing was a valuable "bargaining chip," which the United States could offer in return for a cessation or at least a significant reduction in North Vietnamese support for the war in the South.[65] Thus the US offer of "mutual deescalation" constituted a politically acceptable substitute for a real negotiating position. It appeared to the American public to be a form of "bargaining" which was fair and businesslike, since it was based on mutual concessions. Upon closer examination, of course, it did not involve reciprocity at all, since the United States was offering to stop only its bombing of North Vietnam and not its military build-up and bombing in the South, while demanding that the DRV and NLF reduce or end their military effort in the South.

In the context of the Johnson administration's refusal to negotiate on the central issues of the war, the bombing "pauses" of May 1965 and December–January 1965–66 were not means to make a negotiated settlement possible but instruments for achieving a military solution. The first bombing halt, from May 12 to 17, was actually intended to pave the way for a significant escalation of the American war effort, while conveying another signal that the United States was going for a military victory rather than for any political compromise.[66] After the five-day pause had ended, US spokesmen said they had gotten no response from the DRV and concluded that Hanoi was not prepared to make peace.[67]

Some months later it was revealed that the United States had transmitted a secret message to the DRV at the beginning of the pause which appears to have been aimed at discouraging any move toward negotiations by the DRV.[68] The note said that the United States would be "watchful" for "significant reductions" in armed actions by Liberation Front forces, but offered nothing concrete in return for any such response. All it offered was that if there was an appropriate response, there would be a "more extended" bombing pause—but not a halt—at an unspecified later date. The basic message of the note, moreover, was that the United States would end its air attacks only in return for a complete cessation of activities by the NLF. "The United States must emphasize that the road toward the end of armed attacks against the people and Government of Vietnam is the only road which will permit the Government of Vietnam and the Government of the United States to bring a permanent end to their air attacks on North Vietnam." This was clearly not language calculated to open diplomatic channels.

When the DRV did respond diplomatically on the last day of the pause by clarifying its previous "four points" to the French Foreign Ministry, the State Department deliberately chose to ignore the clarification. The DRV clarification, in the words of a subsequent State Department account, "repeated the four points with slight variations from public statements, apparently softening language by indicating that the four points might be the 'best basis' for a settlement and apparently insisting less strongly that their recognition was required as condition to negotiations." The same official account indicates that this left it "ambiguous" whether recognition of the four points remained "preconditions to talks of any sort." [69] But instead of pursuing the matter further through diplomatic channels, the United States chose to interpret Hanoi's public statements denouncing the pause as evidence of a lack of desire for any move toward a peace settlement.

The second bombing pause, from late December 1965 to late January 1966, was also carried out primarily for public relations purposes: to "lay a foundation," as McNamara put it in a memorandum to the President, "in the mind of the American public and in world opinion for . . . an enlarged phase of the war. . . ." [70] But again the administration had to guard against the appearance of a willingness by Hanoi to negotiate which would stimulate pressures for an indefinite halt in the bombing. And this time the task was made harder by the apparent stand-down by main force units of the PLAF, who were reported by military sources in Saigon to have been ordered to avoid contact with US units.[71] Some North Vietnamese units had reportedly pulled back from South Vietnam into Laos and Cambodia.[72]

Again the administration argued that the other side had not responded to the pause. Secretary Rusk, asked in a news conference about the absence of large-scale contact with the main forces of the Liberation Army during the lull, replied that there was "some ambiguity about the matter" and pointed to a "very active contact with the North Vietnamese" at the time of the press conference.[73] Press accounts indicated that there had indeed been a major contact, provoked by a major amphibious landing in an NLF area by US forces.[74]

The Johnson administration further rejected the withdrawal of its troops until the NLF had been destroyed or brought under control by the Saigon government, as the United States and Saigon formally declared in the communiqué which followed the Manila Conference of October 1966. The language of the communiqué, which was to become known as the "Manila Formula," specified that US and other non-Vietnamese troops "shall be withdrawn . . . as the other side withdraws its forces to the North, ceases infiltration and the level of violence thus subsides." The American withdrawal, according to the document, would take place "not later than six months after the above conditions have been fulfilled." [75] As the administration's own spokesman later admitted, this formula actually committed the United States to nothing, since it included "protective language" about the level of violence subsiding.[76] The United States had no intention, in other words, of leaving the South Vietnamese government to fight it out with Southern NLF forces, whose near military victory in 1965 had precipitated the massive US intervention. In order to remove any ambiguity, President Johnson himself declared just before the 1966 elections that the United States would "pull out as soon as the infiltration, the aggression, and the violence ceases." [77]

This totally uncompromising stance reflected the belief of the Johnson administration that the United States could achieve a military victory in South Vietnam, although it might take a period of years to complete the task. Military commanders in the field predicted in April 1965 that, in "perhaps a year or two," the

United States could "break the will of the DRV/VC by depriving them of victory," and that this would lead to a favorable political settlement.[78] A Joint Chiefs of Staff study stated that offensive ground operations coupled with interdiction of infiltration routes "should lead to progressive destruction of the VC/DRV main force battalions." [79] McNamara himself, testifying before the House Appropriations Committee in January 1966, declared: "I think it is a reasonable conclusion that at some point, these rising casualties, and these higher costs, and these increasing strains are going to become so great that they [the DRV] will conclude that they cannot win in the South." When the North Vietnamese reached this conclusion, he said, "they will be unwilling to continue to bear the costs of a program that cannot achieve their objectives." [80] On the basis of this assumption, many US officials believed that the war would end not in a negotiated settlement but in a unilateral disengagement from the conflict by Communist forces. And for the same reason, the administration was not concerned about getting discussions started with the North Vietnamese. Whenever there was any conflict between opening such discussions through a secret channel and the desire to put maximum military pressure on the DRV, the administration chose the latter. This preference for a military solution was the underlying cause of the collapse of two serious efforts through intermediaries to bring about the start of discussions between the DRV and the United States, first in December 1966 and then in February 1967.

The first effort, which became known within the administration by the code name "Marigold," began as an initiative by Italian Ambassador to Saigon Giovanni D'Orlandi to get the United States to spell out in detail its conception of an ultimate political settlement, which would then be passed on to Hanoi through the Polish delegate to the Control Commission, Janusz Lewandowski.[81] In November 1966, Ambassador Lodge did give Lewandowski an oral presentation of the American position on a political settlement, including a discussion of the problem of elections and US troop withdrawals, which was then put into the form of ten points by Lewandowski. But the United States then insisted on amending Lewandowski's language substantially and maintained that the ten points were not a basis for a settlement or even "agenda items" but merely "topic headings." The United States refused to clarify the substance of the points, moreover, until after direct contacts with the DRV had begun.

Lewandowski told Lodge that, after preliminary details were worked out, the Polish government would arrange for formal discussions between the DRV and the United States in Warsaw, and the preliminary meeting was scheduled for December 5. But on December 2 American bombers struck Hanoi for the first time in two weeks. Lewandowski immediately warned the United States that Hanoi would interpret these raids as a sign that the United States was not serious about a peace settlement. Two days later, the United States again bombed Hanoi. Lodge tried to argue that the raids could not have been canceled without compromising the secrecy of the talks. The planned talks were not yet called off by Hanoi, but the days passed without the change in wording which Washington promised to deliver as the basis for the talks. And on December 6, Lodge himself speculated to newsmen that the war would simply fade away rather than being ended by a negotiated settlement.

One week later, on December 13, the Poles informed the American diplomat in Warsaw, John Gronouski, that they were postponing the talks indefinitely. On the same day American planes hit Hanoi once more, this time damaging not only the civilian quarter of the city but the diplomatic quarter as well. The Poles then broke off the talks completely. Clearly, the top officials of the administration were not interested enough in getting talks started to offer even the slightest gesture of good faith. As Chester Cooper commented later, the series of bombings suggested "even to a few people in the State Department that the United States had little interest in serious discussions." [82]

An even more serious case of deliberate sabotage of a diplomatic initiative was the sudden reversal of the US position during the talks in February 1967 between British Prime Minister Harold Wilson and Soviet Premier Kosygin, who were trying to produce a formula for peace talks which would be mutually acceptable to both the United States and the DRV.[83] This episode was especially important because it was the first time that the Soviet Union had expressed any interest in taking any initiative for a peace settlement in Vietnam since the abortive effort of early 1965. Wilson had asked the United States to send an official who could brief him on the current US diplomatic position, and Johnson sent Chester Cooper, who worked closely with Ambassador Averell Harriman on the diplomatic aspects of Vietnam. Cooper presented Wilson with a formula for starting talks under which the two sides would agree secretly that the United States would stop the bombing, and then, after a period of from one to three weeks, there would be acts of mutual deescalation by both sides—the cessation of infiltration by the North Vietnamese and an end to the augmentation of American forces in Vietnam—a formula which visitors to Hanoi believed would be acceptable to Hanoi. The formula was presented orally to Kosygin, who asked that it be put in writing. But when Cooper cabled the State Department for final clearance to give Kosygin a written statement of the "Phase A-Phase B" plan, as it was called, he got back an entirely different version of the American position. The new formula completely reversed the previous order of the phases: the North Vietnamese had to end their infiltration before the bombing was halted. The Wilson-Kosygin initiative was thus aborted even before the Soviet Prime Minister had left London.[84]

After another high-level debate over the conditions under which the United States would undertake a bombing halt, the demand for substantial deescalation by Communist forces in advance of a bombing halt was modified in August 1967 but still fell short of the "Phase A-Phase B" formula. In connection with a contact with the DRV through Professor Henry Kissinger of Harvard University and two Frenchmen, French microbiologist Herbert Marcovich and Raymond Aubrac, an old friend of Ho Chi Minh's, Johnson approved a message with a new formula for ending the bombing of the North: the United States was "willing to stop the aerial and naval bombardment if this will lead promptly to productive discussions between representatives of the U. S. and the DRV looking toward a resolution of the issues between them." [85] The terms "prompt" and "productive," Professor Kissinger explained, meant that the United States would not permit the negotiations to go on indefinitely without progress, while fighting continued, as they had during the Korean War. This implied that the bombing halt, far from being "unconditional," would be conditional on an early agreement to American terms.

Moreover, the message to DRV Premier Pham Van Dong contained the old condition of a reciprocal act of restraint, though in a new form: "We would assume that, while discussions proceed either with public knowledge or secretly, the DRV would not take advantage of the bombing cessation or limitation." Not taking advantage, Kissinger explained to the two Frenchmen, meant no increase of men and supplies into the South above existing levels. It was not clear from the Kissinger letter to the DRV that the United States was prepared to put a similar restraint on its own military build-up. So the DRV would be negotiating under the threat of renewed bombing, while at the same time giving up any further military build-up to support its negotiating position.

The August 1967 formula was hardly one which invited a favorable North Vietnamese response, particularly since it came at a time when Hanoi was increasingly convinced that the United States was planning to step up the bombing in pursuit of a military victory. But despite North Vietnam's angry rejection of the formula, it became part of the public United States diplomatic stance when it was inserted in a speech by the President in San Antonio on September 29, 1967.[86]

This hardening in the American position on a bombing halt was accompanied by an increasing rigidity in the US commitment to a political monopoly for the Saigon government. In late 1966 and early 1967 the administration was becoming locked in more tightly than before to a position of opposing any political role for the NLF in a postwar South Vietnam. The US Embassy encouraged the writing by the Constituent Assembly elected in October 1966 of a new constitution which outlawed not only Communism but "neutralism" as well.[87] Elections were to be used not to offer a choice between conflicting political forces but to confirm the power of those managing the electoral process. By restricting political choice to a field of candidates who were willing to support the US war effort and oppose any political compromise, the Saigon government and the US Embassy insured that the government of the Republic of Vietnam (RVN) would have a Constituent Assembly which would reaffirm its determination to eliminate the NLF by force. The new constitutional structure and National Assembly constituted, in effect, another set of structural obstacles to a negotiated political compromise.

But the administration seemed happy to pay the price of narrowed diplomatic options in order to reassure its South Vietnamese clients that it was irrevocably committed to their survival. Ambassador Robert Komer, chief of the US pacification program in Saigon, defended the new, politically restrictive constitution on the ground that it "reassures the Vietnamese that the US has a real stake in seeing to it that these processes work." [88] Again, the political frailty of Saigon and the American pursuit of military victory ruled out serious negotiations for a political settlement.

4. The Perils of Protracted War

By 1967 the original premises of American military strategy—that the will or ability of the DRV and NLF to continue the war could be broken within one or two years—had been proven wrong. American officials began to accept the fact that the Vietnamese resistance was prepared for a long-term struggle and was capable of sustaining it for a considerable period of time. In October 1966 McNamara, in a memo to the President, declared that he saw "no reasonable way to bring the war to an end soon." The enemy, he noted, had "adjusted" to the US military drive of 1965–66 and had "adopted a strategy of keeping us busy and waiting us out. . . ." Moreover, the enemy appeared to be able to "more than replace his losses by infiltration from the North and recruitment in South Vietnam." McNamara recommended a "military posture that we could credibly maintain indefinitely" and stronger emphasis on pacification rather than attrition of Communist forces.[89]

McNamara's analysis suggested that there was no way of knowing how long it would take to end the war, but it did not conclude that the United States would not win it. Somewhat more optimistic, but still sobering, were the views of General William Westmoreland. In a meeting with the President in April 1967, Westmoreland admitted that "unless the will of the enemy is broken or unless there was unravelling of the VC infrastructure the war could go on for five years." Additional forces, he added, would shorten the war, "but not necessarily in proportion to the increases in strength. . . ." [90] Westmoreland requested an optimum force of 200,000 additional troops, which would have raised the total US forces in Vietnam to 670,000, and warned that unless he received his minimum request of 70,000 additional troops, there was a real risk of losing the initiative in the ground war.[91] Westmoreland denied, however, that the war was a "stalemate"—a word which had obvious and unacceptable political implications. "We are winning slowly but steadily," he told McNamara in a July 1967 briefing in Saigon, "and this pace can accelerate if we reinforce our successes." [92]

But despite the determination of McNamara and Westmoreland to avoid any suggestion of "stalemate," the objective of forcing their adversary to abandon the struggle by breaking the will of the DRV to continue the war or by destroying main force Communist units was being quietly abandoned by early 1967. Apart from its continued ability to recruit in the South, the Liberation Army could still call on a large untapped reservoir of manpower in the North. The Vietnam People's Army of the DRV had increased its regular armed forces from 250,000 in 1965 to as many as 470,000 by the end of 1967, and all but 55,000 remained in reserve in the North.[93] Moreover, it was discovered by Defense Department officials that their foes could control their casualty rate by deciding how often to attack US units, since they initiated over 90 percent of all company-sized clashes.[94]

But while hopes for a clear-cut military victory waned, American officials refused to draw the conclusion that they could not "win." Although there was no longer a well-defined conception of how the Liberation Army would be defeated in the South, it was simply assumed that it would eventually be reduced to manageable proportions by the weight of American power. The Johnson administration went to great lengths during 1967, in fact, to convince the public that it was already on its way to "winning" the war. Westmoreland, in a speech in November 1967, predicted that within two years the enemy would be "so weakened that the Vietnamese will be able to cope with a greater share of the war burden," thus permitting the United States to begin withdrawing its troops. Conceding that it might take "several years" to complete the task, he told the public that the United States was moving into the third phase of the war effort in 1968, the final phase, in which "the end begins to come into view." [95] The administration was thus trying to ease the country into a protracted war by reassuring them that steady progress was being made and the ultimate victory was already certain. This was in line with McNamara's recommendation a year earlier, that the administration "give clear evidence . . . that the formula for success has been found, and that the end of the war is merely a matter of time." [96]

A critical weakness of the emerging strategy, however, was the fact that American public support for the war effort was broad but perilously thin. The American people were not likely to support a war in an obscure part of the world for an indefinite period at a very high cost in American lives as well as in economic distortion. The Johnson administration had recognized this fact in its determination to execute the war with a minimum of social and economic disruption, particularly in its avoidance of mobilization of reserves, as well as in its effort to bring about a quick military victory. But as the war went into its third year, with no end in sight, the cost of the war was already rising toward a political danger point. In mid-1967 the President had been compelled to impose a 10 percent surtax on individual and corporate incomes, specifically to support the war effort.

The American people were rapidly losing their patience. In November 1967 a Gallup Poll showed that 57 percent of those questioned were dissatisfied with the President's handling of the war, while only 28 percent approved.[97] Paralleling this growing doubt about the President's policy was a tendency to question the original military intervention in Vietnam. By mid-1967 public opinion polls showed that 46 percent of the population thought that US intervention had been a mistake, compared with 44 percent who said it had not.[98]

In part the rise in disillusionment with the war was the result of the failure to win an early military victory, despite heavy sacrifices in American lives, against a small and militarily inferior foe. Many people felt that the United States should have brought the war to a conclusion by escalating the war against North Vietnam, while others wanted to pull out altogether. Most people were frustrated without perceiving a clear solution.

A second source of confusion and doubt about the war was the lack of a convincing rationale for the American intervention. The reasons offered by the administration, involving commitments, "aggression," and the test case theory, were too vague and elusive for most Americans. In initiating the American combat intervention, President Johnson had been able to rely on the patriotic reflexes of the American public, but there was no clearly comprehensible interest upon which public support could be sustained for an indefinite period. Opinion surveys in mid-1967 revealed that as many as half the population had no clear idea why the United States was fighting in Vietnam.[99]

At the end of 1967 public dissatisfaction with the war remained inchoate. People were still ready to support any presidential initiative which promised to end the war. As late as 1967, more Americans appeared to believe that the war should be ended through escalation than through withdrawal. But as analysts of public opinion pointed out, the preference for this method of terminating the war was "soft" and could be changed relatively easily. The desire to end American involvement in the war, on the other hand, was "hard." [100] It was striking, for example, that despite an aversion to unilateral withdrawl of US forces from the conflict, most Americans supported a negotiated compromise which met the demands of the DRV and the NLF. In 1966 an extraordinary 88 percent of those surveyed were willing to negotiate directly with the NLF while 52 percent supported NLF participation in a coalition government.[101]

Confronted with this steady erosion of public support for the war, the administration resorted in late 1967 to making Communist China, rather than North Vietnam or the NLF, the real enemy in Vietnam. Although administration officials had frequently complained about the "doctrine of militant revolution" which it said China was promoting in the third world, this did not constitute an image of an enemy which engaged either the emotions or the reason of the American public in a war effort in Vietnam. But on October 12, 1967 the administration's rhetoric sharply escalated. In a news conference, Rusk explained the importance of Vietnam to American security by declaring, "Within the next decade or two, there will be a billion Chinese on the mainland, armed with nuclear weapons, with no certainty about what their attitude toward the rest of Asia will be." [102] Although he drew no specific connection with the Vietnam war, his intention was clearly to suggest that American troops in Vietnam were somehow holding the line against the surge of China's nuclear-armed hordes in the direction of Hawaii.

While Rusk denied any intention of invoking the specter of the "Yellow Peril," the administration had made a deliberate decision to focus attention on the most menacing foe it could portray in order to justify the rising costs in money and lives of the intervention. Rusk's "billion Chinese" statement was followed by five more speeches by administration spokesmen within two weeks, referring to the threat to Asia which an "aggressive" China posed.[103] The campaign to make China the real enemy in Vietnam was yet another signal that the Johnson administration was nervous about whether the home front would hold up in the long war for which it was already preparing. The administration was determined to deflect or halt the disenchantment with the war effort and to hold its shrinking base of support by every available means.

But the quiet, steady shifting of attitude was leading inexorably toward a consensus favoring American military withdrawal from Vietnam. This process of change was sensitive, moreover, to any dramatic development which would crystallize doubts about the soundness of the existing policy. The 1968 Communist Tet Offensive was to be such a development. It would give this unfocused doubt and frustration a direction and theme: that the war could not be won and that the United States should disengage militarily. Out of this first confrontation between the executive branch and the tide of American public opinion would come the first major turn in American policy toward a negotiated settlement.

3: The Paris Talks: Origins
of a Diplomatic Stalemate

We have seen in Chapters One and Two that the views of
the United States and the DRV on bringing the conflict to an end
were entirely asymmetrical: while the United States had always
opposed a negotiated settlement which would compromise its
freedom and that of its client regime to bring the revolutionary
movement forcibly under control, the DRV had viewed such a
settlement as a means of establishing the legitimacy of the
revolutionary organization as a political force and destroying the
legitimacy of a regime which had not emerged from a true
expression of South Vietnamese will. Thus, while American military strategy was aimed at destroying the National Liberation
Front as a political and military force, the military strategy of the
PLAF was aimed only at forcing the United States to withdraw and
eliminating the power of those leaders who represented American
influence in Vietnam.

The year 1968 was a critical turning point in the conflict
because it saw the first move by the United States toward
negotiations under conditions which implied the kind of compromise settlement which it had always sought to avoid. The failure of
American military might to break the back of the NLF after nearly
three years of all-out warfare, which the Tet Offensive dramatically
demonstrated, increased the impatience at home for an early end to
American military involvement. The Johnson administration,
under pressure in an election year to show some sign of progress
toward a peace settlement, agreed to end the bombing in order to
begin peace talks with the participation of the NLF. And while it

vehemently denied that it was according any legitimacy to the Front by permitting it to participate in the conference, the implicit equality between the two South Vietnamese parties at the Paris Conference provided a logical framework for the ultimate settlement.

For the next three years, however, the Paris talks were stalemated by the insistence of the Nixon administration on keeping its clients in power with uncontested sovereignty over all of South Vietnam. The stalemate was a reflection of the military situation in South Vietnam. The PLAF was not strong enough to cause a military-political crisis in Saigon, as long as American ground and air power continued to protect the RVN. So it waited for the Americans to withdraw their combat forces, while trying to protect as much of the previous gains as possible. But the Americans could not destroy the firmly entrenched revolutionary bases in the South either. The result was the prolongation of the war and virtually no diplomatic movement toward a compromise settlement.

1.   The Tet Offensive: Setting the Stage for Negotiations

In a war of innumerable small skirmishes, indecisive battles, and strategic stalemate, the Tet Offensive of 1968 was the first campaign to change the whole complexion of the war.[1] Despite the heavy cost which the NLF undoubtedly paid in lives, it destroyed for most Americans the illusion that the war was being won and that it could be won by military means. And in so doing, it prepared the way for the phase of fighting and negotiating which shaped the final outcome of the war.

The Tet Offensive was a coordinated series of attacks on 34 of the 44 province capitals and some 64 district towns, most of which were held in whole or in part by PLAF troops for periods ranging from a few hours to more than three weeks in Hue. "The initial attack nearly succeeded in a dozen places," said General Earl Wheeler, Chairman of the Joint Chiefs of Staff, in a report to the President, "and defeat in those places was only averted by the timely reaction of US forces. In short it was a very near thing." [2] In Vinh Long, Ben Tre, My Tho, and other towns occupied by PLAF troops, the cost of forcing them out was the destruction of large parts of the towns.[3]

But it was in the former imperial capital of Hue that the offensive achieved its most stunning success. There the PLAF held out in the old walled citadel for more than three weeks, while a revolutionary government, headed by non-Communist Hue citizens who had been active in the Buddhist Struggle Movement against the Ky government in 1966, was formed to administer the city.[4] Before the city was recaptured, the US and GVN bombing artillery had demolished most of its buildings. More than half of the buildings were destroyed and less than a third escaped serious damage. Some 4,000 civilians were left dead in the ruins, mostly from the indiscriminate use of fire power during the counter-offensive.[5]

When ARVN forces abandoned the villages to recapture the towns and cities, the Front moved in to fill the vacuum. "To a large extent the VC now control the countryside," said General Wheeler in his February 23 report.[6] The figures which had shown that the GVN controlled two-thirds of the population were shown to be meaningless. According to a high US official, Gia Dinh, the doughnut-shaped province surrounding Saigon, had been pronounced 90 percent pacified at the time of the offensive. But during the offensive, the Front seemed to have complete freedom to launch its attacks from the province,[7] and three months later, US intelligence concluded that pacification "no longer exists in any significant form" in the province.[8]

As the Tet fighting ebbed, however, American officials argued that the real significance of the offensive was that Communist leaders had expected the war to end with a "general uprising," and that since no such popular uprising had taken place, they had miscalculated the attitude of the people.[9] In his March 13 address President Johnson declared that the Tet Offensive "did not produce a 'General Uprising' among the people as the Communists had hoped."[10] *Time* magazine, reflecting the views of high US officials, said that the Communist notion of a popular uprising had been shown to be a "myth."[11]

Long after 1968, the notion persisted that the failure of the Tet Offensive to cause a "General Uprising" and to overturn the Saigon government had been a crushing defeat for the NLF and the Lao Dong Party. The documentary evidence indicates, however, that the aims of the offensive were far more sophisticated and realistic than was suggested by this view. Far from being conceived as a final lunge for total victory, the offensive was seen by its planners as one element of a broader and longer-term strategy.[12] A circular from the Current Affairs Committee of the Lao Dong Party's Central Office for South Vietnam (COSVN) and the Military Affairs Committee of the Liberation Army Headquarters dated January 31, 1968, when the offensive was still unfolding, emphasized that it could not end the war and that a long struggle lay ahead: "It is imperative to be fully aware of the fact that the general offensive and general uprising . . . is a prolonged strategic offensive that includes many military campaigns and local uprisings to break off all enemy counterattacks and that it is an extremely fierce struggle." [13]

The argument that the failure of South Vietnamese urban dwellers to rise up and overthrow the GVN was a major defeat for the NLF, moreover, misrepresents the meaning of the concept of "General Uprising" in Vietnamese revolutionary strategy. Contrary to the usual American portrayal of the "General Uprising" as a spontaneous show of support for the revolution in response to calls for demonstrations in the streets, internal Party documents on the offensive made it clear that a "popular uprising" could occur only after the revolutionary forces had won uncontested military control. Thus the appeal of the October 1967 enlarged NLF Central Committee Conference emphasized that the mission of the PLAF in the winter-spring offensive was to "actively support" their compatriots in "uprisings" aimed at "shattering the enemy's bonds." [14] The image which Party leaders had of uprisings, whether in the cities or in the villages, was that the armed forces would destroy the resistance of GVN and US regular forces, and then the people themselves would be led to seize local power, not only by demonstrations, but by searching out local "tyrants" of the GVN and setting up a new administration. The "popular uprising" was seen as the way in which power was actually transferred from the "puppet" government to a revolutionary government, and it had two steps: to "annihilate the enemy's political power," and then to "organize our political power." [15]

The close relationship in Communist thinking between the "general uprising" and the success of the military offensive in the cities was confirmed by several PLAF military officers and Party cadres who were taken prisoner in the battle for Pleiku during the offensive and interrogated later.[16] Asked if they had been told that the population would join in a general uprising against the United States, they all answered in essence that it would depend on the success of the attack on Pleiku. A senior captain and battalion commander, who had been a Party member since 1950, said he understood from political officers that after the armed forces had entered the city and the fighting had ended, the people would emerge from their houses and stage mass demonstrations. People stayed in their homes, he said, because they were afraid of artillery and air strikes. A Bahnar tribesman, who was executive officer for an independent company, said he believed that if the battle were "indecisive," those unarmed civilians who had joined the troops on the way into Pleiku would be killed or captured. People were afraid to leave their houses, he recalled, even though the cadres told them Pleiku was liberated. A finance cadre and Party member since 1949 observed that the participation of the population depended on the liberation of Pleiku, and that since the fighting was still going on, people were afraid to go outside their homes.

Plans for urban street demonstrations assumed that the PLAF would gain uncontested control of the city, which it failed to do. Demonstrations in support of US withdrawal and a coalition government were planned for Saigon, once the city was liberated.[17] But during the few days of NLF occupation of the city, in the absence of the decisive military defeat of Saigon's forces, there appears to have been little effort to organize such demonstrations.[18]

While the Party's strategists wanted to hold cities and towns for as long as possible and destroy as much of the GVN machinery as possible, the broader objective of the offensive appears to have been the opening of a new phase of the war: the phase of "fighting while negotiating," which they hoped would result in a coalition government. Apart from the instructions given to officers and cadres, evidence of this objective is also found in the shift in the DRV diplomatic stance just before the offensive and the appearance of a new non-Communist political group which could play a centrist role in a negotiated settlement.

Prisoners taken during the battle for Saigon confirmed that they had been told the offensive was connected with the diplomatic objective of negotiating a coalition government. Soldiers who studied the resolution concerning the attack on Saigon a month before the attack learned that the purpose of the offensive was to "create conditions for negotiations to bring about a neutralist regime in South Vietnam." [19] A district level cadre who headed a military proselytizing section said that COSVN had ordered the attack on Saigon to "force negotiations which would result in the formation of a coalition government." [20]

Just before the offensive, the DRV had conveyed a new diplomatic signal intended to move a step closer to negotiations with the United States. On December 30, 1967 Foreign Minister Nguyen Duy Trinh stated that once there was an unconditional bombing halt, Hanoi "will hold talks" with the United States.[21] Previously, the DRV had said that talks "could begin" if there was a bombing halt. In the context of the approaching offensive, this was a sign that the DRV was making a strong bid for negotiations in return for a bombing halt. Despite the urging of the Soviet Union to start talks earlier and the opposition of the Chinese to any negotiations, the Vietnamese had insisted that the timing of the start of negotiations be determined by their own analysis of the situation in the South as well as in the United States. The shift of tense by Trinh meant that Hanoi believed the right moment for negotiations was about to arrive.

Finally, the offensive was accompanied by the surfacing of a new political front sympathetic to the aims of the NLF but organizationally distinct from it, which the Party hoped could play a role in a negotiated political settlement. In August 1967 the NLF had produced a political program aimed at appealing to non-Communist groups who were increasingly alienated by the military government in Saigon and who opposed US military occupation. The program offered to take "joint action against the common enemy" with others who shared their goals, even if they did not join the NLF.[22] That program was followed by intensive work by NLF cadres among disaffected students and intellectuals and professional people in the cities, quietly preparing the formation of anti-American, anti-GVN "patriotic organizations." Such organizations would not only help to politically isolate the Saigon regime but might play the role of a non-Communist, though anti-American, centrist group in a coalition government.

During the first days of the offensive, political groups appeared only briefly in Saigon but for a full three weeks in Hue, calling themselves the "Alliance of National Democratic and Peace Forces." At the end of April a national organization with the same name was formed, with a membership including many prominent non-Communist figures in Saigon and Hue.[23] By the early summer of 1968 the Australian journalist Wilfred Burchett, who was close to the DRV and NLF delegations, reported that both Hanoi and the Front believed that the Alliance would play an important role in a negotiated settlement. Burchett said the organization "seems to contain the nucleus of some form of coalition government of nationalist and neutralist forces." [24]

The evidence indicates that, whatever else the Party leadership hoped to accomplish in the 1968 winter-spring offensive, it saw that offensive as part of a larger strategy of moving the war into the stage of "fighting while negotiating," with the aim of increasing the pressure on the United States to accept a coalition government. And although the resistance of the US government to negotiating a coalition government proved to be far stronger than Hanoi had hoped, the Tet Offensive did succeed in this larger aim of getting the negotiations started without yielding on any of Hanoi's principles.

2. *Starting the Paris Talks: Negotiating on Negotiations*

The Tet Offensive caught American society and the American political system at a point when they could not easily tolerate another escalation of the Vietnam war. The United States was overextended economically, militarily, and politically in Vietnam. No more troops could be sent to Vietnam without mobilizing, enlarging draft calls, or lengthening the twelve-month combat tour. The dollar was faring badly on the world money market. Secretary of the Treasury Henry Fowler saw dire economic consequences if the 200,000 additional troops requested by General Westmoreland in the immediate aftermath of the offensive were sent to Vietnam.[25] And finally, American public opinion, already increasingly doubtful about the wisdom of the administration's policy in Vietnam, could not be expected to support a higher level of American military involvement there.

The offensive catalyzed differences within the Johnson administration itself between those who advocated a deescalation of the American war effort and a greater emphasis on a negotiated solution and those who insisted that the United States hold to its original objectives and continue maximum military pressure on the enemy.[26] Those who had been doubtful that the United States could win the war found that the Tet Offensive helped to clarify policy issues and strengthened their arguments. And they found the new Secretary of Defense, Clark Clifford, receptive to their arguments.

Meanwhile the domestic political fall-out from the Tet Offensive became clear in the New Hampshire presidential primary,[27] where Senator Eugene McCarthy of Minnesota, challenging Johnson for the Democratic nomination, won more than 42 percent of the vote. It was a signal that the war, which had been a central issue in McCarthy's campaign, threatened Johnson's prospects for reelection.

Later in March Johnson found that his "Senior Advisory Group" of former diplomats, generals, and other officials, which had previously supported his Vietnam policy, had now turned deeply pessimistic. A majority of them advised Johnson that a military solution was no longer possible and that he should press harder for a negotiated settlement. Johnson realized from their response that the country no longer supported the war effort, although he still believed that they were overly pessimistic.[28]

Confronted with the threat of an erosion of public support for his war policy, Johnson made a tactical concession to those pressing for negotiations, announcing a bombing cutback in North Vietnam, coupled with an announcement that he would not run for another term as President. But Johnson and his closest advisers were not willing to seek a compromise solution. Instead, they viewed the bombing cutback as a useful device: "something had to be done to extend the lease on public support for the war," one high State Department official explained. "We were focused on what we could do without significant military drawbacks to make clear to people we were serious about peace." [29]

Johnson and his top advisers did not believe that the DRV would respond positively to the move, since it fell short of their previous demand for a complete bombing halt.[30] The day before the President's March 31 speech announcing the cutback, a cable had gone out to US ambassadors which said, "Hanoi is most likely to

denounce the project and thus free our hand after a short period."
The cable noted that the United States "might wish to continue the
limitation even after a formal denunciation, in order to reinforce its
sincerity and put the monkey firmly on Hanoi's back for whatever
follows." [31]

The Johnson administration was thus unprepared for the
DRV's announcement of its readiness to send a representative to
meet with the United States. While the debate within the
administration over a complete bombing halt raged through the
summer and autumn, no concrete realistic plan for a negotiated
settlement was developed. Instead, the administration drifted
toward a policy of turning the war over to the GVN. As early as
April 1968 Secretary Clifford spoke of a "policy decision" that "the
South Vietnamese will take over the war." [32] In the absence of a
determination to negotiate a quick military and political settlement
this could only mean an indefinite prolongation of the war and of
US involvement in it.

In contrast to the United States' reluctance to seize the
opportunity for diplomacy, the DRV decision to agree to limited
talks in response to Johnson's bombing cutback announcement
underlined the certainty of the Vietnamese leaders that the time
was ripe for negotiations. Having previously said that they would
not participate in discussions with the United States until all
bombing of the North was stopped unconditionally, they now
agreed to public contacts with the United States—but only for the
purpose of "determining with the American side the unconditional
cessation of the US bombing raids and all other acts of war against
the Democratic Republic of Vietnam so that talks may start." [33]

The Political Bureau, which had been given the power to
decide on the timing of negotiations, had waited until they felt the
balance of forces was most favorable both within Vietnam and
internationally to move for peace negotiations. From their perspective, the LBJ bombing cutback must have appeared to be a
recognition that the war could not be won and a gesture to those
pressing for an end to the war.

Despite his continued invocation of the Manila formula, which
called, in effect, for a unilateral cease-fire by the NLF and
withdrawal of all Northern troops as the price for US military
withdrawal, the speech represented, in their view, a first move to get

peace talks started. They wanted to get an initiative which preserved their demand for a full bombing halt and encouraged those in the United States calling for such a halt to press their case.

When the talks finally began on May 13, 1968, there were two problems to be resolved before substantive negotiations could get under way: the complete cessation of the bombing of North Vietnam and the question of who would be represented at the talks and how. The United States immediately demanded some form of "reciprocity" from the DRV in return for a complete bombing halt, as it had from 1965 onward. On June 26, the American delegation presented a proposal under which the United States would stop the bombing "and all other activities that involve the use of force";[34] the DRV would in turn agree to respect the Demilitarized Zone (DMZ), and not carry out any major attack on Saigon, Hue, or Danang. Both sides would pledge not to build up their forces further and to start substantial talks. On the question of representation at the expanded conference, the US delegation said, "our side will include the representatives of the Republic of Vietnam. Your side will include any representatives you will invite." [35]

The DRV delegation refused as a matter of principle to agree to any conditions and demanded that the bombing stop "unconditionally." But the PLAF did undertake a substantial deescalation in June and July, which seemed to meet Secretary Rusk's request on June 21 for a signal from the other side of willingness to deescalate. Not only did the rocket attacks on Saigon stop abruptly in June, but an estimated 25 to 33 percent of the North Vietnamese troops in the South were withdrawn, and those troops remaining were ordered to avoid contact with American forces.[36] DRV representatives at the Paris talks called these moves to the attention of American journalists as well as to US negotiator Ambassador Averell Harriman.[37]

Harriman recommended to the President that the military lull be regarded as the signal that Washington had asked for and that a full bombing halt be carried out, after informing the DRV delegation of what the United States expected in the way of future military restraint. But Johnson again chose to disregard the lull, as he had done during the bombing pause of 1965–66, and he vetoed Harriman's proposal.[38]

In mid-September, however, after four months of talks without any progress, President Johnson changed his mind and approved the earlier proposal by Harriman and Vance: the United States would stop the bombing after a unilateral declaration to the DRV that it would expect certain military restraints to be observed and that substantive talks would begin with Saigon as a full participant under the "our side, your side" formula.[39]

Beginning on September 20 the United States dropped its demand in the private talks for prior agreement on military restraint, and Harriman told the North Vietnamese that the United States would consider an agreement on serious talks, with the participation of the Republic of Vietnam, as a "major factor" in stopping the bombing of the North. Harriman added, according to the DRV account, "We also take note of your views on stopping the bombing without conditions." [40] Then Harriman went on to present the unilateral "understanding" on a bombing halt: if the United States halted the bombing, it expected that Communist forces would not "indiscriminately attack the major cities, such as Saigon, Danang and Hue," and that the North Vietnamese would not abuse the Demilitarized Zone by firing artillery across it or infiltrating men and supplies at high levels through it.[41]

The American delegation repeated its position at twelve different meetings, and on at least one occasion US negotiator Cyrus Vance read from a "talking paper," which he left on the table for his counterpart, Colonel Ha Van Lau, to pick up.[42] Soviet Ambassador Dobrynin in Washington was briefed on the American position and asked to convey it to the DRV, and the Ambassador sent back a reassuring note, without, however, committing the DRV to anything.[43] Throughout this exercise, the DRV delegation reiterated its understanding that the United States would stop the bombing unconditionally. On one occasion, according to Johnson's own account, a DRV representative said that if the United States stopped the bombing, his government would "know what to do." [44] But in the end, the DRV did not agree to any conditions, and the United States concluded a "unilateral understanding," which permitted the DRV to argue that its demand for an "unconditional bombing halt" had been met.

On October 15 Harriman said that the United States was prepared to end the bombing of the North if the DRV agreed to join substantive talks the following day. DRV delegate Xuan

Thuy's reply posed additional conditions for the DRV's participation in expanded talks: "After the U. S. unconditionally stops the bombing and all other acts of war against the Democratic Republic of Vietnam, the DRV side will accept a conference with the participation of four delegations, namely the delegation of the Democratic Republic of Vietnam, the delegation of the South Vietnam National Liberation Front, the delegation of the United States and the delegation of the Saigon administration, to discuss a political solution to the Vietnam problem." [45] The North Vietnamese formula would have ruled out aerial reconnaissance as well as bombing and would have meant an explicitly four-party conference, rather than the "two-sided" conference which the United States wanted. In a later meeting the DRV delegation insisted that the United States agree to a "minute" affirming that the bombing was being stopped unconditionally. According to the DRV account, Harriman assured them on October 21, "There is no question that we have told you that we make no condition, that we will stop the bombing without conditions," but he refused to put anything in writing.[46]

Finally, on October 30, the DRV accepted the US position that there be no written minute of the United States statement that bombing was being stopped unconditionally, having earlier dropped its insistence that the United States use the phrase "all acts of war" and "four-party" conference in its statement on the bombing halt. Harriman then told the DRV representatives that the United States would end the bombing of the North the following evening, and that the negotiations would start on November 6 at the earliest.[47]

Meanwhile, the United States was having trouble getting its own clients in Saigon to agree to the arrangement. The GVN had already let the United States know in the summer of 1968 that it feared any substantive talks in Paris in which the NLF participated could raise the prestige of the Front.[48] But apart from that, President Thieu had to reconcile the needs of his American patrons with the views of the right-wing political elements whose support he had sought to win during the course of 1968. After the Tet Offensive Vice-President Nguyen Cao Ky had attacked both Thieu and the Americans, accusing them, in effect, of being ready to sell out the country to the Communists.[49] Thieu, evidently fearing a possible move against him from the right, tried to preempt the most intransigent opponents of a negotiated settlement by reaffirming the exclusion of the Front from the political process under any circumstances.

When Ambassador Ellsworth Bunker presented Thieu on October 16 with a joint communiqué approving the bombing halt and the expanded Paris talks, Thieu first gave his approval to the communiqué, then changed his mind.[50] He told Bunker that the conditions under which the talks were starting were unacceptable, calling the communiqué a "clear admission of defeat." [51]

After the difficulties with Hanoi were finally resolved, Bunker again approached Thieu about a revised joint communiqué. Again, Bunker and Thieu reached an agreement on a draft communiqué which emphasized that Johnson and Thieu would not recognize the NLF as an "entity separate from North Vietnam." [52]

But then he balked once again at the whole project. At a meeting with Bunker and Deputy Ambassador Berger, Thieu and Ky demanded that the DRV commit itself publicly to the principle that the NLF would not have a separate seat at the talks. As an alternate proposal, Ky suggested that the GVN send a delegation to Paris, but only for "preliminary" talks to establish ground rules for later negotiations on substantive issues—a proposal which would have nullified the US unilateral "understanding" with the DRV. Berger warned that if the GVN insisted that the DRV pledge publicly not to allow a separate seat for the NLF at the talks, the United States could not support the demand. Thieu angrily retorted that Berger sounded like a representative of Hanoi rather than of the United States.[53]

This maneuvering between the Johnson administration and the Saigon regime took place in the context of an approaching American presidential election in which Republican candidate Richard M. Nixon's position on Vietnam appeared more in line with Saigon's interests than that of his Democratic opponent, Hubert H. Humphrey. After this series of agreements and delays, Johnson began to suspect that the Thieu regime was stalling on the peace talks at the suggestion of someone claiming to represent Nixon, thus denying the Democrats the political advantage of a major diplomatic breakthrough in the closing weeks of the campaign.[54] (Given the shifts in public opinion toward Humphrey in

October and the closeness of the vote, it appears that Saigon may well have succeeded by its delaying tactics in putting Nixon in the White House.) So Johnson went ahead and announced the bombing halt and expanded Paris talks on October 31 without Saigon's approval.

In his announcement, Johnson was vague about the nature of the "understanding" which he said had made it possible to stop the bombing of the North.[55] A few days before, he said, "the United States began to get confirmation of the essential understanding that we had been seeking with the North Vietnamese on the critical issues between us for some time." By using the word "understanding" Johnson left the impression with most Americans that the United States had extracted some commitment from the DRV in exchange for the bombing halt, which it had not. The DRV immediately declared that the United States had been "compelled" to stop the bombing "unconditionally." [56] The US representation of the "understanding" as *mutual* rather than *unilateral*, which was heatedly denied by the DRV, was repeated four months later, when Communist forces launched nationwide mortar and rocket attacks against bases and major cities.[57]

On November 2 Thieu declared that the GVN would not attend the Paris talks because it would "not agree to talk with what the Communists call the NLFSV [National Liberation Front for South Vietnam] as an entity separate and independent from the North Vietnamese government. . . ." [58] When the DRV delegation proposed that the United States begin talks with the DRV and NLF, which Saigon could join whenever it was ready, the United States refused.[59]

But the United States could not afford to let Saigon sabotage the talks which it had already agreed to with Hanoi. On November 11 Secretary Clifford threatened publicly to go ahead with negotiations with the DRV if Saigon continued to refuse to attend the talks.[60] Two weeks later, after more American pressure and renewed assurances to the Thieu regime that the United States would not recognize the NLF as an equal and independent delegation at the talks or impose a coalition government, Saigon agreed to send its delegation to Paris.[61]

When the discussions on physical arrangements opened in November, the American spokesman, Cyrus Vance, proposed two long tables which would support the contention that it was a two-sided conference. The DRV delegation insisted on a square table with one delegate seated on each of the four sides, thus showing that NLF was an equal partner in the negotiations.[62] The United States then proposed a round table, which was completely ambiguous as to its political implications. The DRV quickly accepted the compromise.

But the Saigon government, whether because it genuinely felt that the issue was vital or because it hoped to stall until the Nixon administration took office, refused to go along with it. Harriman was unable to come to an agreement with Hanoi on the shape of the table without Saigon's consent, because the decision had already been made that the United States would not negotiate without Saigon. Harriman later recalled, "They [Saigon's representatives] had to be there. We couldn't negotiate the political settlement with the North; we made it clear we would negotiate a military settlement, but the political settlement would have to be negotiated with Saigon." [63]

The result was that the United States backed away from its earlier compromise position and backed Saigon's demand for further concessions from the DRV. Finally, after the United States prevailed upon the Soviet Embassy in Paris to urge more flexibility on its North Vietnamese allies, the DRV conceded the point and accepted a slight alteration of the round table: two rectangular tables placed at opposite ends of the table.[64]

This ambiguous resolution of the issue of the table represented a limited victory for the NLF, since it failed to give Saigon any special status over the NLF, thus reinforcing the Front's claim of equality with Saigon. As Rusk had said three years earlier, to give the Front equal status at the negotiating table was in effect to prejudice the final outcome of the talks, implying as it did an ultimate compromise involving the sharing of power between the two South Vietnamese parties. The US "our side, your side" formula was quickly overtaken by the reality of an NLF which was treated by the news media as a political entity with a significant role to play in the final settlement.

More immediately, however, the preliminary negotiations over the mechanics and procedures of the talks had shown that the United States did not look upon the Paris Conference as a means of disengaging both militarily and politically from Vietnam, but as a means of preserving the legal and political edifice which had been sustained by American military power. To give Thieu a veto over the negotiations was, in effect, to say that there could be no political settlement.

Indeed, the Pentagon and the State Department were still advising the outgoing President that the DRV's willingness to deescalate the war and negotiate was a sign of weakness, and that the United States could force a settlement on its own terms.[65] The military and some others in the national security bureaucracy saw the building up of the Saigon army while gradually phasing out US military involvement as a way of avoiding defeat in the war. And the incoming administration, as the Thieu regime already knew, was not inclined to make political concessions to the other side in order to get a peace settlement. So the war was moving not toward a diplomatic settlement but toward a new phase of diplomatic stalemate.

3. *The Nixon Administration: The Strategy of Coercion*

When Richard M. Nixon assumed the presidency in January 1969, he had some definite ideas about how the war in Vietnam should be ended, and they excluded a settlement which would yield the Thieu regime's monopoly of power. Although Nixon, like many other Americans, had been shocked by the Tet Offensive and was convinced in 1968 that the United States could no longer win militarily in Vietnam, he was unwilling to conclude that it should agree to a face-saving diplomatic arrangement and withdraw. Instead, he was determined to end the war on American terms. His plan was to bring the influence of the Soviet Union to bear upon the DRV in order to force Hanoi to make crucial concessions: withdrawal of North Vietnamese troops and submission of the NLF to a political structure controlled by the Saigon military regime.

Nixon explained his thinking about how a favorable settlement could be brought about in a discussion with Southern delegates at the 1968 Republican convention. "How do you bring a war to a conclusion?" he asked rhetorically. "I'll tell you how Korea was ended. We got in there and had this messy war on our hands. Eisenhower let the word go out—let the word go out diplomatically to the Chinese and the North Koreans that we would not tolerate this continued ground war of attrition. And within a matter of months, they negotiated. . . ." [66]

Just as Nixon believed that the threat of the use of nuclear weapons forced the Chinese to make the concessions necessary to end the deadlock at Panmunjom, so he believed that threats of drastic military action against North Vietnam could bring the concessions necessary to end the Vietnam war. This high-level coercion would require that the other side be put on notice that he was willing to go beyond the gradual and limited escalation of destruction carried out by the Johnson administration.

Another, closely related, element in Nixon's thinking about obtaining a settlement which would preserve the Saigon government intact was the necessity for the active assistance of the Soviet Union. In a speech written for delivery the same evening as Johnson's March 31 address, Nixon had said, "If the Soviets were disposed to see the war ended and a compromise settlement negotiated, they have the means to move Ho Chi Minh to the conference table." The next President, he told the Southern delegates, would have to "sit down with the Soviet leadership quite directly, not only about Vietnam, you have got to broaden the canvas—because in Vietnam they have no reason to end the war." [67]

In order to get the Soviets to take an interest in an early settlement, therefore, the United States would have to convey threats of its intention to reescalate the war at a more serious level than the Johnson administration and also use all of its diplomatic leverage with the Soviets. Talking with speechwriter Richard Whalen, Nixon said, "We have to say [to the Soviets], 'Look, if you go on supporting North Vietnam, we will have to act dramatically. . . .' On the other hand, we have to say, 'If you are willing to give ground and help us out of this morass, it could mean lots of good things.' " [68] That would mean making agreements on other issues, such as arms limitation and expansion of East-West trade, conditional on Soviet willingness to intervene with Hanoi on a settlement.

In Henry Kissinger, Nixon chose a national security adviser whose views on ending the war were compatible with his own. Like Nixon he believed that the United States had committed its prestige in Vietnam and had to resolve the conflict in such a way as to prove its toughness, if not its military prowess. In a 1966 article, he said the issue in Vietnam was preventing a victory by a "third class Communist peasant state" over the United States.[69] Although skeptical, like Nixon, about military victory, he was not willing to compromise on the central issue of sharing power in the Saigon government with the NLF. In a remarkably frank and revealing article in *Foreign Affairs*, published right after he was named as Nixon's adviser, Kissinger conceded that the strategy of military victory had been shown by the Tet Offensive to be a failure, and that some kind of negotiated settlement was therefore necessary.[70] But Kissinger made it clear that he was opposed to the United States' negotiating a political settlement, at least as long as Saigon lacked confidence in its ability to compete politically with Hanoi on equal terms. The United States, he said, "should avoid negotiating about the internal structure of South Vietnam *for as long as possible*"[71] (emphasis added). The reason, as Kissinger admitted, was that Saigon was obviously unwilling to agree to a political compromise with its adversaries, and therefore the United States would be "likely to wind up applying the greater part of our pressure against Saigon as the seeming obstacle to an accommodation," a situation which might result in the "complete demoralization of Saigon. . . ."[72] In particular, he opposed US negotiation about a coalition government, which he said would endanger the stability of the RVN government.[73]

The US negotiating posture, he argued, should be limited to a staged, mutual withdrawal of forces, carried out over "a sufficiently long period so that a genuine indigenous political process had a chance to become established," and with the stricture that "the contending sides in South Vietnam should commit themselves not to pursue their objectives by force while the withdrawal of external forces is going on."[74] Such a negotiating strategy would seek to ratify the balance of military power created by American troops and air power. As Kissinger put it, if the United States could gain "a reasonable time for political consolidation, it will have done the maximum possible for an ally—short of permanent occupation. . . ."[75]

The DRV, of course, would find this negotiating position unacceptable at first. But Kissinger argued that, given its own limited physical resources and small size, and its inability to expel the United States from South Vietnam militarily, it would have no choice but to accept American terms for a settlement as the price for an American withdrawal. The United States could credibly threaten to hold on in South Vietnam indefinitely, he said, if it adopted a strategy which was "sustainable with substantially reduced casualties." [76] Thus he admitted by implication that the major obstacle to his negotiating strategy was American public opinion, and that a strategy for deflating opposition to the war would be central to the policy of the incoming administration.

The policy adopted by the Nixon administration on Vietnam closely followed the lines indicated by both Nixon and Kissinger before taking office. It aimed at a negotiated settlement which would preserve the existing Saigon regime's power and sovereignty intact; it attempted to force Hanoi to accept American terms through the threat of escalation and by getting the Soviets to put pressure on them to make concessions; and it perceived American public impatience with the war as a constraint on policy which had to be removed.

The new administration was quite open in declaring that its major problem was not only to prevent further erosion of public support for the war but to roll back the opposition which had already developed. In one interview, Kissinger stated flatly, "The major problem we have now is to get domestic support during the period of settlement." [77] To another journalist he said, "I think we've got real possibilities of success with our Vietnam policies, but it will take time. . . . This attempt to get peace in Vietnam may involve 15 or 18 moves." [78]

The administration tried to reduce public controversy over Vietnam, which meant reducing the cost to the American people by withdrawing troops, cutting down on casualties, and reducing draft calls. As Secretary of Defense Melvin Laird said in August 1969, a "possible scenario" involved cutting US forces in South Vietnam to 250,000 volunteers who "would be used only in support capacity." Laird said the plan "could reduce political pressure on the administration and help quiet dissent in general." [79] In September the administration announced the withdrawal of 35,000 troops over a period of several months and substantial cutbacks in draft calls. Secretary of the Army Stanley Resor explained in closed committee hearings that the schedule of troop withdrawals was designed to free the administration from domestic constraints. "If we can just buy some time in the United States by those periodic, progressive withdrawals," he said, "and the American people can just shore up their patience and determination, I think we can bring this thing to a successful conclusion." [80]

The desire to contain public and Congressional opposition to American military involvement also necessitated the use of secrecy and deception with regard to military actions designed to put greater pressure on Hanoi as the United States prepared for gradual withdrawal. One of the earliest decisions made by the Nixon administration on Indochina was to initiate a new campaign of bombing against Communist sanctuaries in Cambodia, where the United States had previously not dared to bomb. The bombing campaign, called "Operation Menu," began on March 18, 1969 with B-52 sorties against Cambodia that often constituted more than half of the total daily B-52 operations in Southeast Asia. It was not only kept secret from Congress and the public but from the State and Defense Departments as well, as a system of falsified records was established to hide the Cambodian operation from all but a few men in the American government.[81]

In Paris, the American negotiating position was defined in large part by the official conclusion that, in the words of a cable from the Mission in Saigon in January 1969, "The GVN political system as it is now is probably inadequate for a political confrontation with the enemy." [82] Since Saigon was not ready for a political competition, there could be no serious negotiation on political elements of a settlement.

The administration had to argue that it could not take responsibility for negotiating a political settlement, while defending the Thieu regime's position to the American public as generous and flexible. This was no small task, given the hostility of Saigon to any proposal which would require it to yield its monopoly control over the political process. Secretary of State William Rogers, testifying before the Senate Foreign Relations Committee in March 1969, said that Thieu was willing to assure "all political elements who are prepared to renounce violence and put their views peacefully to the populace for a decision" of their "right to participate fully in the political process under the national constitution." [83] There were so many qualifications in this endorsement of the Front's participation in elections as to render it meaningless. When asked about the requirement that candidates had to participate "under the national constitution," thus making it a GVN election rather than one under neutral auspices, Rogers retreated to the position that it wasn't the administration's business. "[I] would not like to go beyond the statement," he said, "because it is somewhat inconsistent with the position we have taken as a government that we should leave the political decisions to the people in South Vietnam." [84]

A few days later, Thieu issued a statement that those who belonged to the NLF could participate in elections only after disarming themselves, renouncing Communism, and agreeing to live under the GVN constitution.[85] Despite its participation in the Paris Conference, the Thieu regime was still taking the same extreme line that it had taken a year earlier under right-wing pressures.

Nixon continued to put the best face possible on Saigon's position on a political settlement. In a major speech on Vietnam policy on May 14, 1969 he declared again that "the political settlement ought to be decided among themselves and not imposed by outside powers." He endorsed Thieu's offer of "free elections," explaining that Thieu was offering "all political elements" in South Vietnam "full participation in the political life," provided only that they were "prepared to do so without the use of force or intimidation." [86] Nixon did not explain that this meant that Thieu's opponents had to surrender their arms in order to fulfill these conditions.

Despite its willingness to defend even the most inflexible GVN position, however, the Nixon administration was encouraging Thieu to present a more elaborate proposal for free elections, in order to reassure Congressional critics that it was not the GVN which was obstructing a settlement. After many hints from Washington that such a proposal was forthcoming, Thieu finally produced in July 1969 a plan which provided for an "electoral committee" on which "all political parties and groups" would be represented. The committee would have an equal opportunity to campaign and to "observe the polling and counting of ballots," and an international organization would be "set up to observe the elections." [87] The committee envisioned by Thieu clearly would have no power, and this election would still be carried out by the Thieu regime itself, as was quickly confirmed by RVN Foreign Minister Tran Chanh Thanh in a news conference after Thieu's speech. Some aides of President Thieu spoke of the possibility of "elevating" the status of the committee to that of an "elections ministry" in the RVN, making it clear that it would be subordinate to rather than independent of the Saigon government.[88]

By putting the emphasis on the "electoral commission" and "international inspection," however, the Nixon administration was able to obscure the fact that the Thieu regime had no intention of giving up its grip on the administrative structure and its tight political controls. In testimony before the Senate Foreign Relations Committee, Secretary of State Rogers said the proposal would "turn the responsibility for conducting the election to the international supervisory forces as a group to see that the elections are fair." [89] American officials in Saigon regarded the whole notion of "international supervision" of elections in South Vietnam as something of a joke, designed to conceal the government's tight control over the process.[90] Saigon had made it clear that the international body would not "conduct" the elections—the RVN would do this—but only supervise them.

The administration's only diplomatic initiative in its first year was a proposal for "mutual withdrawal" which the US delegation tabled in Paris a few days after Nixon took office: the "major portions" of all "non-South Vietnamese forces" would be withdrawn over a period of one year, after which the remaining forces would "move into designated base areas and would not engage in combat." The United States would "move to complete" the withdrawal of its forces "as the remaining North Vietnamese forces were withdrawn and returned to North Viet-Nam." Moreover, the North Vietnamese withdrawal would have to be verified by an "international supervisory body" before the United States would complete its withdrawal.

But the DRV had already made it clear that there could be no "reciprocity" for the withdrawal of American troops, any more than there could have been for the cessation of bombing of the North. Whether or not the Party leadership believed that Southern troops alone could force the acceptance of a coalition government in the absence of North Vietnamese troops, they could never agree to any formal arrangement which would put their forces on the same level as those of the United States, thus erasing the distinction between the "aggressor" and the "victim of aggression." [91] Despite the DRV refusal to discuss any proposal for mutual withdrawal, however, Nixon and Kissinger were being told by the Embassy and the military that the weakness of the Communists' military position would force them to accept American terms. A cable from Saigon to Kissinger early in 1969 said, "We think the prospects on the ground are bleak enough for them so that they will, in the end, make significant concessions [in terms of their own withdrawal] to get us out." [92]

The Nixon negotiating position of mutual withdrawal and no political settlement thus represented a calculated risk that the Communists would be forced to accept the American proposal. The administration devoted much of its diplomatic effort to bringing pressure to bear on the Vietnamese through the Soviets. One method was to refuse to move forward on negotiations on a strategic arms limitation agreement, in which the Soviets were known to be interested, unless there was progress in achieving a Vietnam settlement.[93] More important was a series of threats to devastate North Vietnam if there was no settlement of the war on American terms. In a series of conversations with Soviet Ambassador Anatoly Dobrynin, Kissinger reportedly issued "veiled threats" to resume the bombing of North Vietnam—and to go beyond what the Johnson administration had done—if the DRV did not agree to the American proposal for mutual withdrawal.[94] Nixon alluded to these threats in a news conference on March 4, 1969. The Soviets, he said, "recognize that if [the war] continues over a long period of time, the possibility of escalation increases." Nixon expressed the belief that Moscow "would like to use what influence it could appropriately to help to bring the war to a conclusion." [95]

Nixon also made oblique reference to his threats against the DRV in his May 14 address: "I must also make clear, in all candor, that if the needless suffering continues, this will affect other decisions." [96] And just as Nixon was presenting the speech on television, Kissinger was explaining to Dobrynin that the above sentence meant that if the Russians didn't "produce a settlement," the United States would "escalate the war." [97]

The Nixon administration's diplomacy of "linkage" and coercion proved, however, to be fruitless. Not only did the Soviets refuse to put pressure on the Vietnamese to accept an American-imposed solution; they also gave diplomatic recognition on June 13 to the Provisional Revolutionary Government, which had been formed by the NLF and the "Alliance of National, Democratic and Peace Forces" a few days earlier. And in October, the Soviets signed a communiqué endorsing without reservation the NLF's ten-point program for a peace settlement.[98] Diplomatic observers in Moscow noted a certain "irritation" with "American approaches to the Soviets with a view to obtaining their intervention with Hanoi and the NLF. . . ." [99]

In launching this effort to enlist the Soviets on behalf of the American proposal for ending the war, Nixon and Kissinger had ignored the advice not only of Ambassador Harriman, who had dealt with Soviet diplomats in Paris during 1968, but also that of the US Ambassador in Moscow, Llewellyn Thompson. Both Harriman and Thompson had warned that the Soviets, while interested in a political settlement of the Vietnam conflict, were partisans of the DRV and would assist in the negotiations only to the extent that they saw an American willingness to negotiate a genuine compromise. "They're going to take Hanoi's side in these negotiations," Harriman said. "If we can come to some agreement with Hanoi, I think they'll be very helpful in smoothing out some of the rough spots." The Soviets would "urge them to give in on some of the less important details. But they won't take our side in supporting the Thieu government, for instance." [100]

Ambassador Thompson, in a message to the State Department at the end of 1968, also cautioned against expecting too much from Soviet intervention with the Vietnamese. The Soviets, he said, had "openly and privately pressed for talks looking toward a political solution," but they would use their leverage on Hanoi only "with caution, letting Hanoi call the signals." He noted that support in the Soviet media for the DRV and NLF negotiating positions was "vocal and unequivocal, and we think it is unlikely that the Soviets will go far in pressing Hanoi toward concessions unless the talks are near breakdown." [101]

Apart from a healthy skepticism that the Nixon administration would actually carry out the threat to escalate the war beyond the Johnson administration's policy, given the state of American public opinion, there were other reasons why the Soviets would not budge from their support for the DRV-NLF position on ending the war through a coalition government. In the first place, Soviet support for the DRV had already paid off in terms of DRV support on key issues in the socialist world such as the invasion of Czechoslovakia, and neutrality on Sino-Soviet issues. And the issues which divided the United States and the DRV at the Paris Conference were still matters of principle, rather than of detail or degree, as when the Soviets (and Chinese) had prevailed upon the Viet Minh at Geneva to agree to the seventeenth parallel rather than the sixteenth or even lower on the map, as the military demarcation line.

After the Soviet recognition of the Provisional Revolutionary Government (PRG) in June 1969, the Nixon administration appears to have quietly given up its efforts to get a settlement by way of Moscow. On June 19 Secretary Rogers told Ambassador Dobrynin that the United States was prepared to begin negotiations on strategic arms limitation on July 31.[102] The idea of forcing a quick negotiated settlement, which had never been emphasized publicly, was allowed to expire.

4. *1970–71: The Illusion of Negotiations from Strength*

The latter half of 1969 saw a significant shift in the object of the Nixon administration's diplomacy on Vietnam. The emphasis was no longer on getting Hanoi to accept an early agreement on American terms, but on getting it to accept a military and territorial balance which was beginning to tilt in Saigon's favor. The administration was less concerned about an agreement for mutual withdrawal of troops than about preventing any attempt by the PLAF to take advantage of US troop withdrawals to reverse the progress of the Vietnamization program. Particularly after Nixon's November 3, 1969 speech, which had temporarily succeeded in blunting the pressure for a quick US military withdrawal, the administration felt that time was on its side and that it could afford to wait for the DRV to come around to acceptance of less favorable terms.

This strategy depended on explicit public threats to retaliate against any renewed Communist offensive. "If at a time that we are attempting to de-escalate the fighting in Vietnam," Nixon said in a

January 1970 press conference, "we find that they take advantage of our troop withdrawals to jeopardize the remainder of our forces by escalating the fighting, then we have the means—and I will be prepared to use those means strongly—to deal with that situation more strongly than we have dealt with it in the past." [103]

The invasion of Cambodia in May 1970 was aimed in part at buying time by destroying temporarily the Communist base areas in the border area of Cambodia.[104] But it was also used by Nixon to try to increase the credibility of his threat to attack North Vietnam for any renewed offensive. "This action . . . puts the enemy on warning," he declared on May 10, 1970, "that if it escalates while we are trying to de-escalate, we will move decisively and not step-by-step." [105] A series of air strikes on antiaircraft installations and base areas in the southern region of North Vietnam, blandly called "reinforced protective reaction" by the administration, was also apparently intended to underline further the threat of massive bombing against the DRV.[106]

By the spring of 1970 there were signs that the Nixon administration believed it could maintain a military balance in South Vietnam which would leave the DRV and PRG no choice but to agree ultimately to a settlement which would deny them a share in national power. Nixon's April 20, 1970 statement on further troop withdrawals made no reference to the electoral proposal which had been so highly publicized the year before.[107] Instead, he said, "a fair political solution should reflect the existing relationship of political forces within South Vietnam." These words, which departed from the rhetoric about free elections previously used by the administration, were the first hint that it was thinking in terms of a political arrangement which would be based on the NLF keeping control of the territory it then occupied.

Nixon further stated: "We recognize the complexity of shaping machinery that would fairly apportion political power in South Vietnam." The idea of "apportioning political power" could only mean the acceptance of a territorial status quo as the basis for a political settlement. That idea coincided with a plan which had been seriously discussed within the Nixon administration since early 1969, variously termed a "territorial accommodation" or "leopard spot confederal" solution.[108] In essence the plan would have allocated formal power over geographical areas already under de facto NLF control to the local revolutionary committees, in return for their acceptance of the formal sovereignty of the Republic of Vietnam over the area, and guarantees of free movement for certain civilian officials of the RVN through the area. The RVN would "confirm" the local revolutionary government, grant it veto power over all appointments in the area, accept PLAF military units as the Popular Forces (ARVN)/self-defense units, and allocate seats in the RVN lower house to areas controlled by the revolutionaries.

The plan was explicitly designed to reflect the realities of territorial control in the cities and countryside. It would thus have given legal status to a situation created by five years of combat by half a million American troops and daily attacks by American jet bombers and B-52s against the PLAF and the Front's zone of control. Moreover, as one elaboration of the plan pointed out, it would have kept the NLF out of the cities, out of the central government, and therefore out of national power. It would have undermined the claim of the Provisional Revolutionary Government to be an alternate government and reduced it to the status of a communal group, like the Hoa Hao and Cao Dai, both of which had considerable local autonomy within the framework of RVN sovereignty.[109]

Given these advantages to the United States and GVN and disadvantages to the other side, it is not surprising that Thieu, hardly a supporter of political compromise, found the plan acceptable. For it would have guaranteed him not only a political monopoly in his own zone of control but also nominal sovereignty in the zone controlled by his enemies. "Sometimes," Thieu was quoted as saying, "you have to give up a leg to save the body." [110]

For the same reason, the PRG could not accept any such plan as the basis for a political settlement. To agree to Saigon's sovereignty over the territory actually under PRG control would mean giving up the struggle to overthrow a regime which the revolutionaries viewed as illegitimate. Indeed, the formation of the PRG itself in June 1969 had demonstrated that the Front was determined to force the dissolution of the RVN constitutional structure as part of the settlement. For, by claiming governmental status, it was putting itself in a stronger position to demand that neither side should impose its regime on the country during the interim between peace and a new election.

The Nixon administration was implicitly demanding that the other side accept such a "confederal" solution when on October 7, 1970 it proposed an in-place cease-fire divorced from a political settlement.[111] Kissinger, in a background briefing, told reporters that this meant, in effect, the acceptance of the PRG's control over areas where it had "military superiority." [112] Such a cease-fire would have left the PRG with a choice of a political settlement along the lines of the "territorial accommodation" plan outlined above or no settlement at all. As Kissinger had written in 1968, "a formal cease-fire is likely to predetermine the ultimate settlement. . . . Cease-fire is thus not so much a step toward a final settlement as a form of it." [113]

Not only did the October 1970 proposal try to freeze the PRG legally into a diminished zone of control *without* a political settlement at the central government level, it also demanded cease-fires in Laos and Cambodia, where the left-wing forces were on the offensive despite heavy US bombing. Again, this Indochina-wide cease-fire was to take place without any negotiations involving the Pathet Lao and Sihanouk's Royal Government of National Union in Cambodia. In other words, the principle of cease-fire without political settlements was extended throughout Indochina.

On May 31, 1971 Kissinger presented a secret proposal to the DRV in Paris.[114] It added to the previous plan an expression of willingness to agree on a deadline for the complete withdrawal of US troops in return for the repatriation of US prisoners. The date for withdrawal was not set in the proposal but was to be negotiated. Kissinger would later describe this offer as an extremely risky one which could have become a "trap" for the United States if Hanoi had accepted immediately, and claimed that he was "amazed" at Le Duc Tho's abrupt rejection of it.[115] A careful analysis of the proposal suggests, however, that it was carefully conceived, like its predecessors, to yield nothing of substance. It is true that the plan did not specifically call for the withdrawal of North Vietnamese troops, as had previous US proposals. But this was more than compensated for by the fact that it would have committed the DRV to both an Indochina-wide cease-fire and acceptance of the legitimacy of the Thieu regime as the sole sovereign power in South Vietnam even before the date for US withdrawal was negotiated. It would have left the United States free to insist on putting the date for the completion of withdrawal *after* a cease-fire (as it did, in fact, propose a few months later).

The hardening of the American diplomatic posture in 1970 and 1971 indicated a mood of growing confidence within the administration that it could force the DRV into a strategic corner by deterring the Communists from acting decisively to improve their military position in the South. But as 1972 was to demonstrate, the absence of any major military challenge to the Vietnamization and pacification programs was the result of a strategic decision by Hanoi to husband its strength and wait for the right moment to strike another decisive blow. It was a matter of choice and not a lack of will or capability which held back the PLAF.

In the late summer of 1968 the Lao Dong Party leadership decided to shift temporarily to a defensive military posture, abandoning the general line of "continuous offensive" which had characterized the Liberation Army's strategy since the beginning of the war against the United States in 1965. A speech by Truong Chinh, published in September 1968, signaled the new military line. "We must attack the enemy with determination to fight and win," he wrote. "But at times, under certain circumstances, we must shift to the defensive to gain time, dishearten the enemy and build up our forces for a new offensive." [116]

By late September revolutionary forces in the South were beginning a significant withdrawal of main force units. Five divisions of North Vietnamese troops—from 40,000 to 60,000 men—were withdrawn into North Vietnam and Laos, half of them going as far north as the twentieth parallel.[117] This may have been due in part to the difficulty of supplying troops in that area, but it was also clear that the DRV was interested in ending the bombing of the North and getting negotiations started. They were willing to signal to the United States that a tacit understanding on the Demilitarized Zone was possible. So this first phase of the military lull had the diplomatic objective of bringing about a bombing halt and substantive negotiations.

By the end of 1969 Communist troop strength had fallen by as many as 40,000 men, according to the State Department, and the PLAF adopted new tactics to conserve manpower.[118] In the only serious offensive of the entire period, from February to April 1969, usually only one battalion of troops was committed to a single battle, in contrast to the regimental-sized operations of 1968.[119] In 1970 and 1971 the military stand-down by the PLAF was even more pronounced, as commanders were ordered to conserve their main force troops and not to risk being targeted by US air power.[120]

In part, this shift to a defensive posture in the South reflected the feeling of the Vietnamese leaders that the war had entered a new and more complicated stage in which the political struggle in South Vietnam and domestic opinion in the United States were increasingly favorable to the NLF's objectives. They saw public opposition in the United States to the American military involvement in Vietnam as a noose which would gradually tighten around Nixon's policy, forcing him eventually to withdraw enough combat troops to alter the balance of forces within South Vietnam. The Nixon administration's policy was to buy time, hoping that the DRV would be tempted to negotiate in order to avoid having to face a stronger GVN at the end of the Vietnamization process. The task of military struggle, then, was no longer the same as it had been in 1965 or even in 1968. The revolution had to have a military posture which would wait out the American withdrawals and watch for the right moment, politically and diplomatically, for resumption of the offensive.

Moreover, by the end of 1969, the Party leaders saw new opportunities for political struggle in the urban areas to weaken the Thieu regime and thus strengthen the hand of the PRG in reaching a political settlement. They saw signs that the process of "Vietnamization" of the war, which meant prolonging it indefinitely, would increase the opposition to Thieu among urban strata rather than reduce it. Starting in 1970, the Party would put greater emphasis than ever before on the urban groups who demanded peace and opposed Thieu but had no affiliation with the Front as a vital component of the anti-US movement.[121]

Another reason for the shift to the defensive lay in the limited success and high costs of the series of offensive waves in 1968 following the Tet Offensive, when the PLAF command ordered its main force units to attack the cities in order to achieve the greatest political results. The high level of casualties associated with main force attacks was raised significantly in 1968 as the US air war reached a new level of intensity and the B-52 became the primary weapon of the American air armada.[122] Significantly, it was intensive B-52 strikes which were credited with disrupting the third wave of the 1968 offensive.[123]

The military lull was costly to the PRG in terms of territorial control. When the pressure from the PLAF main force units was reduced, a larger proportion of US and ARVN combat troops were thrown into pacification operations, and hundreds of formerly contested or NLF-controlled villages were militarily occupied.

As it consolidated its control, the Saigon government conscripted every adult male into its armed forces, thus increasing the size of ARVN to 1.1 million men from about 700,000 in 1968.[124] By late 1970 the Lao Dong Party was conceding in its internal documents that Saigon had indeed made major gains in control of land and population, while emphasizing that, in the process, "the enemy was forced to resort to dictatorial and fascist policies, which deepened the contradiction between the people of various strata, including personnel of the puppet army, on one hand, and the US-Thieu-Ky-Khiem clique, on the other." [125] Combined with the devastation and depopulation of the NLF zone by US and GVN bombing and shelling, the success of the RVN pacification program compressed the NLF into ever smaller areas of the countryside, especially in the Mekong Delta.[126]

Lao Dong Party leaders accepted these temporary setbacks in the South not because they lacked the capability to challenge the existing balance of forces but because they chose to wait for the most opportune moment to resume the offensive. The military battle had not been won, as the Nixon administration's diplomatic posture implied; it had simply been put in suspension by the other side.

5. DRV/PRG "Peace Cabinet" Diplomacy

The aim of the struggle in South Vietnam, from the revolutionary standpoint, was to force the United States to withdraw from Vietnam not only militarily but politically as well. Whether the DRV might have been willing to settle for something less than a coalition government in the early stages of the negotiation is a question which is unanswerable, since the United States was not offering any compromise between the preservation of the Thieu regime's sovereignty and a coalition government to replace it. And the DRV, perceiving that Nixon was still trying to achieve the elimination of the NLF from South Vietnamese politics, had no interest in proposing any compromise short of its ultimate objective.

Under these circumstances, the diplomacy of the revolutionary side in Paris served a dual purpose: to put forward a comprehensive plan for an overall settlement of the war, while at the same time using the talks as a platform to push for complete US military withdrawal and to encourage political opposition to Thieu in South Vietnam. The NLF ten-point program of May 8, 1969 called for the formation of a provisional coalition government, which would include representatives of all those "social strata and political tendencies in South Vietnam that stand for peace, independence and neutrality," to carry out elections.[127] The provisional coalition would be worked out by consultations among all those who embraced these principles. In order to make the point that this formula was not meant to exclude anyone except those who continued to rely on the United States to carry on the war, the program specified that the coalition could include "all persons, no matter what their political beliefs and their past may be, provided they stand for peace, independence and neutrality. . . ."

The United States argued that this position demanded, in effect, that the United States "overthrow" the Thieu government. From the perspective of those on the other side, however, the NLF plan demanded only that the United States stop imposing Thieu's government on South Vietnam. While the plan called on the United States to give up its support for an uncompromising anti-Communist faction, it did not demand a surrender to the NLF. For it also offered a principle which could be used to ensure that an interim coalition was not an instrument for Communist domination: "During the period intervening between the restoration of peace and the holding of general elections," it said, "neither party shall impose its political regime on the people of South Vietnam." Despite the demand for a government which exluded Thieu, Ky, and Khiem, therefore, there was considerable area for negotiation and compromise.

But until the Nixon administration indicated that it was ready to compromise on the Saigon regime's control over the political process, the DRV refused to begin bargaining. Central Committee spokesman Hoang Tung later explained, "It is normal for the two parties to approach each other and find out what the cards of the other side are. If the Americans weren't going to put forward any cards, we were not going to do so either." [128]

The Nixon administration *was* interested, however, in beginning private talks, in order to indicate to the American public that some progress was being made toward a settlement. Hanoi's negotiators exploited this desire to push the United States on the principle of total withdrawal. At the beginning of September 1969, about one month after a secret meeting had taken place between Kissinger and DRV negotiator Xuan Thuy, Thuy communicated to Kissinger through an intermediary, Professor Joseph Starobin, that the DRV would enter into private talks if the United States would accept "the principle of a complete and total withdrawal and show its good faith by withdrawing 100,000 troops." [129] Thuy made the same point publicly the following day though in less explicit terms. In an informal talk with newsmen, he said that if the United States would accept the principle of complete withdrawal and actually withdraw 100,000 troops, North Vietnam "would take this into consideration." [130]

The DRV and NLF also used the talks as a means of calling attention to the fact that the Thieu regime was still committed to a military resolution of the conflict and was therefore the main obstacle to a political settlement. They called publicly for a "peace cabinet" which would break the deadlock on a political settlement and permit negotiations between the GVN and the PRG and other groups for the formation of a provisional coalition government. "As long as the present regime remains in power in Saigon, the conference will not make progress," said Xuan Thuy.[131] DRV diplomats suggested several names of moderates and even anti-Communist political figures in Saigon, including former Chief of State Duong Van Minh, as acceptable leaders of a GVN cabinet and added that there were also men in the Saigon administration who were acceptable.[132]

While the DRV refused to carry on private talks with the United States in Paris as a symbolic reminder that there would be no diplomatic settlement without American acceptance of the principle of total unconditional withdrawal, it was willing to keep high-level channels of communication with the United States open. Early in 1970 Kissinger asked to talk secretly with Le Duc Tho, the

"Special Adviser" to the DRV delegation at Paris and a senior member of the Lao Dong Party Political Bureau. The DRV agreed, and in February 1970 Kissinger and Tho met for the first of four sessions over a period of six weeks.

Tho used the secret contacts with Kissinger to drive home the point that the DRV would not negotiate an agreement which did not include unconditional US military withdrawal and that the DRV would never accept the legitimacy of the Saigon regime. After four sessions, Kissinger knew privately that there was no common ground between the two sides on a diplomatic settlement. After the invasion of Cambodia two more conversations were held between Kissinger and Xuan Thuy, but again Kissinger offered no new negotiating cards, and the DRV stood by its previous demands.[133]

The only change in the DRV and PRG position was a proposal on September 17, 1970 which for the first time defined the provisional coalition as having three distinct segments: one representing the PRG, one with representatives of the Saigon administration who "stand for peace, independence and neutrality" (and explicitly excluding Thieu, Ky, and Khiem), and one with "persons of various political and religious forces and tendencies standing for peace, independence, neutrality and democracy, including those who, for political reasons, have to live abroad." [134]

As US troop withdrawal continued in 1970 and 1971 the DRV attention increasingly centered on the problem of US insistence that the Thieu regime was the only legitimate government of South Vietnam. The next diplomatic move by the DRV was prompted by the prospect that this obstacle to a settlement might be removed by the very electoral process which the United States itself had created by the constitution of 1967, written under the aegis of the American military intervention. By the summer of 1971 it appeared that those political elements inclined toward a peace settlement were coalescing around the candidacy of retired General and former Chief of State Duong Van Minh for the presidential election scheduled for October 1971. With Minh widely considered in Saigon to be a "peace candidate," the elections could be an opportunity to bring a shift in the Saigon government in the direction of the "peace cabinet" which the PRG had been demanding—if the United States was willing to permit it to happen by visibly withdrawing its support for Thieu before the election. The United States could thus resolve the deadlock over South Vietnam's political future while remaining consistent with the American pledge not to "impose" a coalition on South Vietnam.

This was the context in which Le Duc Tho, meeting secretly with Kissinger on June 26, 1971, offered a new comprehensive nine-point proposal.[135] For the first time, the DRV offered to release all military men and civilians captured during the war simultaneously with US troop withdrawals, both to be completed by the same date. The DRV proposal also made it clear, however, that any cease-fires in the three countries would have to be the subject of agreements between the parties in each country, not determined by an agreement between the DRV and the United States. Most important, the proposal reformulated the political demand to call on the United States to "stop supporting Thieu-Ky-Khiem so that there may be set up in Saigon a new administration standing for peace, independence, neutrality and democracy."

On July 1 the PRG published a seven-point statement which called on the United States to "stop all maneuvers, *including tricks on elections*, aimed at maintaining the puppet Nguyen Van Thieu" (emphasis added).[136] The intention of this language was clear: the United States could prove its willingness to respect free choice by withdrawing political support from the Thieu regime before the election.[137] This pointed suggestion took on special significance in light of NLF broadcasts and captured documents indicating that the Lao Dong Party was urging South Vietnamese not to boycott the presidential election, as it had in 1967, but to use it to defeat Thieu.[138] The PRG statement suggested that the Communist leaders saw the 1971 election as a way out of the diplomatic impasse which had developed at Paris.

There was ample reason for the United States to consider a change in its previous policy of support for Thieu in the political situation of mid-1971. Since June, Thieu's main opponent in the election, Big Minh, had been arguing explicitly that the US attitude of public "neutrality" constituted, in effect, support for Thieu. Instead of "passive neutrality," he argued, the United States had to adopt a posture of "positive and constructive neutrality" in order to guarantee that the election would be fair.[139] In effect, the PRG demand was simply repeating that of the leading opposition candidate in the race.

Further political developments in Saigon underlined the fact that Thieu himself had no interest in permitting Minh to have any serious opportunity to win. On August 5 the RVN Supreme Court, following orders from Thieu, ruled out Vice-President Ky's candidacy, which Thieu reportedly feared would take hard-core anti-Communist votes away from him and raise Minh's prospects in a fair election contest. And on August 12 Big Minh submitted to the US Embassy a document which he said Thieu had sent to all province chiefs on how to use the GVN administrative and military apparatus to ensure victory for his ticket.[140] The need to ensure a reasonably fair election and the opportunity to reach a diplomatic breakthrough were suddenly converging in August 1971.

When Kissinger met with Xuan Thuy on August 16, however, he presented an eight-point proposal which added very little to the May 31 proposal. It offered to withdraw US and other foreign troops from Vietnam "within nine months after an agreement on an overall settlement."[141] In other words, the United States would leave its troops in South Vietnam in place for as long as nine months after a cease-fire and a political settlement over which the United States and Saigon still had a veto.

But more significant was Kissinger's response to the PRG suggestion that the United States drop its support for Thieu in order to allow the South Vietnamese to choose another leader for the Saigon administration. By Kissinger's own account, his August 16 proposal offered only a "simple declaration of American neutrality"[142] in the election. This was nothing more than the United States had already done, and it had already been denounced by Minh as meaningless. On August 20 Minh pulled out of the race, leaving Thieu to run without opposition. But there was still room for the Nixon administration to maneuver, if it chose to. It could have declared publicly that it could not support Thieu's monopoly of the political process, call on him to resign and allow his Vice-President to organize new elections, in keeping with Article 56 of the constitution.[143] Xuan Thuy had told Kissinger on August 16 that Thieu's withdrawal from the race would be a "favorable opportunity" for a settlement.

But Nixon chose to maintain the status quo. Kissinger, meeting again with Le Duc Tho on September 16, while Thieu was in the midst of his one-man race for the presidency, offered nothing to meet the demand of the other side for American political disengagement from Thieu. It was only on October 11, after Thieu had been elected with 82 percent of the votes, that the United States made its next move in the negotiations.

The revised US eight points of October 11 [144] brought back the 1969 "electoral commission" idea, with two new elements: first, an "independent body representing all political forces in South Vietnam" would organize and conduct the election; second, Thieu and Huong would resign one month before the election took place, with the administration to be headed by the chairman of the GVN Senate. The proposal for an independent commission to carry out the election, while an improvement over Thieu's previous offer, nevertheless failed to reassure the DRV and PRG that Thieu would not nullify the work of any such electoral commission by his control over the police, army, and local administration.* In any conflict between a powerless commission and Thieu's apparatus of control, the latter would inevitably win. As for the pledge of the resignation of Thieu and Huong one month before an election, it offered no guarantee that Thieu would not set his machinery in motion before his resignation and then proceed to ride into power, since it did not promise that he would not be a candidate. Moreover, the US plan did not address itself to the NLF demand for a guarantee against reprisal after the war, for democratic liberties, and for the release of political detainees and freedom of movement.

The American eight points of October 11 also offered a new and more complicated formula on the complete withdrawal of US forces. The United States was willing to withdraw all of its forces and those of its allies, "except for a small number of personnel needed for technical advice, logistics and observance of the ceasefire" within seven months of the signing of a statement of principles based on the document. The release of American prisoners and "innocent civilians"—a phrase devised to exclude

---

* Secretary Rogers seemed to admit these weaknesses in the October 11 proposal in his news conference on February 3, 1972. When asked how the administration would "get around the problem that not only the police power but the army, the administration, the provinces, the secret police, etc., etc., would remain in the hands of a pro-American South Vietnamese government," Rogers could only say that if the other side "want to discuss that, we are prepared to discuss it, and we are flexible about it. *We realize the difficulties*" (emphasis added). (Quoted in I. F. Stone, "The Hidden Traps in Nixon's Peace Plan," *New York Review of Books*, March 9, 1972, p. 15.)

prisoners detained for their participation in the struggle against the United States and Saigon—would be completed at the same time. This meant that both the cease-fire and the political settlement would be left for later negotiation, while the United States maintained a residual military force of advisers and technicians and continued its air strikes from outside the country, but after the United States had gotten back its prisoners of war—the only remaining major incentive for the United States to negotiate seriously on a political settlement.

After receiving the proposal from the United States, the DRV indicated that the 1971 phase of the talks had come to an end, by failing to send Le Duc Tho to another meeting with Kissinger before the end of the war.[145] Nixon's continued support for Thieu left no room for diplomatic maneuver in the existing conditions. But the DRV was not yet prepared to abandon the demand for Thieu's ouster without attempting to change the military and political context of the negotiations first. After more than three years of maintaining a defensive military posture in the South, the Vietnamese leaders believed that the "opportune moment" had come to deliver a decisive military blow which would force the United States to make concessions in Paris and usher in the final phase of the negotiations.

4: Hanoi Pushes for an Agreement

The spring offensive of 1972, like the Tet Offensive of 1968, was aimed at breaking a stalemate and moving the conflict to a new stage. The Lao Dong Party leaders were determined to force the United States to accept what it had been resisting for more than three years: the end of its client regime's claim to exclusive sovereignty over South Vietnam. The reduction of the Saigon regime to a status equal to that of its opponents would provide an acceptable basis for ending the war. Along with the complete withdrawal of US military personnel from South Vietnam, it would shift the balance of forces sharply in favor of the revolution.

The Party used military power to the maximum while playing its negotiating cards in such a way as to obtain the best settlement possible. The Vietnamese leaders believed that the offensive would be a crippling blow to Nixon's Vietnamization policy and that the United States would have to agree to a coalition government, but they were prepared to arrive at any settlement which would legitimize the PRG as an equal sovereign government in South Vietnam.

The DRV had not reckoned, however, with Nixon's ability to manipulate détente with the Soviet Union and China for his own internal political benefit, thus nullifying, in effect, the damaging political impact of the offensive and the reescalation of American military involvement in South Vietnam. By showing that he could take unprecedented military measures against North Vietnam without jeopardizing détente, Nixon was able to regain public confidence at home in his ability to end the war, and to resist the

DRV demand for a transitional coalition, which would have signified a clear-cut defeat for the American effort.

Nevertheless, by pushing hard for a coalition during five months of negotiations and then finally dropping that demand in October, DRV negotiators were able to make more attractive to Kissinger their minimum demand for a settlement which would put the PRG and RVN on an equal basis and commit Thieu to a political process which would critically weaken his position.

But as the negotiations neared completion, the interest of the United States in the survival of its client government in Saigon emerged once again as an obstacle to final agreement. Fearing that Thieu was still not strong enough politically to compete on equal terms with the PRG and his non-Communist rivals, Nixon decided to postpone the signing of a peace agreement until some weeks later and to demand more advantageous terms for Saigon. Meanwhile, the United States began pouring in new military supplies which would increase the attractiveness to Thieu of a continuation of the military struggle. Neither Thieu nor the Nixon administration was yet reconciled to a real political compromise with the Communists.

1.   The Spring Offensive

The Lao Dong Party's strategy for ending the war had always assumed that a military and diplomatic stalemate would be broken by a decisive victory which would force the United States to accept a diplomatic settlement based on a coalition government. Contrary to the analyses published by US officials and some foreign observers, their decision to withdraw main force units from the battlefield did not represent the victory of a faction favoring "protracted guerrilla warfare" or "political struggle" over a "regular force" faction in the Lao Dong Party's leadership.[1] For the North Vietnamese leaders never gave up the idea of another offensive in which their main force units would play the leading role, and they repeatedly stated during the long military lull that they were only preparing for the next offensive.[2]

The only question for the Party leadership, therefore, was that of the timing and targets of a new main force offensive. In 1970 and 1971 such an offensive would have been premature, for the United States was still in the process of reducing its troops, while PLAF

troops, including thousands of youths sent North by the NLF in
1969, were undergoing training and slowly accumulating stockpiles
of ammunition and other supplies in their base areas along the
Cambodian and Laotian borders.[3] By the end of 1971 there was not
a single Communist main force division in South Vietnam. Six of
the PLAF divisions which had previously fought in the South had
been pulled back to Cambodia, two to Laos, and three to North
Vietnam.[4] All these divisions were to participate in the 1972
offensive, along with additional divisions from the North.

Nineteen seventy-two was the logical year for an offensive
aimed at bringing the war to an end. US ground combat forces
would be drawn down to only a few thousand men by April 1972
and would no longer constitute a significant factor on the battlefield. So the PLAF could aim their attacks at the regular units of
ARVN. And political pressures on the Nixon administration to
agree to a settlement would be at their peak during a presidential
election year.

Like the Tet Offensive, the 1972 offensive was conceived as part
of a larger political and diplomatic strategy. But the military
objectives of the offensive would be different from those of Tet in
1968. While it would attempt to seize as much territory as possible,
the main objective would not be to capture province capitals, but to
destroy as much of ARVN's fighting capability as possible and thus
show that Nixon's policy of Vietnamization was doomed to failure.
This would increase the pressure on the United States to negotiate
an agreement before the 1972 election. At the same time, it would
tie down a large part of the ARVN main forces on a few major
battle fronts and permit the revival of guerrilla warfare in areas
where it had been dormant, thus disrupting pacification and
increasing the influence of the revolutionary forces in previously
GVN-controlled villages.[5] It was planned both in order to have the
greatest impact on American policy by heavily damaging ARVN's
main force divisions and to contribute to a substantive change in
the military-political balance of forces in South Vietnam.[6]

The offensive was launched at the end of March where it was
least expected: directly across the Demilitarized Zone at the main
ARVN defense line. After three days of intensive shelling, one
PLAF division attacked the firebases under heavy cloud cover and
quickly destroyed the newly-formed ARVN 3rd Division. One of

the three regiments defected to the PLAF, along with their officers, and the rest of the division retreated so hastily that the 110 heavy artillery pieces at the firebases were captured by the Communists intact.[7]

PLAF forces then opened offensives against two other outer security perimeters, one northwest of Saigon and the other in the central highlands.[8] The outer Saigon defense belt stretched from Tay Ninh province through Binh Long and Phuoc Long provinces. The PLAF drove into the district capital of Loc Ninh in Binh Long on April 5 and inflicted heavy casualties on the ARVN 5th Division, which fell back, again leaving large numbers of tanks and guns to the PLAF in Loc Ninh.[9]

The next move was to encircle and threaten the main point in the defense line, An Loc, which was being held by one regiment of the 5th Division. By mid-April PLAF troops had entered An Loc with tanks and held part of it for several days. Between April 14 and April 24 the PLAF attacked and overran two key bases on Highway 14 in the central highlands, and finally captured the entire complex, including the 22nd Division headquarters.[10] The 22nd Division's troops "got scared and ran," according to US officials, when the PLAF attacked at night with tanks.[11]

At the same time, PLAF troops overran two district towns in Binh Dinh province without a fight, as forty percent of the 22nd Division's 40th regiment was reported to have deserted. Three districts with a population of about 200,000 people reverted to the revolutionaries, who had deep roots in the province going back to the Viet Minh period. Some 8,000 militiamen—about 200 platoons—changed sides overnight.[12]

At the end of April the main thrust of the offensive shifted back to the Quang Tri front, where the PLAF began a drive toward the province capital after a three-week pause. On April 28 they overran Dong Ha and began immediately shelling Quang Tri city.[13] By April 29 the city was surrounded, and the remnants of the 3rd Division as well as the elite Ranger Division began to flee in panic.

Reaching Hue, the ARVN troops became a drunken mob, wrecking and looting shops and raping women. The Marines and Rangers beat up and sometimes even killed soldiers of the hapless 3rd Division. Stalls in the US-financed central market were looted and then the whole market was set afire. The next morning, tens of thousands of people, including Saigon government civil servants, began jamming the road south toward Danang.[14]

But after capturing the main defense base west of Hue late in April, the PLAF paused, failing to press its offensive against a city which was ill prepared for a full-scale assault. The expected attack on Hue never occurred. The PLAF strategy appears to have been not to occupy Hue but to tie down ARVN's main force units—including its strategic reserves—on that battle front and to inflict as much damage as possible on them, opening up the countryside to renewed guerrilla warfare and political action.[15] All of ARVN's remaining strategic reserves, including elements of the Marines, the Airborne, and the 7th Division from the Mekong Delta, were sent to the Hue front.[16] A similar strategy appears to have been behind PLAF deployments around An Loc and Kontum. This was, in fact, the view which prevailed among senior military officers in Saigon.[17]

If this was indeed the strategy of the offensive, it was an unqualified success; during the first month of the offensive, the PLAF forced Saigon to commit its entire strategic reserve—10,000 Airborne troops, 13,000 Marines, and 34,000 Rangers—to those three areas.[18] This meant that there were no main force ARVN units to spare in responding to the renewed threat of PLAF guerrilla attacks. When the ARVN 2nd Division was withdrawn from Quang Ngai and sent to the Quang Tri front in April, it left the province open to the PLAF guerrillas. In the following weeks the guerrillas removed 40,000 people from Saigon's "resettlement villages," established uncontested control over 50,000 others, and destroyed Saigon's pacification program in villages with 275,000 more. In Quang Nam and Quang Tin, similar guerrilla actions ended Saigon's control over tens of thousands of people.[19]

Meanwhile, with the entire ARVN 21st Division and one regiment of the 9th Division tied down on the road to An Loc, and five other regiments busy guarding infiltration routes from Cambodia, the Communist guerrilla movement exploded once more in the Mekong Delta. Hundreds of militia posts were overrun or abandoned under pressure.[20]

Faced with a shortage of military manpower in the Delta and fearing a major shift in the balance of power there, the United States again decided to use saturation bombing as a strategic weapon. In the province of Dinh Tuong, where the upsurge of

PLAF guerrilla activity was greatest, US B-52s flew an average of more than two raids each day.[21] Each mission consisted of from three to thirty-six planes, with thirty tons of bombs per plane. The result of this, the heaviest use of B-52s in the heavily populated Delta of the entire war, was a massive increase in death and injury to innocent civilians, as the bombs fell on their fields and around their homes.[22]

In Quang Tri city, during May and June, the PLAF prepared its defenses against the expected ARVN counterattack, digging in behind the nineteenth-century walled citadel, surrounded by a shallow moat. They hoped to lure ARVN's best units into the battle to recapture the city, and thus inflict heavy casualties on them.

At the end of June ARVN forces finally began their counter-offensive. For a month, Saigon's Airborne Division assaulted the citadel without success. It was decimated in the process, and had to be replaced by the Marine Division on July 27. More than six weeks later the Marines finally recaptured the citadel, but only after many of their battalions took 40 percent casualties. When the battle was over, the Marine Division was judged no longer combat effective.[23] Meanwhile in August the PLAF had moved two of its divisions from the Quang Tri front into the Que Son valley in coastal Quang Nam province to take control of an entire district with a population of 20,000 people.[24]

In the 1972 offensive, Communist forces inflicted unprecedented losses on ARVN, particularly its strategic reserves. According to US intelligence estimates, ARVN lost some 70,000 troops during the first three months, which did not include the heavy losses suffered during the ARVN counteroffensive of July, August, and September. Twenty thousand of these were due to desertion or defection to the PLAF. In addition to these main force losses, the Saigon government lost an estimated 70,000 local militia or civil guard troops either in casualties or by desertion or surrender to the PLAF.[25]

During the same period, US intelligence estimated that some 70,000 Communist troops, including guerrillas, had been killed or wounded in the fighting, with relatively few defections or surrenders to Saigon.[26] For the first time since the direct US military intervention, PLAF losses on the battlefield appear to have been substantially less than those inflicted on the Saigon army.

In terms of land and population, the offensive also dramatically reversed the trend of the previous three years, although it was far from restoring the PRG zone to its pre-1969 dimensions. Nearly 1,400 hamlets were *officially* conceded to the PRG by October 1972, while only seven had been conceded before the offensive.[27] Equally important was the dramatic increase in "contested" hamlets, for which no figures were released. The Communist political organization, under tremendous pressure from Saigon's military forces until 1972, was able to surface once again in many areas, thanks to the renewed activities of PLAF guerrillas.[28]

All of these accomplishments added up to a substantial shift in the balance of forces in South Vietnam which put the PRG and NLF in a stronger position for a postwar political struggle. But in the context of American and world politics, in which Soviet and Chinese détente policies appeared as a critical reality, this shift was not sufficient to force the negotiation of a coalition government.

2. US Escalation and Détente Diplomacy

The Communists were threatening to challenge successfully the balance of power which Nixon had publicly proclaimed he would protect with American military force. Nixon turned immediately to his B-52s to warn Hanoi that the punishment planned for the DRV would go far beyond the Johnson administration's military pressures against the North. On April 6, as US B-52s began to step up the bombing of the North, Admiral Thomas Moorer, Chairman of the Joint Chiefs of Staff, said that the bombing would continue to move northward, toward the heavily populated Red River valley and the Hanoi-Haiphong area, unless the offensive was halted.[29]

On April 15 the second phase of the effort to coerce the DRV began, as B-52s, originally intended to carry atomic weapons, carried out raids for the first time against the city of Haiphong for three straight days. The administration was clearly threatening North Vietnam with the devastation of its population centers or, even worse, of its irrigation and flood control system, if it continued its offensive and resisted American terms for a settlement.

This intensification of threats against the North was accompanied by a return to the previously discredited effort to get the Soviet

Union to prevail on the North Vietnamese to halt the offensive and make negotiating concessions. After arriving in Moscow on April 20 Kissinger tried to get Brezhnev to agree to limit Soviet arms deliveries to North Vietnam, and to lean on the DRV to accept a new negotiating proposal which Kissinger would present at the next secret meeting in Paris. Brezhnev refused to use his arms shipments as leverage on the Vietnamese, saying that he had no choice but to support their cause. As for the negotiations, Brezhnev said he was sure the North Vietnamese were ready for "serious" talks.[30]

Kissinger then used his main bargaining chip with the Russians, repeating his threat to take "whatever steps are necessary" to prevent a Communist military victory.[31] He undoubtedly pointed to the B-52 raids on the city of Haiphong as an indication of what lay in store for North Vietnam if they pressed their offensive further. The threat to bring the DRV to its knees through bombing was reemphasized a few days after Kissinger's return from Moscow when Nixon, asked about the possibility of bombing the dikes, carefully left this option open for the future.[32]

Kissinger still hoped after the meeting that the Soviets would press the North Vietnamese to be more flexible in the negotiations, although the Russians had said only that they believed the North Vietnamese were prepared to negotiate seriously.[33] A new meeting was arranged for May 2 between Kissinger and Le Duc Tho. The Soviets immediately informed the DRV of the Kissinger-Brezhnev meeting, including Kissinger's threats, through a high Party official and aide to Brezhnev, K. F. Katushev, who flew to Hanoi after Kissinger's visit.[34]

But the DRV was unmoved by these threats, as it had been in previous years. The leaders of the Lao Dong Party still hoped for substantial concessions by the United States at some point, as the United States recognized that Vietnamization could not succeed and that it could not end the war on its own terms. The offensive was then at its crest with no sign of letting up, and the Americans had been forced into taking escalatory steps which reminded the American public that the war was not winding down. Moreover, the Americans, who had walked out of the Paris talks in March, had agreed to return to the negotiating table in spite of the offensive. So when Kissinger presented the American proposal for a complete withdrawal of US troops four months after a cease-fire and the return of the POWs, Le Duc Tho dismissed it as essentially a restatement of the October 1971 position.

The fall of Quang Tri and the disintegration of Saigon government morale in Hue formed the backdrop for the decision to carry out a military action which the Johnson administration had rejected for four years: the mining of the port of Haiphong. Although Nixon presented the move to the public as a way to "stop the killing" by keeping weapons "out of the hands of the international outlaws of North Vietnam," [35] intelligence specialists pointed out that this move, even combined with the maximum bombing of road, rail, and water traffic in the North, could only slow down and not stop the flow of weapons into North Vietnam and then to the South. For although supplies from the sea could be stopped, this would not prevent the shipment of military material overland through China, the route by which 90 percent of North Vietnam's military supplies had come in the past. [36]

But Nixon and Kissinger had a different set of considerations. They were less concerned about their ability to cut off the weapons supply of the DRV than about their ability to reassure the American people that the administration was taking what appeared to be decisive steps to end the war. The crucial question for them was whether the mining and escalated bombing of North Vietnam would jeopardize the planned summit meeting in Moscow in May.

They had good reason to believe that, while Moscow might not actively intervene to put pressure on North Vietnam, it also would not permit Vietnam to interfere with its broader diplomatic strategy of détente with the United States. The Soviet response to the sinking of a Soviet freighter during the B-52 raids on Haiphong on April 15 had already indicated that the Soviets were too committed to détente to make Vietnam a major issue in relations with the United States: they had failed even to issue a public protest. [37] The Soviets were similarly mild-mannered about the mining of Haiphong. Soviet minesweepers stationed in the Pacific, only a few days' sailing from Haiphong and capable of sweeping away the American mines, did not even venture toward North Vietnamese waters. [38] And the planning for the Moscow summit went on uninterrupted.

This cautious Soviet reaction to the Nixon administration's

reescalation of the war, which would have exposed the Soviet Union to a worldwide attack from the Chinese a few years earlier, was made easier by the fact that China itself was also avoiding any dramatic gesture of protest against the American moves. The Chinese reception of Nixon in Peking only three months earlier had already suggested, in fact, that China had a serious interest in establishing a new relationship of friendship with the United States, even though it continued to oppose the Americans in Vietnam.

The new Chinese posture toward the United States was the culmination of a policy shift which began at the end of 1968, as China faced two hostile great powers which were implicitly or explicitly coordinating their policies against it. One faction in the Chinese leadership had backed a foreign policy of hostility to both the Soviet Union and the United States. But with the fall of Lin Piao, a new line emerged in Peking aimed at closer relations with the United States as a counterweight to the Soviet threat, which was closer at hand and more concrete. The Chinese put out signals that they would be happy to have the US President visit China, and the result was Kissinger's secret trip to Peking in July 1971.[39]

This momentous shift in China's foreign policy did not imply any willingness to lessen its material support for the Vietnamese revolutionaries or to press them to settle for anything less than the terms demanded at the Paris talks by the DRV. Chinese material support actually increased significantly after 1970, as China began to supply not only light armaments and ammunition, as in the past, but heavier equipment as well—primarily 32 mm. antiaircraft batteries and trucks. From 1971 to 1973 the Chinese provided ten trucks for every one supplied by the Soviet Union. In just three years the proportion of trucks in the DRV originating in China rose from one out of four to three out of four.[40]

Kissinger had found during his 1971 trip to Peking that the Chinese were still insisting on American withdrawal from Vietnam as a condition of normalized American-Chinese relations. Chou En-lai told him that Vietnam, not Taiwan, was the primary obstacle to improved relations.[41] On the eve of Kissinger's visit, the Chinese government published an essay on Mao's 1940 work *On Policy,* in which Mao had emphasized the importance of a "dual policy" combining alliance and struggle with those who opposed the main imperialist enemy. The implication was that the Soviets were the main enemy, that the Americans would be useful allies against that threat, but that the Chinese would continue to struggle against the United States where its policies were imperialist, as in Indochina.[42] The Shanghai communiqué during the Nixon trip to China also reflected the fact that the Chinese would continue to oppose American intervention in Indochina as a basic principle of their policy. The statement of Chinese views on Vietnam once more supported the Vietnamese demand for a coalition government in South Vietnam.[43]

Why, then, did the Chinese agree to the Nixon visit at a time when negotiations remained deadlocked and Nixon was pursuing a policy of Vietnamization aimed at maintaining the Thieu regime in power? They believed that the United States was not only a declining power in the world and in Asia, but would inevitably be defeated in Vietnam. The continued withdrawal of US troops in 1971, despite the obvious military debacle of the ARVN invasion of southern Laos, and the American eagerness for rapprochement with China appeared to confirm the Chinese view that the United States was retreating from its former aspiration to maintain hegemony in the area.[44]

The Chinese, like the Soviets, were unwilling to reverse the process of rapprochement with the United States in order to protest B-52 strikes on Haiphong and the mining of North Vietnamese ports. The May 11 statement by the People's Republic expressed "utmost indignation" and condemned the escalation "strongly." It also pledged support for the Vietnamese war of resistance until "final victory." [45] But they were less concerned than the Vietnamese (as indeed they always had been) about the time frame within which it would take place.

The failure of the Soviet Union and China to react strongly to the Nixon escalation was a serious blow to the Lao Dong Party's military-diplomatic strategy for obtaining a favorable settlement of the conflict in 1972. They had expected the United States to begin full-scale bombing of the North after the offensive in the South began; in December 1971 and January 1972 the army had carried out a special training program for antiaircraft and civil defense forces, and air raid shelters were prepared for a new onslaught from the air.[46] And whether or not they were prepared for the mining of Haiphong, they expected that the Nixon administration would be forced to pay a price for such escalation in North Vietnam in terms of its diplomatic relations as well as in terms of American domestic opinion, thus eroding its position at the negotiating table and increasing the likelihood of concessions in Paris before the end of the year. What they were not prepared for was a serious American escalation *without* major diplomatic and political setbacks for Nixon.

It was not that the Vietnamese leaders expected the Soviets or Chinese to react with threats of military action. The DRV had always made it clear that it was not interested in foreign military involvement of any kind in Vietnam, except in circumstances of a ground invasion or the use of nuclear weapons. For that would have defined the issues more in terms of socialism vs. capitalism rather than of Vietnam's right to independence and self-determination.[47] What they did expect from fraternal socialist countries was some diplomatic step which would make it clear that there could be no détente while the United States continued its intervention in South Vietnam and carried out a war of destruction against North Vietnam. The cancellation of the Moscow summit by the Soviets and a public warning by China that the evolution of Sino-American relations would be frozen until the United States ended the bombing and mining of the North would have put Nixon on the diplomatic defensive, reduced his prestige at home, and revived Vietnam as a central campaign issue.

Indeed, the Vietnamese felt that a stronger stand against Nixon's hard line policy would have constrained him from taking the actions he did in April and May. As they analyzed the situation, Nixon's Indochina policy was on the ropes. The combination of a successful offensive in the South, growing impatience in the United States to end the war and bring home American POWs, and Nixon's own election campaign would inevitably force him into a corner in which the only way out was to give in on the issue of coalition government and negotiate an agreement before the election. The Nixon trips to Peking and Moscow, said *Nhan Dan*, were like "throwing life preservers to a drowning pirate."[48] Lao Dong Party Central Committee member Hoang Quoc Viet later revealed to a Japanese interviewer the bitterness felt by the Vietnamese at their socialist allies: "Why was it necessary to extend help to Nixon, who might have fallen with one more stroke?" he asked.[49]

It was frequently asserted by administration spokesmen that the Soviets had helped to bring about a settlement by putting pressure on the Vietnamese to give way in the negotiations with Kissinger. But Soviet détente policy fell short of outright pressure on the DRV. At the Moscow summit meeting between May 22 and May 30, Kissinger and Nixon again pressed Brezhnev to persuade North Vietnam to accept the American peace plan. Brezhnev again strongly backed Hanoi's demand for a coalition government without Thieu, and demanded that the United States end all "acts of war" against the DRV.[50] Kosygin, in an emotional statement, denounced the bombing and mining, bitterly recalling that he had been in Hanoi when the United States first bombed it in 1965.[51]

Despite later American claims that there was an "implied understanding" that the superpowers had to take steps to end the war, the evidence strongly suggests that the Soviets, like the Chinese, were unwilling to use their arms supplies to push the DRV to make concessions in the negotiations with the United States, which was the only way they could have compelled the North Vietnamese to alter their stance in Paris.* Chinese aid to the DRV was dramatically stepped up, as even the Soviets, who had long tried to belittle China's military aid, admitted. And although the Chinese refused to allow Soviet ships to unload at Chinese ports for transshipment overland to North Vietnam, they received ships of East European registry, and there was nothing to prevent the Soviets from having their goods delivered by East Europeans.[52]

The Chairman of the Joint Chiefs of Staff, Admiral Thomas Moorer, later referred to the "heavy resupply of war materials" by both the Soviet Union and China during the summer.[53] The roads from the Chinese border were clogged with vehicles moving constantly, night and day, with military supplies. One French correspondent in North Vietnam during early September described "endless convoys" of brand new Soviet and Chinese trucks, carrying

---

* According to North Vietnamese sources, when Soviet President Nikolai Podgorny arrived in Hanoi in mid-June, with the news of a new Kissinger diplomatic initiative on Vietnam—the idea of a tripartite electoral commission to organize elections—he also brought an offer of sophisticated new Soviet missiles, provided that the Vietnamese would accept Soviet technicians to operate them. The Vietnamese refused on the ground that the presence of foreigners manning their air defenses would be damaging to their own people's pride, which was one of their primary sources of strength. (T. J. S. George, "Landslide Logic," *Far Eastern Economic Review,* November 11, 1972, p. 12.)

everything from ammunition to Soviet antiaircraft missiles south-ward. He also saw evidence that the DRV had a plentiful supply of fuel, despite the bombing and blockade, thanks to a recently completed pipeline from China.[54]

The weakening of Soviet and Chinese opposition to the American intervention in Vietnam was no less harmful to DRV interests, of course, because it took indirect rather than direct form. But when the Lao Dong Party leadership finally decided to sacrifice its central demand for the replacement of the Thieu regime by a coalition government in order to get a settlement, it was because of its evaluation of the existing balance of forces and not in response to pressure from the Soviets or Chinese to change its negotiating stance.

3.   *Breakthrough in Paris*

The Vietnamese leaders had hoped that Nixon would be forced by the spring offensive to be more accommodating on the issue of a coalition government. But Hanoi also entered this final phase of the negotiations with greater diplomatic flexibility than it could afford during the years of the military lull, when it was resisting Nixon's pressures to accept terms favorable to Thieu.

For Hanoi regarded a settlement in 1972 as being in the interests of the revolution. Its leaders realized that American air power had become a major factor in the balance of forces in the South, and that the PRG and its followers needed to be free from the constant threat of B-52 attack in order to permit not only the normalization of the PRG zone but also the strengthening of the PLAF in the South. Furthermore the North itself badly needed a respite from war after seven years of being unable to devote its resources fully to production and economic development. The time had come to end the war, and they were prepared to ease their own demands on the political arrangements, provided that the agreement still represented a net gain for the struggle in the South rather than a defeat. As a spokesman for the DRV later explained, they were ready to end the war "even if there was a compromise, but a compromise which permits us to make a step forward." [55]

Thus the decision was made in the early stage of the offensive, if not before, that the DRV delegation would try to negotiate one of three possible agreements in 1972, depending on the circumstances: an agreement between the United States and the DRV, under which the war would continue without American forces; an agreement which would replace the Thieu regime with a transitional coalition; or a cease-fire agreement which would permit President Thieu to remain in power while explicitly recognizing the PRG as a legally coequal administration.[56] This decision, revealed to Party leaders in the South in the late spring of 1972, indicates that the Communist leaders were completely realistic in their assessment of the range of possible outcomes. They hoped for a major breakthrough in American policy, but they were prepared, if circumstances demanded it, to accept any compromise which did not foreclose the continuation of the struggle or affront their basic principles.

The first step in the DRV's determined effort to bring about an early settlement was a significant modification of the proposal for a tripartite coalition government. In a move clearly timed to take advantage of the initiative which the Communist forces held on the battlefield, the DRV made it clear in the meeting on May 2 that, once Thieu resigned or was removed, the Saigon government could name whomever it wished to its segment of the coalition government. Despite this revision, Kissinger asserted on May 9 that the DRV was still demanding that "all the organized non-Communist forces would have been disbanded by definition" before a cease-fire, and the formation of a coalition government.[57]

On May 12 Le Duc Tho held an extraordinary press conference in Paris to answer Kissinger's representation of the DRV position in the talks. Tho declared, "What we want in South Vietnam is a three-segment government of broad national concord reflecting the real political situation of South Vietnam," and asserted that the DRV and PRG delegations had repeatedly told Kissinger in private meetings that they did not intend to impose a Communist government on South Vietnam. Asked by a journalist if it was fair to say that no Saigon generals or members of Thieu's cabinet could participate in that tripartite government, Tho replied, "Concerning the tripartite government, the segment belonging to Saigon is chosen by themselves; whomever they wish to choose, they can choose, in the segment designated for them, but it can't include Thieu." [58] In interviews with the *New York Times*, DRV and PRG negotiators denied that their proposal demanded the disbanding of the Saigon administration or army.[59]

The significance of this shift from the DRV's earlier demand, that all participants in the coalition must have renounced a pro-American and anti-Communist position, could not have been lost on Kissinger; it was an attempt by the DRV to meet his earlier complaint that the Communists had demanded a veto over who could be represented in the government.[60] The DRV was clearly indicating in the first weeks of the new offensive in the South, therefore, that it was ready to go further than ever before to negotiate a compromise political settlement.

This proposal for a tripartite coalition with built-in guarantees against domination by one side or the other was not the final position for the Lao Dong Party leaders. But by mid-June they had reason to believe that the United States might have to agree to such a compromise before the presidential election, in spite of the failure of the Soviets and Chinese to support them in the face of Nixon's escalation. Kissinger's offer of a tripartite electoral commission not only represented an improvement over the previous conception of an electoral body offered by the United States but suggested, for the first time, that Kissinger was willing to bargain on political issues without bringing Thieu into the process. There was also the rise of George McGovern as a serious contender for the Democratic nomination for president. McGovern's "repeated successes" in the primaries, said *Nhan Dan* on June 10, showed the "great intensity and scope of antiwar feelings among the American people." [61] There was reason to hope, moreover, that the public pressure on Nixon would increase further as it was realized that the war would not be settled in Peking and Moscow.[62] All these factors encouraged the DRV to play out their revised coalition formula for as long as possible in the hope that the Nixon administration would decide in the end to accept it in order to end the war before the election.

But there were also ominous indications that Nixon, fighting against time and believing that Soviet and Chinese détente policies gave him a free hand for the time being, was attacking North Vietnam's flood control system in order to force it to accept US terms for a settlement. Although Nixon administration officials repeatedly denied that dikes were targeted by US planes, there was no dispute over the fact that a considerable number of dikes had been damaged from April on, and that the United States was making no special effort to avoid hitting them.[63] In the context of the Nixon administration's repeated threats to spare no target in North Vietnam unless the DRV came to a settlement, every new instance of bombs dropped on or near a dike could only be interpreted by Hanoi as a suggestion of even heavier bombing to come when the water level of the Red River reached its peak in July and August.

The North Vietnamese feared that Nixon might try to provoke major floods and then blame them on the poor maintenance of the dike system by the DRV. This fear was intensified in early July when high State Department officials, in interviews with the *New York Times*, said that there was a strong likelihood of flooding in the North but said the dike system itself would be responsible rather than bombing.[64] And the following day, Secretary Laird said Hanoi was carrying out a propaganda campaign to "relieve themselves of the responsibility with their own people for their failure to adequately repair this system since the major flooding last year." [65] This claim that the DRV had not done everything possible to repair the dikes after the 1971 floods was strongly denied by Daniel Mandelbaum, a specialist on dike building who did research for the French Ministry of Public Works and who inspected the dike system of North Vietnam in August.[66] Nor were the Vietnamese comforted by an "intelligence report" released by the State Department on July 29, which claimed that only a series of overlapping craters across the entire top of a dike could cause a breach in the dike—a judgment not supported by independent specialists in the field, who pointed out that near misses could cause grave damage to the dikes, particularly during high-water periods.[67] In August specialists on the dike system pointed to the pattern of bombing of the dikes since April, in which 54 of 58 dikes hit in the Red River Delta were situated in the eastern part of the Delta, where most villages were lower than the river and therefore most vulnerable to inundation, in contrast to the western or "high" delta.[68]

The mood of DRV officials in July and August, therefore, was grim. They remained convinced that Nixon was threatening them with devastation in order to force their hand diplomatically. Nguyen Minh Vy, a ranking member of the DRV delegation in

Paris, declared that the United States believed that "after several million people have been killed by the dikes breaking, Vietnam will give in." [69] During the July and August sessions, DRV negotiators repeated their willingness to allow the Saigon government itself to name its part of the coalition, inviting Kissinger to suggest ways in which each side could be confident that the other would not impose its will through the coalition.[70] They called the transitional coalition by other titles to satisfy the American objection to the idea of coalition government, but Kissinger complained that it was still a coalition government, by whatever name.

By the end of August it became apparent that American bombing would not cause any flooding in the North. The water level of the Red River was four inches lower than it had been in 1971, and by the end of the month it had already begun to recede.[71] The DRV could again negotiate without the biggest gun of all at its head.

The talks remained stalemated by Kissinger's refusal to discuss any coalition government—even one which explicitly met his earlier objections. Despite Kissinger's repeated assertions that the United States was prepared to discuss any political solution which did not impose a Communist regime on South Vietnam, it is clear that he continued to take the position through August that a political settlement could only be negotiated *after* and *separately from* a cease-fire, US withdrawal, and exchange of military prisoners. The Lao Dong Party's theoretical journal *Hoc Tap*, in an article published in September on the negotiating positions of the two sides, was obviously commenting on Kissinger's posture in the secret meetings when it complained that the United States still wanted "political questions" to be "solved only some time after the settlement of what it calls 'military questions'." The *Hoc Tap* article further charged that the United States was "aiming at liquidating the revolutionary administration," an apparent reference to Kissinger's insistence that his "electoral commission" had to operate within the framework of the Saigon government's constitution, which was created under the aegis of the United States and which refused to recognize the PRG as legally equal to the Saigon government.[72]

Faced with Kissinger's unwillingness to negotiate on a formula to insure that neither side would dominate a coalition regime, the

DRV decided to publicize its revised coalition government formula, which was still virtually unknown in the United States. On September 11, four days before the next Kissinger-Tho meeting, the PRG released a new statement explaining its proposal for a tripartite government of national concord. The three components, said the statement, "will be in equal strength and on equal footing" and the Saigon side, "without Nguyen Van Thieu," would "appoint its people to participate in the government of national concord." The statement also stated publicly for the first time the DRV-PRG position that a settlement had to reflect the "reality" of "two administrations, two armies and other political forces." [73]

The publication of the PRG statement was meant to put Nixon on the defensive at home. But the US delegation in Paris coolly declared that it was "nothing more than an undisguised attempt to put the Viet Cong in power in South Vietnam without an election." [74] At the next meeting with Tho on September 15, Kissinger again refused to discuss the means by which either side could be prevented from dominating the other, and issued a new threat of even more drastic military action against the North after Nixon's reelection if there was no settlement.[75]

After his return to Washington, Kissinger told a news conference that the "basic principle" of American policy was to refuse "as a result of the negotiations to impose a particular form of government that guarantees predominance to one side." [76] This remark was the first of many misrepresentations of the negotiations which Kissinger would make before their conclusion, since he had systematically avoided discussing that very principle in Paris for months. Asked about the DRV-PRG argument that their proposal would not permit either side to dominate the coalition, Kissinger responded elusively, "The question is not what was said, but what the actual consequence of it is."

But the tripartite coalition government formula, with guarantees against domination by either side, was about to be superseded by a new proposal which made the final concession to the Americans by dropping the demand for a coalition government altogether. The decision to deal this last negotiating card was prompted by the recognition of two realities which together added up to a balance of forces unfavorable to the DRV's original objective. The first was that Nixon had succeeded in consolidating his political position at home, by virtue of his summit meeting in Moscow more than anything else. As a later analysis of the campaign pointed out, Nixon's policy in Vietnam had been in serious trouble in April, before the bombing and mining and the Moscow summit. But by mid-July Nixon had reestablished public confidence in his Vietnam policy by a two to one margin. For the American public, Nixon's policy was judged "successful" because he had been able to handle the Russians. McGovern, deprived of his major issue, never had a chance of being elected.[77] All this was apparent to Hanoi by mid-July.[78]

The second reality was that the offensive in the South, despite the significant gains in the first three months and the heavy losses inflicted on Saigon's best divisions, had not achieved as much as it needed to in order to force more concessions from Nixon. By the end of the summer, the PLAF offensive still had enough push to capture additional territory, as it did in Quang Nam and Quang Ngai. But the original expectation that even more land in the Mekong Delta could be wrested from Saigon and another significant part of the Saigon army put out of action were not met.[79]

The Party leadership was ready, therefore, to accept the continuation of the Thieu regime under conditions which would deprive the RVN of its claim to exclusive sovereignty over South Vietnam and obligate Thieu to loosen his grip over the political life of the Saigon-controlled zone.

During July, August, and September, according to US sources, there had been significant modifications of position on both sides revolving around a tripartite body which would conduct elections. These officials said the DRV tried out several formulas which they no longer called a coalition government, but which Kissinger still regarded as having the functions of a government. The United States had proposed a tripartite electoral commission which still did not have the responsibilities and prestige that the DRV demanded. Out of these discussions emerged the "National Council of Reconciliation and Concord," a protean institution whose conception owed something to both delegations.

Both DRV and US sources agree that by September 26 the DRV had dropped its demand for Thieu's replacement. But its formulation of the National Council was still rejected by the United States as a "de facto coalition government." Nevertheless, after the

September 26 meeting, Ambassador Bunker informed Thieu that the DRV appeared to be moving toward an acceptable formula for a settlement.

The detailed draft which Le Duc Tho presented to Kissinger on October 8 contained the concession on the National Council of Reconciliation and Concord which Kissinger had been waiting for. It defined the Council as an "administrative structure" whose functions were confined to administering the election and promoting the implementation of the agreement. It was also the first complete draft agreement ever presented by either side in the five years of talks.

The DRV draft, which was submitted in English, had nine chapters and twenty-two articles.[80] The key political provisions were contained in chapter 4, dealing with internal South Vietnamese matters. It provided that the government of South Vietnam would be determined by general elections within six months under international supervision, and it obligated the South Vietnamese parties to "achieve national reconciliation and concord" and to "ensure democratic liberties." Among the questions to be decided between the two South Vietnamese parties was to be the mutual reduction of military forces. It also obligated the United States to refrain from supporting "any political tendency or any personality" in South Vietnam. Civilian detainees were to be released, along with captured military personnel, at the same time as the US troop withdrawal, according to chapter 3 of the draft—a major point in past PRG programs.

The problem of relations between the two zones of Vietnam was covered in chapter 5, which provided that reunification would be carried out "step by step through peaceful means" and that civilians could move freely between the two zones in conformity with the principle of Vietnam's unity, which was specified in chapter 1. In the very first article of the agreement, the United States was pledged to respect the "independence, sovereignty and territorial integrity of Vietnam as recognized by the 1954 Geneva Agreements."

The cease-fire provisions prohibited any movement of military forces which would come in contact with those of the other side or extend the area of control. The United States and other foreign states were obligated to withdraw all military personnel, and the South Vietnamese parties were prohibited from accepting additional military personnel, advisers, or war supplies.

Kissinger believed that the draft had made the concessions which he had been waiting for by dropping the demand for a coalition government. He agreed to make it the basis for negotiating the final agreement. He ordered his staff to write a counterdraft based on the DRV draft and sent a cable to the White House outlining the contents of the DRV proposal and asking for permission to negotiate on the basis of it.[81] The following morning the approval was received, and thus began three days of the most intensive negotiations in the entire history of the Paris talks.

The US counterdraft made several substantive revisions in the DRV proposal. The United States demanded that the language on civilian detainees be revised so that the release of American prisoners of war would not depend on that of Vietnamese political prisoners. And the DRV cease-fire provision, which required that all aircraft be grounded and all ships remain at anchor, was amended to permit training flights and movement by ships which were not "acts of force." [82] But the spirit and substance of the DRV draft survived the three days of negotiations, and surprisingly little of the language was changed.

The three days of negotiations were followed by an all-day session on October 11 during which experts from the two sides compared the English and Vietnamese texts to insure that they were consistent. The two delegations had agreed that both the English and the Vietnamese texts would be equally authoritative. Far from being a technical session, this session was a matter of tough negotiating of many politically sensitive terms. The American linguistic experts were fluent in Vietnamese but were not as sensitive to some of the political nuances of Vietnamese terms as their DRV counterparts. This is one reason why the DRV succeeded at the October 11 session in getting US agreement to terms which the United States would later demand be changed. It is also clear that Kissinger was driving the staff to complete the text, and ordered the experts to compromise where necessary in order to get agreement. Both the superiority of the North Vietnamese negotiators in knowledge of Vietnamese and the political decision by Kissinger were factors in the negotiation of a Vietnamese text which was later deemed unsatisfactory by Nixon, according to sources familiar with that session.

By the end of October 11, Kissinger and Tho had agreed on most of the chapters in the draft and even on a tentative schedule for completion of the negotiations. The DRV delegation had initially proposed a mid-October date for signing; Kissinger had proposed on October 9 that the bombing and mining end October 18, that the text be initialed October 19 and signed one week later. The DRV accepted Kissinger's revised time-table, but two days later Kissinger revised the schedule once more so that the final date for the signing would be October 30. Again the DRV agreed.[83]

By October 12, only two issues remained unresolved. The first was the release of Vietnamese civilian prisoners, on which the DRV was pressing for an unambiguous commitment, which the United States resisted. The second was the provision for replacement of war material. The United States was pushing for a liberal one for one replacement, while the DRV wanted more restrictions on American military assistance to Saigon. These problems were left to be resolved in another session after Kissinger returned from conferring with Nixon.[84]

When this round of talks was completed, the DRV believed they had a commitment from Kissinger that Saigon would not be permitted to obstruct the agreement. Kissinger had repeatedly stated that the United States was representing Saigon in the bilateral negotiations, and that Thieu would not have a veto over the settlement, according to DRV officials. The United States and the DRV had agreed that the DRV would initial the draft with the concurrence of the PRG, and the United States would initial with the concurrence of the Saigon government. All four countries would sign the agreement in a later ceremony.[85] Tho insisted that Kissinger commit the United States to meet the revised time-table, so that there would be no chance of the agreement falling apart after the election. Despite Kissinger's denial on October 26 that the United States had agreed to a firm date, he would plaintively ask a friend a few weeks later, "Please explain to me why I wanted this date."

With the DRV draft proposal, which opened the way to an extraordinarily rapid agreement on most basic issues, a momentum was established toward a final signing before the November presidential election. Indeed, the DRV regarded the late October date for the signing as an integral aspect of the draft agreement. After five years of nonbargaining in Paris, on October 12, a peace agreement suddenly appeared within the grasp of the two delegations.

But the last steps of the road were to be blocked by yet another resurgence of the very concern for the survival of the US client regime in Saigon which had blocked agreement for four years in Paris. For when the terms of the agreement collided with the interests of the Thieu regime, Nixon was willing to jettison the October compromise and thus imperil the whole agreement.

4.   *"Peace Is at Hand": The False Peace of October*

With a nearly completed text in hand, Kissinger returned to Washington on October 12 to get Nixon's approval of what had been negotiated so far and to seek further instructions. The tenor and content of the discussions held by Nixon and his advisers over the next three days have not been revealed, although there was reportedly a consensus, at a meeting on October 12, that while the draft was "basically acceptable," there were "a number of provisions" which would have to be "tightened." [86] There is reason to believe that serious objections to the draft and the plan to sign it on October 31 were raised during these three days. General Alexander Haig and John Negroponte of Kissinger's own staff believed that the agreement contained a number of provisions which were too favorable to Hanoi and should be renegotiated. They objected to the speed with which it had been drafted, which they felt was the result of Kissinger's eagerness to get an agreement before the election.[87] Furthermore, William Sullivan, the only high State Department official except for Kissinger himself who was involved in the negotiations, argued that the draft contained a number of weaknesses.[88] In particular Sullivan, who negotiated the 1962 Geneva Agreement on Laos, insisted that it make more concrete provision for policing of South Vietnam's borders by the International Commission of Control and Supervision, in order to halt infiltration of men and supplies.

Moreover, it was clear to those who had followed Thieu's stance toward the negotiations that he would never willingly accept an agreement based on the Kissinger-Tho draft. Despite his previous public endorsement of US proposals for an electoral body, with PRG representation, to carry out elections, Thieu began to balk at such an institution when he learned that serious negotiations were going on over a tripartite electoral commission. Thieu argued that it could be transformed into a coalition government and rejected it, complaining that the United States wanted to negotiate a settlement just when he was winning the war. On September 13 Bunker tried to persuade Thieu to go along with the American proposal but again Thieu flatly rejected it.[89]

Kissinger, then in Moscow, saw Thieu's obstinacy as a threat to the negotiations and cabled Nixon, warning him that unless the United States was prepared to go ahead with the proposal over Thieu's opposition, the talks could collapse before the election. He wanted permission to present the proposal at the September 15 session. On September 14 he received Nixon's approval.[90] Two weeks later, on the eve of another visit to Saigon by Haig, Thieu publicly declared his opposition to any tripartite electoral commission, or, for that matter, to any electoral commission which would be independent of his own regime, thus reversing his earlier agreement to the October 1971 American proposal.[91]

But the electoral commission was not the only issue on which Thieu had broken with the United States. He had also made it clear throughout 1972 that he would not go along with the dropping of the earlier demand for mutual withdrawal of North Vietnamese and US troops. A high Saigon government official later said his government had pointed out to the United States "several times" that mutual withdrawal had to be included in any peace agreement to get his government's approval—most recently during General Haig's visit from October 1 to 4.[92] US officials admitted later that Thieu's strong objections to the American proposal for an in-place cease-fire rather than for mutual withdrawal of troops was well known.

Now, in mid-October, the White House faced the problem again: would it override Thieu's opposition to the agreement, using the full weight of American leverage to force him into line? Or would it bow to Thieu's objections and demand further concessions —to insure his willing acquiescence? The latter course, as Kissinger had pointed out earlier, carried a grave risk of the complete breakdown of the talks, with the North Vietnamese charging that the United States was using Thieu's refusal to participate in a political settlement to sabotage the negotiation of an agreement. The former course, however, would risk an all-out attack by Thieu charging that the United States was betraying his government's anti-Communist struggle.

But there was another problem attached to an early signing of the agreement: the United States had planned to turn over vastly greater quantities of airplanes, tanks, and other weaponry during 1973 to complete a Vietnamization program which would prepare the Saigon government to handle not only Southern Communist forces but Northern troops as well. Signing the agreement as agreed by Kissinger and Tho would mean that Thieu would not get the additional equipment before the cease-fire.

Weighing all these considerations against Kissinger's diplomatic handiwork, Nixon was persuaded that he should not use the leverage at his disposal—including the threat to sign a separate cease-fire agreement with Hanoi (of which Thieu had expressed fear when he condemned the idea publicly in August) [93] and the threat of an aid cutoff—to override Thieu's opposition to the agreement. Nixon's refusal to put pressure on Thieu meant that he was giving the Saigon government veto power—just what Kissinger had pledged to the DRV he would not do.

It also meant that Nixon was putting off the signing of the agreement until after the election, when he would have more freedom to deal with both Hanoi and Saigon. On election day *Washington Post* diplomatic correspondent Murray Marder, talking with a White House official, asked if the White House was dismayed that there had been no agreement before the election. "We never intended to wrap this up by election day," the official replied. He explained that the President wanted to avoid a preelection cease-fire which would not work, and thus avoiding charges that he had rushed into an agreement for political purposes. The President decided, said the official, to risk what he thought would be the "lesser hazard" of North Vietnamese charges of bad faith in the negotiations.[94]

This explanation, which sought to put Nixon's decision in the most statesmanlike light, omitted any mention of the more controversial reasons for it. What is important, however, is this authoritative source's confirmation of the fact that the decision had been made by Nixon *before* Kissinger's trip to Saigon, ostensibly to persuade Thieu to fall in line. For this fact brings into sharper focus what the administration's own account has tried to obscure: that it was not Thieu who sabotaged the October agreement and derailed the scheduled signing, but Nixon, who judged that the terms and timing of the agreement were too unfavorable to his Saigon client state. Thieu's opposition to the agreement, which came as no surprise to Kissinger, was not the cause but the occasion for delaying the signature and asking for "one more round" of negotiations.

On October 16, as Kissinger flew to Paris for another session of the negotiations with Xuan Thuy, Army Chief of Staff General Creighton Abrams was ordered to South Vietnam, ostensibly to check on the progress of Vietnamization, but in fact to find out what additional arms would be needed by Saigon's armed forces in order to make a cease-fire acceptable.[95] Before the end of the month a massive airlift of planes, tanks, and ammunition would begin, based in part on Abrams' recommendations.

Kissinger, meanwhile, was ordered to stand firm on the two issues which had not been resolved in the earlier round of negotiating—Article 7, dealing with the replacement of armaments, munitions, and war materiel, and Article 8(c), dealing with the release of civilian detainees. The North Vietnamese had insisted that the release of American prisoners of war be linked with the release of Vietnamese civilians held in Theiu's jails and prisons, by making the release of both obligatory within sixty days of the agreement. They had also wanted limits on US military aid to Thieu which would be tighter than the one for one replacement provision proposed by the United States. Nixon and Kissinger probably felt that the failure to reach agreement on these two key issues would provide a convenient delay in the time-table for signing.

Thuy did give up his effort to link the release of American POWs and Vietnamese civilian detainees, but he continued to press for unambiguous language guaranteeing their release within ninety days. The Americans insisted on language which Thieu would use to avoid releasing the prisoners: "The two South Vietnamese parties will do their utmost to resolve the questions within ninety days after the ceasefire comes into effect." Kissinger offered his own assurance that the United States would use its influence with Thieu to see that the prisoners were released within ninety days. But Thuy insisted that the commitment to release the prisoners be made explicitly in the agreement.[96] Kissinger left to catch his plane for Saigon with neither of the two remaining problems resolved.[97]

But the DRV, anxious to insure that there would be no slip in the schedule, accepted the US position on both issues by cable after the October 17 meeting to complete the text.[98] The DRV also demanded confirmation from Nixon that the United States considered the text complete and would go ahead with the time-table for ending the bombing and mining, the initialing and signing. Nixon had to answer immediately; the bombing and mining were to end on October 21, according to the schedule agreed to earlier. A negative answer might trigger public charges by the DRV which would have compelled the Nixon administration to explain its policy to the American public.

So Nixon tried a complicated tactic by which he apparently hoped simultaneously to gain time and to reassure the DRV that the United States would not go back on the October text. The DRV has said, and the United States has not denied, that on October 20 Nixon sent a secret message to the DRV Premier Pham Van Dong, which said, in part, "The United States side appreciates the good will and serious attitude of the DRVN. The text of the agreement can now be considered complete." [99] But the cable also raised a number of what the DRV later called "complex questions" on which it asked the DRV to state its views. The message also requested that the time-table be delayed by two days, so that the bombing and mining would end on October 23 and the initialing would take place on October 24.[100] Nixon and Kissinger may have hoped that the Lao Dong Party Political Bureau would require several days to study the message and to agree on a reply.

Within twenty-four hours, however, the DRV had responded fully to the questions and sent its answer to Nixon, thus displaying an astounding ability to work out differences and arrive at a common position in a very short time. The response agreed to Nixon's request for another alteration in the time-table, but warned that this was the last time such a delay would be permitted. The cable, according to the DRV account, "stressed that the US side should not give any other reason to change again the schedule agreed upon." [101]

In Saigon, meanwhile, beginning on October 19, Kissinger was engaged in an angry confrontation with Thieu, who demanded wholesale revision of the text. Kissinger, deprived of the diplomatic leverage inherent in the fact that more than 85 percent of the financial and military resources Thieu used to stay in power came from the United States, knew that Thieu would not accept the draft, which he now read and analyzed for the first time. "We were not prepared to lower the boom on Thieu in October," one American diplomat recalled. Another US official admitted that, while the ferocity of Thieu's reaction to the text was unexpected, Thieu had been expected to "demand some revisions that we could get." Thus Kissinger's aim in the October meeting was not to get Thieu to agree to sign the draft agreement on schedule, but to minimize the changes which the US delegation would have to demand when they returned to the negotiating table once more after the election.

On October 22, in spite of his knowledge that Kissinger and Thieu were discussing what kinds of changes in the agreement would have to be renegotiated, and that there would be no signing before the election, Nixon sent a cable to Pham Van Dong, expressing satisfaction with the DRV response to his questions, and reaffirming that the United States would go ahead with the October 31 signing, on the basis of the October 20 draft.[102] Nixon and Kissinger were attempting to create the impression in Hanoi that the United States was firmly committed to the agreement. They apparently assumed that, when the United States sent a message the following day asking for a delay and further negotiations, it would create confusion and uncertainty in Hanoi and that some Communist party leaders, thinking that there was still a strong possibility that the October agreement could be maintained basically intact, would recommend against public charges of bad faith. They were being advised by intelligence specialists that the North Vietnamese Political Bureau was seriously divided over the negotiations. Hanoi had already agreed to three changes in the schedule by the United States, suggesting to these analysts that the "doves" were in control of things.*

The following day, Kissinger sent another cable to the DRV, saying that the United States was having difficulty getting its ally to go along with the pact and that some further negotiations would be necessary. The North Vietnamese were invited to suggest a date for a new meeting, and nothing was said about the previously agreed time-table. But there was no explicit reneging on the pledge to sign by October 31, and the cable promised that the United States would end all bombing north of the twentieth parallel on October 25—a move which Kissinger believed might help quiet Hanoi's fears that it was being deceived about American intentions.[103]

But this maneuver represented another in a long series of miscalculations about the Vietnamese leaders. It underestimated both the unity of the leadership and their ability to see through the Nixon-Kissinger diplomatic strategy. It was immediately apparent to the Communist leaders that they had been deceived by Nixon, who wanted to use the October draft for political purposes while prolonging the negotiations until after the elections, when the pressure of public opinion would slacken. For if the United States was going to permit Thieu to obstruct the agreement, this meant that it was going to demand substantive changes going to the heart of the October draft.

There was only one way to put pressure on Nixon to sign the draft agreement, and that was to reveal to the American public Nixon's refusal to sign an already completed agreement. So on October 26 the DRV startled the world by publishing a statement outlining the draft agreement of October 20 and the process of the negotiations—the October 8 DRV initiative, the time-tables, and the secret cables between Nixon and Pham Van Dong.[104] The statement charged that the Nixon administration was using Thieu's objections as an "instrument of the United States to sabotage all peaceful settlement of the Vietnam problem," and warned that the US October 23 cable had "created an extremely serious situation

---

* CIA official George Carver, the agency's most influential analyst of North Vietnamese affairs, was then pressing the theme of a factional split in the Party leadership between Le Duan's faction and Truong Chinh's faction. Even one year later, he was still so preoccupied with the idea of such a factional division that he spent the better part of an hour explaining it to a Washington journalist who had come for a briefing on the military situation.

which jeopardizes the signing of the 'Agreement on Ending the War and Restoring Peace in Viet Nam.' "

Thus the Nixon administration had found it impossible to maneuver in such a way as to avoid provoking both Saigon and Hanoi. Now, only two weeks before the election, it stood accused of being ready to sign an agreement which Saigon found unacceptable while at the same time it was charged with breaking its promise to sign the agreement on October 31. Kissinger, who had brought on this crisis, was ordered to go before the television cameras to undo the political damage.

Kissinger had to accomplish two things in his October 26 press conference: he had to take the heat off Nixon from the right by demonstrating that the projected agreement represented a major defeat for the Communists and a victory for the United States and Thieu; and he had to neutralize the charge that he was delaying an agreement which he had promised to sign. Kissinger cleverly insured that the headlines would focus on the promise of peace rather than the question of the Nixon administration's good faith in the negotiations. "Peace is at hand," he declared; an agreement was "within sight" and could be achieved with only one more round of negotiations taking three or four days.[105] He began by emphasizing that Hanoi had agreed to solve military problems in advance of a definitive political solution, "which was exactly the position which we had taken all along."

Then Kissinger sought to defuse the issue of bad faith and delaying in signing the agreement. Here his statements were both self-contradictory and inconsistent with the detailed account broadcast by the DRV the previous day. Nor did he challenge the accuracy of the DRV account, saying he had "no complaint with the general description of events as it was given by Radio Hanoi." He noted that the DRV had demanded a date for signing the agreement as a condition of their October 8 proposal. Kissinger later referred to "the acceptance on our part of the North Vietnamese insistence on an accelerated schedule." Nevertheless, Kissinger argued that there had been a "misunderstanding" on Hanoi's part and that there was never an unconditional commitment to sign by a certain date: "It was . . . always clear, at least to us, and we thought we made it clear in the records of the meetings, that obviously we could not sign an agreement in which details remain to be worked out simply because in good faith we had said we would make an effort to conclude by a certain date. It was always clear that we would have to discuss anything that was negotiated first in Washington and then in Saigon."

But regardless of whether Kissinger's earlier acceptance of a time schedule was conditional as he claimed, the situation on October 23 was completely different. For it was no longer a question of "details" remaining "to be worked out"; the United States had already agreed formally to accept the text as complete and had agreed to the October 31 signing date. Kissinger did not address himself to the two cables from Nixon to Pham Van Dong, but continued to imply throughout the press conference that there had been no acceptance by the United States of a completed text. He was never asked by the press about those documents, and the question of reneging on a promise to sign the existing text was lost in the general excitement over the idea that "peace is at hand."

Kissinger did his best, of course, to avoid the suggestion that the United States was raising issues which would be opposed by the DRV, conveying the impression that the matters remaining to be negotiated were either clarifications or "technical" matters.

To justify the need for further negotiations with the DRV, Kissinger pointed to "certain ambiguities that were raised by the interview that the North Vietnamese Prime Minister Pham Van Dong gave to one of the weekly journals in which he seemed to be, with respect to one or two points, under a misapprehension as to what the agreement contained. . . ."

The interview referred to was given by Premier Dong to Arnaud de Borchgrave on October 19.[106] A careful reading of the interview shows that Dong's answers did not misrepresent the October text. When asked whether Thieu would be part of the Saigon government's component in a tripartite coalition government, Dong avoided any answer which would either confirm or deny the promise of a coalition government in the text or Thieu's role. Instead, he said that Thieu had been "overtaken by events." When de Borchgrave asked about a cease-fire followed by "direct negotiations between the Provisional Revolutionary Government and the Saigon regime," Dong accurately stated that "The situation will then be two administrations in the south and given that new situation they will have to work out their own arrange-

ments for a three-sided coalition of transition. . . ." Dong avoided
the term "coalition government" and even "coalition administration," despite the fact that the text itself used the term "administrative structure." In short, there was nothing in the interview which
went beyond the agreed text.

Kissinger also spoke of "methods by which the international
supervisory body can be put in place at the same time that the
cease-fire is promulgated," failing to mention that what the United
States now had in mind was a major foreign military presence
which would be unacceptable to the DRV. He spoke vaguely of the
relationship of the cease-fires in Cambodia and Laos to the
Vietnam cease-fire and "how to compress the time as much as
possible," without mentioning that the draft agreement said
nothing at all about cease-fires in Cambodia and Laos.

Kissinger said the United States wanted to "make sure that the
Vietnamese text conveys the same meaning" as the English text on
the term "administrative structure" in relation to the National
Council—a reasonable request, except that the US linguistic expert
had already approved the Vietnamese text after going over it in
detail with the DRV delegation all day on October 11. Finally, he
mentioned "some technical problems as to what clauses of the
Geneva accord to refer to in certain sections of the document."

In fact, these were not "technical problems" at all, but matters
of political substance. As would become clear when the November
round of negotiations began, the United States wanted to insert
language from the 1954 Geneva Agreement which would, when
taken out of the whole context of that document, define the
demarcation line between the two zones as an international
political and territorial boundary. As for the problem of Saigon's
signature, it had already been agreed that the DRV and the United
States would initial the agreement with the "concurrence" of their
partners, and that Saigon could then sign the document in the final
ceremony, along with the PRG.

Kissinger's presentation of the problems remaining attempted
to obscure the fact that the United States was reopening negotiations which had already been formally closed on October 22. To the
North Vietnamese Kissinger's press conference could only be read
as confirmation of their fears that they had been manipulated by
Nixon and Kissinger in order to have the appearance of a peace

agreement within sight just before the election, and that the American position would begin to harden as soon as Nixon was reelected. Significantly, Kissinger did not bother to cite Saigon's objections as the reason for requiring further negotiations. He made it clear that the United States would support only those objections with which it agreed and not those which it felt unnecessary, thus confirming Hanoi's view that the United States had merely used Saigon's opposition to the agreement to cover its *volte-face*.

The purpose of the October 26 news conference, however, was not to reassure the North Vietnamese. The publication by Hanoi of the outline of the agreement and its account of the negotiations had marked the failure of that effort. Kissinger's performance was clearly for the benefit of the domestic American audience, who had heard what they wanted to hear about the Paris negotiations. It succeeded in neutralizing the political effect of the DRV charge that Nixon had reneged on his promise to sign a pact already completed, creating a mood of euphoria about the imminence of peace which dulled the nation's desire for close analysis of Nixon's negotiating stance.

Having cleared away the last remaining political obstacle, Nixon and Kissinger began immediately to plan their strategy for the negotiations which would resume after the elections, when they would be free once more to use the threat of massive destruction as the primary means of forcing Hanoi to accept American demands for more concessions. Within a few short weeks, this new hard line would provoke a new diplomatic deadlock and bring on perhaps the most dramatic military and political confrontation of the entire war.

5: Showdown: Hanoi and Paris

After Kissinger's October 26 "Peace is at hand" statement, the requirements of Nixon's Vietnam diplomacy were increasingly at odds with each other. On one hand, Nixon wanted an agreement which would permit Thieu to continue to consolidate his territorial control; this required major revisions in the October draft. But on the other hand, he needed to produce a peace agreement within a relatively short time to satisfy the impatience of the American public with US involvement in Vietnam.

So Nixon would try once more, as he had in 1969 and again in the spring of 1972, to force the DRV to agree to terms favorable to Thieu. Kissinger, meanwhile, would try to keep public opinion in line as he had throughout 1972 by blaming the North Vietnamese for the delay in achieving an agreement and persuading the public of his own reasonableness in the negotiations. The formula had succeeded before in at least gaining time. But Nixon and Kissinger had drawn for too long on the public's desire to believe that the war was ending. Now the general expectation of an imminent agreement which had been generated by Kissinger's October announcement collided with Nixon's last effort to squeeze more concessions from Hanoi.

The DRV delegation in Paris refused to budge from its demand that the October draft agreement remain essentially intact, in spite of Kissinger's repeated threats of terrible devastation. The stage was thus set for a last desperate gamble that the North Vietnamese could be coerced: the destruction of large areas of Hanoi and Haiphong in twelve days of the heaviest bombing of the war. The December bombing, which represented the culmination of Nixon's four-year effort to impose a settlement on the Vietnamese revolutionaries that would leave Thieu safe and secure, demonstrated the fundamental weakness of the American position. For while the brutal bombing of Hanoi could not alter the DRV's determination at the negotiating table, it did bring a final, decisive shift in mood in the United States, from hope to despair, and a determination in Congress to bring the war to an early end.

Having played his last card without success, Nixon lost his room for maneuver. He sent Kissinger back to Paris to sign an agreement even if he had to give up the remaining demands for confirmation of Thieu's sovereignty over all of South Vietnam and for dilution of the tripartite National Council's role and status. Although the Nixon administration tried, of course, to put the best face possible on the agreement, it had lost one of the most important battles of the entire war.

1.   Nixon, Thieu, and the October Draft

Even before his reelection, Richard Nixon had already decided to embark on the risky course of demanding major revisions in the October agreement. The "clarifications" and "technical problems" mentioned by Kissinger on October 26 became "central points" in Nixon's November 2 address and "problems of substance" in the words of Ambassador William Porter in Paris.[1] And in contrast to the three or four days of negotiations to which Kissinger had referred, Secretary Rogers spoke on November 5 of at least "several weeks" to complete negotiations.[2] Nixon had already ordered Kissinger to accept the bulk of Thieu's demands as the basis for the United States' negotiating position.

This decision was bound to create a new crisis in the Paris negotiations, since Thieu's objections to the agreement were not over details or ambiguities, but went to the core compromises which had made it possible to reach agreement in October.

An analysis of Thieu's objections to the agreement leads to the conclusion that his opposition to it from October through January was not merely theatrics but an accurate reflection of his instinctive fears of its political consequences. Thieu immediately recognized upon reading the text of the Kissinger draft that the most damaging aspect of the agreement was its implied acceptance of the presence of North Vietnamese troops in the South. It was not only that the text made no mention of Northern troops; it implicitly agreed that they should be treated as Southern troops. "The Communists resorted to a very crafty use of terms," Thieu later said of the draft agreement, "when they stated that the problem concerning the Vietnamese armed forces in the South would be settled by the two sides in the South. . . . Thus if we want to settle the problem concerning North Vietnamese forces as well as liberation forces we must talk with the liberation front, while the North Vietnamese will be considered as naturally belonging to the liberation front and its government." [3]

In an interview in late December, Thieu explained that the most damaging point in the agreement was the implicit acceptance of North Vietnamese troops in the South: "Officially accepting the presence of 300,000 North Vietnamese troops by juridical agreement, ratified by an international conference, is absolutely unacceptable," he said. "Because it's like recognizing their right to call themselves liberators, their right to say that Vietnam is one country, from Hanoi to Saigon. . . ." The logical consequence of this recognition, Thieu explained, was to portray his government as illegitimate. "It means considering the South Vietnamese army as a mercenary of the Americans." And Thieu recalled telling Kissinger that the agreement would "put the legal government of South Vietnam in the position of a puppet government installed by the Americans!" [4]

The meaning of the October agreement for Thieu, therefore, was that the basic question of legitimacy, over which the war had been fought from the beginning, was being decided in favor of the revolutionary side. Thieu's nephew and chief adviser, Hoang Duc Nha, after refusing at first to answer the question of what Saigon's major objection to the October draft was, finally admitted to reporters that the continued presence of North Vietnamese troops was the "main point," because it "means that our 15 year fight has been senseless." [5] And the Saigon government's permanent observer to the United Nations, Nguyen Huu Chi, said in an interview in December, "It would be very difficult to explain to the army and the people why the North Vietnamese troops were going to be allowed to remain in the south under a peace settlement. . . . It would be very bad for the morale of the armed forces and the people." [6]

Thieu was realistic enough to know that he could not win the withdrawal of all North Vietnamese troops from the South, but his primary concern was to obtain language in the agreement which would be a tacit admission that those troops were in the South illegally. If he could gain that point, he could use it as a pretext to disclaim other provisions after it was signed. He rejected the principle of a negotiated troop reduction and demobilization and demanded instead that the North Vietnamese troops regroup in enclaves and agree to withdraw a portion of their troops, in return for nothing more than the promise that Saigon would demobilize an equal number of its own troops.[7]

A second objection to the draft also related to the legitimacy which it gave to the aims of the DRV and PRG: it failed to establish the Demilitarized Zone as an international boundary between North and South Vietnam. Thieu argued that this further undermined the legal basis of the Saigon government and lent legitimacy to North Vietnam's involvement in the South. Not only had the agreement not mentioned the Demilitarized Zone, but the text put all the emphasis on the US respect for the "independence, sovereignty, unity and territorial integrity of Vietnam as recognized by the 1954 Geneva agreements." Since Communist troops had captured all of northern Quang Tri province in the 1972 offensive, there was no longer any physical barrier between North Vietnam and the PRG in the South. The absence of any legally recognized territorial boundary between North and South Vietnam in the agreement meant that civilian personnel as well as population could move back and forth between North and South as though the division of Vietnam no longer existed.

The third major objection raised by Thieu was the provision for the establishment of a National Council of Reconciliation and Concord. His objection was not confined to the use of the term *co cau chinh quyen* in the Vietnamese text to refer to the Council. The term was supposed to mean "administrative structure," the word used in the English text. But while it can be translated in that way, it can also mean "governmental structure," which suggested to the Vietnamese that it was indeed a coalition government, despite American assurances to the contrary.

Kissinger had already promised during his October visit to clear up this embarrassing oversight when the talks resumed. But that did not satisfy Thieu's fundamental opposition to the whole concept of the tripartite body which would organize and administer elections and promote the implementation of the agreement. For, as Thieu pointed out on September 30, 1972, in explaining his opposition to any electoral commission such as that proposed by Kissinger, it would be a political structure independent of his own regime, and of the constitution of the Republic of Vietnam. It would have "supragovernmental" character and would therefore "nullify the whole parliament, as well as the Supreme Court, because it would be completely independent." [8] A new election, carried out by such a "supragovernmental" body, suggested that a new constitution would result. Thieu had manipulated the existing constitutional structure skillfully in consolidating and maintaining his own political power. Now he was afraid that the agreement would render it irrelevant.

Thieu had a veto within the proposed Council, of course, and could therefore block it from taking any action of which he disapproved. But again, it was not so much how the institution would function on paper but the broader political dynamics which it would set in motion that bothered Thieu. He would be cast in the role of the obstructionist, while both the PRG and his non-Communist opponents called for national reconciliation at the expense of the anti-Communist legal structure.

Thieu appeared to assume that, if the Communists could argue a particular interpretation of the agreement, it would be accepted by most South Vietnamese, and that his own position would be too weak to prevail. In discussing the provision in the October draft in his speech to the National Assembly on December 12, Thieu declared, "This council, having three equal segments with the same number of personnel, will supervise the two existing governments and organize a general election. This means a new constitutional assembly will be elected and there will be a new constitution and a new system determined by the new constitution." [9] This would be the PRG proposal within the National Council, but Thieu's concern over the issue in spite of his own veto revealed the depth of his fears that his own opposition to that argument would be ultimately ineffective.

But the idea that the National Council had a "supragovernmental" character was not merely in Thieu's imagination. The

English text used the relatively innocuous phrase "promote the implementation" of the agreement in describing its function. But the Vietnamese text, as Thieu and Nha discovered when the DRV released the nine-point summary on October 26, used the term *don doc*, which can be translated as "promote," but which had more of a connotation of compulsion, as in "urge," "hurry," or even "push." [10] Furthermore, the fact of its responsibility for organizing and administering elections implied that it was to have the necessary means to carry out these functions, to supervise the governmental personnel of both the Republic of Vietnam and the PRG. One high official of Thieu's government pointed out that it could be expected to have "at its disposition a corps of electoral police, to permit an honest vote." [11] When Thieu attacked the tripartite National Council as an institution which "wipes out our constitution," he was recognizing the fact that, in regard to the provisions of the Paris agreement, the National Council would in fact supersede the RVN constitution. [12]

Thieu had other objections as well. The provision for a demarcation of zones would compel Saigon to give formal recognition to the PRG as an administration. The draft called for the immediate provision of democratic freedoms and the holding of elections within six months, which would force Thieu to go into an electoral competition in an atmosphere of suddenly loosened political restraints. It provided for no cease-fires in Cambodia or Laos, leaving open the possibility of Communist or Communist-dominated governments in those countries and raising the specter of a South Vietnam surrounded by three pro-Communist Indochinese governments. And finally, Thieu complained that the Americans had accepted an agreement which by implication put the blame for the war on the United States and not on the North Vietnamese. The very first article, Thieu pointed out, suggested, by committing the United States alone to respect Vietnam's "independence, sovereignty, unity and territorial integrity," that the United States had previously violated these principles. [13]

From Thieu's viewpoint, then, the October agreement did indeed represent a "sell-out" and a "surrender" to the Communist side on a series of central points. [14] And his fears that it might prejudice the survival of his own regime were not entirely groundless. The Saigon government's continuous attacks on the agreement from late October right up until it was signed were not designed to gain time, and to prepare the population pyschologically for peace. They had, if anything, precisely the opposite effect, demonstrating as they did that Thieu considered the agreement a serious blow to his government. These attacks and demands were intended, rather, to exploit what Thieu sensed was Nixon's reluctance to sign an agreement which was unacceptable to Saigon.

It did not take long for the Nixon administration to accept many of Thieu's most important demands for revision, including the demand for a partial pull-back of North Vietnamese troops. Kissinger said the United States intended to press the North Vietnamese to withdraw some 35,000 combat troops in Quang Tri and Thua Thien provinces. The United States would not ask for a commitment within the framework of the formal agreement, he said, but would seek to "clarify" an informal "understanding" reached during the October negotiations. Kissinger told newsmen that he had expressed concern at the presence of these troops, which he regarded as capable of launching a future offensive against Hue, and said he had the "impression" that the North Vietnamese "understood the need to reduce the number of their forces in the South." [15]

Kissinger's version of the "understanding" on North Vietnamese troop withdrawal was nothing more than an election-eve concoction, designed to reassure the American public that the Nixon administration had won a concession from the North Vietnamese on troop withdrawal at a time when Thieu was attacking the agreement as a "sell-out." There was, in fact, no understanding on the withdrawal of North Vietnamese troops, except that the question of all Vietnamese troops in the South would be negotiated between the RVN and the PRG. Kissinger admitted as much when pressed by one reporter on the precise character of the "understanding." He replied that it was based on no more than his assumption that the North Vietnamese would have to rotate troops to the North and wouldn't be able to send replacements under the agreement. He was actually indicating in advance what one of his demands would be in the November round of talks.

This was only the most publicized of Thieu's demands which the United States decided to present at the Paris talks; others had to do with the Demilitarized Zone and the military demarcation line, the removal of the Provisional Revolutionary Government's name from the preamble and the main text of the agreement, the National Council's functions, cease-fires in Laos and Cambodia, and the definition of zones of control. Collectively, these changes would seek to alter the balance of compromises in the October draft and to take back the US concessions on which the DRV insisted as the price for its willingness to permit the Thieu regime to remain in power.

In addition to the demands which the United States would present on behalf of Thieu, Kissinger also agreed to submit to the DRV a series of "protocols," or implementing documents which would be attached to the October agreement. Ambassador William Sullivan, who had been brought into the negotiations on October 17, prevailed upon Kissinger to bring the State Department's legal adviser, George Aldrich, into the negotiations to draft protocols on the cease-fire, the Four-Party Joint Military Commission (JMC), the International Commission of Supervision and Control (ICCS), and the release of prisoners. These protocols would add fifty-one articles to the existing twenty-two, thus increasing the length of the agreement by more than 200 percent. In addition, they could not avoid raising political questions which had been avoided or resolved in the main text either by ambiguous formulas or by not addressing them at all, particularly in the protocol on the cease-fire. The effect of these protocols was to complicate enormously the task of reaching an agreement.

The Nixon administration seemed confident that it could squeeze substantial new concessions from the DRV if it turned up the pressure—including the renewed threat of massive bombing against North Vietnam's two major cities. Nixon felt that his hand in the negotiations had been strengthened by his reelection, and that the North Vietnamese wanted a settlement so badly that they would not break off the talks. A leading CIA analyst was quoted as saying that the DRV commitment to a settlement was "irreversible." [16]

Presenting the Thieu regime's demands, with few modifications, had the further advantage of stretching out the talks so that the massive military build-up which had begun within a few days after Kissinger's October 26 press conference could be completed before the cease-fire. According to Secretary Laird, the Pentagon was attempting to carry out the entire 1973 military aid program, called "Project Enhance Plus," before the agreement was completed.[17] Although there was no comment on how long this build-up would take or how much equipment was involved, it was learned later that the program involved seventy M-48 and M-41 tanks, and 600 helicopters and fighter planes. By January 1973, Thieu was to have the fourth largest air force in the world, with more than 2,000 planes.[18]

Project Enhance Plus would not be completed until some time in December, so the administration had an obvious interest in delaying the cease-fire for several weeks. But the Nixon administration was interested in more than mere delay in the negotiations. For the new demands predictably created a new diplomatic stalemate in Paris, to which Nixon responded with renewed escalation. It was to be the last act in the drama of Nixon's quest for a clear-cut "victory" over the Vietnamese revolution by diplomacy and military force.

2. *The New Stalemate in Paris*

The DRV returned to the negotiating table on November 20 only reluctantly and with some bitterness. It had argued at first that the United States had to sign the October draft which it had already agreed to, and it sought the support of the Soviet Union and China for that position. The Chinese responded with strong support, issuing a statement on October 30 demanding that the United States "keep its promise and speedily sign the accord with the DRVN. If the U. S. prolongs its aggressive war . . . it must accept all the consequences." [19] The Soviet Union was more cautious. Kosygin issued a statement on October 27 expressing hope that the negotiations would "soon lead to an agreement ending the war," thus appearing to urge the North Vietnamese to make further concessions to the United States.[20] But after East European governments told the Kremlin that it appeared to other socialist countries that the Soviet Union was abandoning the North Vietnamese, the Soviet government did an about-face. On November 5 First Deputy Premier Kiril T. Mazurov, a member of the Soviet Communist Party Politburo, in a major policy speech called on the United States to sign the agreement "as soon as possible" and stated that the Soviets and the DRV had reached agreement "on this particular issue." [21] This position was repeated on November 16, when Politburo member Mikhail Suslov told Le Duc Tho, who was fresh from talks with Chou En-lai in Peking, that the Soviet Union supported the DRV demands that the United States sign the October draft agreement.[22]

The DRV leaders went to great lengths to insure that they had the full support of their socialist allies on the October draft, because they had deep fears that the United States would try to force revision of key points in the agreement. Xuan Thuy announced on November 10 that Le Duc Tho would return to Paris and would meet with Kissinger, but only if the United States did not try to obtain "radical" changes in the October draft.[23] And Le Duc Tho declared on his arrival in Paris on November 18, "If the US protracts the negotiations, delays the conclusion of the agreement, and continues the war, the Vietnamese will have no other way than to resolutely carry on their fight until genuine independence, freedom and peace are achieved." [24]

The presentation by Kissinger of the new American demands at the first meeting on November 20 thus came as no surprise to the North Vietnamese. Despite Kissinger's later claim that he presented Thieu's demands "for the record" and separated them from those supported by the United States,[25] no distinction was made between Thieu's demands and those of the United States delegation. Kissinger presented as many of Thieu's demands as he thought were reasonable, according to an American source close to the talks, letting the North Vietnamese decide which ones had full US support on the basis of how hard the American delegation pushed for them.

The most significant revisions in the October text demanded by Kissinger on November 20 were the following:

1. The United States demanded the insertion in Article 15, on the reunification of Vietnam and relations between North and South, of the sentence, "Pending reunification, North and South Vietnam shall respect article 24 of the Geneva Agreement." Article 24 says, "The armed forces of each party shall respect the demilitarized zone and the territory under the military control of the other party, and shall commit no act and undertake no

operation against the other party and shall not engage in blockade of any kind in Viet Nam." The implication of this language, which was demanded by Thieu, would be that the presence of North Vietnamese troops in the South would be an "act" against the Saigon government and would therefore be illegal. The October draft had made no reference to the Demilitarized Zone.

The US delegation recognized that Saigon wanted to emphasize this provision "simply because it could wreck the negotiations," in the words of one source close to the negotiations. But Kissinger decided that the United States should not "undercut the status of the demilitarized zone," according to this source, so the United States supported Saigon's language, knowing it would probably be unacceptable to the DRV.

2. Also under Article 15, the United States proposed the addition of language severely limiting civilian traffic across the demarcation line. Although US negotiators recognized that North Vietnamese forces would have to be supplied with foodstuffs and other nonmilitary goods, and that the PRG would require material and personnel support from the North, they wished to have language indicating that North Vietnam did not have the right to move civilians freely into the South. "We were trying to have the DMZ as a sanitary corridor," recalled an American official, "with transit rights subject to both Joint Military Commission and the ICCS control." Since the PRG controlled the area adjoining the Demilitarized Zone, however, such stringent controls would deny its claim of sovereignty over the area it controlled.

3. The United States demanded that some North Vietnamese troops withdraw from the South.[26] Kissinger proposed a clause providing for reduction and demobilization of forces by both sides on a one-to-one basis, with language which would have sent demobilized troops back to their original homes.[27] The proposal included provision for international verification of the demobilization and return. The one-to-one troop reduction would have permitted Saigon to increase the numerical superiority of its troops and was thus clearly unacceptable to Hanoi. Furthermore, the United States demanded that the release of civilian detainees in the South be tied to the implementation of this provision.[28]

4. The United States demanded wholesale changes in Article 12, which described the nature and functions of the National

Council, so as to reduce its status to something considerably less than a supragovernmental organ. In the first place, the United States proposed dropping the term "administrative structure" completely, contrary to Kissinger's earlier assurance that the United States merely wished to insure that the Vietnamese term conformed with the English. Second, it proposed that the body be called simply the Council of National Reconciliation and Concord rather than the National Council of National Reconciliation and Concord, because the original terminology suggested a governmental organ, particularly in Vietnamese, where the term *quoc gia*, used for "national," can also mean "state." Third, the United States proposed that the Vietnamese word for "promote" in the phrase "promoting the two South Vietnamese parties' implementation of this Agreement" be changed from the authoritative *don doc* to the more respectful *khuyen kich*, which is usually translated as "encourage." Fourth, the United States insisted that the provision for consultations and the establishment of councils at lower levels be eliminated. And finally, and perhaps most important of all, it proposed the elimination of the "third segment" of the council as an independent entity, by specifying in the text that the "third segment" would be chosen by the two sides, thus making it merely an extension of both. By these demands, the United States was trying to reduce the National Council from a true tripartite body with real authority to little more than an extension of the two-party talks in Paris.

5. The United States demanded that Article 9 specify that the elections would be for the office of President, rather than for a new Constituent Assembly. Thieu had argued that leaving the offices to be determined by negotiation with the PRG would suggest that the political settlement being negotiated superseded his own constitution. (In supporting Thieu on this issue, Kissinger violated his professed principle of not negotiating matters which could be settled in negotiations between the South Vietnamese parties.) The United States further demanded the elimination from Article 9(b) of the deadline of six months within which the elections were to be held, and the elimination from Article 12(a) of the provision that the two South Vietnamese parties would "do their utmost" to reach agreement on internal matters within ninety days after the cease-fire. Thieu opposed an election deadline because it would put

greater pressure on him to loosen the political restrictions against both Communist and non-Communist opponents in his zone of control, as called for in Article 11, making it impossible for him to blame the absence of elections on the Communist refusal to accept his terms for an election. By the same token Thieu apparently felt that the three-month deadline for reaching internal agreement, even with the escape clause "do their utmost," would increase the bargaining power of the PRG in the consultative talks.

6. The United States tried to add a provision for cease-fires in Cambodia and Laos or at least to extract private commitments from the DRV that there would be cease-fires in both countries. The issue of whether the cease-fire in the agreement would cover only South Vietnam or all of Indochina had separated the US and DRV positions in the Paris conference from the beginning, but in 1972 the United States had finally relented and agreed to a settlement in South Vietnam alone. Now it was reopening the whole question.

7. The United States also demanded that all references to the PRG be eliminated from the text of the agreement. Thieu had refused to sign the agreement if the PRG was mentioned anywhere in it, fearing that this would be taken as a de facto recognition of the PRG as an equal political and legal entity. So the United States proposed that the names of the PRG and the Republic of Vietnam, which appeared in the preamble as well as the October text, be replaced by allusions to the "two South Vietnamese parties." The aim of the proposal was to deny the existence of a second government or administration in South Vietnam—one of the central principles of the agreement.

There were other demands of less importance: Kissinger insisted that Article 20(a), which pledged the four parties to "refrain from using the territory of Cambodia and the territory of Laos to encroach on the sovereignty and security of other countries," be amended to read, "the sovereignty and security of one another and of other countries." This was in response to the observation that in the DRV's view, as well as in the agreement itself, South Vietnam was not "another country." Whether it realized it or not, however, the US delegation, in the process of committing North Vietnam not to encroach on the sovereignty of the RVN, also confirmed explicitly that the PRG as well had "sovereignty" over the area which it controlled—the only place in the entire agreement where it was so explicitly stated. Kissinger also asked for references in at least two other provisions to the "sovereignty of South Vietnam," whose political implications in the context of the agreement were not clear.

Kissinger would later claim that the United States had *only* insisted on reaffirmation of respect for the Demilitarized Zone and on references to the "sovereignty of South Vietnam," neglecting to mention the far more important demands listed above.[29] Collectively, they constituted a substantial alteration of the significance of the agreement—precisely what Kissinger would blandly deny to the American public in his press conferences.

The DRV, which had suspected all along that the United States would try to make wholesale revisions in the October agreement, quickly sorted out the minor issues from those questions of principle on which it would refuse to yield. Le Duc Tho agreed to the less important changes demanded by the United States. He accepted the provision for respect of the Demilitarized Zone, but insisted that Article 15 also include the Geneva Agreement's definition of the demarcation line as only provisional and military in character. He agreed to drop the six-month deadline for the elections provided for in Article 11 and accepted the US proposals to add references to the "sovereignty of South Vietnam." He gladly agreed to the change in Article 20(a), presumably recognizing it as a further confirmation of the legal equality of the South Vietnamese parties.

But Tho rejected the other US demands for major changes and insisted that earlier American assurances that civilian prisoners would be released by Saigon be reaffirmed rather than making their release conditional on the successful implementation of the demobilization plan.[30] Furthermore, Tho warned, according to an American source close to the negotiations, that if the United States did not retract its demands for fundamental changes in the agreement, the DRV would likewise reopen questions which had already been resolved, and retract some of its own previous concessions.

On November 25 the United States opened up a series of new issues when it presented its protocols to the agreement. Kissinger's October 26 press conference had prepared the DRV for some effort to spell out the operations of the International Commission in greater detail, but the North Vietnamese were not prepared for these documents, which added three more significant demands to those already put forward by the United States on November 20.

First, the United States proposed not only that the ICCS investigate alleged violations at the request of one of the parties to the agreement with the consent of both parties and inspect the US withdrawals and incoming replacements for war materials, but that it also ensure that no troops and supplies be brought in except through the points of entry designated in the agreement. The United States demanded a large number of ICCS posts along the border with Laos and Cambodia as well as along the DMZ. As an American official close to the talks explained later, the United States wanted a sufficient number of posts so that they would constitute a *deterrent* to infiltration, even though the ICCS could not physically accomplish what seven years of bombing and half a million US troops had failed to bring about. The United States also proposed that the ICCS be composed of 5,000 men who would have the right to carry side arms. To the DRV delegation, this proposal conjured up images of a foreign occupation force.[31] It was offered, according to the US official, only as an opening bargaining move, in the knowledge that the United States would finally have to settle for a smaller number. The US draft further proposed that the ICCS have free movement along the border with Cambodia and Laos and in the DMZ, similar to that provided in the 1954 Geneva Agreement.

Second, in its protocol on the cease-fire, the United States proposed that the points of entry for the replacement armaments, munitions, and war material permitted under Article 7 be named in the text. In the previous draft, the modalities of the entry of these replacements into South Vietnam had been left to be determined after the signature of the agreement. One reason the DRV did not wish to designate their points of entry in advance was simple and straightforward: to do so would have invited a massive military move by Saigon to deny them points of entry. But there may have been another reason as well: by making the designation of points of entry something to be done after the cease-fire, the DRV and PRG would gain important bargaining leverage to get the implementation of provisions which were most important to them—such as the demarcation of zones and a complete standstill cease-fire.

Finally, in the cease-fire protocol, the United States demanded a provision on the determination of areas of control which would have completely overthrown the October compromise on the problem. The DRV had always insisted that the agreement had to be based on recognition of the reality of "two administrations, two areas of control and three political forces." The October draft had provided that the Joint Military Commission would "determine the areas controlled by each party," which assumed negotiations based on the realities of both military and administrative control. But the US draft protocol proposed that the areas of control be defined only by a census of military forces—their location, strength, and deployment. To determine zones of control without considering the factor of administrative organization would obviously favor Saigon.

At the same time, the American proposal would have attempted to gain a major military advantage for Saigon by compelling the PRG to declare publicly the strength and location of every military unit—including guerrillas, who would have to be organized in regular units or disbanded. The US draft provided that within seventy-two hours after the cease-fire the parties "shall form all regular and irregular armed forces into identifiable units," complete with commanding officers, uniforms, and a roster. "Each party shall insure that those armed forces not in an identifiable unit will be promptly disarmed." The result of the DRV's acceptance of this proposal would have been not only to give up its claim to most of the PRG's territory and population but to offer Saigon's air force a list of targets to bomb.

Kissinger made it clear that the United States was serious about getting most, if not all, of these new demands. In both the November 24 and November 25 sessions, according to the DRV account, which was never challenged, Kissinger threatened in blunt language that "the war would be intensified" unless Hanoi yielded on the major revisions he had demanded.[32] Kissinger was quoted by one North Vietnamese diplomat as saying that the bombing would be "savage."[33] An account based on American sources confirms that Kissinger threatened the bombing of the Hanoi-Haiphong region by recalling that the bombing above the 20th parallel had been halted on the assumption that negotiations would proceed "seriously."[34]

The DRV responded by warning the United States that it was

jeopardizing the whole agreement by its demands for major revisions. A *Nhan Dan* editorial on November 27 declared that "If the U. S. side nurtures dangerous designs and is intent on [going back on] the points agreed on, our people, with the sympathy and support of the fraternal socialist countries and all mankind, are determined to fight on until total victory." The commentary referred to the "arrogant claims advanced by U. S. lackey Nguyen Van Thieu" but did not refer directly to the new American demands at the peace talks, in conformity with the agreement not to reveal the contents of the secret talks. But a Liberation Radio broadcast on November 28 went directly to the most important principle violated by the new US demands, when it said, "The U. S.-puppets have no right to divide our country and our nation. Neither can they turn the provisional military demarcation line into a permanent frontier that cuts our country in two."

On November 29 Agence France-Presse's Hanoi correspondent, Jean Thoraval, filed an analysis of North Vietnamese thinking based on talks with diplomats close to the DRV. "By putting off the date for signing the cease-fire agreement," Thoraval wrote, "the Americans are believed here to be trying to improve their negotiating position, firstly by strengthening the military potential of their South Vietnamese allies and secondly by attempting to weaken their adversary by massive bombing raids against their supply lines south of the 20th parallel." These American moves, he said, had "resulted in the hardening of the attitude of the North Vietnamese. . . ."

Thoraval noted that a "significant development" was the resumption of demands in broadcasts by Hanoi and the PRG for the ouster of President Thieu. Without mentioning specifically the new American demands in Paris, he concluded, "According to observers this suggested that if the United States was questioning the fundamental principles behind the October cease-fire agreement, the North Vietnamese and their allies were prepared to cancel their concessions, among them a softening of their attitude toward the South Vietnamese leader." [35]

The United States was thus forewarned that Hanoi planned to retract earlier concessions in response to the American turnabout on a series of fundamental issues. The evacuation of children from Hanoi, beginning on December 4, the day before the negotiations resumed in Paris, further underlined the DRV's refusal to give in on matters of principle.

On December 4 the DRV delegation began withdrawing earlier concessions, hoping that this would make the American delegation realize that it had to drop its new demands in order to move the negotiations toward an agreement.[36] It did not yet reopen issues settled in the October agreement, however, but only withdrew a few concessions on lesser points, such as elimination of the six-month deadline for elections, and acceptance of a provision that both sides would respect the Demilitarized Zone, made in the previous round of negotiations. But the North Vietnamese did threaten to reopen issues which had been resolved in October, particularly the release of American POWs. This issue was raised anew by PRG chief of delegation Mrs. Nguyen Thi Binh in an interview with Agence France-Presse on December 8. Madame Binh referred to a "divergence of interpretation" over the prisoner release question. It was the PRG understanding, she said, that the prisoners in Thieu's jails would have to be freed if American prisoners were to be released. But she added, "the U. S. interpretation is that the two things are not connected." [37]

The strategy of taking back previous concessions and threatening to go even further did bring changes in the American negotiating posture. During the week from December 4 to 11, the United States dropped its insistence on the regroupment of PLAF main force units into enclaves and one-to-one troop reduction and gave up the proposal for elimination of the ninety-day period for an agreement on internal South Vietnamese matters. Regarding cease-fires in Laos and Cambodia, the United States settled for an assurance that the DRV would use its influence with the Pathet Lao to obtain a cease-fire in Laos within two weeks after the Paris Agreement was signed—a cease-fire which the DRV itself was eager to have.[38] But on Cambodia there was no such understanding. Kissinger pressed Tho to give assurances that the revolutionaries would negotiate with Lon Nol or at least agree to a de facto cease-fire, but Tho stood firm on his refusal to commit his Khmer allies to anything.

The United States' most important retreat, however, was on its earlier demand for language from the Geneva Agreement which would bind each party to "commit no act and undertake no operation against the other party. . . ." Instead the United States accepted the DRV language for Article 15(a), specifying that the military demarcation line at the 17th parallel "is only a provisional and not a political or territorial boundary, as provided for in paragraph 6 of the Final Declaration of the 1954 Geneva Conference."

Nevertheless, after a week of very hard bargaining, the United States still stood by its demands for the addition of tough restrictions on civilian movement across the demarcation line, major changes in the National Council, and elimination of all references to the PRG in the preamble of the agreement. And during each of the sessions Kissinger repeated the Nixon administration's threat to unleash American bombers on Hanoi and Haiphong.

On December 11 the North Vietnamese began the second phase of their effort to compel the United States to return to the October draft. While making it clear that they were prepared to sign on the basis of the October draft, they now withdrew one of the major concessions which had made the earlier agreement possible. They returned to their pre-October demands for a linkage between the release of American prisoners and the release of Vietnamese civilian detainees.[39] Tho proposed that the period during which the two sides were to "do their utmost" to release all civilian detainees be reduced from ninety days to sixty days, so that release of military and political prisoners would have identical time frames.

Finally, after several delays, the DRV submitted its counterdraft of the protocols on December 12. These protocols differed from those of the US delegation in several ways. In addition to their versions of the protocols on the cease-fire, the ICCS, the Four-Party JMC, and the prisoners, they submitted three additional protocols on withdrawal of US troops, removal of mines from DRV waters, and the Two-Party JMC, which the American protocols had not addressed. Their protocol on US troop removal detailed the requirement for dismantling bases and removing war material, and prohibited the use of American military advisers or technicians in the guise of civilian contract personnel, which the United States had been reported to be planning. The most significant feature of the protocol on mine deactivation was that it obliged the United States to take responsibility for the DRV's inland waterways as well as its coastal waters. The United States had previously planned to clear only the ports of North Vietnam.[40]

The DRV protocol on the ICCS differed sharply from that of the United States, providing that the total number of personnel be limited to 225 and that the ICCS teams should be able to move only with the permission of members of the Two-Party JMC. And the DRV protocol on the cease-fire rejected the US proposals which would have forced the PRG to define its zone of control in terms of regular military units and to name in advance the ports which it wished to use for receiving shipments of military goods.

The following day, December 13, the two sides discussed the protocols for the first time. Kissinger refused to give way on the major points. He accepted, with some revisions, the DRV protocol on mine removal, but rejected the DRV protocol on US military withdrawal and refused to spell out in any more detail the formation and operation of the Two-Party JMC, which was to be composed of the two South Vietnamese parties. He argued once again that the United States could not, as a matter of principle, negotiate matters which were properly negotiated only by the two South Vietnamese parties—a principle which he had no difficulty in violating in other cases in favor of Saigon. Le Duc Tho indicated that the DRV interpreted American unwillingness to agree to a protocol on the Two-Party JMC, as it did on the Four-Party commission, to mean that the United States did not want the Two-Party commission to come into existence, and made it clear that the DRV was very concerned about the Two-Party JMC's being established.

Little progress was made in reconciling differences on the protocols. It was agreed that three members of the US delegation would stay in Paris to continue discussions with North Vietnamese negotiators on the counterdrafts, while Kissinger and Le Duc Tho would exchange messages.[41] But the negotiations on the main text itself were still at an impasse, and before he left this last session on December 13 to fly back to Washington, Kissinger once more stated that if the North Vietnamese did not agree to the American demands for a settlement American bombers would be unleashed on a new scale.[42] Both sides knew that the next move was up to the United States.

On December 14, one participant in the negotiations recalls, "there were very few differences marked in pencil on my draft." But those which remained were central to the agreement: the modalities of civilian movement, the status of the PRG and its zone of control, and the nature of the National Council. The North Vietnamese had not caved in when confronted with the clear threat of heavy bombing of their two major cities. Kissinger, briefing Nixon that morning, had to report that the talks were at a stalemate unless the United States gave up its remaining demands for revision.

In the five weeks which had passed since his reelection, Nixon had threatened to use force to get better terms for his clients. When Kissinger told him that the choice was to back down or face a refusal by the DRV to go forward with the negotiations, he decided immediately to bomb Hanoi.[43] According· to a report emanating from Saigon, Nixon sent an ultimatum to Hanoi on December 15: yield on the outstanding issues within seventy-two hours or face the bombing of Hanoi and Haiphong.[44] According to the North Vietnamese, however, the ultimatum arrived only on December 18, shortly before the first wave of American bombers appeared on their radar at 7 P.M. Hanoi time.[45] Le Duc Tho had arrived from Paris only three hours earlier.[46]

Before the bombing began, however, Henry Kissinger again went before the public to explain why there was an impasse in Paris. Although no one knew it then, Kissinger was justifying the bombing that would begin two days later. The purpose of Kissinger's December 16 press conference was to blame the stalemate in the talks on Hanoi. But he could not discuss Hanoi's intransigence on fundamental issues, since that would raise anew the question of what issues still divided the two sides and how they arose. Instead he had to portray Hanoi as carrying out a "charade," accusing it of raising "one frivolous issue after another," and thus intentionally preventing the talks from moving to their conclusion.[47]

In explaining again why agreement was not possible in October, Kissinger added to the familiar need for "clarification" and "linguistic difficulties" a new reason: an alleged plan for a massive Communist effort to launch an attack throughout South Vietnam to begin several days before the cease-fire would have been declared and to continue for some weeks after the cease-fire came into being. By refusing to sign in October, Kissinger was arguing, the United States frustrated a Communist plan to massively violate the cease-fire. In fact, however, a Communist document captured in October and released by USIS in November indicated clearly that the final offensive which the Communists planned was *not* to continue beyond the cease-fire deadline.[48]

Then Kissinger sought to shift the responsibility for the impasse in Paris to the DRV. The negotiations, Kissinger said, "had the character where a settlement was always just within our reach, and was always pulled just beyond our reach when we attempted to grasp it." He did not mention the American demands for major changes in the October agreement and the DRV warnings about them, saying only that the DRV did accept *some* of the US proposals in the November round. He then charged that the DRV had withdrawn "every change that had been agreed to two weeks previously."

Kissinger asserted that following more serious negotiations, the two sides were so near agreement on December 9 that "if the other side had accepted again one section that they had already agreed to two weeks previously, the agreement could have been completed." He indicated that the acceptance which he sought was related to the US demand for "some reference in the agreement, however vague, however elusive, however indirect . . . which would make clear that the two parts of Vietnam would live in peace with each other and that neither side would impose its solution by force." Kissinger was referring here to the issue of movement by civilians between the two zones—an issue on which the DRV had never agreed to the American demand, as we have seen.

Kissinger's dissimulation on the reason for the diplomatic impasse was followed four days later by another briefing by Kissinger and William Sullivan, this time on an unattributable basis. They repeated essentially the same deceptive account of the stalemate, professing puzzlement as to why the North Vietnamese were interested in delaying a settlement. They offered various explanations, from an expectation that they could exploit public and Congressional war-weariness in the United States to factional conflict in the Lao Dong Party Politburo.[49]

Nixon and Kissinger hoped to use public confusion and frustration over the failure of the peace talks to bring an agreement to their advantage by portraying the enemy as stalling. In fact, of course, it was the US delegation which had been stalling, presenting a long list of new demands and then giving up some of them while the massive airlift of tanks, planes, and other new equipment was being completed. But Kissinger's press conference was aimed at building public support for one last effort at coercion of the DRV through the bombing of North Vietnam's remaining urban enclaves, Hanoi and Haiphong.

3. *The Battle of Hanoi*

Since the beginning of 1969 Richard Nixon had used the threat of unprecedented devastation of North Vietnam for a variety of diplomatic purposes: to prod the DRV into moving toward terms acceptable to the United States, to deter any move to upset his Vietnamization policy, to warn Hanoi to call off its offensive, and finally to accept American terms for a revised settlement. The December bombing was the logical culmination of his heavy reliance on this ultimate sanction to gain leverage over the Vietnamese revolutionaries.

The retribution which Nixon and Kissinger had so often threatened was to be swift, sudden, and brutal, unlike the Johnson administration's cautious and gradual escalation. Nixon was hoping that intensive attacks on the only two remaining urban agglomerations in North Vietnam would force Hanoi to accept his terms for an agreement. And if the suddenness and indiscriminateness of the bombing of those cities frightened the rest of the world, Nixon told columnist Richard Wilson on December 18, so much the better. "The Russians and Chinese might think they were dealing with a madman and so had better force North Vietnam into a settlement before the world was consumed by a larger war. . . ."[50]

All 200 B-52s in Southeast Asia—one-half of the entire B-52 fleet—were involved in the effort.[51] And three-fourths of all the Strategic Air Command's combat crews were mobilized to participate in the campaign.[52] There were also F-111s and F-4s carrying out strikes in the area, but Linebacker II was an operation planned around the B-52.

American officials acknowledged that the attacks were "aimed at crippling the daily life of Hanoi and Haiphong and destroying North Vietnam's ability to support forces in South Vietnam."[53]

The target list was not limited to military objectives but included political, social, and economic targets as well, including the water infiltration plant for Hanoi and factories manufacturing textiles and noodles.[54] It was accepted by the planners that populated areas of Hanoi and Haiphong located next to the targets would simply be wiped out. The B-52 was, of course, a weapon for destroying a large area, not for hitting a specific building or other target. The *Baltimore Sun* pointed out that the usual three-plane mission would drop 276 500- or 750-pound bombs in a rectangular area a mile and a half long and a half mile wide. The result was that little remained within the target area except rubble.[55]

Nixon clamped an unprecedented complete blackout on the targets and the actual destruction done by the B-52s in Hanoi and Haiphong.[56] But foreign journalists saw the remains of an entire residential neighborhood in Hanoi razed by B-52s on the night of December 26-27. Kham Thien district in the heart of Hanoi had been home for 28,198 people. Most of them had fortunately been evacuated to the countryside already. What remained was a swath of destruction about a mile and a half long and a half mile wide, within which only a few houses without roofs or windows remained standing.[57] The main train station, which was located in Kham Thien, had already been demolished one week earlier, along with the bus station.[58]

Although Kham Thien was apparently the most heavily destroyed residential area, it was not the only one. Telford Taylor, chief prosecutor at the Nuremberg war crimes trials, who saw the ruins of a housing project in the An Duong district, wrote, "Some 30 multiple dwelling units covering several acres had suffered 20 or more hits leaving fresh bomb craters 50 feet in diameter and virtually total destruction of the homes." [59]

The most famous target of Linebacker II, however, was the Bach Mai hospital on the southwest edge of Hanoi. The 900-bed hospital, composed of many buildings spread over five acres, was the country's most complete, modern health facility, with 250 doctors and 800 medical students.[60] According to Telford Taylor the hospital was "completely destroyed." [61] A French doctor who was a visiting instructor in genetics at the hospital had photographs of the damage showing the destruction of many buildings. According to hospital officials, Bach Mai was hit by three bombs on

December 19 and more than 100 bombs at 4:00 A.M., December 22.*

After nine days of heavy bombing, French correspondents reported seeing "craters and uprooted trees" in the main streets of Hanoi, which were delaying the movement of ambulances and rescue teams. More and more of the remaining families were moving into the diplomatic section of the city in the hope that they would be safer from B-52 attacks.[62] The pattern of bombing in and around Hanoi suggested to the North Vietnamese that the purpose was to paralyze the city and isolate it from the rest of the world (Gia Lam, North Vietnam's only international airport, was destroyed by the bombing, but planes continued to take off and land). The bombing appeared to be aimed at leaving Hanoi, in the words of one DRV official, "without any electricity, traffic or relations abroad, and its voice shut—a complete blockade by air. . . ."[63]

If that was the strategy of Linebacker II, it was a failure. Despite the fact that the Radio Hanoi transmitters were struck four times in three days, the station was only off the air for nine minutes before resuming with a standby transmitter. Similarly, although 80 percent of the city's electrical power was wiped out, Hanoi had many small power generators with which it could replace power facilities destroyed by the bombing in order to carry out essential services.[64] DRV authorities claimed that, because of previous evacuation of the city and Hanoi's effective system of air raid shelters, only 2,200 people were killed in the capital—far fewer than the 5,000 to 10,000 deaths estimated by US intelligence.[65]

In fact, the idea of coercing the DRV by destroying or paralyzing its urban centers was illusory. For it failed to take account of either the psychology of the North Vietnamese or their capacity to adapt successfully to an all-out war of destruction.

The North Vietnamese had from the beginning of the war expected that their cities would be destroyed, and had made plans to deal with that contingency. In 1966 Jacques Decornoy told of

---

* Pentagon spokesman Jerry Friedheim, asked about the reports of the destruction of Bach Mai, replied on December 28 that the Department had "no information" that indicated any attack on "any large 1,000 bed civilian hospital." On January 2, he admitted that there had been limited damage to the hospital. Only ten months later, after considerable prodding by the Senate Subcommittee on Refugees, did the Pentagon admit that the hospital was indeed virtually destroyed in the December bombing. (*Boston Globe*, December 28, 1972 and September 2, 1973.)

PLAF soldiers throw down the RVN flag and prepare to hoist the PRG flag over the Administrative Office of Quang Tri after its capture on April 27, 1972.

The Kham Thien neighborhood of Hanoi, a workers' housing area, was destroyed by US B-52s on December 26 and 27, 1972. In the foreground, a single bomb crater.

The Kham Thien neighborhood of Hanoi, a workers' housing area, was destroyed by US B-52s on December 26 and 27, 1972.

Bach Mai Hospital, North Vietnam's largest, was mostly destroyed by more than 100 bombs on the morning of December 22, 1972. The Pentagon at first denied any knowledge that it had been hit, then admitted "limited" damage.

The ARVN 3rd Division abandoned these artillery pieces in its hasty retreat from fire bases guarding the northern defense line along the DMZ as the spring 1972 Communist offensive began.

Le Duc Tho speaking informally with members of the delegation in Paris.

Special Adviser Le Duc Tho at ease in his personal quarters in Paris.

Henry Kissinger and Le Duc Tho after their
last private meeting at Gif-Sur-Yvette, January
13, 1973, before signing the Paris Agreement.

Le Duc Tho and Henry Kissinger exchange pens after initialing the Paris
Agreement on January 25, 1973.

PRG Minister of State Nguyen Van Hieu and the RVN Deputy Premier, Nguyen Luu Vien, chiefs of delegation to the Two-Party political conference at La Celle–St. Cloud, Paris, exchange credentials before the first session on March 19, 1973.

The US delegation to the Four-Party Joint Military Commission, led by General Hugh Woodward (center) at a meeting in February 1973.

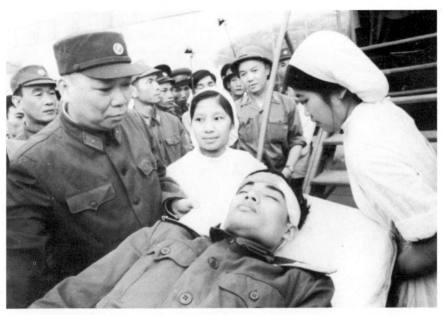

North Vietnamese General Nguyen Don looks at a DRV soldier who was injured in the mob attack on the DRV military delegation in Banmethuot, February 8, 1973.

Lieutenant General Tran Van Tra, Chief of the PRG delegation to the Four-Party Joint Military Commission, visits soldiers with the North Vietnamese delegation at Tan Son Nhut airbase, Saigon. DRV General Le Quang Hoa is at left.

The last American troops board the plane to return to the United States at the Danang airfield under the watchful eye of a North Vietnamese army observer, March 29, 1973.

Residents of Loc Ninh hold posters and banners denouncing US and Saigon violations of the Paris Agreement.

In many areas under PRG control, such as this village in Binh Dinh
province, Saigon's bombing and shelling remained intense after the Paris
Agreement, and bomb shelters were often as big as the house itself. (Photo
by Charles Benoît)

A PRG village chairman in Hoai
Chau village, Binh Dinh province,
shows off his hand-lettered copy of
the Paris Agreement in October
1973. (Photo by Charles Benoît)

People take their homes on their backs as they leave a Saigon government refugee "resettlement site" to return to their old homes in the PRG zone.

being startled to hear the Vietnamese sitting with him in a Hanoi hotel lobby say, "This lobby in which you are now sitting—we already consider it destroyed. We are ready. We are accepting it all beforehand." [66] And in 1972, at the height of the offensive in the South, DRV officials were certain that the United States would still destroy Hanoi and Haiphong in a last spasm of violence before the end of the war. American visitors were reminded that Ho Chi Minh wrote before he died that the two cities would be destroyed just when they were closest to victory.[67] Factories, schools, universities—everything but the skeleton of the urban centers—had already been moved to the countryside. In fact, the government itself had moved its decision-making headquarters out of the city into areas which were safe from American bombs, and high officials traveled back to the city only to receive foreign dignitaries.[68]

More important than the failure of the bombing to disrupt the functioning of government in North Vietnam, however, was the damage which the North Vietnamese were able to inflict on the US air armada, which had only lost one B-52 in the war before Linebacker II. During 1972 the DRV had been secretly making radical improvements in the capability of its radar system for tracking US planes, increasing its coverage from an extremely low percentage of the incoming planes to a very high percentage. North Vietnamese scientists had made the improvements without the help—or the knowledge—of the Soviet Union, according to DRV officials.

Armed with this new capability for foiling the electronic countermeasures used by US bombers to evade the antiaircraft missiles around Hanoi, the North Vietnamese prepared their defense of the capital meticulously. The respite between October 25 and December 18 was used to build up the supply of antiaircraft missiles, and by the time the bombing began the capital was ringed by an estimated 850 SAM missile launchers.[69]

The result of Hanoi's strategic surprise was a toll of B-52s which shocked US strategists. In the twelve days of bombing, the DRV claimed to have brought down thirty-four B-52s.[70] The US claimed only fifteen were lost and that this was less than had been expected.[71] But it was unofficially leaked to the press by Pentagon officials who were obviously unsympathetic to the use of the strategic bomber fleet over Hanoi and Haiphong that this figure did not include planes which had gone down at sea or planes which managed to get back to their bases but were actually put out of action. A high administration source was quoted as saying that the actual number of B-52s damaged seriously was "nearer to what Hanoi says than what we have been saying." [72]

Pentagon officials, who had expected to lose few if any B-52s, conceded privately that they could not accept losses at this rate much longer.[73] Although Admiral Moorer would later call Linebacker II "the greatest devastation of the war" to North Vietnam,[74] it was actually the US Air Force which suffered the most serious loss, since the B-52s were no longer in production and could not be replaced.* Within a few days, the mounting air losses were bringing strong pressure on Nixon from the military to end the bombing soon.[75]

Meanwhile, the bombing brought opposition of unprecedented intensity in countries normally friendly to the United States. Not only the government of Sweden, which had long been openly critical of US policy in Vietnam, but the governments of Denmark, Finland, Belgium, Italy, Canada, Australia, New Zealand, and Japan openly expressed varying degrees of hostility or dismay toward the bombing, and the governments of Britain and West Germany were under strong pressure to express their opposition as well.[76] Even Pope Paul, who had been previously reluctant to criticize the United States in Vietnam, deplored the "sudden resumption of harsh and massive war actions" in Vietnam.[77]

Perhaps even more important, there was evidence that the bombing was threatening Nixon's détente with the Soviet Union and China. Immediately after the battle of Hanoi began, the United States was in contact with both governments, seeking their help in bringing Hanoi back to the negotiating table in a more cooperative mood.[78]

---

* The feelings of shock and bewilderment at the heavy losses which the DRV inflicted on the US strategic bomber fleet were apparent in the statement of Congressman Daniel Flood of the House Defense Appropriations Committee in a hearing with Admiral Moorer just ten days after the bombing was halted: "My, my, my . . . that the . . . Department of Defense, the Pentagon, that they were going to be handcuffed by some little country called North Vietnam and completely knocked off balance, good gravy . . . here this little backward, these gooks . . . are knocking down your B-52s like clay pigeons, with all the sophisticated hardware which was beyond our own ken, being run by 'gooks.' This is some kind of lesson." (*Department of Defense Appropriations*, Hearings before a Subcommittee of the Committee on Appropriations, House of Representatives, 93rd Congress, 1st Session, 1973, p. 30.)

But in contrast to their reactions to the events of April, both the Soviet Union and China now not only strongly reaffirmed their support for the Vietnamese negotiating position but also suggested that they would put opposition to American policy in Vietnam ahead of their desire for improvement in relations with the United States. On December 21, with Truong Chinh in the audience, Brezhnev devoted a substantial portion of a three and a half hour speech to the Vietnam issue, in which he "emphatically stressed" that the future of Soviet-American relations depended on "the question of ending the war in Vietnam." [79] In early January *Pravda* revealed that the Soviets had stepped up deliveries of antiaircraft sales and jet fighter planes to the DRV during the December bombing, thus confirming US intelligence of such an increase in military assistance.[80]

Peking was even more disturbed by the US *volte-face* of October and November. The Chinese made it clear, both in public and in private communications, that they were not interested in any further negotiations with the United States as long as the bombing continued.[81] The state of Sino-American relations was described by one US official in January as "frozen as hard as before the President went to China." [82]

On December 29 the first anti-United States mass rally in more than a year was held in China to condemn the bombing.[83] Hanoi thus achieved a diplomatic united front with its socialist allies at a time when the United States faced the open opposition of many countries that were friendly or militarily allied with it.

The December bombing further seriously eroded the Nixon administration's already shrinking political support at home for continuing the war. There was a wide consensus among political figures, editorialists, and other opinion-makers that the bombing was an outrage. Typical of the reaction was a *Los Angeles Times* editorial which said that "of all the willful uses of arbitrary power, this is one of the most shocking because the means used are so grossly disproportionate to the ends sought." [84]

There were clear signs that Congress did not support the resumption of the bombing north of the 20th parallel and would move quickly to end the war through legislation. Senators' polls by *Congressional Quarterly* on December 21 opposed the renewed bombing by 45 to 19, with 9 expressing no opinion, and favored legislation to end US involvement in the war by a similar 45 to 25 margin.[85] Republican Senators Charles Mathias and Clifford Case issued statements condemning the bombing and warning that they would urge the Senate to end the war through legislation.[86] Chairman of the House Ways and Means Committee Wilbur Mills predicted that in 1973 Congress would approve legislation forcing the United States to withdraw its forces from Indochina.[87]

Nixon thus found himself under pressure not only from foreign allies and adversaries, but from Congress and even his own military leaders, to end the bombing and go back to negotiations once more. He had insisted when the bombing began that it would go on "until a settlement is arrived at", apparently assuming that the North Vietnamese could be forced to negotiate while their capital was being bombed.[88] But after five days of bombing he altered that position to insist on some indication from Hanoi that it would negotiate "in a spirit of good will and in a constructive attitude." [89] This was a formula which would permit Nixon to end the bombing at any time without loss of face, should he decide that it was necessary.

On December 30, after domestic and foreign pressures had continued to build for several more days, Nixon gave in. The White House press spokesman avoided any mention of the bombing when he said on December 30: "The President has asked me to announce this morning that negotiations between presidential adviser Dr. Kissinger and special adviser Le Duc Tho and Minister Xuan Thuy will be resumed in Paris on January 8. Technical talks will be resumed on January 2. That is the extent of the announcement." [90]

It was only under questioning that the spokesman said, "The President has ordered that all bombing will be discontinued above the 20th parallel as long as serious negotiations are under way." Despite the implied threat of a renewal of bombing if the North Vietnamese did not agree to the US demands, it would have been difficult for Nixon to repeat the December bombing.

The White House was silent on the reason for the reversal of Nixon's earlier threat to continue the bombing "until a settlement is arrived at." But the White House plan for forcing the acceptance of its demands for a revised agreement had clearly been foiled by the unexpected military reverses over Hanoi and the surprisingly strong political reaction at home and abroad. According to Lao Dong

Party Central Committee spokesman Hoang Tung, the crucial factor in defeating Nixon's effort to rewrite the agreement was the strategic surprise which Hanoi's antiaircraft units had in store for the US bomber fleet. "If we had not been able to bring down the B-52's," he said, "the situation might have been different. Their side would have made other steps forward to impose their conditions." [91]

As Kissinger and Le Duc Tho prepared to return to the negotiating table in Paris, Nixon's bargaining hand had been greatly weakened. His last major bargaining chip had been used to no avail, and now his administration was under even more intense pressure than before to reach agreement without much delay. Far more than in the October or November-December rounds, the DRV was in a position to reject American demands.

Later the administration would do its best to persuade the US public that the bombing had made the North Vietnamese more cooperative at the peace table.* A Gallup poll taken some weeks later showed that 57 percent of those polled believed that the Christmas bombing had contributed to the peace settlement.[92] In an ironic way, it was true: by its political and military failure, the bombing of Hanoi and Haiphong made the Paris Agreement possible. For it forced Nixon and Kissinger to accept the very terms which they had rejected in October, November, and December. While the threat of massive bombing had seemed to give Nixon leverage over the North Vietnamese, the battle of Hanoi showed how that apparent strength could be transformed into diplomatic weakness.

4. The Last Round in Paris

The mood of the DRV delegation as it returned to Paris on January 7 was grave—a mood reflecting not only the death and

---

* In an interview with CBS News, Kissinger was asked whether he wasn't leaving the public with the "assumption . . . that without that kind of heavy bombing the North Vietnamese would not have become serious—your term—and that therefore one could conclude that it was the bombing that brought the North Vietnamese into a serious frame of mind?" Kissinger replied carefully that the bombing "came at the end of a long process in which they too had suffered a great deal." He added that, on the eve of his own trip to Hanoi, it would "not serve any useful purpose for me . . . to speculate about what caused them to make this decision." (Transcript of "A Conversation with Henry Kissinger," CBS News Special Report, February 1, 1973, p. 7.)

devastation caused by the bombing of Hanoi and Haiphong, but its determination to hold fast to the principles of the October draft. Le Duc Tho, usually jovial in public, was grim-faced as he read his statement at Le Bourget airport. "The decisive moment has come," he said. "What matters now is either to resolve the Vietnamese problem and sign the treaty that was agreed upon or else continue the war. The American administration must make a definite choice; the responsibility rests entirely with it." Denouncing the bombings of December, Tho said they had "achieved no result" but had only "deepened [the Vietnamese people's] hatred and tightened the bonds of its unity." [93]

This statement set the tone for the new round of talks which began on January 8. In contrast to their behavior at previous sessions, the North Vietnamese did not greet Kissinger and the American delegation when they arrived at the villa in suburban Paris. And Tho repeated his condemnation of the bombing, according to the North Vietnamese account, "in a harsh and bitter tone unprecedented in the more than five years of negotiations." The American delegates even had to ask Tho not to speak so loudly, fearing the newsmen outside the villa would hear him.[94]

When the discussion of the remaining issues began, Tho made it clear that his government was not prepared to capitulate on any of them. On the nature of the Demilitarized Zone and the demarcation line, the character and role of the National Council, and the mention of the PRG, the DRV delegation reaffirmed its previous positions. The Americans would have to accept their position, or try to find alternatives to the previous US position which would be acceptable to the DRV. Fortunately, Kissinger appears to have been given enough negotiating flexibility to reach agreement despite North Vietnamese refusal to yield on these issues.

On the issue of the modalities of civilian movement between the two zones, which touched not only the nature of the demarcation line but also the question of sovereignty within South Vietnam, the United States had demanded that stringent control be exercised over nonmilitary movements across the border. The DRV denounced the proposal as a scheme to divide the country in spite of the US agreement to the principle that the line was only temporary and military in character.

Finally, the United States agreed to a formula which would call on "North and South Vietnam" to negotiate the modalities of civilian movement across the "Provisional Military Demarcation Line." Since the parties to these negotiations were not specified, the language left the PRG and DRV free to negotiate the matter of civilian movement. Indeed, since the PRG controlled the area adjoining the line, it implicitly authorized such negotiations. As an American official later admitted, it was the only way to get around DRV refusal to accept specific limitations on freedom of movement.

The issue of the National Council of Reconciliation and Concord was still unresolved in several respects. The United States and Thieu still hoped to deprive it of stature and practical effectiveness. They wished to soften the Vietnamese term for its function of "promoting" implementation of the agreement, to eliminate the establishment of councils at lower levels, to drop the word "National" from its title, and to eliminate, in effect, the "third segment." In the end the United States gave up four of its five demands. It agreed to the original *don doc,* with its connotation of compulsion regarding the South Vietnamese parties; it agreed to restoration of the word "National" in the National Council; it agreed to the original provision for consultations on the establishment of councils of reconciliation at lower levels. And the United States dropped its demand for specifying that the "third segment" would be named by the two sides rather than by consultation as the DRV wished. US officials say that the American delegation agreed to drop the demand while putting on record their "understanding" of the third segment as being nominated by the two sides. The DRV, they say, tacitly accepted this US interpretation as part of the agreement to drop the US demand. But the DRV nevertheless argued after the agreement that the third segment had to be chosen on the basis of consultations with those supporting neither party.

The one point on which the DRV did yield was the elimination of the term "administrative structure" in describing the National Council. Nevertheless, the functions of the Council remained unchanged, and the phrase was so ambiguous that many observers assumed that its elimination represented a compromise between the US demand for a Vietnamese term meaning "administrative structure" and the DRV demand for a term meaning "governmental structure."

The third remaining issue in the text of the agreement was the refusal of the US demand that all mention of the PRG be eliminated from the preamble or the text. This demand was rejected by the North Vietnamese as an obvious attempt to "negate" recognition of the PRG as a coequal party, which was inherent in the October draft. The DRV offered a compromise under which the GVN could sign a document which did not specifically mention the PRG except in the signature page, but the United States would have to explicitly recognize the PRG by signing a document referring to it in the preamble. The United States resisted this solution, arguing that multilateral treaties didn't usually name the parties in the preamble. "We had hoped we wouldn't have to end up with a complicated signing ceremony," recalls one official. "We felt it was an issue which we would leave to the GVN, so we put pressure the other way—on the North Vietnamese."

For the DRV, it was necessary to force the United States to accept the explicit mention of the PRG in order to reinforce the principle that the United States was recognizing two administrations as well as two armies and areas of control in South Vietnam. The United States ultimately conceded the point, and the result was that the signing ceremony embraced two documents, one signed by the United States and the DRV "with the concurrence" of the RVN and PRG respectively, the other signed by all four parties. The former specifically mentioned the PRG in its preamble; the latter did not.

After the US demands were dropped, the DRV quickly put aside the single major new demand which it had on the table at the outset of the January talks: to change the period for the release of political prisoners from ninety days to sixty days, thus implicitly linking it with the release of American POWs. Since the DRV had been willing to sign the October draft without revision, it had always been clear that this demand was merely a device to emphasize to the United States the seriousness of demanding major revisions in a draft which had already been agreed to.

On January 13 the main text of the agreement was agreed to by both sides, and Kissinger flew back to Washington to brief Nixon. The negotiators then turned their attention to the protocols, which had been discussed at only one session before the January round began. Here the major sticking points were the US proposal for a major peace-keeping force with freedom of movement rather than a relatively small corps of monitors which would act only with the concurrence of both sides in the South; the US insistence on the designation of points of entry for war material in advance of the cease-fire; and the delineation of zones on the basis of military forces alone rather than administrative control. And again, the last few days of negotiation saw the United States giving up most of its demands.

On the designation of ports of entry, the United States gave up its demand that it be done in the agreement, in advance of a cease-fire. Instead it accepted the DRV proposal that the two South Vietnamese parties would "agree on these points of entry within fifteen days after the entry into force of the cease-fire." Each party was permitted a maximum of six points of entry. The PLAF was thus left free to attempt to capture ports just before the cease-fire, without giving Saigon advance notice of its objectives.

The American proposal to insert in the cease-fire protocol a provision that the Two-Party Joint Military Commission should base its determination of the areas of control on a complete census of military forces on each side also ran into determined opposition from the DRV delegation. They saw the proposal as yet another attempt to deny the reality of "two administrations" in the South, as well as to give Saigon complete information on the size and location of its military forces, which could then be used to plan both air and ground attacks on the PRG zone. The United States finally dropped the demand and accepted the original language of the October agreement that the Two-Party Joint Military Commission "shall determine the areas controlled by each party. . . ." The DRV agreed, however, to add to this the phrase "and the modalities of stationing," which implied that the location of military forces would be subject to negotiation.

The protocol on the ICCS, on which Kissinger had put so much emphasis in his press conference, also failed to meet US expectations. Although the size of the International Commission, at 1,160, was actually greater than the United States had expected to get, the figure was part of a compromise under which the DRV agreed to a higher figure for ICCS personnel in return for a greater number of Two-Party Joint Military Commision personnel (825 for each party) than the United States and Saigon desired. More important, however, was the fact that the protocol provided for only five inspection teams on the borders of Laos and Cambodia and only a single reinforced team below the DMZ. "The distribution of border posts was not all we had hoped for," an American official admitted later. In effect, the United States had won no more than a token international supervision of the lines of communication between North and South Vietnam, and not the effective deterrent to military movements which it had sought.

Nor did the final protocol go as far as the United States had wanted in the freedom of movement which it granted to ICCS personnel. It gave the commission "such movement for observation as is reasonably required for the proper exercise of its functions as stipulated in the Agreement," which implied that movements of ICCS personnel had to be limited to agreed investigations. Moreover, the anti-Communist members of the Commission would not be able to carry out their own investigations. Article 18(f) provided that the ICCS "shall operate in accordance with the principle of consultations and unanimity," which meant that no investigations could be undertaken to which all members did not agree.

The DRV also won the other major demands which it had made in its own draft protocols: for more detailed articles on the formation and operation of the Two-Party Joint Military Commission, on withdrawal of US troops and dismantling of US military bases, and for clarification of US intentions regarding civilian personnel working for the Saigon military forces. The United States refused to have separate protocols on these issues, but did agree to include more details on both subjects in the Protocol on the cease-fire and Joint Military Commissions.

The DRV delegation, fearing that the United States and the Saigon government would try to prevent the Two-Party Joint Military Commission from becoming operational, demanded that the protocols include a provision that, pending agreement between the South Vietnamese parties on the formation and operation of the Two-Party JMC, the delegations of the two South Vietnamese parties serving with the Four-Party JMC at all levels "shall continue temporarily to work together as a provisional two-party joint military commission and to assume the tasks of the Two-Party Joint Military Commission at all levels" until that agreement was reached. In January the United States accepted this as part of Article 12 of the cease-fire protocol.

The protocol also called for a very significant PRG presence in the RVN zone, which the United States had sought to avoid. The United States had proposed, at Saigon's insistence, that the JMC be represented only at each of the four regional military headquarters, and not at all below that level. The DRV had demanded, however, that the JMC have seven regional headquarters and local teams in all forty-one provinces. In the compromise on the size of the ICCS, the United States agreed to seven regional JMC locations and twenty-six subregional locations—a considerable political victory for the PRG.[95]

Another protocol proposed by the DRV was aimed at making more specific the obligation of the United States and other foreign states in Article 6 to dismantle all military bases within sixty days of the agreement. The DRV insisted that the protocol include a provision which would force the United States to withdraw all its war material, except for "communications, transport, and other non-combat material," which would be transferred to the Four-Party JMC or the ICCS, and to "dismantle and remove from South Vietnam or destroy all military bases," including the weapons, mines, and other military equipment on them, "for the purpose of making them unusable for military purposes." The United States intended to evade the terms of Articles 5 and 6 by interpreting "of the United States" in a legalistic way, so as to permit the United States to transfer title to the bases and equipment to the Saigon government *before* the agreement was signed. But, as the State Department's own briefing paper on the legal interpretation of the agreement later admitted, "We did not explain to the DRV negotiators our interpretation of the phrase 'of the United States.' "[96] The DRV, which had no reason to believe that the United States was not still in control of its bases in South Vietnam, viewed its language as foreclosing any effort to avoid the dismantlement of bases and withdrawal of war material. And the United States kept its own intentions secret because it feared the DRV would press for stronger language if it clarified its interpretation.

The DRV continued to insist that the United States pledge itself to remove all civilians performing military roles on behalf of

Saigon, in addition to military personnel, as part of the protocol on the cease-fire. The United States wished to avoid any commitment on such civilians, since they were regarded as necessary to keep the Saigon air force and logistics complex operating after the cease-fire. In the end, the United States gave an assurance to the DRV that it would withdraw within twelve months after the agreement all civilian personnel "working in the armed forces of the Republic of Viet-Nam," and that it would remove the majority of them within ten months.[97] This assurance was not written into the agreement, but was made explicitly and on the record.

By January 20 the last substantive matters were resolved, and the two sides adjourned to study the language of both English and Vietnamese texts before the final session to reconcile the two texts. William Sullivan left for a vacation in the Swiss Alps. But fifteen minutes after his arrival there, Sullivan received a phone call from Washington. It was Kissinger, who told him that Thieu was not happy with Article 6 of the protocol on the cease-fire. This article had limited civilian police and civilian security personnel of the parties to the use of pistols, except in "unusual circumstances," when they were permitted to carry "other small individual arms." Thieu was demanding that his Police Field Forces, which were armed like military combat units, be allowed to have heavier weapons. Sullivan was ordered to return immediately to Paris to get the article changed.

That evening, after Sullivan's return, the DRV delegation received a phone call from the US delegation, asking that Article 6 be revised to permit the police to carry M-16s. On January 21, the two sides met all day on the question, and the DRV refused to change the existing language. On January 22, the day the two sides were reconciling the English and Vietnamese texts, the United States stated unilaterally that the Police Field Forces would be considered as "paramilitary" forces rather than "civilian police," and would therefore be exempt from the language of Article 6.

The suspicion and tension which had marked the negotiations from the beginning were present even in the last hours before the initialing ceremony on January 23. The two sides had divided up the work of typing up copies of the final text, the DRV delegation taking responsibility for the Vietnamese text and the United States for the English text. Then the two sides convened for a twelve-hour session to check the two texts against each other. The Vietnamese experts discovered thirty typing errors in the English text, which were innocent enough, but they were incensed to find that the US delegation had not numbered the signature pages. They immediately suspected that the United States planned to declare later on that the agreement was void, since the signatures were not part of the agreement, and demanded that the page numbers be typed in.[98] This suspicion was symptomatic of the total distrust with which the DRV delegation viewed Nixon and Kissinger. The American delegation quickly typed the page numbers in.

Before the initialing ceremony, however, Kissinger added one more statement of intentions to the record. He read a statement that until the Cambodian insurgents agreed to at least a de facto cease-fire the United States would continue its bombing in Cambodia. Then Kissinger, seated in front of an enormous mirror, with Le Duc Tho across from him, initialed the agreement. America's longest war was about to come to an end.

6: Implementing the Paris Agreement: I

In 1954 the DRV had reached a peace agreement with France which the Vietnamese hoped would permit them to resolve the conflict and reunify the country peacefully. But they had found once again, as in 1946, that words on paper did not bring peace when the interests of a great power were contrary to the letter and spirit of the peace agreement. In January 1973 the actual interests of the governments which signed the agreement would once more be the key factor in determining whether or not the agreement would lead to peace.

The situation was in some ways directly parallel to that which prevailed at the time of the Geneva Agreement of 1954: a great power had been forced to sign an agreement in order to end an unpopular war—an agreement which both sides regarded as insuring that the client Vietnamese government would be defeated in a political contest if its terms were carried out. And in order to avoid precisely such a political defeat, the United States and its clients pursued policies aimed at nullifying the central provisions of the agreement.

Like France in 1954, the United States signed the agreement in order to regain its domestic tranquillity but was unwilling to support its full implementation. Believing that the Saigon regime was still too weak to enter into peaceful political competition, the Nixon administration supported Saigon's open defiance or evasion of the political provisions. And as in the 1954–59 period, Chinese and Soviet restraints and the DRV's own need to avoid renewed war were counted on to permit Saigon to take the offensive against the revolutionaries in the South. Finally, the United States was prepared to back up this policy of force with the threat of its own reintervention, again repeating its policy after Geneva.

Thus the pattern of interests and policy followed that of the post-Geneva period. But in 1973, the position of the revolutionary movement in South Vietnam was incomparably stronger than it had been in 1954. The Communists now had a powerful army in the South instead of a defenseless political organization, and they could push back when conditions were ripe for such a push. Moreover, the tide of popular and Congressional opposition to US military involvement did not recede after the signing of the Paris Agreement, and it threatened to tip the balance against Nixon's policy of protecting the interests of his Vietnamese clients by military threat. For these reasons the results of US policy after the Paris Agreement would be quite different from that which followed the earlier Vietnam peace agreement.

1.   The DRV and PRG: The "New Phase" of the Struggle

After more than a dozen years of armed struggle, the DRV signed an agreement which accepted for the time being the existence of the Saigon government. The Vietnamese leaders as pragmatic revolutionaries had accepted the fact that the balance of forces within Vietnam and in the world outside, which had always been their guide to the timing of both offensive action and compromise, did not yet allow the replacement of the Thieu government by a coalition including representatives of the PRG. "We cannot exterminate imperialism at one time and in a single battle," said *Hoc Tap*. "We drive it back step by step and destroy it part by part." [1]

Having accepted "two administrations" as the basis for the settlement, there were powerful reasons for the Party leadership to abandon the military offensive and rely on political struggle to achieve its goal of replacing Thieu with a broad coalition government. In the first place, the DRV had already decided that when a settlement was reached, it would begin once again the rebuilding of its war-torn economy. Immediately after the agreement, the DRV reorganized its economy along peacetime lines and reoriented its cadre structure around economic reconstruction, which it called the "central task" of the North in the "new phase" of the revolution.[2] So the Party did not wish to provoke the return of American bombers by being drawn into a renewal of main force warfare in the South. In spite of broad opposition to Nixon's bombing in December, Hanoi had reason to fear that he would again defy Congress and the public to reintervene in the conflict.

Under these circumstances, the Party's primary concern was to achieve a stable peace and consolidate the gains of the more than twelve years of armed struggle. So it was in the interest of the Party to dampen the level of military conflict as much as possible and base its strategy in the South on the demand for strict implementation of the Paris Agreement, which not only gave legitimacy to the PRG but also required Thieu to give up his control over the political process as well as over civilian detainees and refugees from PRG and contested areas. A directive issued at the time of the agreement summed up the revolutionary task in the South in the "new phase" as one of mobilizing a "political movement of the masses" in order to "create basic conditions to guarantee the implementation of the agreements, maintain peace and enable the revolution to continue its march forward." [3]

Party leaders had no illusions that the United States would throw its weight behind the implementation of the accords. A COSVN directive predicted that the Americans would not only "maintain by all means and under new forms their military involvement in the South" but would "use their lackeys . . . to sabotage the implementation of the Agreement [and to] unceasingly instigate limited conflicts which include the possibility of a resumption of war. . . ." [4]

DRV leaders used the terms "protracted," "difficult," and "complex" in describing the struggle for the implementation of the Paris Agreement, thus recalling the language used by the Party in discussing the political struggle in the South after Geneva, when defenseless cadres were ordered to avoid the use of armed force altogether.[5] Indeed, for many Party cadres and soldiers, this was all too reminiscent of the line from 1954–59 and the unhappy consequences which it had brought. A provincial cadre in North Vietnam, in an emotional conversation with a visiting group of Americans in January 1975, recalled that at the time the Agreement was being negotiated, "There were people who said, 'We would rather sacrifice a little more and not let things happen again as they did after the Geneva Agreement.' "

To reassure its cadres that the Paris Agreement would not result in a similar disaster, Party leaders emphasized that the situation in the South in 1973 was completely different from the situation in 1954, when South Vietnam "did not have two governments, two armies, two different zones, or fully equipped revolutionary armed forces occupying strategic areas." They also pointed out that the United States had been forced to "recognize" the "reality" of "two governments, two armies and three political forces. . . ." [6]

The Party's strategy of demanding full implementation of the agreement rested not on the assumption that the Saigon regime would willingly carry out the provisions which Thieu did not find in his interest, but on the assumption that his obdurate attitude toward the agreement and his bellicosity in refusing to end the military conflict would further narrow his base of support and strengthen the political movement against him. In a directive issued two months after the agreement was signed, COSVN portrayed the agreement as the main factor defining the political struggle against Saigon:

> The form of the struggle between us and the enemy is: the enemy distorts the Ceasefire Agreement, impedes the implementation of the Agreement, creates suspicion and divisions and hatred among the people, and maintains the tense situation. We disseminate the Agreement broadly, bring out the significance of the Agreement as a great victory, open up the movement of struggle to demand that the enemy implement the Agreement, and follow the trend in demanding peace and national concord among all classes of people—even within the puppet army and puppet government—and this forms our new struggle position in the new situation. [7]

The main thrust of the political struggle was to be concentrated on specific demands, such as freedom of movement and other democratic liberties, or an end to the drafting of young men and the upgrading of local militiamen to the status of regular ARVN troops. [8] The ultimate objective of the political struggle was not simply to raise people's consciousness but to get them to act in defiance of the Saigon government's orders. These actions, which

Saigon considered "illegal," were the higher level of the political struggle, which the Party called the "political violence of the masses." [9]

In contested areas or areas controlled by Saigon people would be urged to "apply by themselves the rights to freedom, democracy, freedom of movement, freedom to earn a living, and disregard the enemy's reactionary policies and regulations." [10] One of the most important tasks was to organize people to return to their former rice fields and orchards despite Saigon government orders to stay away. "Where the enemy tries to stop them," one document says, "they must break out in violent struggles to return to their land." [11] This "political violence" was primarily the work of unarmed civilians, but PLAF guerrillas could be called upon under the new strategy to support a political struggle movement by killing individual "cruel tyrants" or by destroying "enemy units playing the key role in oppressing the people." [12]

The Party also viewed the agreement as providing more favorable conditions in which to carry out its policy of "national reconciliation and concord." In a document written shortly before the Paris Agreement and used by the Party for educating various echelons of Party leadership and members, it was emphasized that "national concord is not just a tactic in order to divide the ranks of the lackeys of the U.S. in the South, but remains our basic policy toward the masses of people living in temporarily occupied areas." [13]

Despite more than a decade of war, destruction, and violent struggle, the Lao Dong Party still regarded those in the Saigon army and government as sharing its aspirations for national unity and independence from foreign influence. In a ten-point declaration on January 25, 1972, the PRG had said that families whose members had been "forcibly enlisted" in ARVN were considered as "unfortunate victims of the American policy of aggression" and pledged that there would be "no discrimination whatever toward them. . . ." Saigon soldiers were permitted to visit families in their native villages in the PRG zone and leave again if they wished, while the families were eligible to receive land under PRG land programs.[14]

The Party's study document on its "national concord policy" at the time of the agreement promised amnesty to all those who had worked for the Saigon government's political and armed organs and were prepared to renounce their past. It said that such persons "must have a place in the people's hearts," and that the revolutionaries would "use the just cause to persuade them, charity and justice to convert them. . . ." [15]

Since Hanoi was restrained from using all the military power at its disposal, it had a particular interest in a stand-still cease-fire. Despite their expectation that Saigon would violate the cease-fire broadly, Party leaders hoped that Saigon's offensive operations could be contained and that the zones of control could be stabilized. Documents captured or reconstructed by US intelligence indicated that PLAF units were ordered in January to fight only in defense of the PRG zone and not to launch attacks on the RVN zone.[16]

PLAF military policy was to be reassessed by Party leaders after the first few weeks of the cease-fire. The orders to military units were apparently valid for the first sixty days, and there was no major public pronouncement by the Party on long-term political and military strategy toward the agreement until the April issue of *Hoc Tap*. Whether the PLAF could hold to its completely defensive posture or retaliate by striking at ARVN units in their rear bases, and whether main force units should be committed to battle, would depend on how serious the threat from Saigon would be and how well the PLAF could cope with it under the existing policy.

From the viewpoint of the Party leadership, therefore, the Paris Agreement represented a long-term political solution which they knew would not be achieved until the overall balance of forces shifted toward the revolution. In the meantime, the Party was content to rely on political struggle to weaken the Thieu regime and to try to stabilize the cease-fire as the basis for the implementation of the whole agreement.

2.   *The RVN: Thieu vs. the Paris Agreement*

For President Nguyen Van Thieu and the government of the Republic of Vietnam, the signing of the Paris Agreement was a bitter pill, which was swallowed only under duress. Thieu had been convinced, when the negotiators were reaching agreement on the October draft, that he could maintain the military initiative with continued air support from the United States.[17] And he had viewed the October draft as a grave blow to his chances for survival. Reassured by Nixon that the United States would back his demands at the negotiating table, Thieu did not use the months of November and December to prepare the population under his control for the impact of the October terms. Instead, he threw his propaganda apparatus into a massive effort to indoctrinate the population on the evils of the draft agreement.

Some 5,200 military officers and cadres from the Thu Duc military school were sent into the countryside to preside over village meetings, at which Saigon's opposition to the draft accord was explained in exhaustive detail.[18] Thieu had been so sure that Nixon would not force him to sign the October draft that he had toyed with the idea of promising to respect a cease-fire but refusing to accept the political settlement prescribed by the October draft, as Ngo Dinh Diem did in 1954.[19] In early December *Tin Song*, known to reflect the views of the presidential palace, published a story that "observers" did not believe the United States would sign an overall settlement with the DRV without the "consent" of the Saigon government because, without it, "such a cease-fire could not be respected." [20] At the same time, Saigon government sources began to circulate the idea that the RVN might give its consent to, but not sign, an agreement between the United States and North Vietnam, recognizing the cease-fire but not the political provisions of such an agreement.[21]

When the January round of negotiations obtained only one of the many revisions which Thieu had demanded in October and November, Thieu had to be threatened with a cutoff of US aid and a separate peace between the United States and the DRV to get him to sign. On January 17, Nixon wrote in a private letter to Thieu, "Your rejection of the agreement would now irretrievably destroy our ability to assist you. Congress and public opinion would force my hand." [22] Three days later, Nixon sent him an ultimatum. The United States would sign the agreement with or without him. "I must know now whether you are prepared to join us on this course," wrote Nixon, "and I must have your answer by 1200 Washington time January 21, 1973." [23]

Thieu then agreed to sign the pact and at once made an about-face in his public position toward the agreement, seeking to present it to his public not as a "surrender" but as a "glorious victory" for his government.[24] In order to make this argument, Thieu had to ignore the actual terms of the agreement and misrepresent the provisions related to the issue of his own sovereignty and the unity of Vietnam. In his January 24 speech Thieu declared, "I tell you that I believe this is solely a ceasefire agreement, no more no less," [25] implying either that there were no political provisions or that they were not binding on him. He went on to argue that the Communists had been forced to "recognize that North and South Vietnam are two countries, two separate countries among the four in Indochina," and that "in South Vietnam there is one legal government." [26] The agreement had, of course, explicitly contradicted his first claim and had both South Vietnamese parties, in effect, as "legal governments."

Thieu's interest in misrepresenting the central provisions of the agreement made the problem of distribution of the text a touchy one in the Saigon zone. The text was published in Saigon newspapers and was available to the public at the government press office, but no effort was made by the Saigon government to familiarize the public with its specific terms, in marked contrast to the DRV, which broadcast the text repeatedly over Hanoi radio at dictation speed.[27] Instead, the RVN circulated to middle- and lower-ranking officials its own bizarre interpretation of the agreement. The Army's psychological warfare branch issued a "summary" of the agreement—but not the full text—to officers who were sent into the villages to be in charge of information activities. "When people ask us about the peace agreement," one of them told a reporter, "we tell them that this is nothing more than a cease-fire in place, and the people are supposed to stay in place." [28] Thus the cease-fire provisions were turned into a denial of the freedom of movement guaranteed in Article 11.

Thieu's aversion to any arrangements which would shift the conflict to a political plane reflected his fear that the Communists could defeat him by political methods. Like most other military officers and high government officials of his generation who fought or worked as civil servants for the French until 1954 and then experienced another long period of humiliating dependence on the Americans, Thieu had little confidence in the political strength of his regime and a distinct awe of the Communist political organization.

As chief of state, he had given an interview with an American reporter in 1967 in which he expressed alarm at the possibility that the NLF could gain power simply by returning to their villages as citizens, and then forming a non-Communist political party. "They can call it the Flower party, Royalist party, Salem or Winston party," he said. "Then they can win through elections, first the hamlet, then the National Assembly, the senate, the government." He conceded that South Vietnamese were tired of war and found "negotiations to end the war" an appealing election slogan.[29]

Over the years, Thieu and his colleagues were haunted by the feeling that they controlled the population physically but did not have their loyalty. An ARVN corps commander admitted in a briefing in January 1970 that the RVN controlled 93 percent of the population, but said that this did not mean they controlled the "spirit of the population." [30] Or as one Army officer put it shortly after the October agreement was disclosed, "The problem is that on our side, we're not confident that we can face the Communists in a political, social and economic struggle. We are not sure that the masses of people are with us." [31]

With the loyalties of the vast majority of South Vietnamese still so uncertain, Thieu feared that his regime was highly vulnerable to "subversion"—a term which appeared constantly in Thieu's speeches in 1972 and 1973. In an address to graduates of the National Defense College in August 1972, Thieu warned that, even if the Communists lost the war militarily, they would still be able to "wage subversive campaigns in our ranks" [32] because of "loopholes" in the laws concerning the press, elections, and political parties. Thieu, who viewed the Communists as "very dangerous bacteria within our body," clearly believed that allowing his enemies to enter the political process would "infect" the body politic and threaten to overwhelm its defenses.[33]

The consequence of this political insecurity was that, while the Nixon administration was putting forward peace proposals which envisioned free elections in which the NLF and later the PRG could participate, Thieu was progressively tightening his grip over the population as well as over the political process at every level, while committing himself even more strongly to the exclusion of the left from South Vietnamese politics. During the 1972 Communist offensive, Thieu declared martial law, and then in September 1972 he decreed the end of elections at the hamlet level, after it was discovered that many of the elected village and hamlet chiefs had been cooperating secretly with the NLF.[34] He explained in a speech in August that "if we allow the Communists to operate openly in South Vietnam, we will lose the country." [35] And just as the Paris negotiations came close to final agreement, Thieu was declaring, "We have to kill the Communists to the last man before we have peace." [36]

At the time the agreement was signed, a new tone of hysteria was evident in Thieu's statements and actions, reflecting his heightened fears of Communist-inspired disorder and subversion. "If Communists come into your village," he said on January 24, "you should immediately shoot them in the head." [37] And those who "suddenly begin talking in a Communist tone," he said, "should be killed immediately." [38]

At the same time, Thieu issued new orders to his police and military forces: shoot to kill those who "urge the people to demonstrate, and those who cause disorders or incite other persons to follow communism"; shoot anyone who deserts or incites others to desert; arrest and detain neutralists and people who "incite the people to create disorder and confusion, or to leave those areas controlled by the government in order to go into Communist-controlled zones or vice versa." [39]

Thieu's intention to ignore the political obligations of the agreement were thus well known in advance. What was not generally understood abroad, however, was Thieu's intention to ignore the in-place cease-fire provisions. It was assumed by most foreign observers that the cease-fire was in Saigon's interests, since it would freeze the lines of control in a way which was still favorable to Saigon, in spite of the gains of the 1972 offensive.

But Thieu and his advisers viewed the situation differently. In the first place, they feared that, in a situation where the Communists were concentrating on the "subversion" of his regime, any relaxation of anti-Communist discipline on the part of his troops, police, and other officials would inevitably lead to accommodations between them and the enemy. This in turn could lead to the alienation of ARVN troops and other personnel from his regime and to mass desertion or defection to the other side.[40] And without the shooting war which justified military control of the society from top to bottom as well as restrictions on democratic freedoms, the demands for the restoration of normal political life and civilian government could become irresistible.

Secondly, a standstill cease-fire which would explicitly recognize two zones of control would support the PRG's claim of "two administrations" in South Vietnam. The Saigon government had to be able to argue that the PRG controlled "neither territory nor population, except for its zones of station of troops," and that meant avoiding the recognition of a PRG zone of control by continuing to occupy as much territory as possible.

Finally, Thieu's political survival depended on the vagaries of American policy, and as the United States withdrew its last remaining troops and ended its military operations in Vietnam, Thieu knew that there would be a collective sigh of relief in the United States. If the United States disengaged from the Vietnam conflict not only militarily but also emotionally and politically, he might no longer be able to count on the intervention of US air power when he needed it. Thieu had a fundamental interest, therefore, in preventing this American disengagement by keeping the level of fighting high and, if possible, even provoking the Communists into making a military move which he could use to justify calling on the return of US air power.

Both the close relationship between a cease-fire and the political dynamics of South Vietnamese society and its potential effect on American policy had thus convinced Thieu that a cease-fire would simply play into the hands of the Communists. In November, French correspondent François Debré reported, "The Presidency's closest advisers do not hide . . . their determination to wait for the propitious moment (the moment when the great powers will have averted their eyes) to violate an accord imposed by 'foreign' pressure." [41]

At the moment of the cease-fire, Thieu had thus concluded that a standstill cease-fire was not in his interest, and no government will implement an agreement which it regards as inimical to its interests—unless it fears sanctions which would be brought to bear against it if it violated the accord. In this case, it was the Nixon administration that would determine whether or not Thieu could violate the agreement openly. And Thieu had reason to believe that Nixon would back him in such a policy.

3.   *The United States: Protecting the Client*

After seven years of war against Vietnamese in both North and South Vietnam, the United States had finally agreed to a fundamental compromise with the DRV which at least gave the Thieu regime a chance to survive a postwar political test. In return the United States had pledged that it would withdraw from Vietnam not only militarily but politically as well, and not "impose any political tendency or personality on the South Vietnamese people" (Article 9[c]).

Having arrived at this compromise, the United States could have bowed out of the effort to maintain an anti-Communist regime in Saigon with relative ease. Merely by complying with the spirit and letter of the agreement it had signed, the Nixon administration could have helped to foster a political settlement and save hundreds of thousands of Vietnamese from death or maiming in a prolonged war; it could have transformed the American role from one of destroying and dividing a society to one of healing not only the physical wounds of war but its social and political wounds as well. Such a course would have implied a momentous shift in policy: the replacement of the patron-client ties with the Saigon government by an explicit even-handedness in regard to the contesting parties in the South.

This shift of role from patronage of Saigon to detached guardian of peace was, in fact, the only course that would have permitted the Paris Agreement to restore peace to Vietnam. For as long as the United States remained the sponsor of the Saigon regime, Thieu and his colleagues would ignore the terms of the agreement, knowing that the United States would protect them from the consequences by providing the hardware, technical personnel, and financial aid required to keep the war machine in operation, covering Saigon's violations before the American public, and intervening with air power to blunt any military response by the other side. Only if Saigon were to become merely a dependent rather than a client would Saigon be constrained to comply with the agreement.

But for Nixon, who refused for nearly four years to agree to any settlement which would have permitted the PRG to have an equal chance to determine the terms of an election, an even-handed policy toward the Vietnamese parties to the agreement was out of the question. By the manner in which he had concluded the Paris Agreement—refusing to sign the draft negotiated by his own representative, supporting Thieu's objections, then bombing North Vietnam's only remaining urban centers with B-52s—Nixon had shown his unwillingness to make peace with his Vietnamese adversaries or give up his patron-client relationship with Thieu.

In his radio and television address on January 23, 1973 Nixon indicated clearly that the agreement would bring no change in the US relationship with the Saigon government. He announced that the United States would "continue to recognize the government of the Republic of Viet-Nam as the sole legitimate government of South Viet-Nam." [42] Since the United States had agreed to leave the political future up to negotiations between two parties with an equal claim under the agreement to "sovereignty" within their own areas of control, this declaration already violated the spirit of the agreement. Moreover, it could be read by both South Vietnamese parties as supporting Saigon's position that it still had sovereignty over all of South Vietnam and could legitimately occupy villages administered by the PRG, providing that they were not protected by identifiable PLAF units. The statement that Nixon recognized the RVN as the "sole legitimate government" in South Vietnam bore the seeds of a new war.

Another indication of the direction of the Nixon post-cease-fire policy was the decision, made as early as October 1972, to bring in a large force of "civilians" to run the absurdly large, expensive, and highly technological war machine which the United States had turned over to the Saigon government under the "Vietnamization" program. At one point, it appeared that the Pentagon was thinking in terms of a "civilian" corps of pilots which would be hired as "contract personnel" to fly the C-130s and other aircraft for which Saigon had no trained pilots, thus providing only the thinnest cloak over the open flouting of the provisions barring US military personnel.[43] Apparently this plan was never brought to fruition but in November and December it was leaked to the press that the United States intended to bring in a large force of "civilians" to other jobs previously done by US military personnel—assembling aircraft, teaching aircraft and instrument repair, computer programming. The new corps of thinly disguised military personnel would include both persons hired directly by the United States and those employed by twenty-three corporations given contracts totaling $150 million for military-related work in Vietnam.[44]

Several thousands of these military technicians, many of them recruited directly from the military and officially "retired" for the purpose, entered Vietnam just as the last American troops were being withdrawn.[45] These military technicians may have successfully evaded the restrictions imposed on the United States by Article 5 of the agreement, but their employment also involved the United States so deeply in the Saigon army that it blatantly violated the more fundamental obligation of Article 4: "The United States will not continue its military involvement or intervene in the internal affairs of South Vietnam."

A third indication that the old patron-client relationship was still intact is the secret commitment by Nixon to Thieu that the United States would intervene again immediately if the cease-fire was violated by the Communists. In private letters to Thieu dated November 14 and January 5, and later made public by a former Saigon cabinet minister, Nixon pledged to "react very strongly and rapidly" and then to "respond with full force" to any violations by the North Vietnamese.[46] Thieu's mouthpiece, *Tin Song*, indicated in December that Thieu interpreted these assurances to mean that the United States was prepared to resume bombing of North Vietnam.[47]

All the evidence indicates, moreover, that the Nixon administration was not interested in restraining Thieu militarily, any more than it was willing to push him to accommodate to the political provisions of the accords. On the contrary Nixon and Kissinger apparently believed that Thieu could successfully expand his territorial control without a high risk of a North Vietnamese main force response, provided that the North Vietnamese feared the renewal of American bombing, on one hand, and were restrained by declining levels of Soviet and Chinese military aid, on the other. Nixon had used the December bombing to reinforce his image as someone capable of responding to any challenge to his policy by massive bombing, and despite the opposition from all over the world to this policy, he hoped that it would make Hanoi cautious about any military response to Saigon's pressures against the PRG zone.

At the same time, Kissinger learned from his trips to the Soviet Union and China during 1972 that both socialist allies of North Vietnam intended to reduce military aid substantially after an agreement was reached, implying a veto over any new Communist offensive in the South.* Thieu was reportedly informed by Nixon and Kissinger during his April 1973 visit to the US that Moscow and Peking would restrain the North Vietnamese by reducing military aid.[48]

So the Thieu regime, bolstered by the shipment of some $1.2 billion in new armaments shipped between October and January, would be in a better position to take the offensive, with full US diplomatic support, and the promise of military reintervention if necessary. For both Nixon and Thieu, therefore, the cease-fire deadline would mark not the beginning of peace but the start of a new war under ground rules which they hoped would be advantageous to Saigon.

4.   The Cease-fire War

As the Paris Agreement was being signed, PLAF troops and Communist cadres were launching a nation-wide offensive and "uprising" aimed at increasing the PRG zone of control before the cease-fire took effect. Planned in meticulous detail for months, it was to be the Communists' final offensive effort: a combination of military attacks, overthrow of local RVN governments, destruction of Saigon's control over refugees, and stepped-up efforts to induce Saigon soldiers to revolt against their commanders.

Directives from higher Party echelons emphasized that the military operations in support of the uprising would continue until the cease-fire became effective, after which "we continue motivating the people to rise up and to launch military proselytizing attacks [propaganda within enemy armed forces] . . . in order to

---

* Ambassador Graham Martin referred to the fact that the Soviet Union and China had "significantly decreased their supply of arms to North Vietnam" in 1973 and were "not resupplying them with massive weapons of war" in interviews in 1974 (*Washington Post*, March 15, 1974; "Memoranda of Ambassador Martin," *Congressional Record*, April 4, 1975, p. 2022.) The Defense Intelligence Agency's estimate of combined Soviet-Chinese military aid to North Vietnam in 1973 was $290 million, less than half of the estimated $600 million in arms aid during 1972. (Letter from Defense Intelligence Agency to Congressman Les Aspin, May 18, 1974.)

shatter the enemy force and achieve our basic objective of liberating the rural area." [49] As the cease-fire began, the PRG planned mass meetings celebrating the end of the war and began putting up flags to show that the area was under PRG control, in anticipation of an eventual visit by the International Commission.[50]

From Friday, January 26, to 8:00 A.M. on Sunday, January 28, Saigon time (the cease-fire deadline), the PLAF succeeded in taking control of several hundred hamlets throughout South Vietnam as well as the district town of Cai Lay in Dinh Tuong province. They also managed to get control of the province town of Tay Ninh for a few hours on Saturday, but were driven out later in the day.[51] By the cease-fire deadline, an American official later conceded privately, the PRG still held about 350 hamlets.[52]

In every case where journalists were on the scene at the time of cease-fire or were able to talk with residents of the hamlet in question, the story was the same: PLAF troops entered the hamlet and established control well in advance of the cease-fire; the ARVN then counterattacked, usually with Regional (RF) and Popular Forces (PF) but occasionally with main force units. This attack generally went on for several days before finally recapturing the village.[53]

All over South Vietnam, ARVN recaptured the hamlets it lost before the cease-fire in the same way it always had driven out the PLAF—by pounding them with air strikes, helicopter gunships, and artillery, at a high cost in civilian casualties. In Long Khanh province, the twelve hamlets taken over by PLAF (about one-tenth of the hamlets in the province) were all retaken with air strikes, artillery, and helicopter gunships.[54] In one village, the artillery attack lasted four days, killing sixty civilians but not a single PLAF soldier, according to the residents interviewed.[55] And in Tay Ninh province, where PLAF troops seized the province town as well as twenty-six hamlets in the area surrounding it early on January 26, it took government troops five days to clear the capital and all of the hamlets completely, at a cost of forty civilians killed and 200 wounded, according to Saigon's official estimates.[56]

An RVN spokesman said on Monday, January 29, that the PLAF had seized ninety-five hamlets in the Third Military Region beginning on Friday, and claimed that fifty-two of them had been captured after the cease-fire deadline Sunday morning. But he also declared that Saigon forces, which had cleared only twenty-nine of them up to that time, were going to clear all ninety-five hamlets in the region, in open defiance of the cease-fire.[57] ARVN officers were equally frank in saying that they would ignore the cease-fire in order to reopen major highways cut by the PLAF at the time of the cease-fire.[58] In Hau Nghia province, where the PLAF had cut the road from Trang Bang to Tay Ninh city in about ten places, Colonel Dang Nhu Tuyet, commander of the 50th regiment of the 25th Division, told a reporter shortly after the cease-fire that he was determined to reopen the road no matter how long it took and regardless of the cease-fire.[59] In addition to the mobilization of a number of regiments for these battles, Saigon's artillery and air strikes were later described by US officials as having "reached levels of intensity higher than that experienced during the 1972 spring offensive." [60]

Saigon's own last-minute offensive before the truce, meanwhile, came to a quick and inglorious conclusion at Cua Viet, a former US Marine base at the mouth of the Cua Viet river in Quang Tri which had been captured from the ARVN by the PLAF during the 1972 offensive. Two ARVN Marine battalions drove into the key PLAF base some time around the cease-fire deadline on the morning of the 28th. The Marines themselves claimed that they reached their objective just two minutes before the cease-fire began, and that they controlled the base.[61] But an American source who was in Danang at the time says the ARVN never gained uncontested control of Cua Viet, and by the following day was in full retreat, taking heavy losses, later reported as 91 killed, 238 wounded, and 149 missing.[62]

The most important battle of the immediate post-cease-fire period centered on the village of Sa Huynh in Quang Ngai, where Highway 1 nearly touches the South China Sea. The PRG intended to use Sa Huynh as a point of entry for war material under the agreement. The DRV had insisted that ports of entry be named only after the agreement was signed, in order to prevent Saigon from simply concentrating its forces to seize them before the cease-fire and also to give the PRG itself the element of surprise in capturing a seaport in its pre-cease-fire offensive. Two PLAF regiments seized Sa Huynh on January 26, cutting Highway 1 north of Sa Huynh, and overwhelmed the Regional Forces post two kilometers away from the town.[63] Nearly 300 soldiers at the post apparently gave themselves up to the PRG.[64] ARVN had been caught off guard, in spite of American warnings for months of the danger of such a move in the area.[65]

As ARVN mobilized to recover the town and the highway, its spokesman in Saigon remained silent about what was happening at Sa Huynh for ten full days. Then, on February 6, ARVN's missing in action total after the cease-fire jumped by nearly 400 overnight. The spokesman then claimed that the RF post had been overrun just after the cease-fire. But he still refused to comment on ARVN efforts to recapture the port town and reopen Route 1, still under PLAF control for a twenty-mile stretch.[66]

The Saigon post-cease-fire counteroffensive was not only aimed at recapturing territory lost just before the truce; Saigon also used its jets, helicopter gunships, and artillery to destroy any PRG flags, whether flown on open territory or in populated areas, and to attack well-established PRG hamlets. Anticipating the PRG efforts to show the flag in order to demonstrate to International Commission teams that they controlled the area, Saigon helicopters roamed the countryside in search of PRG flags, then sprayed the hamlets with machine-gun fire.[67]

Ron Moreau of *Newsweek*, Martin Woollacott of the *Manchester Guardian*, and Peter Hazelhurst of the London *Times* were in PRG villages during the first few days of the cease-fire and witnessed shelling and bombing attacks on them by ARVN.[68] One Western cameraman who spent twenty-four hours in a PRG village in early February reported that a helicopter gunship attacked the village for more than a half hour, and that the villagers had predicted to him correctly, within five minutes, the beginning of the regular evening artillery bombardments of the village.[69]

Thieu's military challenge to the agreement was fully supported by the United States, in spite of White House statements calling on both sides to strictly implement the cease-fire. The Embassy informed Thieu that the United States considered it perfectly legitimate for his government to take back all the territory it had lost before the cease-fire took effect, according to an authoritative US diplomatic source. "We didn't expect the South Vietnamese government to stand by supinely," said this official later, arguing that the Communists' pre-cease-fire offensive had given them an unfair advantage.

Back in Washington, meanwhile, the Nixon administration was covering for Thieu. On January 31 Secretary of Defense Elliot Richardson, in his first news conference in the Pentagon, called Saigon's offensive in the first four days of the truce "a process of oscillation back to a posture closer to what [existed] before these [last minute] surges took place," and called it "encouraging." [70]

In Quang Ngai, where Route 1 remained under PRG control both north and south of Sa Huynh, a major battle raged. By February 16, ARVN had thrown two Ranger multibattalions, three infantry regiments from the 2nd Division, and the 4th Armored Unit, supported by aircraft, artillery, and warships, into the offensive aimed at recapturing Sa Huynh.[71] When Saigon finally reestablished uncontested control over the area a few days later, RVN officials claimed that they had never lost control of the town.[72] Supporting Saigon's story, the chief of the US delegation to the Four-Party Joint Military Commission, General Gilbert Woodward, accused the PRG on February 27 of a three-week-long attack on the town which it had controlled since the night before the cease-fire deadline.[73]

Moreover, while the United States joined in calling on both sides to implement the cease-fire scrupulously under the Joint Military Commission, it was at the same time undercutting that appeal by telling the American public that the continued fighting was nothing to be concerned about. On February 16 the Four-Party Joint Military Commission issued an appeal to the military commands of the South Vietnamese parties to strictly respect the cease-fire and reaffirmed the prohibition of the agreement of air combat missions; this could only have been aimed at the Saigon government, which alone had aircraft in South Vietnam.[74] But Saigon's drive on Sa Huynh was stepped up anyway, and air sorties continued at the same level as before.[75] Three days after the cease-fire appeal, Saigon planes bombed the PRG airfield at Duc Co.[76] On February 25 Kissinger, asked about reported cease-fire violations in a television interview, replied that they did not concern him, because, "after all, how are the two sides going to establish areas of control except by testing each other?" [77]

An American official in Saigon later told a newsman that it had taken Saigon three weeks to recapture the 350 hamlets seized by the Communists before the cease-fire "and a few more as well." [78] But Thieu, encouraged by the strong support of the Nixon administration for his post-cease-fire offensive and the absence of any strong Communist reaction, had already decided to go much further. While Secretary Rogers was telling the House Foreign Affairs Committee that both sides were "staying within the territory which has sort of been acknowledged" and that the fighting had been "considerably reduced," [79] Saigon's troops were continuing to expand the RVN zone of control. They moved into areas which were either contested or PRG-controlled, in order to set up new, permanent military bases and establish their control, in violation of Article 2 of the Protocol on the Cease-fire, which prohibited "major redeployments or movements that would extend each party's area of control. . . ." In addition to losing significant chunks of territory in Binh Dinh, Quang Nam, and Quang Ngai provinces during the first three months of the 1972 offensive, ARVN had been forced during the latter half of 1972 to consolidate its troops and bases in many areas where it was stretched thin. It had withdrawn from hundreds of outposts in the Delta and in the coastal lowlands, leaving the areas to PRG influence. "Saigon's attitude was that the agreement was forced on them by the U. S.," one US official explained. They immediately rebuilt outposts along Route 4, in Kien Hoa, all along the coastal lowlands, in all the places where they had pulled back during the 1972 offensive.

Some of these land-grabbing efforts provoked battles with the PLAF. Officials of the US Defense Attaché's office in Saigon told the Senate Foreign Relations Committee staff that ARVN had begun "several operations designed to expand areas of control to which the enemy reacted strongly." [80]

Apart from the desire to confine the PRG to the smallest possible territory and population, there was another, even more compelling, reason for the RVN to grab as much of the land lost to the PRG in 1972 as possible. It had too many refugees in its camps and cities and not enough land for them to farm. The only economically rational solution was to return them to their homes, but most of them were from villages now under PRG control. So in Quang Nam and Quang Ngai, Saigon went on the offensive to regain that territory. "We're trying to grab back land under their control so our people can return to their homes," said one ARVN officer in southern Quang Ngai.[81]

Not all of ARVN's land-grabbing involved areas lost to the Communists during the 1972 offensive. In Kien Hoa province, ARVN forces pushed into a long-time Communist base area south of Giong Trom and began constructing permanent outposts.[82] And by midsummer, emboldened by earlier successes in expanding its control, ARVN launched a new drive to build outposts in the Nghia Thuan valley of Nghia Hanh district in Quang Ngai province, seizing control of an area which had been under NLF and then PRG administration since 1964.[83]

The PLAF, meanwhile, was under orders to try to hold on to as much territory as it could without committing its main force units to battle, thus leaving the initiative to the Saigon army. American officials in Saigon characterize the military posture of the PLAF as "generally defensive" during the first two months of the agreement.[84] The Party's initial two-month assessment resulted in a decision to continue the restraints on the use of military force, forbidding the PLAF from striking into RVN territory. In a secret directive issued in late March, the revolutionaries were urged to use military force, political struggle, and military proselytizing within ARVN in order to "hold the enemy back" and "force him to implement the agreement." [85]

The only exceptions to the defensive military stance of the PLAF to which US and RVN officials could point in the winter, spring, and summer of 1973 were attacks by fire on Tonle Chan, a base near the Cambodian border, and attacks from the banks of the Mekong on RVN ships carrying war material to Phnom Penh at Hong Ngu on the Cambodian border.[86] (Since the PRG controlled the banks of the Mekong, it could claim control over ship traffic under the agreement.)

Tonle Chan, which Saigon publicized for months as the one important cease-fire violation by the PRG, had long been responsible for interdicting Communist use of a supply corridor running from the border area down to the PLAF "war zone D." After the cease-fire reconnaissance teams from the base continued to carry out attacks on PLAF personnel moving through the corridor, while Rangers patrolled deep into the surrounding PRG zone.[87] When

Saigon rejected the PLAF demand that the local ARVN commander meet with his PLAF counterpart to discuss measures to prevent conflict, as provided in Article 4 of the cease-fire protocol, the Communist forces cut off the base from all access except by helicopter and began to shell it.[88]

Party leaders were apparently uncertain that Saigon's offensive thrust could be contained successfully by this military posture. In the first major essay on post-agreement strategy, in the April 1973 issue of *Ho: Tap*, Hoang Tung referred to the "possibility of actively repulsing the plot of the counterrevolutionary forces to renew the war," thus "maintaining and strengthening the peace." But he also referred to the "possibility of the enemy renewing the war," which meant that Saigon might threaten to push the PRG from its "leopard spots" of control in the Mekong Delta and other populated areas, forcing the Communists to launch a major counteroffensive.[89]

This restrictive military policy in the face of Saigon's expansion of control caused some morale problems within Communist ranks in the south. In its March 1973 directive, COSVN reported that "in many areas," people were "still confused about the application of the struggle principles and methods in the new situation, while the enemy is infringing on us . . . and is secretly causing us a number of losses and difficulties. . . ."[90]

While confirming the initial policy of limited and localized responses to Saigon's military pressures, the March 1973 directive also emphasized the importance of increasing the military potential of the PLAF. "Opposition to the enemy will not win victory," it warned, "unless there is change in the ratio of military forces between us and the enemy." Only if there were such a change, it said, "can every enemy plot for obstruction and instigation of conflict be stopped or dealt with in a timely fashion should he adventurously instigate the civil war, and can we force the enemy to implement the Ceasefire Agreement and defeat him."[91]

Even though it was forced to give ground to ARVN in the early months of the cease-fire, then, the Party was looking to a gradual change in the military balance to ultimately force Saigon back to the Paris Agreement. By improving the lines of communication in the PRG zone, by building up a sophisticated new logistics system in Quang Tri, and by recruitment of more troops in the South, particularly guerrilla and local forces, which had long been under strength, the Party hoped to force the conflict back to the political plane, where it felt it had a decisive advantage.

5.   *The Return to Bomber Diplomacy*

The Nixon administration's decision to support Thieu's efforts to expand his area of control by force required that it continue to rely heavily on the threat of renewed bombing in order to "deter" a Communist military response. And having committed itself to gaining a military advantage for Thieu, the administration also intended to use that threat to force North Vietnam to slow down its infiltration of troops into the South to a trickle.

The DRV had no intention of giving up its personnel replacement operations or its resupply operations while Saigon was trying to eliminate the "leopard spots" of PRG control in the heavily populated Mekong Delta and central coast. In the first weeks of the agreement, the DRV continued to move personnel replacements and war material into the South in spite of the restrictions of Article 7. It had been precisely to insure that provisions intended to work under conditions of a cease-fire would not be used to give military advantage to the Saigon side in a continuing war that the DRV negotiators had chosen the wording of Article 7 carefully in their original draft agreement. Article 7, as drafted by the DRV and accepted by the United States in the October 22 draft, provided that the restrictions on resupply and reinforcements would come into force "when there is enforcement of a ceasefire."

When the State Department's legal adviser, George Aldrich, was brought into the negotiations in November, according to officials close to the talks, he pointed out that this language gave the North Vietnamese an escape clause to continue reinforcement and resupply efforts if there were violations of the cease-fire. The US delegation tried to redraft Article 7 in the November and December negotiations, but the DRV stood by its original language, and the United States did not press the point. This did not mean, however, that the Nixon administration was prepared to give up its argument that Article 7 applied regardless of compliance with the cease-fire. "We always anticipated there would be violations of the cease-fire," one official said later, "and we didn't intend to leave the North

Vietnamese an excuse to continue resupply just because six days didn't go by without a shot being fired." The administration's public statements made clear its intention to force Hanoi to comply fully with the limitations of Article 7, even while the war was being carried into the PRG zone in the South.

The first indication of administration intentions regarding Article 7 was a statement by the US delegation to the thirteen-nation conference in Paris on the Paris Agreement on February 27, saying the United States had "continuing evidence that there are gross violations on the Communist side that include infiltration of several thousand North Vietnamese forces into South Vietnam since January 28." [92]

The administration's next public move was to give the public the impression that the DRV was carrying out a major, illegal military build-up. On March 10, the Defense Department commented that some 250 tanks, some weapons, and "about 30,000 persons" had been spotted moving through Laos, and that some supplies had moved through the Demilitarized Zone to the South as well.[93] The Pentagon said it had no definite information on how much had actually entered the South. Two days later, the Pentagon revised its estimate to 300 tanks and said 30,000 men had been observed on the Ho Chi Minh trail "since the first of the year." [94]

The use of this time frame was irrelevant, of course, to the consideration of the cease-fire agreement. From November on, the DRV had rushed to get as many tanks and military personnel into the South as possible before the truce deadline, in response to the major US build-up of Saigon's army in the months before the agreement, which had approximately doubled ARVN's tank force to some 450 tanks.[95] In fact, Pentagon officials admitted privately that all but "several thousand" of the troops and virtually all of the tanks had entered South Vietnam before the cease-fire or were bound for the Cambodia border area. Moreover, they said, the movement of tanks down the trail had already stopped. The only continuing movement of equipment into the South in March was the truck traffic carrying supplies to the PLAF.[96] But all of these facts were overlooked and the 300 tanks and 30,000 men were repeatedly mentioned in the press.

On March 13 the State Department issued a statement on the infiltration which again avoided specifically charging the North

Vietnamese with a violation of the agreement, but said the United States was watching the movement of troops and supplies "very closely and with some concern in the context of Articles 7 and 20 of the Paris Agreement." [97]

There were good reasons for the State Department to phrase its statement in such cautious language, for the United States faced more than one legal problem in trying to charge the DRV with a violation of the agreement. Apart from the fact that there was no "enforcement of a cease-fire," which was to precede the actual application of Article 7, no agreement had yet been reached on the procedures and modalities for resupply under that article.

Article 7 of the cease-fire protocol called for the two South Vietnamese parties to "agree on these points of entry within fifteen days after the entry into force of the cease-fire." But according to US officials the PRG, while informally choosing Lao Bao, Gio Linh, and Xa Mat as its points of entry, refused to inform the ICCS officially of its choices until there was an agreement on exactly how Article 7 would operate. The PRG demanded that the RVN and the United States agree that the phrase "of the same characteristics and properties" in Article 7 be taken literally, so that the United States could not bring in any new models of weapons already used by ARVN—particularly of aircraft. Since the United States was already planning to turn over to Saigon F-5E jet fighters, which clearly did not have the same "characteristics and properties" as the F-5As they were to replace, Saigon could not agree to this interpretation of Article 7. So the PRG argued that until there was agreement on the procedures and modalities for the "piece for piece" replacement, there was no point in naming their points of entry officially.

In its secret briefing paper on the meaning of various provisions of the agreement, the State Department had originally interpreted Article 7 to mean that there could be no acceptance of replacement equipment by either side until entry points were officially designated.[98] But it reversed itself after the negotiations on the modalities of Article 7 bogged down and began shipping war material to the RVN anyway. The United States justified its action by arguing that it interpreted Article 7 to permit such shipments in advance of agreement on procedures and modalities governing the implementation of the provision.[99] The DRV and PRG could, of course, make the same argument.

But Nixon did not want to be tied down by legal niceties. He believed that he could force the North Vietnamese to cut down their resupply to troops in the South by the threat of renewed bombing. On October 11 Secretary Rogers announced that SAM-2 antiaircraft missiles which had been set up at the PLAF base at Khe Sanh, and which the US delegate to the JMC had implicitly threatened to remove by air strikes if necessary, had been removed.[100] Nixon apparently saw their removal as a sign that the DRV would back down when the United States threatened to use force. The following day the order went out from the White House to prepare the ground for a presidential threat on the North Vietnamese infiltration into the South.[101]

On March 15 Nixon threatened for the first time to take unilateral action if necessary to force the DRV to stop its use of the trail network and the DMZ to move military equipment into the South.[102] Asked how concerned he was about the reports of cease-fire violations, Nixon again minimized the significance of the fighting and denied that any serious violations of the standstill cease-fire had occurred. "As you ladies and gentlemen will recall," he said, "I have consistently pointed out in meetings with you that we would expect violations because of the nature of the war, the guerrilla nature. . . ." Then he referred to "another violation that could lead to, we think, rather serious consequences. . . . And that is the reports that you ladies and gentlemen have been receiving from your colleagues in Vietnam with regard to infiltration . . . reports of infiltration into South Vietnam of equipment exceeding the amounts that were allowed under the agreement." Nixon answered a follow-up question on the infiltration of troops by saying that they "could be simply replacement personnel" and therefore he was less concerned about it—again indicating that there was no evidence of a North Vietnamese troop build-up after the cease-fire.

Nixon then declared: "Our concern has also been expressed to other interested parties and I would only suggest that based on my actions over the past four years, that the North Vietnamese should not lightly disregard such expressions of concern, when they are made, with regard to a violation." Members of the White House staff interpreted the statement for reporters as a warning to the DRV that the United States would resume bombing if the infiltration continued.

By the first week in April, the focus of the administration's concern shifted sharply in the wake of a stunning offensive by the Khmer National United Front, now fighting without any North Vietnamese combat units to assist them, against the failing Lon Nol government. On April 7 Nixon sent General Alexander Haig to Indochina to assess the situation. The White House said the trip was prompted by the President's concern over the failure of North Vietnamese troops to withdraw from Cambodia, the "level of violence in Cambodia," and "ongoing violations of the ceasefire in South Vietnam." [103]

The decision to make Cambodia an issue involved the administration in even deeper legal and political waters than did the infiltration issue. For in order to issue threats against North Vietnam over the Cambodian situation, the administration had to misrepresent the nature of the Paris Agreement's provisions concerning Cambodia.

Although the Vietnamese Communist military command had already pulled back its last remaining combat unit from the Cambodian conflict around the time the agreement was signed,[104] it had not withdrawn from its base areas in the border region. Nor was it obliged to by the Paris Agreement. Article 20 called on all foreign countries to "put an end to all military activities in Cambodia and Laos, totally withdraw from and refrain from reintroducing into these two countries troops, military advisers and military personnel, armaments, munitions, and war material." But the provision was notably lacking in any deadline for the fulfillment of these obligations. As State Department Legal Adviser Aldrich told a Congressional committee immediately after the agreement, "The timing of the obligations in article 20 . . . is deliberately left unspecified and those obligations do not take effect until agreed upon by the Laotian and Cambodian parties. *Thus the withdrawal of foreign forces from Laos and Cambodia and the cessation of bombing in those countries, are objectives, not present obligations*" (emphasis added).[105]

It was under this interpretation of Article 20 that the United States justified the continuation of American bombing in Cambodia, which had resumed early in February.[106] In declaring its freedom to continue its military activities in Cambodia until a cease-fire was concluded between the Cambodian parties, the United States had at the same time conceded the right of the North Vietnamese to maintain a military presence in the country until that time. Now the administration wanted to have its cake and eat it too. While continuing its own bombing until a Cambodian cease-fire, it now appeared to be demanding immediate withdrawal of North Vietnamese troops.

But this was not the primary object of the administration's pressures on the DRV in April. Faced with the distinct possibility of the collapse of the Phnom Penh government, Nixon hoped to force North Vietnam to get its Khmer allies at least to call off their offensive and perhaps even to agree to a de facto cease-fire. This much was apparent from background statements to the press suggesting that the North Vietnamese were violating an "understanding" by failing to secure a Cambodian cease-fire. CBS News reported on April 9 that administration officials claimed a secret understanding had been reached in Paris on a cease-fire in Cambodia and were "angry" with the North Vietnamese for failing to honor it.[107] On April 15 the *New York Times* reported that Kissinger was known to feel that Hanoi had violated an "understanding" by "not putting its influence behind a prompt truce in Cambodia."

These reports, which could only have emanated from Kissinger himself, were aimed at strengthening the administration's hand in its effort to coerce the DRV on the Cambodian question. But Kissinger again misrepresented the record of the Paris negotiations. During the Paris negotiations the DRV delegation had consistently refused, despite strong pressure from Kissinger, to give any assurance that there would be a cease-fire in Cambodia. They pointed out that Sihanouk's Royal Government and the National United Front regarded the Lon Nol regime as an illegitimate usurper and refused to negotiate with it. And on January 21, 1973 Sihanouk himself had said his government would not accept any cease-fire agreement reached at Paris.[108] Sihanouk was willing to offer a temporary cessation of offensive operations as a gesture toward negotiations with the United States, but not a permanent cease-fire vis-à-vis the Lon Nol regime.[109]

Failing to obtain any agreement from the North Vietnamese,

Kissinger finally read a unilateral statement on Cambodia, announcing that Lon Nol's forces would suspend all "offensive operations" and the United States would suspend its bombing in Cambodia. He further stated that "if the other side reciprocated, a de facto cease-fire would thereby be brought into force in Cambodia," but that "if the Communist forces carried out attacks, government forces and United States air forces would have to take necessary countermeasures and that, in any event, we would continue to carry out air strikes in Cambodia as necessary until such time as a cease-fire could be brought into effect." [110] As in 1968, the United States had issued a "unilateral understanding," which was nothing more than a statement of its own intentions.

The administration also continued its pressure on Hanoi to halt its resupply and troop reinforcement. On April 11 the Pentagon spokesman restated the Department's position on the significance of military infiltration into the South, which it now called a "sizable" violation of the agreement.[111] In contrast to earlier Pentagon statements, which had avoided charges of massive infiltration of tanks or troops following the cease-fire, it now claimed that the "bulk" of Communist weapons which had moved down the trail network, including about half of the estimated 400 to 500 tanks believed to be in South Vietnam, had entered the South after the agreement took effect.

This statement was flatly contradicted by sources at US Support Activities Group (USSAG) in Thailand, where photoreconnaissance and other intelligence data on Communist forces in Indochina were interpreted. Intelligence officials there told Senate investigators that "relatively little" of the equipment sent down the trail during the entire November 1972–April 1973 period actually entered South Vietnam after the cease-fire. This statement applied to the total of 341 tanks, 173 artillery pieces, and 146 antiaircraft weapons sighted on the trail network during the entire dry season.[112]

The Pentagon also repeated its earlier statement that 30,000 fresh troops had been sent toward the South since the beginning of the year. What the spokesman did not reveal was the fact that only 7,000 combat troops were estimated to have entered South Vietnam during the two months following the agreement—hardly enough to even cover losses due to casualties in combat during that period.[113]

And there was evidence of the movement of two North Vietnamese divisions, the 304th and 308th, from Quang Tri province back to North Vietnam, which would have reduced Communist troop strength in the South by 5,000 to 10,000.[114] Finally, the number of combat troops believed to have begun the trip south after the agreement was so small (2,500) as to indicate a DRV willingness to accept further reduction in North Vietnamese troop levels in the South.[115]

While the Pentagon was trying to build a case for major violations of the agreement by Hanoi, administration officials let it be known that they were considering approaches to the Soviet Union and China, US air attacks on SAM sites and the PLAF logistics base at Khe Sanh, or renewed mining and bombing of North Vietnam. These officials also revealed that Saigon had requested permission to carry out systematic ground and air attacks against "troop and weapons concentrations"—thus revealing not only Saigon's eagerness to resume full-scale war but also the veto over Saigon's military policy which the administration could still exercise if and when it chose to. The administration, according to these sources, was considering agreeing to this request, thus removing the last limitation on Saigon's operations.[116]

The stories of an "understanding" on Cambodia, Pentagon allegations of DRV "violations," and the revelations by high administration officials about the "options" being considered were all part of a carefully orchestrated crisis, creating the atmosphere for more concrete acts of threat and coercion which were to follow.

The first serious overt act against the DRV came on April 17 when the United States suspended its mine-clearing operations of coastal waters off North Vietnam, bringing a public protest from the DRV that the move was a violation of the agreement. The State Department announced that the move was in response to alleged North Vietnamese violations and that the chief US representative to the meetings with the DRV on reconstruction aid was being recalled for "consultations." Secretary Rogers remarked to a meeting of business leaders that the administration was "committed to the full implementation of the agreement, including the provisions on withdrawal of foreign forces from Cambodia and the cessation of infiltration activities." [117]

The administration sharpened its threat to resume bombing

against the DRV when it announced that it had begun carrying out military reconnaissance flights over the North. American officials admitted this was a violation of Article 2 of the agreement, which called on the United States to "stop all its military activities against the territory of the Democratic Republic of Vietnam. . . ." It was again justified by the State Department as a response to a "material breach" of the agreement. Officials said privately that the purpose of the move was to warn Hanoi that the United States was taking "preparatory steps for renewed bombing." [118]

At the same time, the United States sent a formal note to the DRV, which both responded to North Vietnamese charges of US violations of the agreement and set forth the administration's charges against North Vietnam.[119] The note began by charging that the DRV had sent military equipment to the South without regard to Article 7 and built roads in Laos which did not approach any of the designated points of entry. Neither of these actions, of course, could be considered violations of Article 7, in the absence of either "enforcement of a cease-fire" or agreement on the modalities of resupply under that article.

The note also stretched previous Pentagon claims even farther than before, asserting that 400 tanks and armored vehicles and 30,000 troops had entered South Vietnam after the cease-fire agreement. As noted above, these claims bore no relationship to the administration's intelligence data. In contrast to the assessment of the Defense Attaché's Office that the Communists had been in a defensive posture militarily, the note charged PLAF forces with attacks on "hamlets, villages and Republic of Vietnam military positions throughout the country, in an obvious effort to expand the area controlled by forces under North Vietnamese command."

As for Cambodia, the note carefully avoided charging an outright violation, but stated that the DRV and "Cambodian forces under its control" had carried out a "total military offensive" in Cambodia "despite obligations assumed by the Democratic Republic of Vietnam in Article 20 of the agreement and Article 8 of the Act of Paris." But it did not say what "obligations" were relevant to this implied charge of a violation of the agreement.

On April 25 Kissinger himself renewed the charge that the DRV had "cynically violated" what he called an "unconditional" commitment to withdraw from Cambodia and Laos.[120] But six days later the Senate Foreign Relations Committee, which had obtained a copy of the State Department's own briefing paper contradicting Kissinger's claim, forced Secretary Rogers to admit, under questioning, that the DRV had not violated Article 20.[121] Nor was his fall-back position that Hanoi had violated the "spirit of an understanding" very convincing to the Committee, since Rogers revealed to the Committee that the "understanding" was purely unilateral.

The failure of the administration to put forward a clear-cut and consistent case for a violation of the agreement by the DRV in Cambodia left Congress cold to any resumption of bombing in North or South Vietnam. After eight years of direct military involvement in Indochina, Congress and the public wanted to get out—not to jump back in. By the end of April the administration was struggling to continue the bombing of Cambodia, which influential senators were now calling illegal. Freed from the constraints of active US participation in the Vietnam conflict, Congress was about to strip Nixon of his power to make war in Indochina as he pleased. On May 4 the House Democratic Policy Committee, chaired by House Speaker Carl Albert, voted eighteen to three to support the cutoff of funds for the bombing of Cambodia. On May 10 the entire House followed suit, paving the way for the vote on July 31 to cut off all bombing of Cambodia and prohibit further military action in Indochina without prior Congressional authorization.

This Congressional opposition would probably have prevented even a strong administration from using its bombers for diplomatic leverage over Hanoi. But even as he embarked on this round of bomber diplomacy, Nixon was desperately trying to save his presidency from the unraveling of the Watergate cover-up. Nixon's speech of April 30, announcing the resignation of Kleindienst, Dean, Haldeman, and Ehrlichman, marked the beginning of the decline of Nixon's authority and credibility with Congress and the American public. Although administration officials continued to issue threats of possible renewed bombing from time to time, they did so with steadily diminishing conviction. The keystone of Nixon's strategy toward the agreement had been broken, and it was only a matter of time before the entire structure of US policy would crumble from its own inherent weakness.

7: Implementing the Paris Agreement: II

1. The Failure of Enforcement: The Joint Military Commissions

The mechanism established by the Paris Agreement to insure its implementation was as fragile as the compromises on which the agreement itself was based. The foundation of the enforcement machinery was not an international authority with power to compel the parties to carry out their obligations but two bodies composed of the parties themselves: the Four-Party Joint Military Commission (US, DRV, RVN, PRG) and the Two-Party Joint Military Commission (RVN, PRG). The primary responsibility for ensuring full implementation of the cease-fire, the American withdrawal, the exchange of prisoners, both military and civilian, and the demarcation of zones of control rested on the delegations of the parties to these two bodies. The International Commission of Control and Supervision (ICCS) could investigate and report to the parties on violations of the cease-fire, but it was only the parties themselves who could keep the peace.

The Four-Party JMC had the responsibility under the agreement to "deter and detect violations, to deal with cases of violations, and to settle conflicts and matters of contention between the parties" relating to the cease-fire and other provisions. It was supposed to send teams to investigate alleged violations and "assist the parties in finding measures to prevent recurrence of similar cases." It could only carry out this mandate, however, by agreement among all four parties. The body had no authority over any of the parties, and could only recommend specific actions to them. It could operate, therefore, only to the extent that each of the parties wanted it to.

The Saigon government not only wanted to resist the recommendations of the Four-Party JMC; it wanted to prevent it from becoming operational at all. What Thieu feared was that the officers of the PLAF, after years of carefully guarded secrecy in their constantly shifting headquarters, would emerge from the jungle to establish a legal PRG political presence under the aegis of the JMC, not only in Saigon but at regional and local JMC sites. Both sides understood that the JMC would confer a significant political advantage on the PRG in establishing its status as legally coequal with the Saigon government under the agreement, thus undermining Saigon's claims to legitimacy and making the political struggle against Thieu's regime more effective.

The chief of the PRG delegation was Lieutenant General Tran Van Tra, who appeared for the first time in public when he walked into the JMC meeting at Tansonnhut airbase on February 2. A fifty-four-year-old former peasant from Quang Ngai province, Tra had eluded enemy troops and B-52s for almost ten years in his headquarters near the Cambodian border, first as Commander-in-Chief of all revolutionary armed forces in the South and later as commander of the crucial Fourth Military Zone, which included Saigon and the provinces around it. He had been the key figure in planning both the Tet Offensive and the 1972 offensive's thrust at An Loc.* Once a shadowy figure whose picture was not even available to American intelligence men, he would soon be chatting amiably with diplomats and reporters at Saigon cocktail parties. Thieu's concern about the presence of Tra and other previously "Faceless Viet Cong" in Saigon was reflected by his forbidding the publication in the Saigon press of pictures of the Communist delegations or even of parts of news stories describing their uniforms.[1]

Even before the first PRG delegation arrived at Tansonnhut airport on a South Vietnamese Air Force C-47 from Bangkok, Saigon had already planned its first tactic to block the PRG from

---

* It was a measure of the American ignorance of the Vietnamese revolutionary movement that the US press reported—presumably on the basis of official US briefings—that Tra was a "North Vietnamese general" who was "claiming he was really a Southerner." (*Washington Star-News*, February 25, 1973.) In fact, Tra had spent virtually all of the two long armed conflicts, first against the French and later against the Americans, in the Saigon area, regrouping to the North in 1954 only because it was required by the 1954 Geneva Agreement and thus becoming, temporarily, part of the "North Vietnamese" army.

establishing its JMC delegations in the Saigon-controlled zone. It had already been agreed in Paris that the Communist delegations would not need to present travel documents or sign official RVN forms to enter the country by air, but RVN officials boarding the plane refused to recognize PRG travel documents, since that would have conceded that the PRG existed as a government, and they insisted that the delegates sign RVN immigration forms. Saigon was thus trying to force the PRG's delegates to deny its own sovereignty while recognizing that of Saigon. Both the PRG and DRV delegates refused to sign the forms and remained on their plane for twenty hours, as both Saigon and US officials continued to negotiate with them. Only after the personal intervention of Ambassador Bunker himself was Saigon forced to give in and let them disembark without signing the immigration forms.[2]

But this was only the first step in Saigon's effort to prevent the PRG from deploying its JMC teams to Saigon's province and district towns. The agreement called for the Four-Party JMC to be represented at seven regional headquarters, each of which would supervise joint military teams at twenty-six locations within the RVN zone. These local teams were to carry out the day-to-day work of investigating truce violations and solving problems relating to the cease-fire. In recognition of the fact that it would take both time and carefully worked out arrangements to establish the local Four-Party joint military teams, particularly in order to provide for the movement of the PRG delegates to the field sites, the agreement allowed fifteen days for the completion of the task. Although forty PRG representatives and 800 DRV representatives were flown from Hanoi to Saigon by US C-130 transport planes between January 28 and February 8, the bulk of the PRG personnel would have to be picked up at designated sites by US aircraft.[3]

This procedure provided Thieu with one means of obstructing the deployment of the PRG teams to the field sites. When the PRG designated a location and time for the pickup of its personnel for the JMC regional sites in Hue and Phan Rang early in February, the RVN shelled or bombed the sites.[4] According to US officials, the Saigon government argued that the sites were not in PRG-controlled territory, and that by having their people picked up at those sites, the PRG was trying to establish a territorial claim.[5] In fact, Saigon often tried to deny PRG control of any area it could reach either by ground forces, air strikes, or artillery. In Binh Thuan province, the province chief claimed everything within the range of his big artillery pieces (nearly ten miles) as RVN territory and refused to allow PRG personnel to be picked up within that area. According to the PRG, on February 4, in Binh Thuan province, the United States not only failed to pick up the PRG military teams at kilometer 26 on Route 8, but permitted Saigon troops to hit the spot with artillery and then occupy it.[6] The PRG finally agreed to be picked up well outside the range of the chief's artillery.[7]

American sources on the Four-Party JMC do not deny that some of these attacks occurred at sites clearly within the PRG zone of control, and that the effect was to discourage the PRG from deployment of its personnel to the pickup sites. "There was clear evidence that the ARVN was initiating artillery strikes to get them [PRG personnel] before they were picked up," said one US official. These sources say the US delegation to the JMC believed the PRG had a valid reason for complaint and for failing to deploy their personnel.

Saigon's strategy of discouraging PRG presence in its towns and cities was also evidenced in its treatment of DRV and PRG delegations once they arrived at both Central JMC headquarters and Regional Commission locations. Local RVN officials were ordered to treat the Communist delegations as virtual prisoners rather than as diplomatic representatives of parties to the peace agreement, in the hope that they would choose not to submit to the indignity and give up on the JMC. Communist delegations were given uncomfortable quarters, denied rudimentary facilities such as phones, kept under armed guard, and surrounded by barbed wire and mines. As an officer attached to the US delegation said, the PRG compounds "gave the impression that the PRG and DRV were held captive." [8]

It was more than just an impression. The Communist delegates were forbidden to leave the compound except on official investigations and at first were denied any contact with the outside world. At My Tho, representatives of the four members of the ICCS tried to visit the DRV and PRG delegations to the regional JMC but were prevented from doing so by guards who cited "security reasons." When they finally obtained permission to get into the compound, they found them living in uncomfortable and unhygienic conditions, and prevented from leaving the building.[9] And at the Can Tho regional JMC headquarters, non-Communist sources on the ICCS confirmed that Communist complaints of inadequate facilities, including a lack of communications equipment and no freedom of movement, were "valid." [10]

In Saigon, where the danger to the RVN of a visible Communist presence was greatest, its treatment of the DRV and PRG was also most heavy-handed. Saigon was particularly eager to ensure that the Communist delegates would not be able to communicate any information about Saigon's violations of the cease-fire to the Western press during those early days. They prevented the PRG delegates from communicating with their military commands in the field and isolated the PRG and DRV delegations from the press. On February 8 Saigon detained twenty-three newsmen and confiscated their press cards when the journalists tried to talk with North Vietnamese and PRG delegates.[11] And on February 17 Saigon warned newsmen that they could be shot if they tried to seek interviews with the Communist delegations, because MP's were authorized to fire at anyone "improperly on the base." [12]

All of these actions by the RVN were clear violations of Article 16 of the Protocol on the Joint Military Commissions: "The Joint Military Commissions and their personnel, while carrying out their tasks, shall enjoy privileges and immunities equivalent to those accorded diplomatic missions and diplomatic agents." But Saigon's strategy of frustrating the deployment of PRG personnel went one step further, by communicating an explicit threat to the physical security of the PRG delegations once the Americans and North Vietnamese had withdrawn. It did so by staging incidents in which rock-throwing threatened injury to the Communist delegations during hostile demonstrations and actually did injure some of them.

The first such incident occurred on February 8, as the DRV and PRG delegates arrived at the local Joint Military Team site in Banmethuot in the central highlands. A crowd, waiting at the compound where the delegates were to be housed, began throwing rocks after the Communist delegates had left their helicopters. Eight DRV officers were injured, two of them suffering head injuries.[13] Saigon's chief of delegation, Lieutenant General Ngo

Dzu, said the incident had occurred because the crowd was "infuriated at Communist violations of the ceasefire in their province." [14] But the RVN made little effort to hide the fact that such demonstrations were part of its treatment of enemy delegates. Saigon's military briefer warned that his government could not "use guns to repress our own people to protect the Communists." [15]

This incident confirmed the fears which the Communists had already held regarding the danger to their personnel in the JMC delegation. The PRG in particular had approached its deployment to the field with the greatest caution from the start, knowing that the physical danger to their men would increase once the United States lost interest in the operations of the JMC. Some PRG officers, for example, appeared at field sites in North Vietnamese uniforms, ostensibly as DRV delegates. One US official recalled later that there were reports that the DRV delegation at the regional JMC headquarters in Danang included some officers identified as people from the area rather than as North Vietnamese. These officers wore North Vietnamese uniforms in order to insure that physical safety would be assured before emerging as PRG delegates.

The Banmethuot incident was a clear indication that Saigon would not shrink from physical violence against Communist delegates. The DRV immediately announced that it would send no more of its people to the field until there were adequate guarantees of security as well as improvement in living conditions. That was just what Thieu wanted, of course, and he ordered more such "spontaneous demonstrations." On February 25 two rock-throwing demonstrations against the DRV delegates took place, one in Hue, the other in Danang.[16] Three thousand demonstrators, carrying banners, posters, and rocks, were brought in buses and trucks from the city itself to the camp housing the DRV delegations outside Danang. Meeting no opposition from Saigon MP's, they climbed over the gate and pelted the barracks with rocks. In Hue, meanwhile, rock-throwing demonstrators injured five North Vietnamese officers in their compound.

After the Danang and Hue incidents, the PRG suspended its deployment of personnel to the JMC regional and local sites. Although by February 19 the PRG had brought in about 200 of their personnel from the field, this number never rose above 215 out of the 825 authorized for the JMC. PRG personnel occupied four of the seven regional sites but no local team sites when they suspended the deployment.

The DRV delegation not only withdrew its personnel from Danang and Hue but decided to use the only real leverage it had with the United States—the threat to delay the release of US prisoners from the North—to demand that its delegations receive the treatment guaranteed by the agreement. The DRV press spokesman told reporters that the United States was encouraging the Saigon government not only to violate the cease-fire and delay the return of civilian prisoners but to harass the JMC delegations of the PRG and DRV. The Americans cared only about getting their prisoners back, he said, warning that there would be no further release of American prisoners until the United States and Saigon showed that they would "correctly implement" the agreement.

The US delegation had been privately minimizing the importance of the problem of privileges and immunities as well as security for the Communist delegations, while disclaiming any responsibility for such problems.[17] In an earlier letter responding to Communist complaints, the chief of the US delegation, General Woodward, had defended the quarters provided by the RVN and remarked that "until the cease-fire becomes stable, there will be some unavoidable risks [in deploying JMC teams to the field] which the United States delegation has already accepted in deploying its own personnel." [18] In other words, the United States had no interest in the difficulties of the Communist delegations at the hands of the Saigon government.

The DRV threat to halt the release of the US prisoners brought the angry retort from the United States that the agreement did not link the release of prisoners with any other part of the agreement, except withdrawal of American and other foreign troops.[19] But despite its demand that the prisoner release continue without any conditions, the United States was compelled to make at least a show of responding to the Communist complaints concerning Saigon's failure to observe the cease-fire and its treatment of DRV and PRG delegations. The US delegation to the JMC made it clear to Saigon that it had to halt all incidents of violence against the DRV and PRG personnel.

General Woodward also assured General Tra that the United

States would insure against any future RVN attacks on PRG personnel at the pickup points by occupying them with Four-Party JMC personnel before and during the pickup.[20] But by this time the PRG had decided that the JMC was not a very good investment of manpower. Since the United States had used its leverage over Saigon only after the threat to delay releasing American prisoners, they may well have feared the eventual capture of their officers by Saigon at the field sites. General Tra did not respond to Woodward's offer.

On the problems of living and working conditions at the DRV and PRG compounds and freedom of movement, Woodward pressed Saigon to make some concessions to demands for fulfillment of the privileges and immunities clause of the agreement. "We emphasize that they should have at least some access to the press, and that they had the right to meet individuals and leave the compound," said a member of the US delegation later.

But while trying to meet the Communist demands sufficiently to avoid a complete breakdown of the agreement's machinery, the United States also shared Saigon's interest in keeping the PRG delegates under control and out of sight as much as possible. The US delegation told the Communist delegations that complete freedom of movement was unrealistic because of the need to provide security, citing the incidents at Banmethuot and Hue to support the argument. For a few weeks, the United States actually acted as a "broker," as one official put it, trying to find a compromise between the two sides. "It was a matter of degree," he said. "We wanted a little more freedom, but not going as far as the DRV wanted. We were interested in the privileges and immunities question only because it was a roadblock to the prisoner release."

The JMC's Subcommission on Procedures received eighteen specific demands from the DRV delegation concerning Saigon's treatment of the DRV and PRG delegations immediately after the Hue and Danang incidents. The United States prevailed on the RVN representative to accept some of them, modified others, and rejected some of them completely, and after two weeks of negotiation, on March 19 the Four-Party JMC agreed for the first time on a number of policies to guide the implementation of the protocol.[21]

The text of the agreement reached on March 19 contained eight points, six of which dealt with the "privileges and immunities" of the delegations.[22] It obligated each party "in its area of control" to "do its utmost to ensure maximum safety" for JMC personnel. The delegations were authorized to "contact diplomatic agencies, local authorities, suppliers, medical organizations and transportation companies." The problem of access to the press was to be discussed by press officers of the four delegations, who ultimately agreed to allow the PRG to have a weekly press conference at its quarters at Tansonnhut. Meanwhile the United States took steps to improve the physical facilities occupied by the DRV and PRG delegations.[23]

But the March 19 agreement brought little change in practice in Saigon's treatment of the DRV and PRG delegates, who were still in virtual detention, surrounded by armed guards, floodlights, and barbed wire, invisible to the South Vietnamese people. And the PRG, knowing that the Americans had forced a temporary compromise on Saigon in March only in order to obtain the release of its own prisoners, were not even confident that their physical safety would be protected. There was no move by the PRG to resume the deployment of their personnel to the JMC sites. At the end of March, General Tra told Woodward that he needed to visit Hanoi for liaison purposes, but he never returned to Saigon. Woodward told aides that he thought Tra had come to Saigon in the belief that the PRG would have at least a visible presence in the Saigon zone, and had become disillusioned with the JMC.

The stalemate in the establishment of the JMC in the field ruled out any role by the Commission in investigating local violations or resolving local disputes. Neither side requested a JMC investigation of an alleged truce violation until the PRG asked the Commission to investigate the situation at Sa Huynh on February 19. The Four-Party JMC agreed to send a delegation to Danang to determine how the investigation should be carried out.[24] But before the delegation arrived, the tide of battle unexpectedly turned, and Saigon succeeded in reoccupying the town. The PRG no longer wanted an investigation then, since it would have confirmed Saigon's control over the town. The PRG and DRV delegations, by raising procedural questions, delayed the start of the investigation for two days.[25] Then on February 22, the United States and RVN broke off the discussions and their delegates left Danang by helicopter for Duc Pho district town without the Communist delegations. From there they drove in twelve cars, including those with the PRG and DRV flags, to Sa Huynh, where they carried out their own investigations.[26] The Communist delegations naturally refused to accept the results.

The Four-Party JMC was equally unsuccessful in getting compliance with the other provisions of the cease-fire agreement. Early in February, after several days of continued fighting, the Commission began discussing how to make the cease-fire effective. The DRV and PRG delegations proposed at the JMC meeting on February 5 that the four parties appeal to the commanders-in-chief of the two South Vietnamese armies to meet to discuss measures to bring about a "temporary cessation of hostilities," and that the cease-fire order be transmitted to all units by loudspeaker, radio, and other means of communication.[27] This proposal was rejected by Saigon, which argued, according to US sources, that the means of communicating the cease-fire should be left up to the parties. The Communist delegations also proposed that the appeal include repetition of Article 4 of the protocol on the cease-fire, calling on commanders of opposing forces in direct contact to meet in order to "reach agreement on temporary measures to avert conflict and to insure supply and medical care for these armed forces." [28] Thieu was afraid that contacts between local unit commanders would bring about local accommodations, with the result that the PRG would claim that Saigon had recognized its zone of control. He had ordered all unit commanders to refuse such meetings.[29] The US position, according to one US official close to the negotiations, was that it did not object to the PRG/DRV proposal, but it was not prepared to force Saigon to accept it. The result, as indicated in the previous chapter, was that the February 16 cease-fire appeal had no effect on Saigon's offensive operations.

With the expiration of the sixty-day period, the Two-Party JMC was supposed to take full responsibility for maintaining the cease-fire. The DRV, fearing that the United States and Saigon would try to avoid the establishment of the Two-Party JMC, had succeeded in obtaining language in the protocol providing that the delegations of the two South Vietnamese parties to the Four-Party JMC would also assume the functions of the Two-Party JMC at all levels. The two South Vietnamese parties were to come to agreement as soon as possible on the organization and operation of the Two-Party JMC. The two South Vietnamese delegations would continue to function as a provisional Two-Party JMC until an agreement was reached. But the Saigon government's attitude of total hostility toward the presence of PRG delegates within its zone, and its determination to deny the PRG the status of a coequal party under the agreement, meant that even this provisional Two-Party JMC could operate only in the most limited fashion.

In addition to the tasks which it inherited from the Four-Party JMC, the Two-Party JMC had one responsibility on which the possibility of a stable cease-fire rested: the demarcation of zones of control between the PRG and the RVN, as called for in Article 3(b) of the agreement. Like the National Council and the JMCs, this touched the political sensitivities of the Thieu regime, for recognition of a PRG zone of control would be used as evidence of its sovereignty as a government. Thieu had insisted that the United States avoid any implication of PRG sovereignty in Article 3 by demanding that the demarcation of zones be based solely on the size and deployment of military forces of the South Vietnamese parties. The DRV had rejected the proposal and the United States finally dropped it. But when the PRG and RVN met early in February to discuss the demarcation of zones of control, the chief of the Saigon delegation, General Ngo Dzu, again demanded that the PRG submit a list of all its military units, their size, commanders, and locations. When General Tran Van Tra pointed out that PLAF units had never occupied fixed points like those of the ARVN, Dzu said there would be no demarcation of zones of control.[30]

Saigon's position was that it would recognize only a perimeter of control around fixed military installations, in keeping with its argument that the PRG "controls neither territory nor population except for its zones of stationing of troops."[31] Robert T. Walkinshaw, US Consul-General in Bien Hoa after the cease-fire agreement, recalled later, "As far as the RVN was concerned, the VC owned no property in the Third Military Region," and added that he would "never agree" that the PRG "controlled territory."[32] Saigon's refusal to recognize the reality of a PRG zone went so far that, when the PRG chose sites for the return of prisoners, Saigon complained that it had "selected various return sites in the zone under temporary Communist occupation with a view to deceiving the RVN into tacitly recognizing its zone of control." [33]

Although Thieu refused to recognize the existence of PRG-controlled territory, the State Department had colored maps prepared in 1973 which showed an approximation of the de facto zones of control of each of the two parties. The maps, one of which was shown to the author by a State Department official in 1974, showed that the PRG was conceded significant territory in all four military zones. The official said, in fact, that the map did not differ in any major way from a rough map of the PRG zone which was published in the DRV magazine *Vietnam Courier* (see map, p. ii).

As long as Saigon refused to recognize that a PRG zone existed, it had a pretext for encroaching on contested and PRG areas, arguing that it was merely "consolidating its control" over its own zone or contested areas. The refusal to delineate zones of control was thus the crucial indicator of Saigon's preference for an ambiguous continuation of the fighting rather than for a cease-fire with stable, mutually recognized demarcation lines.

In June 1973 Kissinger, his ability to credibly threaten intervention in Vietnam much reduced, met in Paris with Le Duc Tho. While Kissinger pressed Tho for agreement by the Two-Party JMC on the supervision of replacements of military supplies, Tho pushed hard for strict enforcement of the cease-fire and the demarcation of zones of control. And in an effort to escape from the captivity of Saigon's military camps, he demanded the relocation of the Two-Party JMC headquarters at all levels. After a full week of discussions, during which cable traffic between Washington, Paris, and Saigon was reported to be very intense, an agreement was finally produced on June 13 which marked only slight progress, and left the main issues of implementation still unresolved.[34]

The United States agreed not only to new cease-fire orders but to a paragraph directing the commanders of military units at "places of direct contact" to meet within twenty-four hours of a new cease-fire deadline in order to arrange a local cease-fire—one of the Communist demands from the start. It agreed to the demand that the PRG delegation to the Two-Party JMC be given more dignity and status by liberating it from the prison-like atmosphere of its barracks at Tansonnhut and elsewhere. "The headquarters of the central Two-Party Joint Military Commission shall be located in Saigon proper or at a place agreed upon by the two South Vietnamese parties where an area controlled by one of them adjoins an area controlled by the other," the communiqué said. Similarly, regional and local JMC headquarters were to be located at sites agreed to by the PRG either in the towns named in the original protocol or in places between the two parties' zones of control.

Kissinger was reportedly ready to make some concessions to the DRV on the demarcation of zones of control, but Thieu warned that he would not sign or be bound by any agreement between the United States and the DRV which compromised his position on the issue.[35] The final communiqué, also signed by the PRG and RVN, simply called upon the Two-Party JMC to determine the areas controlled by the South Vietnamese parties and the modalities of stationing "as soon as possible." It also directed the Two-Party commission to discuss "movements necessary to accomplish a return of the armed forces of the two South Vietnamese parties to the positions they occupied at the time the cease-fire entered into force. . . ."

The June 13 communiqué did not mark any change in the attitude of the Saigon government toward the cease-fire or the JMC, and the new agreement quickly broke down. No new orders were transmitted to ARVN troops, and Saigon was still unwilling even to have local commanders meet.[36] The provisions for negotiation of the locations of the JMCs were quickly stalled when Saigon refused to agree to move the JMC headquarters either into Saigon or to a location between the PRG zone and the Saigon zone.

Although the Kissinger-Tho meetings had aimed at preventing the JMC and the cease-fire itself from becoming a dead letter, Saigon's strategy had been from the beginning to let them die a slow death. By refusing to agree to relocation of the JMC headquarters, it was well on its way to achieving that goal. The last substantive discussions on the issues of privilege and immunities, the cease-fire, demarcation of zones, and periodic replacement of military supplies took place in August 1973, after which, US officials say, the two South Vietnamese parties stopped negotiating with each other.

2.   *The Irrelevance of International Supervision: The ICCS*

By his emphasis in both October and December press conferences on the importance of insuring that an effective international supervisory body would be in place when the cease-fire took effect, Henry Kissinger had contributed to the popular impression that the ICCS was crucial to successful implementation of the cease-fire. In fact, however, none of the parties to the agreement had any illusion that the International Commission of Control and Supervision would have anything but a marginal influence on the cease-fire and other military provisions of the agreement. The final agreement did not achieve what Kissinger had promised, for the ICCS could not expect to be deployed to its field locations for two weeks, during which time the cease-fire lines of January 28 would be shattered in hundreds of places throughout the country.

Thieu heaped scorn on the ICCS before the agreement was even signed, calling it "useless and helpless," [37] and had no intention of stopping his own military operations just because of the possibility of ICCS investigations. The DRV and PRG hoped that ICCS teams would visit PRG villages and recognize them as part of the PRG zone. Communist cadres carefully prepared villagers for such visits, in an apparent misunderstanding of how the supervisory body would function.[38] But the Party leadership had no faith that the ICCS would restrain Thieu militarily.

Cynicism about the capability of an international supervisory body in Vietnam to prevent cease-fire violations was well founded. The experience of the old International Control Commission set up by the Geneva Agreement of 1954 had shown clearly that "peace observation" missions, as opposed to real "peacekeeping" missions, were capable of insuring the implementation only of those aspects of the peace agreement which both sides clearly wanted to have implemented, such as regroupment and exchange of prisoners, and not those which one or more parties had no interest in implementing, such as the ban on reprisals in the South, and the ban on introduction of armaments in both zones.[39]

Despite the Geneva Agreement's provision for freedom of movement for the ICC, the Diem regime had simply refused to permit any investigations when it did not wish to expose its violations, and the DRV did the same in order to keep secret the extent of its own rearmament after the agreement. The ICC's failure to prevent renewed warfare was not the result of failure to accuse either side of violating the agreement. But since the Commission had been unable to ensure the implementation of the political provisions for elections and a ban on reprisals, the Lao Dong Party had ultimately supported the use of armed force in the South, in spite of any legal objections by a majority of the Commission's members. The United States likewise simply ignored the ICC conclusion that it was violating the Geneva Agreement by setting up a military command and bringing massive amounts of new weapons into South Vietnam.

In view of the low respect which all parties had for any international supervisory body, there was no chance that the new ICCS could compel an unwilling party to comply with the Paris Agreement by the threat of finding and reporting violations. Because of the complexity of the cease-fire, moreover, the determination of specific violations would not be as simple as it had been after Geneva.

The Paris Agreement itself had implicitly recognized the irrelevance of the ICCS in the enforcement of the cease-fire. It was not expected to make definitive judgments against either side, as was suggested by the composition of the new body. It abandoned the troika format of the old commission, which had represented an effort at impartiality with its "neutral" chairman, India. The new commission was frankly bipartisan, with Hungary and Poland sympathetic to the Communist side, and Canada and Indonesia sympathetic to the United States and Saigon. The ideological cleavage within the ICCS, combined with the unanimity rule, insured that there would be few investigations on which the ICCS did not submit equally divided opinions.

The United States clearly viewed the ICCS not as an instrument for enforcing the cease-fire but as a means of influencing the American public. It built its ICCS strategy around the prospects of getting wide publicity for the views of the anti-Communist members of the Commission, who could submit "different views" to be forwarded to the JMC when the ICCS could not reach unanimous agreement. The key to this strategy was the knowledge that Canada would be the dominant member of the Commission by virtue of its ability to publicize its views through the media. Washington took no chances in its efforts to enlist Canada's participation in the Commission, even going so far in November 1972 as to tell Canada that the other three members of the ICCS had already accepted, and that the agreement could collapse unless the Canadians accepted membership, all of which it knew to be untrue.[40]

Canada's carefully cultivated image of impartiality and fairness, which was an asset for the United States and Saigon in terms of world opinion—particularly American opinion—concealed a firm commitment to the Saigon regime's survival. Having been chosen as the representative of Saigon's interests in the first ICC, Canada had tried to reconcile this role with scrupulous fairness in judging the facts in any particular investigation.[41] For the most part, its findings of fact in particular investigations had been fair enough. But the Canadian understanding of the origins and character of the conflict derived from the same perceptions as that of the United States. The Canadians, like the Americans, blamed the war on the Vietnamese revolutionaries, rather than on Western military and political intervention in the Vietnamese revolution.

The official line of the Canadian Ministry of External Affairs had always been that the division of Vietnam was merely the natural result of a conflict between the anti-Communist Vietnamese "community" and the Communist Viet Minh, and that the role of the French and the Americans was somehow merely incidental.[42] Canada made no secret of its belief that the division of Vietnam was necessary to maintain peace, and that any negotiated settlement should be based on a progressive reapplication of the Geneva Agreement's cease-fire terms—but not its political terms.[43]

Canada needed no coaching from the United States, therefore, when its ICCS contingent arrived on the scene at the end of January. The chief of the Canadian delegation, Ambassador Michel Gauvin, a veteran of the first ICC delegation in 1954–55, was well known as an anti-Communist zealot, particularly with regard to the DRV. He immediately adopted what was called an "open-mouth" policy, which was supposed to mean that the commission's business would be made known to the rest of the world. But Gauvin's favorite theme was the presence in the South of North Vietnamese troops, which he referred to as "foreign troops" —a term which even the United States eschewed after the agreement. He did not hesitate to criticize the agreement itself for

failing to call for the removal of Northerners from the South.[44]
Unencumbered by having to defend an agreement negotiated by
the United States, the Canadians could thus be even more partisan
in their support of Saigon's views than the Americans.

On one occasion the extreme hostility of the Canadian delegation toward the DRV and PRG caused it to go so far in accusing
the Communists of bad faith as to appear somewhat ridiculous. It
began with the flight of two helicopters carrying an ICCS team of
eleven persons, including two PRG liaison officers, from Hue to Gio
Linh and Lao Bao, the sites of two ICCS border posts, on the
morning of April 7. The four-kilometer-wide flight corridor over the
PRG zone was chosen by PRG local authorities to follow Route 9
all the way to Lao Bao. But the helicopters, guided by a PRG
liaison officer who had little or no experience navigating from a
helicopter, strayed from Route 9 to follow a new road not found on
any maps.

PRG authorities were extremely sensitive about intrusions on
their air space, particularly in this area, which was on the edge of
the Khe Sanh plateau, where the major PLAF logistics center was
located. This concern had been heightened by the fact that the
Saigon government had been carrying out commando operations in
the area, while the United States was known to be taking aerial
photographs of it.* The helicopters were fifteen miles off course
when they were fired on by PLAF troops. One was hit by a
heat-seeking missile and crashed in the jungle, killing all nine men
aboard. The other landed safely and the survivors were taken to a
nearby construction camp.[45]

Before a thorough investigation of the helicopter incident had
even begun, the Canadian delegation categorically rejected the
PRG account of the incident, claiming that the helicopters were
definitely in their flight corridor when forced down.[46] When the

* Complicating the problem of air corridors still further was Saigon's use of helicopters
with ICCS and JMC markings for reconnaissance and military missions. The PRG
complained in mid-April that an aircraft with ICCS markings had been flying from Pleiku
every day with no apparent ICCS mission. (Los Angeles Times, April 15, 1973.) They also
charged that a helicopter bearing JMC markings had strafed the PRG zone in Chau Tranh
district, Kien Tuong province. (Liberation Radio, March 16, 1973.) These charges were lent
credence when an ICCS regional team from Can Tho found a Saigon government helicopter
with "vestigial ICCS markings" at the airfield in Vi Thanh, Choung Thien province.
According to an ICCS source, the ICCS team wrote a letter of protest on April 28 to the
RVN, saying that these markings endangered the safety of ICCS personnel.

ICCS carried out its own on-the-spot investigation, it discovered that the PRG had been right: the helicopters had been fifteen miles away from the prescribed flight corridor when they went down.[47]

Instead of admitting a mistake, however, Ambassador Gauvin used the incident to launch a renewed attack on the legality of North Vietnamese troops in the South. There was a "reasonable possibility," he said on April 13, that the helicopter had been shot down by "troops whose presence in South Vietnam is not provided for in the Paris Agreement." This formula attempted to turn the agreement's tacit acceptance of their presence into a condemnation of it. Gauvin went on to assert that it was "evident that the self-determination of South Vietnam cannot be expressed if outsiders take sides in support of one South Vietnamese party against the other."[48]

US Embassy officials then tried to discredit the ICCS investigation by insisting that they had information that the Communists had moved the wreckage of the ill-fated helicopter, using a huge Soviet "hook" helicopter, in order to support the PRG claim that it was off course. Gauvin declared that it was "not beyond the realm of possibility."[49] And even after a second investigation by the ICCS showed that the helicopter could not possibly have been moved, the Canadian delegation still refused to sign the report, which had been endorsed by the other three members of the Commission. Instead Canada insisted that the ICCS condemn the PRG for a formal violation of the truce agreement if it refused to grant five-mile-wide air corridors for ICCS helicopters.[50] The agreement had said nothing about the width of air corridors, of course, and the PRG, which agreed to increase the corridors from two and one half to three miles, said that it could not adequately man and supervise more than that.[51] Only late in May, after the incident had ceased to be newsworthy, did the Canadian delegation quietly agree to a report stating that the helicopter had been off course.[52]

In contrast to the flamboyant Canadian style of sensational charges and intense courting of the Western press, the other members of the Commission seemed uninterested in making the ICCS a forum for propaganda attacks. Despite their obvious role in protecting the interests of the DRV and PRG within the Commission, Poland and Hungary made no effort to issue press statements amplifying DRV and PRG charges of US-Saigon violations. They preferred to play a more defensive role, insuring that the Commission's machinery would not be used against the DRV and PRG in other ways. They did not hesitate to use their "different views" within the Commission to back up PRG and DRV charges, as when they filed a final opinion concerning the ICCS helicopter incident which hinted that CIA-chartered pilots had deliberately flown off course to use the mission to gather intelligence on the PRG zone.[53] But they realized, perhaps, that they could not hope to compete with Canada in press relations, so they didn't try.

The Indonesians were even less inclined to make propaganda statements, despite their basic alignment with the United States and Saigon. Although the Indonesian military delegation was made up mostly of officers who had participated in the 1965 massacre of suspected Indonesian Communist sympathizers, the diplomats on the delegation preferred to avoid public confrontation and deplored the Canadian style of diplomatic grandstanding.[54] The chief of the Indonesian delegation even took issue with the Canadian effort to portray the Commission as always split into two blocs, with Poland and Hungary on one side and Canada and Indonesia on the other. The Indonesian delegation, he pointed out in a press conference in late April 1973, had often voted with Hungary and Poland against Canada.[55]

The ICCS was divided into two hostile blocs, however, over the question of what could be investigated and whether or not the Commission would operate on the basis of unanimity. In two test cases, the Canadians were blocked by the Communist delegations from establishing the precedent that investigations could be carried out whenever requested by one of the parties, regardless of opposition from one or more members of the ICCS.

The United States and Saigon called for an ICCS investigation on February 26, charging that the North Vietnamese had committed a "blatant violation" of the cease-fire by setting up three SAM-2 sites near what had once been the US Marine base at Khe Sanh, which had been under Communist control since the start of the 1972 spring offensive. Saigon's representative to the JMC produced aerial photographs showing the Khe Sanh area on January 24, three days before the cease-fire, and again on February 18, to show that the missiles had not been present before the cease-fire. He charged a violation of the ban in Article 7 on the introduction of weapons into South Vietnam except to replace those used up or destroyed. The DRV did not deny that there were SAMs at Khe Sanh but pointed out that they had had SAM-2 batteries in Quang Tri province for some time before the cease-fire.[56]

At the ICCS meeting on February 28, Canada argued that the Commission had to carry out an investigation, because the agreement called for it to investigate at the request of any of the parties. But Poland and Hungary refused, arguing that there were "inadequate grounds" for such a request.[57] They noted that no evidence had been presented that the missiles were not already present in the South at the time of the agreement. (In fact, North Vietnamese troops had used SAM-2s in large numbers below the Demilitarized Zone during the early phase of the 1972 offensive, reportedly firing some 800 missiles at US and Saigon planes.)[58] And in any case, an investigation at Khe Sanh obviously would not prove that the missiles had been brought into the South after the cease-fire.

From the DRV and PRG viewpoint, then, the US and Saigon request for an investigation of the Khe Sanh missiles was nothing more than a bid to go on an intelligence expedition into the most sensitive military area of the PRG zone. The PLAF command was just beginning to transform Khe Sanh into a major logistics complex, the first major Communist military base in South Vietnam which was not camouflaged deep in the jungle. The DRV had insisted on the unanimity rule within the ICCS to prevent just this kind of use of the body for intelligence purposes.

The United States knew, of course, that there would be no investigation by the ICCS deep in PRG territory at Khe Sanh, and it actually had no idea whether or not the missiles had been brought into the South after the cease-fire, as was noted later by columnists Evans and Novak.[59] The threat by General Woodward to take "such actions as [the United States] deems appropriate" if the missiles were not removed was aimed at putting pressure on the North Vietnamese, and the request to the ICCS for an investigation was merely an adjunct to that move.

Although the ICCS was blocked from carrying out the investigation, Canada's vocal criticism of the Communist delegations on the ICCS for voting against it effectively reinforced the impression in the United States that the Communists were paralyzing the truce enforcement mechanism in order to cover a massive violation of the agreement.

A second major rift within the Commission between Communist and anti-Communist members began in early May over the interrogation of North Vietnamese prisoners by Canadian and Indonesian regional delegations in Can Tho. The RVN had presented the prisoners to the ICCS in support of their charges that North Vietnamese were infiltrating into the South after the cease-fire. The Polish and Hungarian delegates at Can Tho refused to participate in the interrogation without approval from their delegations in Saigon, but the Canadians proceeded immediately to question the prisoners anyway, along with the Indonesians.[60] They were trying, in effect, to force the repeal of the unanimity rule which had been applied up to that time, by acting without Polish and Hungarian concurrence.

The Canadian delegation had been eager to document North Vietnamese infiltration ever since its arrival in Saigon. External Affairs Minister Mitchell Sharp, on returning from a trip to Vietnam in March, had declared that Canada wanted the ICCS to act to confirm the reports from US and Saigon intelligence of such infiltration even though he admitted that the ICCS had not been asked to observe or given permission to observe the reported infiltration.[61] So they leaped at the opportunity to prove the point when the prisoners were offered to them by Saigon.

Reports on the Canadian and Indonesian interrogation, which suggested that some North Vietnamese had come into the South after the cease-fire, were quickly leaked to the Western press.[62] But the Polish chairman of the ICCS refused to forward the reports, which the Canadian delegation insisted were "different views," as ICCS documents, arguing that the investigation was never authorized and that it exceeded the mandate of the Paris Agreement. Canada replied again that the Commission had a "mandatory obligation" to carry out investigations, and that the unanimity rule therefore did not apply. Canada, supported by Indonesia, threatened to walk out of the Central ICCS meetings and bring all business to a halt unless the documents were accepted as "different views" and forwarded.[63]

When Canada again became Chairman of the Commission on

June 1, Gauvin announced that he would hold no further meetings until the Communist delegations agreed to this demand.[64] The Canadians were thus saying, in effect, that the Commission would have to throw out the unanimity rule or there would be no Central ICCS, at least for the month of June. The deadlock did indeed close down the ICCS in Saigon for the entire month. According to a Canadian official, the PRG delegation to the JMC made it clear to the Canadians that it was unhappy that the ICCS was being deadlocked, suggesting that it still believed it had more to gain than to lose by the operation of the Commission.

By this time, however, Canada had already announced that it was going to leave the Commission at the end of July, so there was no reason for the Communist delegations to permit it to establish a precedent allowing unilateral investigations. Moreover, Indonesia began to dissociate itself from the Canadian position. The Indonesian Department of Foreign Affairs issued a statement denying that Indonesian delegates in the regional or subregional headquarters had been authorized to participate in any investigation initiated by the Canadian delegation.[65]

By the end of June, Canada was ready to give up the fight. "The Canadian government decided it didn't want to leave the Commission in a deadlock," said one Canadian official later. "The only way we could see to break it was to take unilateral action." So Gauvin called a meeting on the last day of June and announced he was unilaterally forwarding the "different views" on two reports concerning North Vietnamese prisoners to the JMC. In the guise of an arbitrary action, Canada was backing down, for it had been unable to force the rejection of the unanimity rule. The Poles and Hungarians objected to the move, and the Indonesians dissociated themselves from it. "In fact," says the Canadian official, "I think they were privately relieved."

The single most important obstacle to the full functioning of the ICCS was the fact that the PRG delegates to the Four-Party JMC had not been deployed to regional and local sites, because of the RVN's openly hostile actions against them. The PRG did send a delegation to the Region VI Four-Party JMC headquarters in Can Tho, but it warned immediately that, until the problems of security and diplomatic privileges and immunities were resolved, it would take no actions except for "securing accommodations" for its people. The Polish and Hungarian members of the ICCS in Region VI took the position that investigations could not be carried out without liaison officers and written guarantees of safety from the four parties, thus blocking ICCS action until the PRG delegation to the JMC had become fully operational.[66] The PRG was clearly determined that the status of its delegates be clarified before agreeing to give full cooperation to ICCS investigations.

In keeping with its position, the PRG delegation in Can Tho made no requests for investigations of Saigon truce violations for some weeks. During the first two months of the agreement, all of the twenty-one requests for investigations in Region VI came from the RVN. (The PRG did, however, inform the ICCS of alleged RVN cease-fire violations in the Region.)[67] Later, the PRG decided that it could not afford to let Saigon monopolize the ICCS investigative function and did begin initiating requests. By the end of May 1973, the PRG had made ten requests for investigation from the field.[68]

According to figures provided by the Polish delegation in July 1973, the RVN had made 924 requests for investigations through June, while the PRG had made eighty-five.[69] But while no statistical breakdown on the nature of the requests from each side was available, a Canadian source in the ICCS confirmed that virtually all of Saigon's complaints concerned individual cases of shelling, mining, or assassinations, while most of the PRG complaints charged "nibbling operations," that is, military operations aimed at taking control of an entire area, whether formerly contested or in the PRG zone. In the Can Tho region, for example, Saigon's six requests to the ICCS for investigation up to March 9 all involved acts of sabotage or shelling rather than movements of the PLAF on the ground.[70] The nature of the complaints submitted by the two sides therefore, provided a significant indication of the difference in their military policies.

The problem of finding violations of the cease-fire was obviously quite different, depending on whether it was requested by the RVN or the PRG. In the case of Saigon-requested investigations, it was usually easy enough for investigators to conclude that a shell or mine had exploded, but an inference usually had to be made that it was caused by the PRG. Local Saigon government officials, eager to prove their case, often went so far as to place the tail fins of Communist mortar shells in the shell holes, which looked impressive but was an obvious trick.[71] The Hungarians and Poles routinely refused to accept the inference that the shell or mine was caused by the PRG, thus insuring that there would be no "reports" from the ICCS accusing the PRG of cease-fire violations.[72]

The Canadians, on the other hand, went to the opposite extreme of assuming PRG responsibility for every bomb, grenade, or mine which exploded, even when there was no positive evidence of it and substantial grounds for doubt. In a bizarre case involving a Cao Daist who was killed by a bomb hidden in some meat which he had bought at a market, the Canadian and Indonesian delegations in Can Tho were able to conclude that the PRG had assassinated the man, basing their decision on nothing more than the uninformed assumption that the PRG wished to kill Cao Daists.[73] The report on the investigation of Saigon's charge, written by the Canadian delegation, declared that the victim "fell within the scope of the PRG political assassination program . . . not only because he was a Cao Daist but also because his assassination can be presumed to be a part of the PRG effort to weaken the natural leadership class and social fabric of an RVN-controlled community." Since the investigation had produced absolutely no evidence of Communist hostility to the Cao Daist, this conclusion was based completely on the Canadian government's distorted view of the Vietnamese Communist movement's doctrines and mode of operations, acquired from two decades of reliance on official French, American, and anti-Communist Vietnamese sources of information and analysis. In fact, the NLF and PRG had never targeted leaders of religious groups for assassination in order to weaken the "social fabric" or "natural leadership class" of the "RVN-controlled community." On the contrary, Communist policy had been most careful to maintain a correct, if not cordial, attitude toward religious figures. This report, presented by the Canadian team in Can Tho as a "typical" ICCS investigation of an assassination complaint, showed how the Canadian hostility to the Communists colored its investigations.

Since most PRG complaints to the Commission involved Saigon's land-grabbing operations, it faced an entirely different sort of problem in proving Saigon's violations: once Saigon had succeeded in taking control of a particular area, it was a simple matter to arrange for witnesses to testify to the Commission that the

RVN had controlled the area at the time of the cease-fire. This difficulty was illustrated by the ICCS investigation in Sa Huynh, which the PRG had requested when it still held the town but lost interest in when Saigon recaptured it.

When the investigating team arrived in Sa Huynh they received written statements from fourteen villagers, all supporting the story presented by the District Chief that Saigon troops had held on to the town until January 29 before the Communists captured it. All of the statements, prepared in advance, were on paper apparently taken from the same note pad and were quite similar in form. The Canadian delegation was obviously not convinced, but it chose to call it a case of inadequate evidence. "It's clear there were violations," said one of the Canadian members in Sa Huynh, "but on which side it is difficult to say, when we cannot contact the other side." [74] No villager, of course, was likely to expose himself to reprisals by telling the ICCS anything which contradicted the official RVN account. So the report of the investigation was bound to be inconclusive. The Hungarians and Poles insisted on a statement pointing out that the investigation was incomplete, since only one side of the story had been heard. The Canadians argued that it should be forwarded to the JMC without comment. In the end, "different views" were forwarded to the JMC rather than a single report.[75]

The PRG also failed to get a unanimous finding of a violation when it charged that US planes had bombed the town of Loc Ninh in early May. The ICCS team talked to several seriously wounded Loc Ninh residents and to the doctor who treated them, all of whom testified that a US swing-wing jet had strafed the main street of the town on May 12.[76] The Canadian delegation again called the evidence "inconclusive." They also objected so strongly to a friendly crowd of villagers who held signs protesting the air attacks and applauding the arrival of the ICCS that they threatened not to carry on any further investigation there unless they could do so "free from political propaganda and harassment." [77]

Apart from the difficulty of getting the Canadian and Indonesian delegations, who leaned over backward to protect Saigon and the United States nearly as much as the Poles and Hungarians did for their allies, to agree that its charges were accurate, the PRG's requests for investigations were frequently blocked either by

Saigon's refusal to permit them or by difficulties of transportation into the PRG zone. At the end of May, for example, the PRG asked the ICCS to investigate its charge that the RVN had built new military posts in territory which the PRG had controlled for years along Route 2 between Xuan Loc and Vung Tau. The Saigon government, which had complained that Communist forces were mortaring its outposts as well as the barracks which it had built for the troops who manned them and their families, for once agreed to the investigation. But after the ICCS regional team and two PRG liaison officers had assembled at Xuan Loc to begin the investigation, an ARVN colonel told them that his government could not assure their safety. And when they tried again the next day, they were told that the RVN would not be able to assure their safety at any time in the future to carry out the investigation. The investigation had to be called off.[78]

In other cases, where the PRG requested investigations to take place in territory which it still controlled, the ICCS could only reach the area by helicopter and demanded a five-mile-wide air corridor. The PRG, which had offered a three-mile-wide corridor, said that it could not adequately supervise a wider one because of the problem of communicating with all of its armed personnel in a short time. According to one report, "dozens" of investigations requested by the PRG in April and May were blocked by this problem.[79] Only in the case of US bombing at Loc Ninh did the PRG decide that the investigation was so important that it changed its position on the width of the air corridor.

Given these political and physical realities of the Commission's investigative role, it is not surprising that, of the seventy-nine investigations ordered by the ICCS during its first two months of operation, only nineteen were actually completed, most of which were of RVN complaints, and that not a single unanimous report on a cease-fire violation had been forwarded to the JMC.[80] More surprising is the fact that by the end of July, when Canada left the Commission to be replaced by Iran, the two anti-Communist delegations had agreed on ten occasions that Saigon had violated the cease-fire.[81]

But the results of the ICCS investigations, which were on the whole inconclusive and, in any case, were never published, had no influence on the policies of either side. The publicizing by Canada of US and RVN charges concerning North Vietnamese infiltration and missiles at Khe Sanh had far more political impact on the situation than all of the investigations combined, since it helped shape American public and Congressional views of who was violating the cease-fire. For the United States and Saigon it was a triumph of public relations over the legal and political realities of the Commission's operations.

3. *US Obligations and the Paris Agreement: Withdrawal,
Mine Deactivation, and Postwar Aid*

Apart from its general responsibilities within the Four-Party JMC to investigate truce violations and resolve problems relating to the cease-fire and truce machinery, a number of provisions in the agreement obligated the United States to carry out specific actions relating to its long and heavy military involvement in Vietnam: the withdrawal of its troops, bases, and war material, the deactivation of mines in North Vietnam, and the negotiation of an agreement with the DRV to provide postwar reconstruction assistance.

The provisions of the agreement relating to the withdrawal of US troops and war material and the dismantling of American bases in South Vietnam were to be implemented within the framework of the Four-Party JMC and under the supervision of the ICCS. The agreement obligated the United States to provide the JMC and the ICCS with "general plans" for the troop withdrawal, and with "necessary information" on plans for base dismantlement.

But when the Four-Party JMC met for the first time, the DRV and PRG were still in the dark as to US plans for dismantling its extensive system of bases around the country, and it was one of the first things that the Communist delegations asked about. They were shocked when General Woodward announced that the United States had no bases to dismantle or equipment to withdraw, because they had all been turned over to Saigon already. "General Tra seemed to be genuinely surprised," said an American official.*

---

* Despite the fact that the American negotiators in Paris had kept the DRV ignorant of US plans for evading the language of Articles 5 and 6, Kissinger and Sullivan informed General Woodward, who was also in Paris in January, that the DRV understood that the United States intended to turn over legal title to all the bases and equipment before the agreement was signed. The US delegation therefore used Tra's obvious surprise to "imply that the North Vietnamese had not informed them of the understanding in Paris," according to an American source close to the JMC.

No public announcement had been made as the United States quietly and methodically transferred the title on not only all the bases but most of the equipment on them to the Saigon government and then had them officially "loaned back" to the United States. This process continued throughout January, according to a knowledgeable US source, even as the protocol itself was being negotiated. As far as the rest of the world knew, the bases were still in American hands when the agreement was signed on January 25.

The DRV and PRG naturally regarded this as a trick to evade Article 6. Even weeks after the United States announced that it no longer had any bases to dismantle, it was still manifestly in control of major bases such as Tansonnhut Air Base. "We come out of our quarters here at Tansonnhut every day and we see nothing but Americans at 7th Air Force Headquarters and it's a cynical argument to say it's a Vietnamese base," a DRV official remarked bitterly. The DRV complained to the ICCS, but the Canadians defended the US position, arguing that the ICCS could only deal with "possible breaches of the cease-fire committed after January 28." [82] So there was little the DRV could do about the American maneuver except to threaten to discontinue its own implementation of the agreement, and this the DRV was reluctant to do.

The United States also stirred opposition not only from the DRV but from the ICCS as well by its failure to provide sufficient information to either the JMC or the ICCS to permit control of the withdrawal of its troops and equipment. In response to an inquiry from the ICCS, General Woodward took the position that the US obligation was fulfilled by providing a general schedule of withdrawals and statistics on withdrawals already carried out, and that no "direct involvement" of either the JMC or ICCS was necessary.[83] In other words, the United States, which had always sought strong international enforcement and inspection as part of the agreement, refused to have any inspection by either control body of its own withdrawal. This position was clearly contradicted by the language of Article 16, which refers to "ensuring joint action" within the Four-Party JMC in implementing the withdrawal provisions, and of Article 18, which refers to the "control and supervision" of those withdrawals by the ICCS.

Even the Canadians were shocked by this attitude. They pointed out to General Woodward that the ICCS had the right under the agreement to inspect the US withdrawals on the spot. After Ambassador Gauvin himself had talked with Ambassador Sullivan, the United States finally gave in on inspection of the troop withdrawals. After February 20, both the ICCS and the JMC were on hand when US troops were put on planes to return to the United States.[84]

But the United States continued to evade the control of both the JMC and ICCS on the withdrawal of its equipment. "We had to compromise on personnel, but we never did on equipment," one US official said later. The United States, he explained, foresaw objections which they wished to avoid by keeping the JMC and ICCS away from the process. Not the least of these, of course, would be that much of the equipment was being turned over to Saigon in the same way the bases were, rather than removed from South Vietnam. In March, the DRV requested an ICCS investigation of this aspect of the withdrawal, as well as the failure to dismantle bases and the introduction into South Vietnam of "military personnel in disguise." [85] But nothing came of the request, because of Canadian opposition.

One of the least known aspects of the implementation of the Paris Agreement was what the US Navy called "Operation End Sweep"—the removal or deactivation of the mines which had been dropped in North Vietnamese coastal waters and inland waterways during the 1972 offensive.[86] It was a unique episode in US-DRV relations, for it involved an effort at cooperation between the two nations rather than conflict. And for the DRV, with its extreme sensitivity to the danger of foreign espionage within its territory, as well as its distaste for having foreign "teachers," it was a distinctly uncomfortable experience. Nevertheless, the DRV wanted the harbors cleared, and wanted the expertise and equipment so that it could clear mines itself in the future.

So on February 5, after preliminary negotiations within the Four-Party JMC, Rear Admiral Brian McCauley, Commander of the Navy's Mine Warfare Force, was flown from Saigon to Hanoi with a staff of fourteen, and then flew in a Russian plane from Hanoi to Haiphong, where they would spend three months conducting the minesweeping operations and negotiating with the DRV. It was the first time that US military men had been in North

Vietnam on a nonhostile mission since the evacuation of Haiphong in 1955.

The North Vietnamese were obviously suspicious of the intentions of the US mine deactivation team, and had decided before they had arrived to minimize their physical presence in every possible way. The protocol drafted by the DRV and accepted by the United States said that, while the United States would be "responsible" for mine clearance on the inland waterways of North Vietnam, the DRV would actively participate, "to the full extent of its capabilities," with the United States supplying the equipment and technical advice. This division of labor would not only keep the US military out of the interior of the country but would also obtain valuable equipment and knowledge from the very people who had laid the mines in the first place. The US and DRV officers who were to negotiate the details immediately divided into subcommittees on coastal and inland waterways.

The negotiations were long and hard. The DRV side felt that the US time schedule for clearing all of the waterways was suspiciously long—180 days, and 40 days for the Haiphong harbor area alone.[87] (A source on the American team later conceded that the United States had no intention of completing the clearing operation before the last US prisoner of war was on his way home.) The DRV side was also dissatisfied with the equipment offered by the United States, which at first did not want to provide helicopters or radio-controlled boats needed to complete the sweeping of the inland waterways.[88] Moreover, the United States refused to clear dud bombs, which could still blow up at any time and therefore continued to endanger waterborne traffic, arguing that they were not covered by the agreement.

It was not until February 25 that the DRV agreed to the US plan for mine clearance. And it did not actually get under way in the main shipping channel until March 6. By the end of March, DRV impatience with the slowness of the clearance of Haiphong harbor was expressed in the form of posters in Haiphong portraying the US team as killing fish rather than detonating mines. The sweeping of Haiphong harbor was still continuing when it was interrupted by the United States on April 17, and was not resumed until after the June 13 communiqué.

By that time the Navy was certain that all the mines either had self-destructed or were automatically deactivated already. The June 13 communiqué specified that the mine clearance operations were to be completed within thirty days. But by July 5, after Haiphong and five other ports had been declared officially open to ship traffic, the North Vietnamese became convinced that all the mines were already deactivated anyway. They informed the United States that they were not interested in any other US sweeping operations.

The clearing of the inland waterways involved two demands by the DRV for training in the use of sweeping equipment and other equipment required to complete the job with reasonable speed. The United States agreed to teach forty North Vietnamese how to use the equipment. During the three weeks of instruction, according to a member of the US team, the Vietnamese pressed the Americans for technical information on the equipment and mines which the United States refused to provide. The most contentious issue, however, was how much equipment would be furnished. The United States did agree to provide motor launches and motors as well as the magnetic pipes used to sweep the mines, but not as much as the DRV regarded as necessary, and only on loan. It seems likely that the North Vietnamese knew that the mines were passing their self-destruct dates, because they never did do any sweeping of the inland waterways.

The final US obligation under the agreement was the provision of postwar reconstruction assistance to the DRV as promised in Article 21. There is a good deal of evidence that the DRV had originally thought that the United States would make good on this promise, and that a process of normalization of relations with the United States would begin, in spite of the ongoing struggle in the South. Americans with the mine deactivation team in Haiphong found DRV authorities, including the head of the Haiphong Administrative Committee, not only discussing the future US economic aid as a foregone conclusion but also assuming that it would open up a new relationship between the United States and the DRV. One American recalled that the North Vietnamese would ask, "When you open your consulate in Haiphong, will you come to visit?"

Kissinger's trip to Hanoi in early February resulted in an

agreement to begin talks on US reconstruction aid on March 15 in Paris. The talks went smoothly, in spite of Nixon's charges about North Vietnamese infiltration, and on March 27 the chief of the US negotiating team, Maurice J. Williams, told Washington that an agreement on government procedures for US aid was virtually complete, the only remaining problem being the method by which the DRV would report to the United States on its use of the assistance.[89] But within the next two weeks, Nixon had decided to use all of his diplomatic leverage with Hanoi to force a cease-fire in Cambodia and a complete halt to the infiltration of troops and civilians. The aid negotiations were the first casualty of this political decision along with the mine deactivation operations.

The June 13, 1973 Kissinger-Tho communiqué called for resumption of the aid negotiations within four days and completion of the first phase within fifteen days after that. Both the DRV and the United States agreed in later statements that the negotiations resulted in a draft agreement governing US postwar aid to the DRV, but that the United States made the signing of the agreement conditional on Hanoi's acceptance of US and Saigon interpretations of several articles of the Paris Agreement. Williams, echoing earlier administration statements on Cambodia, said there could be no agreement on aid to the DRV until there was "a cessation of the fighting and the withdrawal of all foreign forces from Laos and Cambodia." [90] As noted earlier neither a cease-fire in Laos and Cambodia nor removal of forces within a specified time was required by Article 20. In addition, according to DRV officials, the United States demanded that the North Vietnamese accept Saigon's position on many parts of the agreement. "Thus many clauses would have to be considered as implemented when in fact they weren't," recalled one official familiar with the talks. On July 23, 1973 the talks in Paris on US economic aid broke up with the United States refusing to sign the agreement, and they were never resumed.

Predictably, the DRV and PRG refused to permit the search for bodies of Americans missing in action within their zones as long as the United States continued to regard itself as being unofficially and indirectly at war with both governments. The revolutionaries were determined to hold on to this last negotiating card until the

United States took an active interest in the application of the entire Paris Agreement. The "era of reconciliation" between the United States and the DRV which the agreement had promised seemed no closer six months after it was signed.

8: Political Stalemate and the Shifting Military Balance

1. The Paris Conference: Negotiation or Propaganda

On March 19, 1973 the two South Vietnamese parties met in a castle at La Celle–St. Cloud outside Paris, provided for the purpose by the French government. They were beginning the political negotiations called for in Article 12 to reach agreement on "the internal matters of South Vietnam as soon as possible and to do their utmost to accomplish this within ninety days after the ceasefire comes into effect. . . ."

The final objective of the talks was to produce an agreement on an election for a new government for South Vietnam, which would then integrate the two zones, two armies, and two administrations. But the same political interests which had compelled the Saigon government to resist signing the October draft also made it impossible for the two sides to agree on conditions for such an election. Saigon wanted a minimum of disruption in its own tight control over the political process—and over the Communist and non-Communist activists whom it had jailed. It also wanted all North Vietnamese troops removed before any vote, even as it increased its military pressures against the PRG zone.

The PRG, on the other hand, wanted an opportunity for the political opposition to Thieu to operate freely and to develop its full potentiality before an election. It also wanted a completely effective cease-fire and at least the beginning of a mutual demobilization of military forces. Thus Thieu was willing to agree to an election only under conditions of a wartime status quo, while the PRG would agree only under conditions of peace and liberalization of the Saigon-controlled zone.

Although the timing and modalities of the country-wide election were the central issue around which the discussions revolved, there were six major issues raised by the Paris Agreement on which the RVN and PRG took contradictory positions: the standstill cease-fire, the guarantee of democratic freedoms, the formation of the National Council of Reconciliation and Concord, the release of detained civilians, the reduction of armed forces, and elections.

As Kissinger pointed out in his June 1973 news conference, the North Vietnamese had insisted on an election within a specific period of time, but the United States had refused, at the insistence of Saigon.[1] Thieu was afraid that an election conducted by the tripartite National Council and without the political controls which had existed throughout his regime would be a disaster for him. In December 1972 Thieu had revealed that he tried to get the United States to demand an entirely different electoral scheme in the November round of negotiations. "We have proposed," he said, "that a popular referendum be organized and supervised by the U. N. We will rely on the results of this popular referendum to decide the percentage of the composition of the commission in charge of organizing the elections of the new president and vice-president of the Republic." Then, he explained, the new President would form a "coalition" based on the number of votes for each candidate in the election.[2] Thus the PRG as well as third force groups would be excluded from the conduct of the election and would have only token representation, if any, in the new government. The United States considered Thieu's electoral proposal so unrealistic that it did not even bother to present it along with Thieu's other demands for revision in November.

When the Paris Agreement was finally initialed, the Thieu regime's first response was a statement by Thieu's nephew and palace adviser Hoang Duc Nha that the RVN would not agree to any new elections until North Vietnamese troops had been withdrawn from the South. Nha made it clear at the same time that Saigon would reduce its own troops only on a one-for-one basis.[3] In effect, Thieu was demanding that the PRG leave its zone defenseless, since the RVN had more than four times as many men under arms as the PRG did. Saigon sources also said the RVN would demand that the elections be for President and Vice-President rather than for a new Constituent Assembly, thus forcing the PRG to recognize the legitimacy of the existing constitutional structure— a point which the United States had unsuccessfully demanded at the Paris talks on Thieu's behalf.[4]

As the talks began on March 19, Saigon's first move was to propose an agenda composed of three points: the general election provided for in Article 9(a), the composition of the National Council, and the question of armed forces in South Vietnam.[5] Saigon's demands on those three issues constituted the essence of its proposal for the agreement on internal matters. The PRG countered by proposing an agenda which included the implementation of the cease-fire, the return of all captured and detained civilians, immediate ensurance of full democratic liberties, and establishment of the National Council, in that order. The first three points were not even proposed for discussion by the Saigon delegation. The PRG delegation said that the discussion of an electoral law and mutual demobilization of forces had to await the implementation of these four provisions of the agreement, which were either to be carried out immediately, or, as in the case of the return of civilian prisoners, to be completed within ninety days, if possible. The remaining two problems, they argued, were not given the same urgency in the text of the agreement, which said only that agreement was to be reached on all internal matters within ninety days.

PRG chief of delegation Nguyen Van Hieu pressed the full implementation of the cease-fire as the precondition for the resolution of the political problems and complained about Saigon's efforts to increase its areas of control, its continuation of bombing operations, and its refusal to demarcate zones of control. Nguyen Luu Vien responded that the two parties were not in Paris to discuss cease-fire violations, which were the responsibility of the Joint Military Commission.[6] Hieu ridiculed Saigon's desire to discuss elections while the war still raged. "The house is burning, threatening everything inside," he told the press. "We propose to extinguish the fire. The other side pretends not to see the fire, and suggests that we discuss how to decorate the living room." [7]

The PRG demanded that the return of civilian personnel and

the restoration of democratic liberties be resolved before the two parties proceeded to those issues which were to be decided by negotiation between them. Given the importance of tight control of all dissidents to Thieu's power, both sides knew that these obligations would on balance hurt the Saigon government. The United States had successfully avoided any linkage of the time periods for the release of US prisoners of war and for the release of civilian prisoners, in order to deprive the DRV of its major leverage for insuring the implementation of Article 8(c), and Thieu was determined to maintain his control over the tens of thousands of potential PRG personnel.

For the PRG, the release of RVN personnel was much less of a political sacrifice. The scale of arrest and detention by the Communist side had always been much smaller than on the US and RVN side, particularly after the establishment of the US Phoenix program for capture or killing of Communist cadres in late 1967. Moreover, most of the Saigon government personnel captured by Communist security personnel were not detained for long periods, but were put through indoctrination courses in the detention camp and then released. For the Party believed that all but a small minority of RVN personnel were capable of changing sides. Those officials who were involved in the RVN's repressive apparatus and who were considered to have committed serious crimes were more often assassinated than imprisoned if they ignored warnings to desist.

Similarly, the implementation of the guarantee of democratic freedoms in Article 11 also presented far more difficulties for the RVN than for the PRG. It was within the Saigon-controlled zone that the non-Communist opposition to Thieu as well as the bulk of the voters in any election were located. If the political monopoly held by Thieu's machinery in this zone could be broken, it would weaken the RVN far more seriously than the 1968 and 1972 offensives combined. Those who had remained in the PRG zone after eight years of assault by the US air force were almost without exception supporters of the revolution; any active foes of the NLF and PRG had long since moved to the Saigon zone. The PRG had little to fear, therefore, from an overt propaganda effort within its zone by pro-Saigon groups before an electoral campaign. The Saigon delegation, on the other hand, treated Article 11 with open contempt, declaring that the article did not apply to the RVN because its constitution provided that democratic freedoms were to be restricted during wartime, and that the war was still continuing.[8] In short, the Thieu regime held its own constitution to be superior to the agreement.

Moreover, while the Saigon government tried to prevent pro-Communist civilians from moving into its zone and refugees from returning to old homes under PRG control, the PRG encouraged its people to move freely between the two zones, both to trade and to carry on low-level political work in the Saigon zone.[9] Charles Benoit of the Ford Foundation, who visited the PRG zone in Binh Dinh, was struck by the complete absence of the curfews, barbed wire, checkpoints, and military posts which the RVN used to restrict civilian movement.[10]

On the formation of the National Council of Reconciliation and Concord, the PRG delegation made the same proposal which it had made in the negotiating of the Paris Agreement itself: that the two sides issue joint or separate statements expressing their willingness to enter into consultation with organizations and individuals of the "third political force." The PRG defined this "third force" to include all those who supported neither party but did support the agreement itself. The RVN demanded that the composition of the third segment be determined by nomination of the two South Vietnamese parties to the agreement, half of them by Saigon and half by the PRG, which would have had the effect of denying the existence of a "third force" as an independent entity.[11] It was an essential part of Thieu's catechism that anyone who did not support his regime was supporting the Communists, so that there could be "no such thing as a third force in South Vietnam." [12] To admit the existence of political forces not aligned with either party to the agreement was to admit that his own regime merely represented one political faction rather than the entire non-Communist political spectrum.

The irreconcilable positions taken by the South Vietnamese parties on the National Council and the demobilization of forces, and Saigon's flat refusal to carry out Article 11 and its denial that it held more than a few thousand civilians affiliated with the PRG, left the negotiations at La Celle–St. Cloud stalemated after seven meetings, without agreement even on an agenda. On April 25, with only two days remaining before the three-month deadline, both sides presented formal proposals. The RVN delegation presented a draft "agreement on principles" containing ten articles, which was to be followed within thirty days by a more detailed agreement.[13] It offered an election within four months after the signing of the document, for an "organ representing the people of South Vietnam in order to decide the political future of South Vietnam." This organ would in turn "decide on the government structures, both Central as well as local."

This formula successfully avoided the question of whether or not the election would be within the framework of the existing constitution or would be for a Constituent Assembly. The joker in this seemingly liberal election offer, however, was that Saigon was willing to remove its tight restrictions on personal and political liberties only thirty to sixty days before the elections, and then only after the PRG had left itself defenseless by demobilizing all Northern troops without a proportionate ARVN demobilization. Article 9 of the proposed text stated:

> When the overall agreement is signed, simultaneous with the implementation of Articles 2 and 7, Chapter II of the Paris Agreement, and parallel with the withdrawal of non-South Vietnamese armed forces referred to in Article 8, above, the two South Vietnamese parties will get rid of all restrictions due to the wartime situation, regarding the democratic freedoms referred to in Article 11 of the Paris Agreement.

The reference to Article 2 was curious, since this article merely calls for observance of a cease-fire, but does not even contain the specific obligations of the two sides in observing the cease-fire, nor does it refer to the demarcation of zones. Article 7, however, was one on which the United States was then exerting maximum pressure on the DRV and PRG. Despite failure to agree on the modalities of replacement of war material, the United States was trying to force the Communist side to designate points of entry and introduce war material only through those points. By mentioning Article 7, therefore, Saigon was posing yet another unrelated precondition for implementing Article 11.

The restrictions on democratic liberties were to be removed "parallel with" the withdrawal of North Vietnamese troops, and that withdrawal according to Article 8 was to take place in two phases, the first beginning with the signing of the final detailed agreement and lasting for thirty days, and the second lasting thirty days after that. Thus, even if the PRG capitulated completely on North Vietnamese troop withdrawal, Saigon would not have to end its tight control over every aspect of South Vietnamese life until sometime during that *second* phase of withdrawal. And since the general election was to take place thirty days after the completion of the second phase of troop withdrawal, opponents of the regime would have between thirty and sixty days to make up for many years of political repression—far too little time for opposition groups to organize a nationwide political organization for electoral competition, even assuming that Saigon carried out in good faith the pledge to eliminate its political controls. Even Ambassador Bunker told Thieu that he should allow more time between the removal of political restrictions and elections, according to an authoritative US diplomatic source. Furthermore, the RVN proposal pointedly omitted any mention of the release of civilian prisoners any time before such an election.

The aim of this proposal was to permit the RVN to point to its offer of a quick election within four months and its rejection by the Communist side, particularly for the purpose of demonstrating its good faith to the US Congress. The hope was, of course, that few people would read the whole text and discover why both the PRG and "third force" opposition groups did not consider it a serious election proposal.

On the same day, the PRG released the text of its six-point program.[14] The PRG again proposed that each of the political problems be resolved one at a time and that each be implemented immediately, as soon as agreement was reached, before going on to the next problem. When all of these problems were solved, the two sides would go on to the issue of elections and the Vietnamese armed forces in the South. The PRG proposal also specified that the general elections would have to be held for a constituent assembly, rather than for the presidency as the RVN proposed.

These April 25 proposals remained the official positions of both sides until January 25, 1974, when Nguyen Luu Vien presented a new, revised time-table on behalf of the Saigon delegation, which increased the period between the complete restoration of democratic liberties and the actual elections by thirty days—an apparent concession to criticisms of the previous proposal.[15] Otherwise, the RVN proposal remained unchanged.

The last significant development in the talks in 1974 was a PRG statement on March 22 which supported the holding of general elections "no later than one year after the establishment of the Council." [16] But the PRG continued to point out that under the agreement, an election law, including the date for the general elections, could only be written by the National Council, with the participation of an independent third segment. It wanted to shift the focus of attention back to the issues of democratic freedoms, release of civilian prisoners, and the right of groups and individuals not aligned with either party to have a voice in the political future.

In one sense the "third force" represented a third party in the Paris talks. For, even though it was physically absent, the political role of the third force was being taken into account in the proposals of both sides. The PRG assertion that the third force was indeed an independent entity was borne out by the fact that so many individuals who had once seen the future of South Vietnam being determined within the framework of the RVN regime now no longer recognized the Saigon government as the sole arbiter of the country's destiny. The leaders of organizations calling for national reconciliation and peace and denying the exclusive sovereignty of the RVN had come from the anti-Communist political, social, and intellectual milieu of urban South Vietnam, and most had come from the major institutions of non-Communist Vietnamese society: the army (General Duong Van Minh), the national assembly (Ly Quy Chung, Ho Ngoc Nhuan), the Catholic Church (Fathers Nguyen Ngoc Lan and Phan Khac Tu), the bar (lawyers Tran Ngoc Lieng and Mrs. Ngo Ba Thanh), the university (Professor Chau Tam Luan), and the RVN government itself (former Foreign Minister Vu Van Mau). The evolution of a third political force, far from being a result of Communist manipulation, was an expression of the political weakness of Thieu's sterile anti-Communism, which had failed to crush the Vietnamese revolution but had brought political dependence and economic and social chaos to the Saigon-controlled zone.

While the leaders of the third force did not share the revolutionary outlook of the Communists, the Party leadership saw them as sharing the objective of overthrowing a regime implanted and maintained by a foreign power. The Party was prepared to let these non-Communist opponents of Thieu play an important role in the transition from war to peace. And if there ever was an electoral contest for a new Constituent Assembly, the Party would throw its support behind them wherever necessary in order to defeat candidates of the reactionary right—just as it had been ready to do in 1971. The policies of the PRG and the Thieu regime toward the third force once again dramatized the contrast in Vietnamese politics between the maneuverability of the revolutionary left and the total inflexibility of its Vietnamese and American opponents.

2.   Hostages of War: Political Prisoners and Refugees

Almost all South Vietnamese had an immediate personal stake in the successful implementation of the Paris Agreement. It could have meant the beginning of a new life free from the death and destruction as well as the heavy economic burden of the war. But it was the refugees and civilian prisoners who had the most to gain from the strict application of the agreement. For the stakes involved their own freedom from the prisons, interrogation and detention centers, refugee camps and towns of the RVN zone. For tens of thousands of civilian prisoners and hundreds of thousands of refugees who were prevented from returning to their homes, Thieu's defiance of the agreement meant primarily the prolongation of the US-Saigon system of police repression and population control.

When the RVN was called upon to submit its list of civilian prisoners, only 5,081 names were offered,[17] including 320 students and intellectuals who publicly claimed to belong to the "third force" and not to the PRG.[18] This was of course only a small fraction of the total number of prisoners who fell under the protection of Article 8(c). Statistics given to *Newsweek* magazine in 1971 by Colonel Ly Trong Son of the RVN National Police showed that more than 43,000 civilians had been sentenced as "Communists" in the period from July 1968 through 1971 alone.[19] This flood of prisoners *began* at a time when the RVN prison system was already seriously overcrowded.[20] The vast majority of those sentenced were not charged with a specific crime but were held under a procedure permitting detention of prisoners up to two years

merely for being considered a "threat to national security." This
"An Tri" (detention) sentence could be renewed indefinitely by the
"Province Security Committee." [21]

During 1970 and 1971, An Tri cases were being reviewed at a
rate of about 10,000 a year, and in more than a third of these cases
the detainees were held for at least an additional term, ranging
from less than a year to two years.[22] The number released during
these two years was about 11,000—less than the number of
additional prisoners sentenced, which totaled about 14,000 in the
same period.[23] During the 1972 Communist offensive, moreover,
there were tens of thousands of new arrests, and at least 14,000 more
persons were sentenced or sent to prison to await sentence.[24] So
from 1968 to the beginning of 1973, it seems clear that the total
prisoner population was continuing to increase.

But despite this increase, the number of prisoners reported by
US and RVN officials to be in the forty-one national and provincial
"correctional centers" actually dropped off, from a peak of about
34,000 or 35,000 in mid-1969 to about 30,000 by mid-1971.[25] And
even after the increase of 1972, the total was still said to be about
35,000.[26] How could the RVN continue to arrest and sentence
detainees faster than they released them and still have the same
number of prisoners as three years earlier?

The answer seems to be that the additional prisoners were being
detained outside this system of "correctional centers" in a variety of
makeshift detention facilities: jails, interrogation centers, and
detention camps. The very existence of most of these facilities was
denied by the Saigon government in order to hide the actual
number of civilian prisoners which it held.

One part of the auxiliary detention system used by Saigon for
the growing number of prisoners was a series of rudimentary camps,
controlled by the province chiefs, dispersed around the countryside.
Two of these camps were discovered by an International Red Cross
team, which was informed of their location by religious authorities
in early 1973. The camps, called Thoi An and An Loi, were in two
different districts of Phong Dinh province, but when the Red Cross
asked one of the district chiefs for permission to visit the camp in his
district, he denied its existence. Nevertheless, two Red Cross
officials, Conradin Pernier and Dr. Erik Karup-Pederson, visited
the camps anyway on March 25 and 27, 1973, and again on April 5

and 6, 1973.[27] Pernier described them as consisting of six or seven tents each, surrounded by barbed wire about a meter high and guarded by soldiers. They held a total of 277 persons, 120 in Thoi An and 157 in An Loi. Most had been in the camp for about two years, according to Pernier's report. But some had been in one prison or another for at least three years. Except for some thirty-five persons in the second camp, none of the prisoners received any food from the government authorities; they had to rely entirely on their families. There were at least two cases of paralysis of the lower limbs due to a lack of vitamin B, and according to Dr. Karup-Pederson, some 40 of the 157 detainees at An Loi camp had one kind of illness or another.

There is no way of knowing how many such detention camps, which Saigon officials called "readaptation camps," existed throughout the RVN-controlled zone, or how many thousands were being held in them. But the fact that Phong Dinh province had two such small camps, each in a different district, suggests that there were a number of them widely dispersed throughout the country in order to keep them secret.

In addition to those in detention centers controlled by the province chief, there were thousands more in interrogation centers and other detention facilities run by the police. While the RVN denied heatedly that there were any jails at district or village level,[28] the chief of the US Public Safety Division in Vietnam told the author in a May 1971 interview that there were some 8,000 to 10,000 persons in jails, with space for 2,000 to 4,000 more.[29] A large number of people were also held in interrogation centers, one of which was located in each province capital, along with eight major centers in Saigon. In mid-1969, the American adviser to the RVN Director of Prisons said that about 10,000 detainees were held in interrogation centers.[30]

On the basis of statistics furnished by the RVN and the United States, the fact of an ever-increasing population of prisoners and detainees, and the knowledge that there were an unknown number of detention camps not even acknowledged by Saigon or the United States, the number of detainees was clearly considerably greater than the 38,000 admitted by the RVN after the agreement was signed.[31] Robert Shaplen, a journalist not given to accepting information from pro-NLF sources, wrote in January 1973 that the ranks of political prisoners had increased to "at least seventy thousand." [32]

Of these prisoners, a considerable proportion were explicitly nonaligned with either party. The approximate number may be gleaned from the fact that the Saigon government offered in April 1973 to hand over to the PRG "21,007 common criminals" if the PRG would accept them as being "part of the insurgent movement." [33] Saigon's reason for making this offer appears to have been to prevent non-PRG political activists from being able to operate freely within the RVN zone of control. By any reasonable interpretation of Article 11, these individuals should have been allowed to return to their homes within the Saigon zone.

The Saigon government denied that it held either civilian personnel or non-PRG political prisoners, except for those on its official list of 5,081 Communists. Even before the agreement was signed, the RVN began to systematically reclassify these prisoners as "common criminals." The US Embassy, in a letter to the Senate Subcommittee on Refugees on April 3, 1972, said, "Before and since the ceasefire, the GVN has been converting A and B category 'An Tri' detainees to common criminal status by the expedient of convicting them of ID card violations or draft-dodging." [34] These detainees, it explained, were those who, according to the Saigon government, held "important positions" in the Communist infrastructure. Saigon then claimed that these detainees could not be protected by the Paris Agreement. An official statement from Nha's office in April 1973 said, "Naturally, common criminals belong to governing national law, which no alien or foreigner has the right to interfere with." [35] This move was carried out with the full support of the US Embassy, according to a high-ranking American diplomat, despite the fact that Article 8(b) of the protocol on prisoners explicitly stated, "The detaining parties shall not deny or delay their return for any reason, including the fact that captured persons may, on any grounds, have been prosecuted or sentenced."

The reclassification came after Military Courts and Province Security Committees carried out mass proceedings to convict the detainees of new common law crimes. At Con Son Prison, a Military Court reportedly judged some 1,500 detainees at the rate of 100 persons per hour.[36] Most of the younger detainees were forced to join the Saigon army—also in violation of Article

8(b)—and when they refused, they were convicted of the common law crime of "disobedience to orders." [37] Wherever possible, prisoners were forced to put their fingerprints on confessions of such common law crimes.[38]

The statement from Nha's office further explained that the RVN defined "civilian personnel" to mean only individuals holding "responsibility in an organizational structure, as for example: a civil servant, a cadre." And it declared that, in accordance with this definition, "The Communists cannot receive anyone they want to as their 'civilian personnel,' because if they want to be classified in this way, prisoners must produce papers (a certificate or identification card) recording clearly their position in a Communist organization or agency." [39]

This interpretation of "civilian personnel" in the Paris Agreement was very far removed from the language of Article 7(a) of the protocol on prisoners, which said, "The term 'civilian internees' is understood to mean all persons who, having in any way contributed to the political and armed struggle between the two parties, have been arrested for that reason and have been kept in detention by either party during the period of hostilities." The purpose of this broad language was clearly to cover all prisoners who had been arrested and detained because of their role in the conflict, official or unofficial. Yet Saigon, after arresting them on the flimsiest evidence of "Communist activities," was raising the Kafkaesque demand that the prisoner himself provide documentary proof of being a Communist agent in order to be released!

Saigon did release some 5,000 persons considered "low level supporters" of the revolutionary side during the first six months of 1973, but this was no more than had been released in previous years under the US-initiated "parole" program.[40] And these prisoners were still treated like criminals. They were forced to report regularly to the police, denied freedom of movement, and their families were threatened with retaliation if they engaged in any political activities.[41]

The Saigon government sought to justify its refusal to release the vast majority of the civilian detainees it held by arguing that the PRG admitted holding only 637 RVN civilians when in fact it had detained thousands more. Saigon published a thick paperback book to back its claim that nearly 17,000 government cadres had been abducted by the Communists since 1954, along with 50,000 civilians.[42] But a close reading of the book does not support the RVN argument that many thousands of RVN personnel remained in detention camps in the PRG zone. The vast majority of the government cadres listed—as many as 75 to 80 percent of them—were clearly not abducted at all but surrendered voluntarily to the PRG during the 1972 Communist offensive, when the PLAF gained control over large areas of the countryside. In virtually every case, when a new village was taken over by the PRG, the local self-defense forces and other cadres changed sides and became part of the PRG government structure. For example, 1,243 persons, or over 85 percent of the 1,461 government cadres listed as abducted in Quang Tri province, simply happened to be in villages and towns captured by the PLAF in the early phase of the offensive, as ARVN fell back virtually without a fight. Similarly the list of policemen allegedly abducted includes 171 in Hoai An and Hoai Nhon districts of Binh Dinh province, where it is known that policemen and other self-defense forces changed sides after the PRG took control, again without a fight, 82 policemen in Loc Ninh who also became the local PRG police force, and 117 who were absorbed into the PRG apparatus in Quang Tri during the offensive. Another 58 policemen are listed as having been abducted in Hue during the Tet Offensive of 1968, when it was reported that most of the RVN policemen were formed into a revolutionary police force.[43] These names include more than half of the total of 825 policemen listed as abducted.

In some cases, self-defense forces make up just over half the total, and most were again involved in the 1972 offensive. The document explicitly admits that many of the cadres listed voluntarily left with the Communist forces. Seventy-two of the self-defense forces listed in Quang Ngai and forty in Quang Tin are followed by the comment "Chay Theo Viet Cong," which means that they fled voluntarily with the retreating PLAF forces. Most of the remaining number of self-defense forces are shown to have been missing after a battle, so that there is no basis for concluding that they were being held against their will.

In short, the RVN list, which does not include any of the 50,000 civilians claimed, provides no evidence of thousands of RVN cadres being incarcerated by the PRG. While it is impossible to determine from the information provided how many of those listed were actually "arrested" by the NLF-PRG, it is clear that the bulk of the names on the list were not relevant to the problem of releasing civilian detainees.

Other statistics provided by the US Mission lent support to the PRG claim that it held only 637 RVN civilian detainees. During the four years from 1966 to 1969 only 1,045 RVN civilian personnel were reported abducted by the NLF, an average of 261 each year.[44] This compares with the total of 17,310 actually sentenced to prison by Saigon in the year 1969 alone. As noted above, the NLF generally held RVN personnel for "reeducation" rather than punishing them with long imprisonment. Most of those who were sent to "thought reform" camps were detained for less than six months.[45] Because of the difference in scale between the PRG and RVN detention systems and the rapid turnover in the PRG system, the figure of 637 RVN civilian prisoners seems to have been reasonable.

The US Embassy, coming to the defense of its client, denied that there were significant numbers of prisoners outside the major national and provincial "correction centers," as claimed by non-Communist South Vietnamese concerned with the problem of civilian detainees. The Embassy declared that its "sources" supported the Saigon government's claim that there were "no district or village jails." It did acknowledge that there was an "informal lock-up capacity," but insisted that the number held there was "certainly very small these days." [46] As for interrogation centers, the Embassy suggested a "maximum estimate" of 1,000 detainees held there, while admitting that this was "just a guess." [47] How accurate the guess was may be judged from the fact that while the Embassy was asserting that the Quang Ngai interrogation center was "largely empty," American Quaker personnel in Quang Ngai were reporting that the center continued to hold over 1,000 detainees.[48] The Embassy claimed to be unaware, of course, of the hidden detention camps scattered around the country, such as those discovered by Red Cross workers.

While claiming to have made an independent inquiry on the subject, the Embassy had in fact simply accepted the word of the Saigon government and passed it on to the American public. As a result, the United States became a party to the RVN cover-up of the actual number of political prisoners held in its prisons, jails, interrogation centers, and detention camps.

From the American assurances that the interrogation centers and local jails had been virtually emptied, one would suppose that Saigon had ended its system of An Tri arrest and detention. But in fact, an An Tri system was not only continuing; the procedures for arrest were made even easier. Whereas previously three separate accusations of the suspect were required for arrest, beginning in late 1972 only a single accusation was sufficient.[49] Only now the charge was to be "disturbing the peace" rather than "Communist activities."[50]

Equally tragic in its human consequences was the plight of those refugees in the RVN zone who were unable to return to their homes in contested or PRG-controlled areas. The freedoms of movement and residence were two of the most important among those guaranteed by Article 11 to those living in both zones of control in South Vietnam. During the course of the war, well over two million refugees left areas under NLF-PRG control, not because they were anti-Communist or pro-RVN, but because of the heavy bombing and artillery attacks against the zone, and the physical danger and economic hardship which the war imposed on them there. At the time of the cease-fire there were some 641,000 people in RVN refugee camps, most of whom had fled from their homes during the heavy fighting of 1972.[51] Virtually all of these people wanted to go home, if they would be safe from war and Saigon government reprisals.

But Saigon's interest in maintaining control over these people and denying them to the PRG made a dead letter of these freedoms as it did of all of Article 11. For one of the Saigon government's priority tasks in the period immediately following the cease-fire deadline was to discourage and restrain refugees from leaving their RVN-controlled camps. At the time of the signing of the agreement, a press dispatch from Saigon reported that "informed sources" had said the RVN had "no intention of letting refugees return to areas which remain under Communist control. . . ."[52] And from Danang, a correspondent quoted American officials as saying Saigon's troops and police had been ordered to "restrain the refugees, forcibly if necessary."[53]

The RVN used a variety of methods to coerce refugees to

remain in place. In Quang Ngai, loudspeaker trucks warned refugees in and around the province town that they would be shot if they tried to leave the RVN zone in order to return to their old homes.[54] The police used informers in the refugee camps in order to pinpoint Communist agents or overt sympathizers, thus preventing any organized movement within the camps to return to PRG or contested areas.[55] If any member of a family failed to return to the camp by the 7 P.M. curfew, the head of the family was detained by police and ultimately imprisoned, since it was assumed that the missing person had joined the Communists.[56] Identification cards were confiscated from refugees known to have pro-PRG sympathies, so that they would be arrested automatically if stopped by police outside the camp.[57]

When refugees did try to move to the PRG zone, they were subjected to reprisals. A former AID refugee official, Edward L. Block, told of reports of a boatload of refugees trying to return from Danang to the PRG-controlled part of Dong Ha. The refugees were intercepted by a Saigon government coastal patrol, and were never heard from again.[58] In some provinces, the ARVN ground forces burned down houses and destroyed rice fields in PRG areas which were newly settled in order to discourage people from trying to live there. Artillery fire was also used to harass people who returned after the cease-fire to areas outside Saigon's control.[59] According to Dr. Wells Klein, who investigated the refugee program for the Senate Subcommittee on Refugees in March 1973, most of the approximately 10,000 rounds of artillery fire which fell on the PRG zone every day was not connected with any particular military operation, but was "harassment and interdiction fire" against the PRG zone in general.[60]

Saigon operations against the PRG, police controls, and fear of renewed war kept most of the refugees under RVN control in spite of the Paris Agreement. Refugees in Quang Ngai province told an American journalist they feared reprisals if they tried to go back home, and said they would have to have guarantees against arrest or harassment by ARVN troops before they would feel safe in doing so.[61] But fear of renewed fighting in the PRG-controlled zone was also a factor in holding them back. One old refugee farmer, when asked immediately after the cease-fire if he would go back home, said, "If I hear airplane motors overhead, I'm afraid I won't have the courage to go back. I'm still afraid of airplanes." [62] And refugees interviewed in Binh Long province in February said they might go back to their own homes, now under PRG control, if they thought it would be "calm." But they had fled from their homes during the 1972 Communist offensive because of the heavy bombing which followed the PLAF advance and they were still afraid of having to repeat the experience. "When the Viet Cong come, we leave automatically," said one woman, "because we know the airplanes will come and bomb." [63]

Saigon took advantage of the reluctance of most of the refugees from PRG-controlled or contested areas to defy its orders in order to relocate them to gain control over previously unpopulated and contested areas. Some of the refugees from Central Vietnam and Region II were to be moved hundreds of miles to Region III; others were to be moved out on the margin of the PRG zone of control—and in some cases into PRG territory occupied by ARVN after the cease-fire. In either case, the refugees became pawns in the RVN's effort to expand its area of control. And while the resettlement was in theory "voluntary," the refugees had little choice when the RVN authorities told them the camps were closing down and they would receive no more food.[64]

Although US and Saigon officials later denied that refugee resettlement was carried out with the extension of RVN control in mind, a letter from the US Consul General in Region III, Mr. Robert L. Walkinshaw, to the RVN Corps Commander, Lieutenant General Nguyen Van Minh, on April 13, 1973, made it clear that the United States and Saigon had precisely that in mind in selecting resettlement sites. Referring to refugees from other regions who were to be resettled in Region III, Walkinshaw said, "The people will move into areas that were previously considered marginal, thus secure the area, improve movement and security along major routes of communication, develop the agriculture and economic situation in the province concerned, and bring economic viability to the country as a whole. . . ." [65]

Edward Block, in testimony before the House Foreign Affairs Committee, said that "almost every resettlement" established in Quang Ngai and Binh Dinh provinces had "pushed the GVN deeper into contested areas; in many instances, areas where the GVN had no military presence prior to the cease-fire." [66] In Binh

Tuy province, both the American adviser and Saigon troops confirmed that the site chosen for the Dong Den resettlement camp had been considered to be under PRG control at the time of the peace agreement.[67] In most cases, the RVN set up military outposts near the resettlement sites to provide security, thus violating the standstill cease-fire.[68] The result was almost invariably a PRG military response against both the outposts and the settlement aimed at discouraging the people from remaining at the sites.

In these marginal settlements, the refugees were in theory supposed to become self-sufficient. But more often, refugees found that they were being shifted from government handouts to the brink of starvation. Thousands of refugees who were moved by Saigon from Binh Dinh, Quang Nam, and Quang Ngai to Tay Ninh had to pay more money than most of them had in order to obtain a piece of virgin land. There was no employment for 80 percent of them, and the government provided no food. The refugees were left to forage for roots, which were often poisonous. More than half of the refugees decided to make the long trip back to Central Vietnam on their own, trying to escape the threat of starvation at these RVN resettlement sites.[69]

Those who were moved to what were called "return to village" sites in Quang Tri, Quang Nam, and Quang Ngai were frequently no better off. Living behind barbed wire and guarded by ARVN soldiers, the inhabitants of these settlements were allowed to leave the camps only between 7 A.M. and 5 P.M., if their land was under RVN control.[70] And if, as was often the case, their land was several kilometers away, they could not farm it adequately because of the lack of time. If the land was under PRG control, they were not allowed to farm it at all.

American lawyer Robert C. Ransom visited one such "return to village" site in Quang Ngai, where 750 families were prohibited from farming the land because of the presence of Communist forces. Because of RVN incompetence and corruption the people had not received the money, roofing, or rice allowance they were promised, and they were desperately trying to stave off starvation by eating chopped banana stalks.[71] Refugees at the Cam Thanh "return to village" site in Quang Nam were in the same situation, and they too were found eating chopped banana stalks and fearful of starvation.[72]

Those remaining in RVN refugee camps were only slightly better off. At Son Tra camp, Binh Son district, Quang Ngai, food distribution in the camps, which had always been irregular, became even more infrequent. Earl and Pat Martin of the Mennonite Central Committee, who visited the camp in the spring of 1974, observed hunger and malnutrition which was "much worse" than anything they had seen in their previous experience in the province from 1966 to 1969. One old man told them, "They have imprisoned us here. It's like they have put us in a cattle pen and left us here to starve." [73]

It was probably hunger that drove many refugees to take the risk of arrest and torture to try to slip into the PRG zone. According to Mai Ngoc Duoc, the Deputy of the National Assembly from Quang Ngai, as many as 10 percent of the people in the GVN zone had moved to the PRG zone by March 1974 to escape starvation. Many refugee families living in villages in contested areas on the edge of the PRG zone, according to Duoc, asked the PRG to surround their village and take them back to their old homes. [74] The problem of hunger and starvation in Central Vietnam was not limited to refugees. One village chief in Quang Ngai told a journalist that the Vietnamese staple food—rice—had almost disappeared from the diet of most of the people, because they could not afford to buy it. [75] But it was the refugees who were hardest hit.

Saigon's forcible retention of control over refugees may have temporarily denied population to the PRG zone, but it also strengthened the political hold of the Communists over these refugees. In "relocation centers" such as Than Thuy, ten miles south of Danang, where the people had been forcibly moved by US troops in 1969 after their village was burned, the refugees' hatred of the Saigon government had clearly increased during the four years at the new location. Living in tin shacks on a barren stretch of sand near an RVN-controlled highway, without gardens or trees, the 2,000 people of Than Thuy were still only a mile away from their old homes and they resented not being allowed to return. They may once have grumbled about the political controls and economic burdens associated with life under the NLF. But after four years in virtual captivity under the Saigon government, they were more likely to recall NLF rule with genuine fondness. One man complained to a visiting journalist about the tight control exercised over their lives by the RVN and declared that under the Communists they had enjoyed "more freedom and a higher standard of living"—a judgment in which most others at Than Thuy concurred. The political implication of the sense of oppression felt by refugees held by threat and coercion is reflected in the fact that the hamlet, considered "contested" when it was relocated in 1969, was then considered by RVN authorities to be 80 percent pro-Communist.[76]

3.   "Preemptive" Attacks and the PLAF Counteroffensive

Up to October 1973 the Communists had held back from any major military thrust which would be used by Saigon to accuse them of causing the breakdown of the cease-fire. In the PRG zone, in Quang Nam, Quang Ngai, Binh Dinh, the central highlands, and the northern Delta, the PLAF had essentially permitted ARVN to occupy its zone, resisting only with guerrillas and local troops and refraining from a strong, coordinated counteroffensive. But beginning in October 1973 the Party authorized a shift in military policy which permitted PLAF main force units to strike back at rear bases and at other points of its own choosing, in response to Saigon's nibbling operations. This shift would ultimately reverse Saigon's territorial and population gains and give the PRG a decisive military advantage which would ensure the steady erosion of Thieu's position.

This revised Communist military policy coincided with new military initiatives by the Thieu regime which appeared to be aimed at provoking a Communist offensive that would justify the formal renunciation of the agreement by Thieu, if not the return of American air power to the conflict. In the summer of 1973 Saigon was already carrying out one of its biggest operations of the post-cease-fire period, moving two regiments of the 22nd Infantry Division and three battalions of Rangers into northern Binh Dinh in August to seize twenty square miles of rice land from the PRG. The offensive was of such magnitude that some US officials feared it would trigger a major military response by the Communists.[77]

Several considerations weighed heavily in Thieu's inclination toward an early and open break with the agreement. First, the very fact that he had to continue negotiating with the PRG over the political outcome in South Vietnam impaired his regime's legitimacy and lent credibility to the idea that there were indeed two administrations in the country, both with equal legality and an equal voice in determining its ultimate political structure. And his refusal to agree to restore democratic freedoms was attacked by third force figures in Saigon, including members of his own National Assembly, who questioned the right of his regime to decide unilaterally on matters of fundamental political importance. Some members of the Assembly, for example, attacked his carefully controlled Senate elections on August 27 as a violation of the spirit of the agreement, arguing that future elections were to be decided by the two South Vietnamese parties and conducted by the National Council of National Reconciliation.[78] Thieu responded angrily that those who made the argument were seeking to "destroy the legality of the South Vietnamese regime." [79] By having to justify his actions in terms of the Paris Agreement, Thieu was thus put on the political defensive.

Probably more important in Thieu's calculations, however, was his fear of losing the firm American support which he then had from Richard Nixon. As he watched the growing mood of noninvolvement in the United States and Nixon's deepening political crisis, Thieu saw the distinct possibility that both the pledge of US air support and plentiful military and economic aid might disappear within a relatively short time. Thieu, who felt that Saigon faced a military showdown with the Communists eventually in any case, wanted it to come as soon as possible.

The Congressional vote on July 31, 1973 to end all bombing in Indochina, and prohibiting any future military operations there without Congressional approval, had been a blow to his hopes for US air support. But it also made it all the more urgent to bring about a military showdown sooner rather than later, when the United States had disengaged even further from Indochina. Thieu hoped, by launching a concerted propaganda effort, to create in the United States an anticipation of a Communist offensive, and, by carrying out his own "preemptive" attacks against the PRG zone, to provoke a major Communist military move. This counterattack would then be presented to the US Congress and public as a repetition of the 1972 offensive, demanding the intervention of US air power.

At the beginning of October, in a speech in Pleiku, Thieu began to speak of an alleged Communist plan for a "general offensive," claiming that "captured Communist directives" indicated it would be launched in the spring of 1974.[80] US intelligence analysis conceded privately that there was absolutely no evidence at the time for such a claim. But Thieu coupled his charges with calls for "preemptive attacks" by ARVN units against Communist forces, as he traveled from one military base to another.[81] These "preemptive attacks" represented the very military strategy which the White House had mentioned as an "option" in May 1973: operations aimed not merely at expanding Saigon's territorial control but at engaging PLAF main force units. One such attack was ordered at the end of September when three battalions of Regional Forces and two of the 25th Division assaulted a long-standing PLAF base area at Thanh Duc in Tay Ninh province. They were ambushed and retreated with heavy losses. The Saigon military spokesman charged that Communist troops had attacked two ARVN outposts on the road between Tay Ninh and Khiem Hanh district town. But soldiers of the 25th Division told journalists that their posts had not been attacked by the Communists at all, and that the ARVN battalions had been sent into a rubber plantation which they knew was held by the Communists.[82] The RVN continued to cite the imaginary attack on its bases at Khiem Hanh as a major Communist violation of the cease-fire.[83]

During the first week of October Saigon's air force suddenly stepped up its bombing attacks against populated PRG areas in Tay Ninh. From October 3 to 7 over 100 planes attacked the Thien Ngon and Lo Go crossroads, as well as the strategic town of Xa Mat on the Cambodian border. (Xa Mat was one of the three points of entry which the PRG had informally selected for its war replacements, and the bombing there suggested one reason why the PRG had no intention of applying Article 7 in the absence of a cease-fire.) The attack on Lo Go on October 3 killed civilians and destroyed homes, gardens, and rice fields.[84] It was the beginning of an intensive bombing campaign against the PRG zone in the Third Military Region.[85]

Meanwhile, ARVN was carrying out a new nibbling operation in Quang Duc province on the Cambodian border. During October, Thieu moved five regional force battalions, an armored group, and two artillery companies into PRG-controlled areas of the province, setting up new military posts at road junctions and on strategic hills along Route 14 in Quang Duc.[86] During the last week in October and the first week in November, the PRG publicly complained at least five times about ARVN's push into Quang Duc, in broadcasts, a press conference, and a government communiqué.[87]

While the Thieu government was stepping up the pressure against the PRG, the Party leadership was deciding to step up its own military response to that pressure. Directives went at the beginning of October to local units to punish Saigon's offensive operations by attacking not only the units engaged in violating the agreement but their rear bases as well. According to US intelligence sources, however, the directives added that the purpose of such counterattacks was still limited to punishing Saigon's cease-fire violations and that they must not cause the breakdown of the cease-fire itself. In mid-October the PRG issued a warning to Saigon in the form of a public order to the PLAF to counterattack "any place and in the appropriate form" if Saigon did not discontinue its land-grabbing operations.[88] Liberation Radio, in commenting on the new orders, added, "If they attack us in an area, we will counterattack them in the same area and attack in other places as well. If they send aircraft and artillery to bomb and shell our liberated areas, we will counterattack them in the same areas and also directly attack their rear bases." [89]

The PLAF began immediately to roll back some of Saigon's post-cease-fire territorial expansion, attacking illegally built outposts and the rear bases for nibbling operations. On October 12 ARVN troops were forced to withdraw from Bach Ma outpost, which intelligence officials said had been established on a previously unoccupied mountain top after the cease-fire in an effort to push beyond the cease-fire line in Thua Thien province.[90] The PLAF also claimed in October that it forced ARVN to retreat from a number of posts built after the cease-fire in My Tho and Kien Phong provinces.[91]

On November 4 the PLAF overran the newly built bases in Quang Duc as well as two of the three pre-cease-fire ARVN bases in the province, one of which was the command post for ARVN's military operations there. Two days later it overran the last ARVN military outpost in Quang Duc and launched a rocket attack against Bien Hoa air base, the base for the heavy bombing attacks on PRG villages and military units in the Region.[92]

The United States and Thieu made the most of this first significant military response by the PRG under its new policy. The State Department and Pentagon had already been trying to persuade Congress to pass its request for military and economic aid for Saigon, and their strategy was based on a warning, conveyed in private talks with Congressmen, leaks to the press, and carefully phrased public statements, of the possibility of a major Communist offensive within two or three months.[93] And while intelligence agencies can always make honest mistakes in the direction of caution, this was a clear case of deliberately misrepresenting the intelligence available to the administration.

Not only was there no evidence to support such a warning; US intelligence had captured and reconstructed directives from the Lao Dong Party's Central Office for South Vietnam which indicated clearly that the tasks and missions for 1974 excluded any general offensive and reemphasized the importance of forcing Saigon to comply with the agreement. The tasks outlined in these documents, according to a Pentagon official interviewed on October 31, 1973, were to defend PRG territory, to force Saigon to carry out the agreement, to protect rice crops under PRG control, and to obtain rice from government-controlled areas.[94] This information was of course denied to Congress while it was considering the level of military aid to Thieu; it was leaked to the press only after the appropriations for Saigon had passed.[95]

The Thieu government immediately seized on the PLAF counterattacks to move another step toward a complete break in the structure of negotiations which was to make possible an end to the military conflict. Declaring that the "Third Indochina War" had now begun, Saigon announced that it had ordered fifty air force planes to bomb in and around Loc Ninh, the former RVN district town which the RVN believed would eventually become the administrative capital of the PRG zone. The PRG reported that 120 bombs hit the airstrip, a market, and residential areas, destroying a hospital and killing or wounding more than 100 civilians.[96] In succeeding days Saigon's planes also bombed the towns of Lo Go, Thien Ngon, and Xa Mat in Tay Ninh. The bombing of these key towns in the PRG zone continued intermittently throughout November and December.[97] By early 1974 Saigon air force pilots were reportedly angry at what they termed "vengeance bombing," which was militarily useless but risked both planes and pilots.[98]

In addition to its provocative air attacks against PRG towns, Saigon threatened on November 8 to "launch operations deep into their sanctuaries" to punish PRG "violations" of the cease-fire.[99] On November 8 the Saigon press spokesman threatened to break off the military and political talks with the PRG: "If they launch a big offensive—and small attacks around the country could also be considered a big offensive—the negotiations can break up." [100] In other words, further PLAF ripostes to the attacks "deep in their sanctuaries" would be used to justify breaking off the political negotiations with the PRG, and declaring the RVN free of the obligations of the agreement.

The same threat was repeated by Thieu himself on December 28, when he said that he wondered "whether or not we should continue to be at the bargaining tables." [101] And on January 4, 1974 Thieu again raised the specter of a Communist offensive— now discounted publicly by US intelligence—and ordered his troops to carry out operations "in the areas where their army is now stationed." He concluded by declaring, "As far as the armed forces are concerned, I can tell you the war has restarted." [102]

Carrying out Thieu's orders to completely ignore the Paris Agreement in its military operations, ARVN launched a series of major new operations in early 1974 to grab more land and to attack PLAF base areas. In February ARVN began a major operation to gain control of the whole eastern seaboard of Quang Ngai's Mo Duc district and the northern part of Duc Pho district, neither of which it had controlled since 1964. The operations involved building many new military posts, relocating the population to ARVN-controlled enclaves, burning the old villages, and police operations to arrest and detain suspected Communist cadres.[103]

Also in February two division-size operations were carried out in the "Iron Triangle" in the Cu Chi-Trang Bang area west of Saigon, one of the oldest Communist base areas in South Vietnam. Called Operation Quang Trung 1815, it involved twenty-one battalions sweeping the area and setting up new posts. Meanwhile, in the northern Delta, the ARVN 7th and 9th Divisions were launching a major offensive aimed at pushing PLAF main force troops out of their principal base in the region, around Tri Phap village, Dinh Tuong province.[104]

By the end of February 1974 US analysts in Saigon were estimating that the RVN had seized as much as 15 percent of the total land area which the PRG had controlled at the time of the cease-fire, and that Saigon had gained control of a total of 779 hamlets which had been either completely or predominantly under PRG control on January 28, 1973. They claimed a 5 percent increase in the population to which the Saigon government had "dominant access." Thus an estimated one million South Vietnamese had been affected by Saigon's encroachment and "pacification" operations in the PRG zone.[105]

As noted above, Thieu hoped that "preemptive" attacks and stepped-up encroachment operations against the PRG zone would provoke a Communist reaction that would justify the break-off of negotiations with the PRG and the renunciation of the most troublesome aspect of the Paris Agreement for Thieu: the necessity to negotiate on the basis of equality with the PRG. By April 1974, as Congress prepared to hold hearings on economic and military aid to the Thieu regime, there had still been no significant Communist military move which Thieu could use to end the negotiations. Two ARVN outposts in Hau Nghia and Kontum provinces, both of which had been used to try to interdict movement over the communications lines and interfere with road building in the PRG zone, were overrun by the PLAF in the first week of April, but there was still no major effort to take back the large chunks of territory it had lost earlier to Saigon.[106]

With an eye to American public and Congressional opinion as well as to his domestic politics, therefore, Thieu decided to fabricate a dramatic Communist attack on the besieged ARVN Ranger base at Tong Le Chan and turn it into the opening round of the Communist "general offensive." On the night of April 11 Tong Le Chan was quietly and swiftly evacuated—with the help of the PLAF troops, who had obligingly left open an escape route for withdrawing Saigon forces.[107] The following day, Saigon's propaganda organs put out the story that Communist troops had attacked and "overrun" the base, and that this heralded the long-awaited

Communist offensive. "It is obvious," said Radio Saigon, "that in overrunning one of our fixed positions, the Communists have destroyed the significance of the Paris Agreement and given the signal to start their offensive in the coming days." [108]

Saigon then used the phoney Tong Le Chan incident to take the step which it had been wanting to take for months: suspension of the political talks in Paris and resumption of its original rough treatment of the PRG delegation to the JMC. Saigon abruptly withdrew even the limited "privileges and immunities" which had been accorded the Communist delegates under American pressure in March, denying them access to the press, cutting their telephones, and ending the weekly liaison flights to Loc Ninh.[109] The move was aimed at provoking the breakdown of the JMC meetings as well, thus eliminating the last vestige of RVN's obligation under the agreement to treat the PRG as a diplomatic equal. After more than three weeks of isolation, the PRG delegation did walk out of the JMC meeting on May 10, after handing the RVN delegation a note saying that the talks would not resume until their privileges and immunities had been restored. Despite a conditional restoration of these facilities to the PRG on June 7, Saigon still implicitly claimed the right to withdraw them again at any time. By mid-June, the operations of all the bodies set up to implement the accord were in suspension without any prospect of being reconvened.* [110]

May 1974 marked not only the complete breakdown of the political and military talks between the South Vietnamese parties, but the end of the generally defensive posture which the PLAF had adopted since the agreement. Beginning in mid-May, the PLAF launched a series of military moves aimed at regaining territory seized by Saigon and at preventing encroachment and "pacification operations" by keeping ARVN main force units preoccupied with defensive missions. The first major PLAF countermove came in

---

* After the PRG suspended its participation in the Four-Party Joint Military Team, whose sole purpose was to facilitate the search for the missing in action, the RVN resumed the Loc Ninh flights, telephone service was restored, and the PRG delegation was permitted to hold press conferences again. But the RVN also made it clear that the restoration of these privileges and immunities was only to "help the Communist side fulfill its mission of searching for the missing in action" and rejected the PRG demand for an unconditional guarantee of privileges and immunities as an obligation under the agreement. (*Vietnam Press*, June 14, 1974, morning edition; Liberation Radio, June 12, 1974.)

mid-May near the district capital of Ben Cat, twenty-five miles north of Saigon, when Communist troops and tanks overran three militia posts, including one just a mile from the town. ARVN committed its entire 18th Division in an effort to recapture the lost territory, but withdrew from the fight after six weeks and some 2,500 casualties. The PLAF thrust effectively ended ARVN nibbling at the PRG zone in the Third Military Region.[111]

On the central coast, meanwhile, the PLAF began to roll back RVN's occupation of PRG territory by attacks against its military posts in the region. In late April, May, and June, the PRG claimed that its forces had forced Saigon from 290 positions and ended RVN control over more than 100,000 people in the provinces of Quang Nam and Quang Ngai.[112] The heaviest fighting began in mid-July, when two regiments attacked the Nong Son-Trung Phuoc base complex in the Thu Bon river valley southeast of Danang, in coordination with guerrilla actions which regained villages in Duc Duc and Que Son districts which had been occupied by the RVN in 1973.[113] Then on August 7 a PLAF regiment unexpectedly overran the district town of Thuong Duc, also southwest of Danang, which had been the rear base for Saigon's encroachment operations in the area in 1973. Again coordinated guerrilla actions eliminated RVN military posts and government presence from the villages.[114] The RVN sent two brigades of the elite Airborne Division to recapture the areas in the three districts but the counterattack stalled, and the effort in Duc Duc and Que Son districts had to be abandoned.[115]

In Quang Ngai, where ARVN had seized a significant portion of the PRG's villages and farm land in 1973 and early 1974, large areas of Son Tinh, Binh Son, and Tu Nghia districts were returned to PRG control. In Ming Long district, where the PRG had controlled most of the area around the district town and the road leading to it at the time of the cease-fire, only to see it seized by Saigon forces in the summer of 1973, the PLAF not only recaptured their old villages but went on to gain control of the district town itself.[116]

By autumn 1974 it was clear that the balance of forces had shifted in favor of the PRG. With the completion of a road linking the PRG-controlled areas of the central coast, the central highlands, and Military Region III, and the establishment of a major logistics base at Khe Sanh, the PLAF was capable of moving main force units to virtually any battle front within a matter of hours. In the case of Thuong Duc, for example, Communist forces took the ARVN completely by surprise when they appeared at the town.[117] It was primarily this growing equalization in logistics capabilities, coupled with the loss of US fire power, and not the alleged major build-up of North Vietnamese troops in the South, which accounted for the inability of ARVN to hold on to the territory it had acquired after the cease-fire.* In the wake of the PLAF counter-offensive, American analysts said the PRG had regained virtually all of the 15 percent of its zone which Saigon had seized in 1973 and early 1974.

Far more important, however, Thieu's early hopes that a PRG military response to his own offensive would reopen the question of US air power were dashed completely in 1974. As a COSVN directive pointed out to cadres in the South, "When we stepped up the people's warfare in the lowlands and border area, raiding their bases or destroying their subsectors, . . . the puppet army met with lots of difficulties, and the US did not dare intervene openly." [118] In fact, the Nixon administration, in its own death throes at the time of the PLAF counteroffensive, was unable to head off a sharp cut in military to Saigon by Congress, from the original request of $1.4 billion to $700 million. And when Nixon was forced to resign in disgrace, the Party leadership's assessment, in the COSVN directive, was that it "adversely affects the Saigon administration in all respects and drives henchman Nguyen Van Thieu into a state of confusion." [119]

* In the spring of 1974 the number of North Vietnamese combat troops in the South was variously estimated at 150,000 and 160,000 by State and Defense Department officials in public testimony. These estimates did not exceed the estimate of 160,000 which one foreign journalist obtained from careful cross-checking of US and RVN military sources in late November 1972 (*Le Figaro*, November 27, 1972), and which was reliably reported to be the CIA's estimate at the time the Paris Agreement was signed (Tad Szulc, *Washington Post*, January 30, 1973). The alleged massive North Vietnamese troop build-up after the agreement would appear to be a complete myth. For the official estimates in 1974, see testimony of Monteagle Stearns, Deputy Assistant Secretary of State, Southeast Asia, in *Second Supplemental Appropriation for Fiscal Year 1974*, Hearings before the Appropriations Committee, US Senate, 93rd Congress, 2nd Session, 1974, p. 1473; testimony of Major General William B. Caldwell, Director, Plans Policy and Program Formulation, Security Assistance, office of Assistant Secretary of Defense, ISA, *FY 1975 Authorization for Military Procurement, Research and Development and Civilian Personnel Strengths*, Hearings before the Committee on Armed Services, US Senate, 93rd Congress, 2nd Session, Part 4, Manpower, p. 1884.

By September 1974 Hanoi believed that the combination of military victories and the fall of the Nixon administration had created a new political situation in South Vietnam, exacerbating economic problems, encouraging Thieu's opponents to step up their activities in the cities, and making the Thieu regime increasingly unstable.[120] "Contradictions are evident even in the leading organs of the Saigon administration," said Central Committee member Hoang Tung in late 1974. "Between Thieu and [Prime Minister Tran Thien] Khiem, there is no unity of view." At the same time the North Vietnamese thought they discerned signs that the United States was preparing the way for a change of regime, if only to continue the same basic policy, while trying to influence the direction of the urban opposition to Thieu. When right-wing Catholic priest Tran Huu Thanh, formerly a lecturer at the ARVN psychological warfare school, began leading mass street demonstrations against Thieu as head of the "People's Anti-Corruption Movement," Hanoi saw it as a move by the United States to "keep a finger in the anti-Thieu struggle."

These military and political developments, coming on top of Thieu's intransigence in the year of negotiations in Saigon and Paris, brought a change in the public stance of the Communists toward negotiating with Thieu. On October 8 the PRG issued a statement calling on public figures and organizations in the South to work for "an end to the US military involvement and interference in South Vietnam, the overthrow of Nguyen Van Thieu and his clique, and the establishment in Saigon of an administration willing to implement the Paris Agreement seriously."

Two weeks later the United States began a campaign to reassert its support for Thieu, and the anti-Thieu movement in the cities seemed to lose its steam in November and December. But Party leaders continued to feel that Thieu could not survive, even if the new Ford administration wanted to support him. They viewed the ability of the United States to prop up any client regime as sharply reduced by the economic crisis in the United States and the rising opposition to US involvement in Indochina.

The Party leadership's decisions on South Vietnam had always been guided by its appraisal of the "balance of forces" at each juncture, and its determination to seize the right moment for advancing the revolution. They were convinced in late 1974 that the "opportune moment" had come to apply maximum pressure on the United States to drop its support for Thieu. In late December the PLAF began a new drive to capture the capital of Phuoc Long province, and by January 6 the entire province had fallen to the PRG. Party leaders warned that there would be more major defeats for Thieu until he was replaced by a government willing to implement all of the Paris Agreement's provisions.

Yet all the evidence indicated that the Party was still pursuing its basic strategy of using the Paris Agreement as the legal and political fulcrum for achieving the final dissolution of the client regime in Saigon. For the full implementation of that agreement would assure the Party of the achievement of its primary aims in South Vietnam: an end to foreign intervention, a legitimate political role for the revolutionary left in a political system without any popular, well-organized political competitors, and the opportunity to advance gradually toward reunification.

For the United States, meanwhile, the issue of support for the Paris Agreement was posed anew by the shifting balance of forces within South Vietnam as well as by the faltering American economy. To try to continue supporting the Thieu regime's military effort in the face of Congressional unwillingness to provide sufficient funds was to risk further rapid decline in the military situation and possible collapse of morale on the part of ARVN. But to shift US support to a Saigon regime committed to the spirit and letter of the Paris Agreement would represent a clear-cut defeat for the quarter century of US involvement in Vietnam. Whether or not the executive or legislative branch could summon the will to end the war by a conscious decision, it was increasingly clear by the beginning of 1975 that the fate of South Vietnam would be decided by forces larger than the will of those who determined US policy.

Epilogue

Only a few weeks after this manuscript was originally completed in February, the end of the Vietnam war came with stunning swiftness and finality. Both sides had been prepared for a struggle which would continue for many more months. But military pressure by the PLAF against a military and administrative structure which was far more fragile than American officials had ever acknowledged publicly produced a process of unraveling so rapid that the Communist forces could scarcely keep pace.

This process of disintegration, which took place over a period of six weeks, overtook the formula for a political solution which had been outlined in the Paris Agreement and offered by the PRG. Although the shifting balance of military and political forces made it clearer than ever that a tripartite National Council of National Reconciliation and Concord would be dominated by the PRG, this body still offered a way of ending the war by a peaceful transition rather than a military victory for the Communists. But the United States made no diplomatic effort to achieve a political settlement by replacing Thieu until the very last minute, and then only to gain time to evacuate the Vietnamese it had already promised to get out of the country.

By the time a leader was finally brought in who *could have* negotiated a settlement earlier, there was nothing left to negotiate, and the higher echelons of the Saigon administration and army were already in the process of fleeing. Thus Washington chose, in effect, to have the end come through a military victory for the Communist forces rather than a face-saving arrangement such as it had vainly sought in Cambodia. It appeared, in fact, that Kissinger wished to be able to argue that the Communists had never really been interested in a nonmilitary solution, and that the United States had no alternative but to support Saigon's war effort to the end.

The Communist's 1975 dry season campaign, as originally envisioned by PLAF military planners, was aimed at creating stronger pressures for Thieu's removal by further eroding Saigon's control and destroying part of his army. Although it was to include the capture of several objectives with great psychological impact, it was not expected to end the war immediately but rather to lay the groundwork for a war-ending offensive the following year.[1] Nevertheless, it set in motion a dynamic which went far beyond that. For it turned an army which had appeared to be a formidable fighting force into a mob of frightened and demoralized men who made the unspoken decision that the war was over for them.

Despite its massive size and modern armaments, the Saigon army's morale had long since declined to a point where disintegration was an ever-present danger. ARVN was not held together by any commonly held aspirations or cause, nor by any personal bonds of respect and affection between officers and men. It had been able to survive until the Paris Agreement under the umbrella of American power, on which ARVN troops had come to depend. The absence of US air support after the agreement and the growing military potential of the PLAF had created profound doubts that the ARVN could resist a determined offensive effort by the Communists, while PRG propaganda on the Paris Agreement and reconciliation policy had further reduced the willingness of ARVN soldiers to continue fighting. An American consular official in Quang Ngai province, Paul Daley, told a journalist in early March 1975 that he had visited an ARVN unit on the front line and had seen some soldiers taking off on Hondas. When he asked the battalion commander why he let them go, Daley said, the reply was, "What can you do?" The problem was, Daley continued, "These guys think that peace should have come twenty-four hours after the agreement was signed." [2]

Finally, due to soaring inflation, ARVN troops had been reduced more and more to robbery and pillage for their daily economic survival. By mid-1974, 92 percent of the soldiers surveyed by the US Defense Attaché's Office said their pay and allowances were not adequate to provide food, clothing, and shelter for their families. The DAO concluded that the economic crisis had caused a "deterioration of performance, which cannot be permitted to continue, if [the ARVN is] to be considered a viable military force."[3]

Accommodation and outright desertion or defection to the PLAF were rampant in 1974. One ARVN outpost, originally carrying 129 men on its rolls, lost all but twenty-three of them in desertions and defections before it was finally abandoned. When ARVN tried in 1974 to assign local militiamen to the regional forces, which were expected to fight farther away from home within the same province, the result was mass desertion. In one newly formed battalion of six hundred men drawn from the local forces, only three soldiers were left after a few weeks away from their home villages.[4]

The dry season campaign began with a move calculated to have a particularly devastating effect on Saigon's morale: an attack on Ban Me Thuot by troops of the Montagnard autonomy movement, FULRO, which had pledged its allegiance to the government in January 1969 but had drawn closer to the PRG because of Saigon's exploitative policies toward the tribal minorities. On March 10, FULRO troops fought their way into the central highlands capital and on the following day, they gained uncontested control of the city.[5]

Suddenly realizing that the central highlands were indefensible, Thieu ordered an unexpected strategic withdrawal from the remaining highlands provinces, Pleiku and Kontum. But the withdrawal quickly turned into a rout, as the 23rd Division was outflanked and essentially destroyed before it reached the coast. At the same time, Thieu decided to give up the provinces of Quang Tri and Thua Thien in order to establish a new defense line at Danang. He later changed his mind, fearing the political impact of the withdrawal from Hue, and ordered his troops once more to stand and fight for Hue. Although the Marines turned back toward Hue, the 1st Division troops refused the orders and ARVN began to fall apart as they streamed into Danang in complete disorder. Meanwhile, resistance to the PLAF melted away all along the central coast, as Quang Nam, Quang Tin, and Quang Ngai quickly fell without a fight, having been abandoned by their defenders.[6]

The demoralized Saigon soldiers who fled to Danang from

other provinces brought social chaos and panic in their wake, just as they had in Hue in 1972. Their despair signaled to the population of Danang that the city was already lost, and the exodus began almost immediately. Within two days after the fall of Hue to the Communists, most government officials, including nearly all the policemen, had already disappeared from their posts in Danang, and order inevitably broke down.[7] Danang was ruled by horror for three days, as hysterical troops began to shoot civilians indiscriminately in the streets. The worst disorders occurred when Americans attempted to evacuate refugees from the airport and then from the port of Danang. Soldiers shot and killed hundreds of civilians in order to get themselves and their families on to evacuation aircraft. On board an American refugee ship, they beat and raped refugees and killed those who protested.[8] On March 30, Liberation Army troops moved into Danang without resistance and established order within less than an hour, according to eyewitness reports.[9]

The rout continued southward down the coast. In only three days Qui Nhon, Tuy Hoa, Nha Trang, Cam Ranh, and Dalat went through the same sequence of developments: officers and civilian officials pulled out, soldiers began looting, and finally Liberation Army forces arrived to restore order.[10]

By April 2, the PRG found itself master of two-thirds of the country, with its foes in a state of shock. Saigon appeared for the first time to be virtually indefensible with its dwindling and demoralized forces. Six Saigon divisions had been eliminated from the battlefield, including the most reliable combat units, and half of its air force was gone. The PLAF, which had overwhelmingly superior forces around Saigon, was now in a position to force a quick end to the war.

Assessing the new situation, the Party leadership quickly revised its strategy to take advantage of the Saigon government's collapse, in two-thirds of the country. On April 4, the PLAF sent out orders to its units to prepare for an attack on Saigon itself.[11] While making plans for a military take-over, however, PRG officials did not rule out a return to the Paris formula, provided that the United States would replace Thieu with a government which would renounce the violently anti-Communist policies of the past. On April 1, and again on April 2, the PRG offered to negotiate with such a government on the basis of the Paris Agreement.[12] In the latter statement PRG Foreign Minister Nguyen Thi Binh suggested for the first time that General Duong Van Minh would be a logical replacement for Thieu: "We understand that General Minh is ready to negotiate peace, and we are ready to talk with him," she said. On April 9, in a press conference, she again demanded a government which would "insure strict application of the Paris Agreement," offering once again to arrive at a political settlement with such a regime.[13]

But the offer to return to the Paris Agreement's political formula was ignored by Washington and the US Embassy in Saigon. State Department officials had gone out of their way in late March to make it clear to the press that the Peace Agreement was, in their view, "inoperable," and that there was no possibility of a negotiated settlement.[14] In mid-April, Ambassador Graham Martin said in an interview, "There has been no advice from Washington for Thieu to step down." [15] At the same time, Martin was actively discouraging a military coup against Thieu, assuring former Vice-President Ky that Thieu would soon step down.[16] This attitude of determined disinterest in a political solution was consistent with earlier reports from State Department sources familiar with Kissinger's thinking emphasizing that a North Vietnamese military victory was already considered inevitable and that Kissinger's only concern was to appear to be a "good ally" to the very end.

Instead of trying to end the killing as soon as possible by pressing for a change of regime in Saigon, therefore, the Ford administration went through the motions of asking for an additional $722 million in military aid on April 11. Kissinger, in a background briefing for the press, suggested that the administration understood that the war was already lost, and hinted that the posture of all-out support for the Thieu regime was necessary in order to have its cooperation in the evacuation of Americans from Saigon. Kissinger spoke of trying to establish a perimeter around Saigon in the hope of negotiating a cease-fire and evacuating large numbers of Vietnamese from the city. But he did not indicate any intention to work for a political solution by replacing Thieu.[17]

On April 19, with the Liberation Army poised to begin its final drive on the capital, the PRG spokesman at Tansonnhut, Colonel Vo Dong Giang, publicly warned that there would be a military takeover if negotiations were not begun soon by a new government without the "Thieu clique." [18] At the same time, according to US sources, an ultimatum was passed on to the United States through the Hungarian and Polish ICCS delegations demanding that Thieu resign within forty-eight hours and that a new government be established within a few days with which the PRG could negotiate a political settlement. The note gave assurances that during those few days, there would be no military interference with the American evacuation of its personnel.[19]

The ultimatum finally mobilized the Embassy to action. It needed more than forty-eight hours to evacuate the Americans and South Vietnamese who had been promised evacuation. The Embassy immediately put intense pressure on Thieu to step down. As a high Embassy official put it, "The old man had to lean on him substantially." [20] On the evening of April 21, Thieu announced his resignation and was soon on a US military plane bound for Taiwan. The PLAF, which was conceded to be in a position to attack the city at will, then reduced its military activities to a minimum.

For the next six days, as the military lull and the stepped-up US evacuation continued, Thieu's successor, the ailing, seventy-one-year-old Tran Van Huong, who had been closely identified with Thieu's rule for many years, seemed unable or unwilling to turn the government over to General Duong Van Minh, who could have negotiated peace. Not until April 27 did the National Assembly finally vote unanimously to turn the Presidency over to Minh. But by that time the lull had ended and with it any chance for a negotiated settlement.[21] As the PRG began its "Ho Chi Minh" campaign to take the city, the PRG delegation in Paris raised the new demand that the Saigon army and administration be dissolved.[22] And even as Minh was being inaugurated, virtually the entire military and civilian leadership of the Saigon government was fleeing the country in the US airlift.[23]

After futile attempts to get the PRG representatives at Tansonnhut to negotiate with him, Minh ordered his troops to surrender on April 29. Liberation Army troops entered Saigon shortly thereafter to find that the Saigon Army in and around the city had vanished into history, leaving tens of thousands of boots, helmets, and uniforms lying in the streets and sidewalks.[24] Within hours of the departure of the last American, the military and administrative apparatus which the United States had spent more than twenty years and billions of dollars building up and protecting had ceased to exist. The quarter-century effort by the United States to prevent the completion of the Vietnamese revolution was ending in complete victory for the revolutionaries. When the revolutionary troops entered the presidential palace, General Minh told them that he was ready to meet with them to "hand over the administration." But the PLAF officer responded, "One cannot hand over what one does not control." [25]

Now that the whole experience of the Vietnam intervention is behind us, it should be possible to view the policies of the parties to the struggle with greater detachment and to discern certain historical realities which were more or less obscure at the time. Inevitably, the relentless researching of the history of this war will show that the claims of successive administrations about their own policies and those of their adversaries were false or misleading. For it was the kind of war in which dishonorable and ultimately futile deeds were always clothed in the rhetoric of peace.

This study was intended as a contribution to the process of clarifying the record of the Vietnam war, so that the right lessons might be learned from a tragic and ignoble chapter in American history. Some of the major conclusions which emerged from the foregoing narrative and analysis are worth repeating for emphasis:

1. *The US executive's definition of America's interests in Vietnam required that it deny peace to that country from the beginning of its involvement to the very end.* American geopolitical interests were invariably held to be absolute ones which took priority over any consideration of the interests and aspirations of the Vietnamese people themselves. Permitting a political solution at any time which would have given up the right of American intervention would have meant jeopardizing the client regime's chances for survival. Despite many opportunities to resolve the conflict by diplomatic formulas which, in other contexts, would have been regarded as fair and acceptable, the United States invariably chose to rely on force to try to consolidate the power of the anti-Communist regime.

2. *The Christmas bombing of 1972 was probably the most important defeat suffered by the US executive in the entire war.* Although there was no single decisive battle in the fifteen years of war in Vietnam, there

were campaigns which opened up a new phase of the conflict, representing a strategic setback for the United States and a gain for the revolutionaries. The bombing of Hanoi and Haiphong in December 1972 appears to have been the most important such campaign. Intended to facilitate a more favorable agreement and to suggest that the United States could reintervene if necessary, it made such reintervention far less likely. It aroused strong public opposition and provoked Congressional moves to cut off funds for any further bombing. It not only failed to force North Vietnam to rewrite the Paris Agreement in order to make it easier for Saigon to accuse its foes of violations; it also prepared the way for the mid-1973 legislative prohibition against any further military action in Indochina without prior Congressional approval.

3. *The Paris Agreement could not end the war, because Thieu had been assured by the Nixon Administration that he would get full US backing for a policy of avoiding political accommodation and continuing the military offensive.* Thieu had a strong incentive, moreover, to provoke a military confrontation with the Communists while he still had the strong support of the White House. The Nixon administration's backing for Thieu—and especially its pledge to resume bombing in the event of any "violation"—thus had the effect of nullifying the terms of the accord, which depended upon Thieu's having an incentive to make political compromises which he had been adamantly resisting for years. The United States thus rejected an opportunity to bring about a cease-fire and political settlement, to which the Communist leaders were willing to agree for their own reasons in 1973.

4. *The conflict ended in complete military victory for the PRG rather than in a negotiated political solution, because the United States refused to adjust its policy to the new balance of forces reflecting the fact that the United States clearly would not again intervene with air power in Vietnam.* Kissinger and Nixon refused to use their power to force a political change because they found it more compatible with both domestic political needs and foreign policy objectives to lose militarily while playing the "good ally" than to actively seek a political solution to bring an end to the war. The Paris Agreement's formula depended on a US interest in finding a way to end the war short of total defeat; in the absence of such an interest, a Saigon regime whose *raison d'etre* had been to repress the revolutionaries had to be replaced by a regime established by those very revolutionaries.

NOTES

1. Negotiating Peace: The View from Hanoi

1. On the March 6 accord, see Philippe Devillers, *Histoire du Vietnam* (Paris: Editions du Seuil, 1952), chapters 11–13.

2. Quoted in Russell Stetler, ed., *The Military Art of People's War: Selected Writings of General Vo Nguyen Giap* (New York and London: *Monthly Review*, 1970), p. 29. Translated from Devillers, pp. 228–230.

3. See George F. Sheldon, "French Policy and Vietnamese Nationalism since the Second World War," unpublished Ph.D. thesis, University of Chicago, 1949, pp. 141–142; Donald Lancaster, *The Emancipation of French Indochina* (London: Oxford University Press, 1961), p. 154.

4. Vo Nguyen Giap, "The Vietnamese People's War of Liberation against the French Imperialists and the Interventionists," in Stetler, p. 85.

5. George McT. Kahin and John W. Lewis, *The United States in Vietnam* (New York: Dell, 1967), p. 47.

6. Philippe Devillers and Jean Lacouture, *End of a War: Indochina, 1954* (New York: Praeger, 1969), p. 104.

7. George K. Tanham, *Communist Revolutionary Warfare, From the Vietminh to the Viet Cong* (New York: Praeger, 1961), pp. 56, 71.

8. A booklet published by the Party in 1952 admitted candidly, "Economically, we are having a very difficult time at present." *Khang Chien Truong Ky Gian Kho Nhat Dinh Dinh Thang Loi* (The Difficult, Protracted War of Resistance Will Certainly Be Victorious) (Third Interzone Information-Education Committee, 1952). Wason Film 2584, Cornell University Library.

9. "Looking at the World Situation, March 1954," *Nhan Dan*, April 1–5, 1954.

10. "With Regard to the Geneva Conference: A New Success of Our Camp," *Quan Doi Nhan Dan*, broadcast on Voice of Vietnam, April 20, 1954.

11. *Nhan Dan*, April 23–30, 1954.

12. "The Meeting of the Geneva Conference, A Success of the Forces of Peace," Voice of Vietnam, April 27, 1954.

13. See Devillers and Lacouture, chapters 20 and 21.

14. Ibid., pp. 203–204.

15. "Viet Minh Policy Document," probably issued by the Central Committee of the Lao Dong Party to Eastern Interzone of Nam Bo, obtained November 1954. Item 200 in Captured Documents and Interrogation Reports (mimeographed), US Department of State, March 1968, p. 9.

16. Ho Chi Minh, *Nhung Chang Duong Lich Su Ve Vang* (Episodes from a

Glorious History) (Hanoi: Nha Xuat Ban Quan Doi Nhan Dan, 1973), p. 87. Quoted in Carlyle A. Thayer, "Origins of the National Front for the Liberation of South Viet-Nam, 1954–1960: Debate on Unification within the Viet-Nam Workers' Party," paper presented to the Australasian Political Studies Association, Queensland University, July 20–21, 1974, p. 3.

17. "Viet Minh Policy Document," p. 10.

18. Ibid.

19. See Franklin B. Weinstein, *Vietnam's Unheld Elections: The Failure to Carry Out the 1956 Reunification Elections and the Effect on Hanoi's Present Outlook*, Data Paper No. 60, Southeast Asia Program, Cornell University, July 1966, pp. 7–8; Devillers and Lacouture, pp. 286–287.

20. Weinstein, p. 9; Devillers and Lacouture, p. 293.

21. Agreement on the Cessation of Hostilities in Viet-Nam, Appendix 2, Kahin and Lewis, p. 422; Final Declaration of the Geneva Conference . . . , Kahin and Lewis, p. 441.

22. Ibid., p. 442.

23. Weinstein, pp. 26–27.

24. "Viet Minh Policy Document," pp. 5–6.

25. *Nhan Dan*, June 7, 1955.

26. Nguyen Minh Vy, "A Refugee from the North," *Viet-Report*, January 1966, p. 10.

27. Voice of Nam Bo, October 26, 1954.

28. Voice of Viet Nam (Hanoi), November 4, 1954.

29. This report is quoted in Truong Chinh, *March Ahead under the Party's Banner* (Hanoi: Foreign Languages Publishing House, 1963), p. 39.

30. "Duong Loi Cach Mang Mein Nam" (The Path of Revolution in the South), Document no. 1002 in the Jeffrey Race collection, available on microfilm from Center for Research Libraries, Chicago, p. 2.

31. Ibid., p. 7. For a discussion of the significance of this document, see Jeffrey Race, "The Origins of the Second Indochina War," *Asian Survey*, X (May 1970), pp. 364–368.

32. Race quotes a former Party member, who defected in 1965, as saying that the Party did have a program of "extermination of traitors" *(tru gian)*, which relied primarily on Party agents within the Saigon government to finger the Party's enemies as being disloyal to the Diem regime and thus let the government itself eliminate them. Race, p. 369. But it is clear that any such program was extremely limited in scope and did very little to soften Saigon's campaign of repression.

33. "The Path of Revolution," p. 15.

34. Ibid., p. 2: "The revolutionary objective of the South must be the overthrow of the fascist dictatorial government of the US-Diem; and the realization of democratic alliance policy, having a popular democratic character. . . ."

35. Reuter and United Press dispatches, *Bangkok Post*, January 18, 1956.

36. *Nhan Dan*, July 11, 1956.

37. For a review of Hanoi's diplomatic initiatives on reunification and normalization of relations up to July 1957, see the speech by Vice-Minister of Defense Ta Quang Buu, Vietnam News Agency, July 24, 1957.

38. Interview with Vo Nguyen Giap by New China News Agency, September 19, 1957.

39. Interview with Tran Van Dinh, Diem's ambassador to Burma in 1957–58, July 27, 1967.

40. Voice of Vietnam, September 24, 1957.

41. See William A. Nighswonger, *Rural Pacification in Vietnam* (New York: Praeger, 1966), pp. 35–36; David Halberstam, "Return to Vietnam," *Harpers*, December 1967, p. 47.

42. An internal Party document later obtained by US intelligence said that "thousands of Party members were killed." Tinh Minh Nam Bo Tu Sau Hoa Binh Lap Lai Den Nay (The Situation in the South from the Restoration of Peace until the Present), cited in Thayer, p. 15. For first-hand testimony on the Diemist repression, see Joseph Zasloff, "Origins of the Insurgency in South Vietnam, 1954–1960: The Role of the Southern Viet Minh Cadres," Rand Corporation Memorandum, REM-5163-ISA/ARPA, May 1968, pp. 12–13.

43. Translation of a captured document called, "Experience of the South Vietnam Revolutionary Movement during the Past Several Years," referred to by the US government as the "Crimp document" because it was captured on Operation Crimp in 1966, in US Department of State, *Captured Documents and Interrogation Reports*, Washington, D. C., 1968.

44. "Tinh Hinh va Nhiem Vu 59" (The Situation and Tasks for 1959), Document no. 1025 in the Race Collection, was the regular outline of revolutionary strategy for the coming year, sent to the South in late 1958. It continued to speak optimistically of the possibilities for political struggle without resort to arms and blamed the weaknesses of the revolutionary movement on the failure of the Party in the South to take advantage of the "contradictions" within the Saigon administration.

45. "The Situation and Tasks for 1959" document makes the remarkable admission that "A large number of Party members don't truly understand and lack faith in the political struggle line of the Party" (pp. 5–6).

46. According to a high-ranking Party official in the South, who was captured in 1962, some village chapters which had 400 to 500 members during the resistance were reduced to only ten members in 1959, and none of them could safely remain in the village for fear of arrest. Jeffrey Race, *War Comes to Long An* (Berkeley: University of California Press, 1972), p. 99.

47. Le Duan, *Ta Nhat Dinh Thang, Dich Nhat Dinh Thua* (We Will Certainly Win, The Enemy Will Certainly Be Defeated) (Nha Xuat Ban Tien Phong, 1966), p. 7.

48. Thayer, p. 15.

49. "Muc Tieu va Phuong Huong cua Toan Dang, Toan Dan Ta" (The Goal and Direction of the Struggle of Our Whole Party and People), *Hoc Tap*, Binh Duong province, May 25, 1960, Document no. 1038 in Race Collection (emphasis added).

50. Interview with Hoang Tung, Hanoi, December 24, 1974.

51. Le Duan, *On the Socialist Revolution in Vietnam*, vol. 1 (Hanoi: Foreign Languages Publishing House, 1965), p. 48.

52. "Tho Cua Xu Uy Toan The Cac Dong Chi Chi Bo" (Message from the Regional Committee to All Comrades in Party Chapters), April 25, 1960, Document no. 182 in Douglas Pike Collection, available on microfilm from Cornell University Library.

53. Quoted in Zasloff, p. 22.

54. "Situation and Tasks in 1961" (English translation, Document no. 241 in Pike Collection).

55. See, for example, Vietnam Press, June 9, 1960; June 15, 1960; June 28, 1960; July 22, 1960; July 26, 1960.

56. Nguyen Phu Cuong, "U. S. 'Special War' (1961–1965)," *Vietnamese Studies*, nos. 18 and 19, 1968, p. 158.

57. Le Hong Linh et al., *Ap Bac* (Hanoi: Foreign Languages Publishing House, 1965), p. 15; "US State Department Working Paper on the Role of North Vietnam in the South," *Congressional Record*, May 9, 1968, p. H3609.

58. "Resolution of the Third National Congress of the Vietnam Workers Party on the Tasks and Line of the Party in the New Stage," *Third National Congress of the Vietnam Workers' Party*, vol. I (Hanoi: Foreign Languages Publishing House, 1960), p. 221.

59. Minh Tranh, "The Revolution in South Vietnam and National Unification," Hanoi Radio, October 19, 1960.

60. Interview with Hoang Tung, Hanoi, December 24, 1974.

61. T. A., "A Big Historical Victory and the Role of the National Liberation Front Committee," *Chien Dau* (internal organ of the Ba Ria province party branch), no. 4, July 1962, Document no. 48 in Pike Collection.

62. The Polish delegate to the International Control Commission indicated this in a conversation with Donald S. Zagoria in October 1963. See Zagoria, *The Vietnam Triangle* (New York: Pegasus Books, 1967), pp. 108, 277.

63. *Nhan Dan*, July 24, 1962.

64. Douglas Pike, *Viet Cong* (Cambridge: M.I.T. Press, 1967), p. 351.

65. Georges Chaffard, *Les Deux Guerres du Vietnam* (Paris: La Table Ronde de Combat, 1969), pp. 266–270.

66. *Journal de Genève*, August 29, 1963.

67. *Washington Post*, May 12, 1963.

68. Chaffard, pp. 307–308.

69. Mieczyslaw Maneli, "Vietnam, '63 and Now," *New York Times*, January 27, 1975.

70. Ibid.

71. Interview with Tran Van Dinh, Washington, D.C., July 27, 1967.

72. Chaffard, p. 347.

73. Ibid.

74. Document no. 96, *Vietnam Documents and Research Notes*, July 1971, pp. 15, 40.

75. See the report on the diplomatic volumes of the Pentagon Papers in *Washington Post*, June 27, 1972, p. A13.

76. Chaffard, p. 363.

77. Ibid.

78. Ibid.

79. Ibid., p. 427.

80. Ibid., pp. 361–362; Franz Schurmann, Peter Dale Scott, and Reginald Zelnik, *The Politics of Escalation in Vietnam* (New York: Fawcett World Library, 1966), p. 37.

81. Ibid.

82. Chaffard, p. 383; *New York Times*, December 6, 1966; Mario Rossi, "U Thant and Vietnam: Untold Story," *New York Review of Books*, November 17, 1966, pp. 8–13.

83. *The Pentagon Papers, Gravel Edition* (Boston: Beacon Press, 1971), Vol. III, p. 293. (Cited below as *Pentagon Papers*.)

84. "Tinh Hinh Moi, Nhiem Vu Moi" (New Situation, New Task), Information and Training Committee of South Vietnam, 1965, Reorientation Document, Document no. 921 in Pike Collection.

85. *Pentagon Papers*, III, p. 266.

86. Ibid.

87. Le Duan, *We Will Certainly Win*, p. 38.

88. Excerpt from "The Revolutionary Road," Ho Chi Minh's collected lectures originally published in 1926, *Viet Nam Courier*, no. 255, February 9, 1970, p. 4. See also Georges Boudarel, "Essai sur la Pensée Militaire Vietnamienne," in Jean Chesnaux, Georges Boudarel, and Daniel Hemery, eds., *Tradition et Révolution au Vietnam* (Paris: Editions Anthropos, 1971), p. 472.

89. See Vo Nguyen Giap, *People's War, People's Army* (New York: Bantam Books, 1968), p. 72; Giap, "The Vietnamese People's War of Liberation," pp. 88, 89, 104.

90. *Pentagon Papers*, III, p. 291.

91. *Washington Post*, June 27, 1973, p. A13.

92. Ibid.

93. David Kraslow and Stuart H. Loory, *The Secret Search for Peace in Vietnam* (New York: Random House, 1968), p. 93.

94. *Pentagon Papers*, III, p. 291. The authors of the papers judged that "On balance . . . the action-signals were sufficiently numerous and the warnings sufficiently explicit to have given Hanoi a fair awareness that the U. S. was likely to respond to the deteriorating situation by intensifying the conflict" (p. 292).

95. "Nhan Ro Yeu Cau Moi Cua Thinh Hinh, Nang Cao Y Chi Phan Dau vi Trau Doi Dao Duc Cach Mang, Hoan Thanh Tot Moi Nhiem Vu Cong Tac Truoc Mat" (Let's Realize Clearly the New Requirements of the Situation, Raise High the Will to Struggle, to Learn Revolutionary Virtue, and Complete Well Every Task Before Us), Directive from the Lao Dong Party Central Committee, dated January 2, 1965, Document no. 912 in Pike Collection.

96. Le Duan, *We Will Certainly Win*, p. 25.

97. Kahin and Lewis, Appendix 14, pp. 506–507.

98. "Program of the National Liberation Front of South Viet-Nam," in Marcus G. Raskin and Bernard F. Fall, eds., *The Viet-Nam Reader* (New York: Random House, 1965), pp. 216–217.

99. Quoted in Philippe Devillers, "Independence for Whom," *Viet-Report*, January 1966, p. 14.

100. Vo Nguyen Giap, "Once Again We Will Win," in Stetler, p. 273.

101. *Washington Post*, June 27, 1972, p. A12.

102. *Washington Post*, October 2, 1967.

103. The term is used in Vo Nguyen Giap, *Big Victory, Great Task* (New York: Praeger, 1968), p. 100.

104. Ibid., p. 24.

105. Interview with Giap by Jacques Decornoy, *Le Monde*, December 8, 1966.

106. Translation of a letter dated March 1966, to high Party officials in the South, captured by US forces in January 1967, released to the press March 16, 1967, in US Department of State, *Working Paper on the North Vietnamese Role in the War in South Viet-Nam*, May 1968, Annex, Document no. 302.

107. Giap, *Big Victory, Great Task*, pp. 59–60.

108. Speech by General Nguyen Van Vinh to the Fourth Congress of the Central Office for South Vietnam, April 1966, in *Working Paper*, Annex, Document no. 303.

109. "Truong Son on the Lessons of NLFSV Victories," from *Tap Chi Quan Doi Nhan Dan*, June 1967, in Patrick McGarvey, ed., *Visions of Victory: Selected Vietnamese Communist Military Writings, 1964–1968* (Stanford, Cal.: Hoover Institution on War, Revolution and Peace, 1969), p. 126.

110. Resolution of the Fourth COSVN Congress, March 1966, released to the press August 18, 1967, quoted in Melvin Gurtov, "Hanoi on War and Peace," in John R. Boettiger, ed., *Vietnam and American Foreign Policy* (Boston: D. C. Heath, 1968), p. 56.

111. "Truong Son on the 1965 Dry Season," from *Tap Chi Quan Doi Nhan Dan*, June 1966, Hanoi Radio, July 4–7, 1966, in McGarvey, p. 82.

2. *Negotiating Peace: The View from Washington*

1. *Supplemental Foreign Assistance, Fiscal Year 1966—Vietnam*, Hearings before the Committee on Foreign Relations, US Senate, 89th Congress, 2nd Session, 1966, p. 433.

2. *United States–Vietnam Relations 1945–1967* (Washington, D.C.: Government Printing Office, 1971), vol. 8, p. 474.

3. Ibid., vol. 9, pp. 274–275.

4. See Anthony Eden, *Full Circle* (London: Cassell, 1960), pp. 132–133.

5. US delegate Walter Bedell Smith stated at the final meeting of the Conference that the United States was "not prepared to join in a Declaration by the Conference such as is submitted." For the full text of his statement see George McT. Kahin and John W. Lewis, *The United States in Vietnam* (New York: Dell, 1967), Appendix 2, pp. 446–447.

6. *United States–Vietnam Relations*, vol. 9, p. 268.

7. Ibid., vol. 10, p. 697.

8. Ibid., vol. 10, pp. 935–936.

9. *New York Times*, August 9, 1955, cited in Franklin B. Weinstein, *Vietnam's Unheld Elections: The Failure to Carry Out the 1956 Reunification Elections and the Effect on Hanoi's Present Outlook*, Data Paper no. 60, Southeast Asia Program, Cornell University, July 1966, p. 32.

10. Weinstein, p. 32.

11. *The Pentagon Papers, Gravel Edition* (Boston: Beacon Press, 1971), vol. III, p. 503. (Hereafter cited as *Pentagon Papers.*)

12. The former Chief of Staff of the South Vietnamese army, General Tran Van Don, refers to the participation of Lansdale and Rufus Phillips of the CIA in the planning of these operations in his serialized memoirs "Vietnam Qua 20 Nam Bien Co" (Vietnam Through the Events of 20 Years), *Tieng Noi Dan Toc* (Voice of the Nation), Saigon, May 24 and 25, 1971. On the activities of the CIA in connection with the "civic action teams," see William A. Nighswonger, *Rural Pacification in Vietnam* (New York: Praeger, 1966), pp. 35–36.

13. *United States–Vietnam Relations,* vol. 10, p. 1080.

14. For the text see Kahin and Lewis, Appendix 2, p. 427.

15. For an explicit statement of this argument, see the address by Henry A. Byroade on October 30, 1953, in which colonial peoples in Africa were informed that statehood in the twentieth century involved "obligations" such as granting special economic rights to Western European states and participating in the security plans of the anti-Communist bloc. Department of State Press Release no. 605.

16. Paul M. Kattenburg, "Vietnam and U.S. Diplomacy," *Orbis,* XV (Fall 1971), p. 822.

17. Weinstein, p. 38.

18. See Roger Hilsman, *To Move a Nation* (New York: Doubleday, 1967), pp. 413–427. For an even more revealing glimpse of Kennedy administration thinking, see Hilsman's Foreword to Giap's *People's War, People's Army.* For a critique of the body of counterinsurgency doctrine, see Eqbal Ahmad, "The Theory and Fallacies of Counterinsurgency," *The Nation,* August 2, 1971, pp. 70–85.

19. Quoted in Hilsman, p. 415.

20. See the speech by Walt W. Rostow at the US Army Special Warfare school at Fort Bragg, June 1961, in Raskin and Fall, *The Viet-Nam Reader,* pp. 113–114.

21. Hilsman, pp. 431–432.

22. Theodore Sorenson, *Kennedy* (New York: Harper and Row, 1965), pp. 548–549.

23. In a phone conversation with the author on July 18, 1974, Rusk explained why the United States did not make a major diplomatic effort to resolve the Vietnam problem by negotiations as it had in Laos, as follows: "The build-up in Vietnam was still of modest proportions in 1961–62. If the Laotian solution would keep out North Vietnamese, we felt the South Vietnamese could handle the problem."

24. The first Chinese article to discuss the South Vietnamese struggle against Diem in any but the most general terms significantly failed to mention armed struggle at all but instead cited a series of "mass struggles" which consisted entirely of urban street demonstrations against the United States and Diem, suggesting that China was more comfortable with a struggle like the ones in Japan, South Korea, and Turkey during 1960, which had shaken the pro-US governments there but had not offered an excuse for a direct US military intervention. See "Under U.S.–Ngo Dinh Diem Rule," *Peking Review,* April 28, 1961, p. 44.

25. Liao Cheng-cheh, "The Present International Situation and Tasks of the World Peace Movement," *Peking Review*, July 19, 1960, p. 11.

26. New China News Agency, September 2, 1960. For other comments on China's desire to see Vietnam included in a "peace zone," see the article by *Jenmin Jihpao's* "Observer," *Peking Review*, May 16, 1961.

27. *Peking Review*, March 2, 1965.

28. Speech of July 21, 1962, in *Peking Review*, July 27, 1962, p. 9.

29. See New China News Agency, September 23 and October 5, 1962; *Jenmin Jihpao*, October 6, 1962; "Joint Struggle against U.S. Imperialism," *Peking Review*, October 12, 1962, p. 5.

30. Sorenson, p. 649.

31. Ibid., pp. 654 and 656.

32. Interview with Michael Forrestal, New York City, November 27, 1967.

33. Hilsman, p. 480.

34. Ibid., pp. 488 and 493.

35. Bernard Fall, "What de Gaulle Actually Said about Vietnam," *The Reporter*, October 24, 1963, p. 39.

36. Ibid., pp. 39–40.

37. *Chicago Sun-Times*, June 23, 1971. For the story of how this document found its way into public print (it was not included in the Pentagon Papers), see David Wise, *The Politics of Lying: Government Deception, Secrecy and Power* (New York: Vintage Books, 1973), pp. 172–195.

38. *New York Herald Tribune*, September 18, 1963.

39. *Washington Post*, September 19, 1963, p. A11.

40. *Pentagon Papers*, vol. II, p. 759.

41. *Chicago Sun-Times*, June 23, 1971.

42. *Pentagon Papers*, vol. III, pp. 502–503.

43. *New York Times*, July 24 and 25, 1964.

44. *New York Times*, July 26, 1964.

45. *Pentagon Papers*, vol. III, p. 526.

46. *Pentagon Papers*, vol. III, pp. 598–606, 656–666.

47. Ibid., p. 675.

48. Ibid., p. 605.

49. Ibid., p. 597.

50. Ibid.

51. Ibid., pp. 685–686.

52. Ibid., p. 685.

53. Ibid., pp. 689–690.

54. Transcript of a talk by General Nguyen Khanh, Ithaca, New York, December 6, 1973, p. 3.

55. John Gittings, "The Soviet Initiative on Vietnam—A Missed Opportunity?" *Viet-Report*, November-December 1965, vol. 1, no. 4, p. 19.

56. *New York Times*, February 26, 1965.

57. *Department of State Bulletin*, April 26, 1965. Reprinted in Kahin and Lewis, Appendix 13, p. 499.

58. *I. F. Stone's Weekly*, April 19, 1965, cited in Edward S. Herman and Richard

B. Du Boff, *America's Vietnam Policy: The Strategy of Deception* (Washington, D.C.: Public Affairs Press, 1966), p. 42.

59. Herman and Du Boff, p. 42.

60. *New York Times*, February 26, 1965.

61. *Department of State Bulletin*, January 17, 1956, p. 88; cited in Kahin and Lewis, p. 225.

62. *Supplemental Foreign Assistance, Fiscal Year 1966—Vietnam*, Hearings before the Committee on Foreign Relations, United States Senate, 89th Congress, 2nd Session, 1966, p. 665.

63. Rusk declared on June 24, 1965, "We'd be in favor of free elections in both places [North and South Vietnam]." Interview on US Information Agency Television Service, Department of State Press Release no. 167, July 3, 1965, p. 7. President Johnson supported "free elections" in South Vietnam or in both North and South Vietnam in his speech of July 28, 1965. See *New York Times*, July 29, 1965.

64. Philippe Devillers, "Preventing the Peace: Report from an Intermediary," *The Nation*, December 5, 1966, p. 600.

65. See, for example, *Pentagon Papers*, vol. IV, pp. 95–97.

66. As President Johnson said in a message to Ambassador Taylor on May 10, 1965, "You should understand that my purpose in this plan is to begin to clear a path either toward restoration of peace or toward increased military action, depending upon the reaction of the Communists." *Pentagon Papers*, vol. IV, p. 366.

67. *New York Times*, May 19, 1965.

68. For the full text see *Pentagon Papers*, vol. IV, p. 369.

69. Ibid., p. 380.

70. Ibid., p. 33.

71. On the Communist stand-down see *New York Times*, February 3, 1966; *Philadelphia Daily News*, January 28, 1966, cited in Herman and Du Boff, p. 68. On the US offensive during January see *New York Times*, January 10, January 30, February 2, 1966.

72. *New York Herald Tribune*, January 29, 1966, cited in Herman and Du Boff, p. 68.

73. *New York Times*, February 1, 1966.

74. UPI, *Philadelphia Bulletin*, January 28, 1966; *New York Times*, January 28, 1966, cited in Herman and Du Boff, p. 69.

75. *New York Times*, October 26, 1966, cited in Kahin and Lewis, p. 337.

76. On "Face the Nation," February 4, 1968, *Department of State Bulletin*, February 26, 1968, p. 277.

77. *New York Times*, November 5, 1966.

78. Report by McNamara on a meeting with Ambassador Maxwell Taylor and US military leaders in Honolulu, dated April 21, 1965, *Pentagon Papers*, vol. IV, pp. 705–706.

79. Ibid., vol. IV, p. 294.

80. *Supplemental Defense Appropriations, Fiscal Year 1966*, Hearings before a Subcommittee of the Committee on Appropriations, House of Representatives, 89th Congress, 2nd Session, 1966, p. 91.

81. This account of the failure of "Marigold" is based on Kraslow and Loory, pp. 3-88; Cooper, pp. 333-342; Richard Hudson, "The Nearest to Negotiations Yet," *War/Peace Report*, March 1967, pp. 3-4.

82. Cooper, p. 339.

83. See Cooper, pp. 351-368.

84. At the same time, the hardening of the US position was reinforced by a letter sent by President Johnson to Ho Chi Minh, again demanding prior cessation of infiltration from the North before a bombing halt, with no US commitment to deescalation. See *New York Times*, March 22, 1967.

85. This account is based on the *Washington Post*, June 27, 1972, p. A12.

86. *New York Times*, September 30, 1967.

87. For a discussion of the process by which the US-sponsored constitution and elections were brought about, see Kahin and Lewis, pp. 345-459.

88. Quoted in Townsend Hoopes, *The Limits of Intervention* (New York: David McKay, 1969), p. 73.

89. *Pentagon Papers*, vol. IV, pp. 348-349.

90. Ibid., vol. IV, p. 442.

91. Ibid., vol. IV, pp. 463, 512.

92. Ibid., p. 516.

93. Hoopes, p. 105.

94. *Pentagon Papers*, vol. IV, p. 465.

95. Hoopes, p. 102.

96. *Pentagon Papers*, vol. IV, p. 374.

97. Hoopes, p. 97.

98. Don Oberdorfer, *Tet!* (New York: Avon Books, 1972), p. 101.

99. Ibid., p. 100.

100. John P. Robinson and Solomon G. Jacobson, "American Public Opinion about Vietnam," *Peace Research Society (International) Papers*, X (June 1968), p. 71.

101. Sidney Verba et al., "Public Opinion and the War in Vietnam," *American Political Science Review*, LXI, 2 (June 1967), p. 320.

102. See F. M. Kail, *What Washington Said, Administration Rhetoric and the Vietnam War: 1949-1969* (New York: Harper Torchbooks, 1973), p. 29.

103. Ibid.

3. The Paris Talks: Origins of a Diplomatic Stalemate

1. For a journalistic account of the Tet Offensive and its impact on American society and policy in Vietnam, see Don Oberdorfer, *Tet!* (New York: Avon Books, 1972). The following account departs from Oberdorfer's interpretation of the purpose of the offensive.

2. *The Pentagon Papers, Gravel Edition* (Boston: Beacon Press, 1971), vol. IV, p. 547.

3. *National Observer*, March 11, 1968; *New York Times*, February 6, 8, 1968; *Newsweek*, February 19, 1968, p. 34.

4. Douglas Pike, *War, Peace and the Viet Cong* (Cambridge: M.I.T. Press, 1969), pp. 27, 29, 30.

5. "Status of Refugees," official report by the Office of Refugees, US Agency for International Development, Vietnam, May 2, 1968; *Saigon Post*, March 17, 1968. The GVN and the United States later claimed that 1,000 and then 4,000 or more civilians were murdered by the NLF during the occupation. For an analysis of these claims, which concludes that they were false and misleading, see D. Gareth Porter, "U. S. Political Warfare and Vietnam: The 1968 'Hue Massacre'," *Indochina Chronicle*, no. 33, June 24, 1974, pp. 1–13, reprinted in *Congressional Record*, February 19, 1975, pp. S2189–2194.

6. *Pentagon Papers*, vol. IV, p. 548.

7. Interview with a high-ranking US official in Saigon, June 18, 1968.

8. Associated Press dispatch, *South Bend Tribune*, May 10, 1968.

9. This was the argument presented to President Johnson by General Wheeler on February 28, 1968. See *New York Times*, March 6, 1969. Also see *Newsweek*, February 19, 1968, p. 33.

10. *New York Times*, April 1, 1968.

11. *Time*, February 9, 1968, p. 23.

12. This is not to say that many cadres and others who followed the Front during the Tet Offensive did not believe that it was a war-ending offensive. A COSVN resolution issued more than a year later complained that cadres at province and region levels had misunderstood the purpose of the Tet Offensive and thought it was a "one blow affair" which had failed. *COSVN Resolution 9, July 1969*, mimeographed manuscript released by the US Mission in Vietnam (no date).

13. "Circular from COSVN Current Affairs Committee and Military Affairs Committee of the S. V. L. A. F. Headquarters Concerning a Preliminary Assessment of the Situation," in Patrick McGarvey, ed., *Visions of Victory: Selected Vietnamese Communist Military Writings, 1964–1968* (Stanford, Cal.: Hoover Institution on War, Revolution and Peace, 1969), p. 253.

14. Liberation Radio, in Vietnamese, October 30, 1967.

15. Directive from a Party Provincial Standing Committee to a District Committee, November 1, 1967. Viet-Nam Documents and Research Notes, Document no. 28, April 1968, p. 5.

16. This paragraph is based on my notes from Interrogation Report no. 6, one of a series of such reports on interrogations with prisoners taken during the Tet Offensive and made available by the US Embassy in July 1968.

17. Interrogation Report no. 3.

18. This is the conclusion reached by a RAND Corporation study based on 405 interviews in Saigon-Cholon-Gia Dinh after the Tet Offensive. Victoria Pohle, *The Viet Cong in Saigon: Tactics and Objectives during the Tet Offensive*, RAND project no. 9994, May 1, 1968. See especially pp. 40–48.

19. Interrogation Report no. 12.

20. Interrogation Report no. 1.

21. Oberdorfer, pp. 85–86.

22. See George McT. Kahin and John W. Lewis, *The United States in Vietnam* (New York: Dell, 1967), p. 360. For the full text of the 1967 NLF program, see *New York Times*, December 15, 1967.

23. On the personalities who made up the national "Alliance" organization,

see *The Sunday Star* (Washington, D.C.), May 12, 1968; and Robert Shaplen, "Letter from Saigon," *The New Yorker*, June 29, 1968.

24. Edith Lenart, "A Neutral Peace?" *Far Eastern Economic Review*, June 27, 1968, p. 639. Professor Richard Falk and lawyer Malcolm Burnestein, after conversations with DRV leaders in France, said the Alliance could be the central element of a coalition government. *New York Times*, July 9, 1968.

25. Chester L. Cooper, *The Lost Crusade* (New York: Dodd, Mead and Company, 1970), p. 391.

26. Townsend Hoopes, *The Limits of Intervention* (New York: David McKay, 1969), pp. 171–181; *New York Times*, March 6, 7, 1969.

27. Hoopes, p. 182.

28. Lyndon Baines Johnson, *The Vantage Point, Perspectives on the Presidency, 1963–1969* (New York: Holt, Rinehart, and Winston, 1971), pp. 416–418; Hoopes, pp. 214–218; *New York Times*, March 7, 1969.

29. *New York Times*, March 7, 1969.

30. Johnson, p. 421; Cooper, p. 395.

31. *Pentagon Papers*, vol. IV, p. 270.

32. *Washington Post*, April 12, 1968.

33. *New York Times*, April 3, 1968.

34. Johnson, p. 421. This was, as Johnson says, a formula to permit US reconnaissance flights over the North.

35. These were the four points on which the DRV says the United States demanded agreement before there could be a bombing halt. See the text of the DRV statement in Paris, April 20, 1972, *New York Times*, April 21, 1972. The State Department said that the statement had presented only part of the record, but did not challenge any specifics and refused to release its own minutes of the meetings. *New York Times*, April 22, 1972. Chester Cooper confirms the essence of this US proposal, but does not mention the requirement that neither side build up its forces. Cooper, pp. 398–399, 403.

36. Kahin and Lewis, p. 384.

37. Averell Harriman, "Harriman Suggests a Way Out of Vietnam," *New York Times Magazine*, August 24, 1969, p. 74.

38. Cooper, pp. 400–401; Kahin and Lewis, p. 385.

39. Johnson, p. 421.

40. DRV statement, April 20, 1972, *New York Times*, April 21, 1972.

41. *Los Angeles Times*, October 18, 1968, March 9, 1969.

42. *New York Times*, November 11, 1968; *Washington Post*, November 3, 1968.

43. Johnson, p. 518; *Los Angeles Times*, March 9, 1969.

44. Johnson, p. 518.

45. DRV statement, April 20, 1972, *New York Times*, April 21, 1972.

46. Ibid.

47. Ibid. Johnson's account of this phase of the negotiations is consistent with the DRV version. He adds, however, that the DRV originally wanted "weeks" to elapse between the bombing halt and the start of negotiations but finally agreed to only three days. Johnson, pp. 516–517.

48. Johnson, p. 511.

49. *Saigon Daily News*, April 15, 1968.

50. *Washington Post*, November 5, 1968; *New York Times*, November 11, 1968.

51. *Chicago Daily News*, November 5, 1968.

52. *New York Times*, November 11, 1968.

53. *Christian Science Monitor*, November 12, 1968; *Chicago Daily News*, November 5, 1968. Another, similar, version of the story is found in the Drew Pearson–Jack Anderson column, *Washington Post*, November 17, 1968.

54. Johnson, pp. 517–518, 521.

55. *New York Times*, November 1, 1968.

56. *Washington Post*, November 4, 1968.

57. *Los Angeles Times*, February 27, 28, 1969.

58. Saigon Radio, February 2, 1968; cited in Kahin and Lewis, p. 390.

59. *New York Times*, November 6, 1968.

60. *New York Times*, November 14, 1968.

61. *Los Angeles Times*, November 16, 1968.

62. *New York Times*, December 6, 1968.

63. Phone conversation with Averell Harriman, September 12, 1974.

64. Phone conversation with Harriman; *Baltimore Sun*, January 9, 1969; *New York Times*, January 17, 1969.

65. See Hoopes, pp. 227–228; *Christian Science Monitor*, November 4, 1968; *Wall Street Journal*, October 17, 1968.

66. Quoted in Lewis Chester et al., *An American Melodrama: The Presidential Campaign of 1968* (New York: Viking Press, 1969), p. 464.

67. Ibid.

68. Richard Whalen, *Catch the Falling Flag: A Republican's Challenge to His Party* (Boston: Houghton Mifflin, 1972), p. 139.

69. Henry Kissinger, "What Should We Do Now?" *Look*, August 9, 1966.

70. Henry Kissinger, "The Viet-Nam Negotiations," *Foreign Affairs*, vol. 47, no. 2 (January 1969), pp. 211–234. Reprinted in Paul T. Menzel, ed., *Moral Argument and the War in Vietnam* (Nashville: Aurora Publishers, 1971), pp. 147–156.

71. Ibid., p. 155.

72. Ibid.

73. Ibid.

74. Ibid.

75. Ibid., p. 156.

76. Ibid., p. 155.

77. Patrick Anderson, "Confidence of the President," *New York Times Magazine*, June 1, 1969, p. 44.

78. Gerald Astor, "Strategist in the White House," *Look*, August 12, 1969, p. 56.

79. *Time*, August 29, 1969.

80. *Washington Post*, December 3, 1969.

81. For the most complete exploration of the bombing of Cambodia and the cover-up, see *Bombing in Cambodia*, Hearings before the Committee on Armed Services, US Senate, 93rd Congress, 1st Session, 1973.

82. National Security Memorandum No. 1 (NSM-1), *Congressional Record*, May

11, 1972, p. E5023. This is the incomplete text of a long series of questions on Vietnam from Kissinger to various agencies and their answers. The top secret document, completed early in 1969, was leaked to the press in 1972 and entered into the *Congressional Record* by Congressman Ron Dellums (D.-Calif.).

83. *Briefing by Secretary of State William P. Rogers*, Hearing before the Committee on Foreign Relations, US Senate, 91st Congress, 1st Session, March 27, 1969. Rogers' own Department of State had commented in its response for the NSM-1 that the demand for acknowledgment of GVN sovereignty and acceptance of the GVN constitution amounted to "surrender in NLF eyes" and that most GVN leaders knew they were "not realistic." The same leaders, according to the State Department, found it "extremely hard to envisage any softer formula which does not entail risks which they now regard as quite unacceptable." *Congressional Record*, May 11, 1972, p. E5066.

84. Ibid., p. 38.

85. Saigon Radio, Domestic Service, April 7, 1969.

86. *New York Times*, May 15, 1969.

87. Saigon Radio, Domestic Service, July 11, 1969.

88. *New York Times*, July 14, 1969.

89. *Briefing on Vietnam*, Hearings before the Committee on Foreign Relations, US Senate, 91st Congress, 1st Session, 1969, p. 48.

90. Robert G. Kaiser, "Elections Aren't Vietnamese Style," *Washington Post*, July 6, 1969, p. B1.

91. See the comments by DRV delegate Xuan Thuy, *Washington Post*, April 18, 1969.

92. NSM-1, *Congressional Record*, May 11, 1972, p. E5012.

93. Marvin Kalb and Bernard Kalb, *Kissinger* (Boston: Little Brown, 1974), pp. 105–113.

94. Ibid., p. 131.

95. Ibid., pp. 126–127.

96. *New York Times*, May 15, 1969.

97. Kalb and Kalb, p. 134.

98. *Le Monde*, November 5, 1969.

99. Ibid.

100. Harriman, p. 76.

101. NSM-1, *Congressional Record*, May 11, 1972, p. E5025.

102. Kalb and Kalb, p. 113.

103. Press Conference, January 30, 1970, *Public Papers of the Presidents, Richard Nixon, 1970* (Washington, D. C.: Government Printing Office, 1971), p. 37.

104. A study on the political and military situation in South Vietnam as of April 1970 by the Vietnam Special Study Group of the National Security Council staff concluded that if US troop withdrawals continued at their current rate to July 1971, the Thieu regime would begin to lose ground in Binh Dinh, Quang Nam, and several other provinces. Henry Brandon, *The Retreat of American Power* (New York: Doubleday, 1973), pp. 328–329.

105. *Washington Post*, May 11, 1970.

106. *Christian Science Monitor*, May 5, 1970.

107. *New York Times*, April 21, 1970.

108. Two detailed, though unofficial, expositions of such a plan are presented in Samuel P. Huntington, "Getting Ready for Political Competition in South Vietnam," SEADAG Discussion Paper, for presentation at a joint session of the SEADAG Political Development Seminar and Council on Vietnamese Studies, Statler Hilton, Boston, March 29, 1969; and "The Vance Plan for a Vietnam Cease-Fire" (interview with Cyrus Vance), *New York Times Magazine*, September 21, 1969, pp. 30–31, 93–99. For press reports indicating that the plan had been adopted as a possible solution by the Nixon administration, see David Kraslow and Tom Lambert, Los Angeles Times Service, *New Haven Register*, August 1, 1969, and Max Frankel, *New York Times*, June 21, 1969.

109. Huntington, pp. 115–116.

110. Quoted in Kraslow and Lambert, Los Angeles Times Service, *New Haven Register*, August 1, 1969.

111. *A New Peace Initiative for All Indochina*, An Address to the Nation by Richard Nixon, President of the United States, October 7, 1970, Department of State Publication 8555, East Asia and Pacific Series 196.

112. *New York Times*, October 8, 1970.

113. Kissinger, "The Vietnam Negotiations," p. 152.

114. This proposal, the text of which was never made public, was described in President Nixon's press conference on January 25, 1972 and Dr. Kissinger's press conference of January 26, 1972. *Washington Post*, January 26, 27, 1972.

115. Tad Szulc, "Behind the Vietnam Cease-fire Agreement," *Foreign Policy*, no. 15 (summer 1974), p. 27.

116. Truong Chinh, "Let Us Be Grateful to Karl Marx and Follow the Path Traced by Him," serialized on Hanoi Radio, September 16–19, 1968, and translated in Vietnam Documents and Research Notes, no. 51, p. 2.

117. *Baltimore Sun*, October 17, 1968; *New York Times*, January 21, 1969.

118. *Briefing on Vietnam*, p. 5.

119. See Peter Arnett, Associated Press, *Philadelphia Sunday Bulletin*, March 23, 1969.

120. See COSVN Resolution 14, Vietnam Documents and Research Notes, no. 81, July 21, 1970.

121. See, for example, *Study of COSVN Resolution 10*, COSVN Directive 01/CT71, Vietnam Documents and Research Notes, no. 99, October 1971, p. 4.

122. See Raphael Littauer and Norman Uphoff, eds., *The Air War in Indochina*, rev. ed. (Boston: Beacon Press, 1972), p. 281.

123. "B-52 Big Weapon in Saigon Defense," *Washington Post*, August 12, 1968.

124. Fox Butterfield, "Peace Is Still at Hand," *New York Times Magazine*, November 11, 1973, p. 132.

125. *Study of COSVN Resolution 10*, p. 3.

126. See David W. P. Elliott, *NLF-DRV Strategy and the 1972 Spring Offensive*, Cornell University International Relations of East Asia Project, Interim Report No. 4, January 1974, pp. 13–17.

127. *New York Times*, May 9, 1969.

128. Interview with Hoang Tung, Hanoi, December 31, 1974.

129. Text of letter from Professor Joseph R. Starobin to Senator J. W. Fulbright, November 6, 1969, in *Briefing on Vietnam*, p. 158.

130. Ibid.

131. *Los Angeles Times*, May 21, 1969.

132. Richard J. Barnet, "How Hanoi Sees Nixon," *New York Review of Books*, January 29, 1970, p. 21.

133. Kalb and Kalb, p. 151.

134. Full text in *New York Times*, September 18, 1970.

135. For the text released by Hanoi, see *New York Times*, February 1, 1972.

136. "7-Point Statement by the Provisional Revolutionary Government of the Republic of South Vietnam, made public by Minister Madame Nguyen Thi Binh at the Paris Conference on Viet Nam (July 1st, 1971)," Delegation of the PRG to the Paris Conference on Viet Nam.

137. For an analysis of the significance of DRV/PRG initiative, see George McT. Kahin, "Negotiations: The View from Hanoi," *New Republic*, November 6, 1971, pp. 13–16.

138. UPI dispatches, *Saigon Post*, August 20, 28, 1971.

139. *Christian Science Monitor*, June 25, 1971; *Stars and Stripes*, July 8, 1971.

140. For the full text of this document, see *Indochina Chronicle*, no. 5, September 15, 1971, pp. 1, 4–8.

141. Again, no text is available. For description of the August 16 proposal see Kissinger's press conference, *New York Times*, January 27, 1972.

142. Ibid.

143. Szulc, p. 30.

144. Text released by the DRV, *New York Times*, February 1, 1972.

145. Ibid.

4. Hanoi Pushes for an Agreement

1. For a discussion of the "factional" interpretation of the North Vietnamese leadership, see D. Gareth Porter, "How Scholars Lie," *Worldview*, vol. 16, no. 12 (December 1973), pp. 22–27.

2. Ibid., p. 26.

3. John Prados, "Year of the Rat: Vietnam, 1972," *Strategy and Tactics*, no. 35 (November 1972), p. 13.

4. Ibid., p. 9. Another source says that there was "no more than a single Northern division on South Vietnamese territory" by the end of 1971. See Jean Lacouture, "Toward an End to the Indochina War?" *Pacific Community*, vol. 3, no. 2 (January 1972), p. 330.

5. For an excellent analysis of the 1972 offensive, see David W. P. Elliott, *N. L. F.–D. R. V. Strategy and the 1972 Spring Offensive*, International Relations of East Asia Project, Cornell University, Interim Report no. 4, January 1974.

6. For two articles on the North Vietnamese military review which emphasize these aims, see Trung Dung, "Nhung Chuyen Bien Lon Trong Cuc Dien Chien Tranh" (Big Changes in the War Situation), *Tap Chi Quan Doi Nhan Dan* (People's Army Review), no. 5 (May 1972), pp. 1–11; Quyet Thang, "Thang Loi To Lon,

Buoc Tien Manh Me" (Big Victory, Powerful Stride Forward), *Tap Chi Quan Doi Nhan Dan*, no. 4 (April 1972), pp. 70–77.

7. *Time*, April 17, 1972, p. 38; V. B., "The April Offensive," *Vietnam Courier*, June 1972, p. 5. A detailed account of the 56th regiment's defection to the PLAF is found in Nguyen Khac, "Gap Cac Si Quan Phan Chien Trung Doan 56" (Meet the Anti-War Officers of the 56th Regiment), *Doan Ket* (Paris), May 10, 1972, p. 6.

8. The concept of "outer defense" lines, as opposed to the "inner front" of pacification, is presented in V. B., "The April Offensive," pp. 3–5; also see Elliott, pp. 50–51.

9. Prados, p. 15.

10. *New York Times*, April 21, 26, 27, 1972; Prados, p. 15.

11. *New York Times*, April 29, 1972.

12. *New York Times*, April 27, 30, May 2, 3, 1972; V. B., "The April Offensive," p. 6; Tom Fox, "New Offensive?" *American Report*, September 1, 1972, p. 8.

13. *New York Times*, April 30, 31, 1972.

14. This paragraph is based on the account by Judith Coburn in *The Village Voice*, July 20, 1973, pp. 8, 18, 20; *New York Times*, May 4, 1972.

15. Tom Fox, "The Current Offensive: Final Push or Continuing Struggle," *American Report*, June 2, 1972, p. 12; V. B., "The April Offensive," p. 6.

16. Fox, "The Current Offensive," p. 12.

17. *New York Times*, April 29, 1972.

18. Elliott, p. 22.

19. *New York Times*, June 20, 1972.

20. *Baltimore Sun*, April 16, 1972; *Time*, June 19, 1972, p. 24.

21. *Time*, September 11, 1972; *Los Angeles Times*, September 9, 1972, part 1, p. 13.

22. *Time*, September 11, 1972, p. 24.

23. Prados, p. 16.

24. Ton Vy, "The Second Battle of Quang Tri," *Viet Nam Courier*, September 1972, p. 9; Prados, p. 16.

25. Tom Fox, "New Offensive?" p. 8.

26. Ibid.

27. Thuong Duc, "War of Attrition," *Viet Nam Report*, vol. 1, no. 12, June 1972; *Wall Street Journal*, October 4, 1972.

28. See Elliott, p. 52.

29. *New York Times*, April 7, 1972.

30. Marvin Kalb and Bernard Kalb, *Kissinger* (Boston: Little, Brown, 1974), pp. 293–294.

31. Ibid.

32. Ibid., p. 298.

33. Ibid., p. 209.

34. Charles Bartlett, *Washington Star*, June 20, 1972.

35. *New York Times*, May 9, 1972.

36. J. J. Brown, "Mining of Haiphong Port Won't Stop Supplies," Dispatch News Service International, Release no. 323, May 9, 1972.

37. *New York Times*, May 3, 1972.

38. UPI dispatch, *Washington Star*, May 23, 1972.

39. For an excellent analysis of the evolution of Chinese policy toward the United States, see Jim Peck, "Why China Turned West," *Ramparts*, May 1972, pp. 34–41.

40. Wilfred Burchett, *The Guardian*, February 28, 1973.

41. Kalb and Kalb, p. 264.

42. "Unite People, Defeat the Enemy, A Study of 'Our Policy'," *Peking Review*, no. 35, August 27, 1972, pp. 10–13.

43. *Peking Review*, no. 9, March 3, 1972, p. 4.

44. See Peck, p. 38, and David Mozingo, "Why Are the Chinese Being So Nice to Nixon?" *Understanding China* (Ann Arbor, Mich.), vol. 8, no. 6 (November-December 1972), pp. 1, 6.

45. "Statement of the Government of the People's Republic of China," May 11, 1972, *Peking Review*, no. 20 (May 19, 1972), p. 6.

46. Prados, p. 13.

47. Nguyen Khac Vien, "The American War: An Interview with *Jeune Afrique*," in David Marr and Jayne Werner, eds., *Tradition and Revolution in Vietnam*, translated by Linda Yarr, Jayne Werner, and Tran Tuong Nhu (Berkeley: Indochina Resource Center, 1974), p. 161.

48. *Nhan Dan*, August 17, 1972. Translated in *Viet-Nam Courier*, no. 4, September 1972, p. 3.

49. *Tokyo Shimbun*, November 3, 1973.

50. Kalb and Kalb, p. 330; Frank Van Der Linden, *Nixon's Quest for Peace* (New York: David McKay, 1972), p. 196.

51. Tad Szulc, "Behind the Vietnam Cease-Fire Agreement," *Foreign Policy* no. 15 (Summer 1974), pp. 41–42.

52. *Christian Science Monitor*, August 29, 1972.

53. *Department of Defense, Appropriations*, Hearings before a Subcommittee of the Committee on Appropriations, House of Representatives, 93rd Congress, 1st Session, 1973, p. 5.

54. Jean Thoraval, Agence France-Presse, *Christian Science Monitor*, September 7, 1972.

55. Nguyen Khac Vien, p. 149.

56. *Washington Post*, November 12, 1972. This account by Don Oberforder was based on reports by defectors from the Party during 1972.

57. Text of Kissinger's news conference, *New York Times*, May 10, 1972.

58. Excerpts from the original Vietnamese text of Le Duc Tho's press conference, *Doan Ket*, May 31, 1972, p. 7. A slightly different translation from my own is given in the *New York Times*, May 13, 1972, which omits the words "whomever they wish to choose, they can choose. . . ."

59. *New York Times*, May 13, 1972.

60. See text of Kissinger's news conference, January 27, 1972, *Washington Post*, January 28, 1972.

61. *Washington Post*, June 11, 1972.

62. This was the view expressed by high-ranking North Vietnamese diplomat Nguyen Minh Vy to American antiwar movement leaders in Paris in mid-June.

See Dave Dellinger, "Conversations with the Vietnamese in Paris," *Liberation*, August 1972, p. 13.

63. Confronted with eyewitness reports of the bombing of dikes in North Vietnam, a Pentagon spokesman said on June 30 that the dike system was not "targeted," but added, "That doesn't mean that some of them don't get hit by stray weaponry." *New York Times*, July 1, 1972.

64. *New York Times*, July 6, 1972.

65. *Boston Globe*, July 7, 1972.

66. Reuters dispatch, *Washington Post*, August 17, 1972 and *Le Monde*, August 18, 1972.

67. *New York Times*, July 29, 1972. For specialist's views, see the remarks at an international congress of geographers by Professor F. R. Garry, specialist in the geography of Indochina at the University of Montreal, in *Montreal Star*, August 17, 1972.

68. Yves Lacoste, *Le Monde*, August 16, 1972.

69. *The Guardian* (London), July 22, 1972.

70. See George McT. Kahin, *New York Times*, October 26, 1972.

71. Nguyen Khac Vien, p. 152.

72. Huong Nam, "At the Paris Talks: Two Opposing Negotiating Positions," *Hoc Tap*, no. 9 (September 1972), pp. 70–76.

73. *New York Times*, September 12, 1972.

74. *Washington Star*, September 14, 1972.

75. Kalb and Kalb, p. 348.

76. *New York Times*, September 17, 1972.

77. See Daniel Yankelovich, "Why Nixon Won," *New York Review of Books*, November 30, 1972, p. 7.

78. Joseph Kraft pointed out during a visit to Hanoi in July that "The smart money in Las Vegas is not quoting heavier odds against George McGovern's election as President than the Communist leadership here in Hanoi. . . . ," *Washington Post*, July 23, 1972.

79. Hoang Tung later said in a 1974 interview that the offensive "fell short of expectations" both in the destruction of Saigon's forces and the capture of territory in the Delta. Quoted in Tom Hayden, "What Détente Means to the Vietnamese," *Focal Point* (published by the Indochina Peace Campaign, Santa Monica, Calif.), July 1974, p. 3.

80. This synopsis is based on the summary of the draft agreement made public by the DRV on October 26, 1972, published in the *New York Times*, October 27, 1972, and information from official sources concerning other points in the original DRV proposal and the October draft not covered in the summary.

81. Kalb and Kalb, pp. 354–355.

82. Statement by George Aldrich, legal adviser, Department of State, in *Situation in Indochina*, Hearings before the Committee on Foreign Affairs, House of Representatives, 93rd Congress, 1st Session, 1973, pp. 8–9.

83. DRV statement of October 26, *New York Times*, October 27, 1972.

84. Press conference of Xuan Thuy, October 26, *Washington Post*, October 27, 1972; Kalb and Kalb, p. 360.

85. News conference of DRV spokesman Nguyen Thanh Le, October 27, 1972, *New York Times*, October 28, 1972; Nguyen Minh Vy, quoted in Richard Barnet, "Peace: Why the Delay?," *American Report*, November 6, 1972, p. 7; *New York Times*, November 5, 1972.

86. Szulc, p. 54.

87. Kalb and Kalb, p. 357; Joseph Kraft, *Washington Post*, January 9, 1973. Haig reportedly had not supported even the tripartite electoral commission proposed by Kissinger earlier in the year. Szulc, p. 50.

88. *Le Monde*, November 1, 1972.

89. Szulc, pp. 48–49.

90. Ibid., pp. 49–50.

91. *Chinh Luan*, October 1, 1972.

92. *Washington Star-News*, November 10, 1972.

93. Tom Fox, "Cease-Fire a Possibility in Vietnam—Thieu Worries," Dispatch News Service International, Release no. 410, August 16, 1972.

94. *Washington Post*, November 9, 1972.

95. Associated Press dispatch, October 16, 1972.

96. *Baltimore Sun*, November 11, 1972. Mrs. Nguyen Thi Binh of the PRG delegation, in speeches in October and November, frequently referred to the US "responsibility" to "put pressure on Thieu" to release the political prisoners.

97. Kalb and Kalb, pp. 360–361.

98. DRV statement of October 26. This part of the DRV account is confirmed by administration sources.

99. Interview with Xuan Thuy, *New York Times*, November 5, 1972. Administration sources refuse to comment on the question of US commitments to the DRV during this period of the DRV account, leaving little doubt that the DRV account is essentially correct.

100. DRV statement of October 26.

101. Ibid.

102. Ibid.

103. Kalb and Kalb, pp. 377–378.

104. DRV statement of October 26.

105. Text of Kissinger's news conference, *New York Times*, October 27, 1972.

106. "Exclusive from Hanoi," *Newsweek*, October 30, 1972, pp. 26–27.

5. Showdown: Hanoi and Paris

1. *New York Times*, November 2, 3, 1972.

2. *New York Times*, November 6, 1972.

3. Address to the National Assembly, Saigon Radio Domestic Service, December 12, 1972.

4. "Thieu," An Interview with Oriana Fallaci, *New Republic*, January 30, 1973, p. 17.

5. *Boston Globe*, October 30, 1972.

6. Interview with Kingsbury Smith, Hearst newspapers, *Baltimore News-American*, December 17, 1972.

7. "Thieu," pp. 17–18; Associated Press dispatch, *Baltimore Sun*, November 10, 1972; *Daily Telegraph* (London), November 13, 1972.

8. *Chinh Luan*, October 1–2, 1972.

9. Saigon Radio Domestic Service, December 12, 1972.

10. For the Vietnamese text of the nine-point summary, see *Nhan Dan*, October 26, 1972.

11. *Le Figaro*, November 10, 1972.

12. *New York Times*, November 1, 1972.

13. *Le Figaro*, November 23, 1972. The text of the final agreement amended Article 1 by adding the words "and all other countries" after the United States.

14. *New York Times*, November 1, 1972.

15. See *New York Times*, November 1, 1972; *Washington Star-News*, November 1, 1972; Associated Press dispatch, *Baltimore Sun*, November 2, 1972. Kissinger is named as the source of these stories in *Philadelphia Evening Bulletin*, November 5, 1972.

16. *Christian Science Monitor*, November 10, 1972; for a similar account of the administration's perceptions of North Vietnam's readiness to yield further in the talks, see *Wall Street Journal*, November 17, 1972.

17. *Washington Star-News*, November 6, 1972.

18. *Washington Post*, January 17, 1973; Stanley Karnow, "We Aren't Out of Vietnam," *New Republic*, November 17, 1973, pp. 19–20.

19. *New York Times*, October 31, 1972.

20. *New York Times*, October 28, 1972.

21. *Baltimore Sun*, November 7, 1972.

22. *Baltimore Sun*, November 17, 1972.

23. *New York Times*, November 11, 1972.

24. Vietnam News Agency, November 19, 1972.

25. Tad Szulc, "Behind the Vietnam Cease-fire Agreement," *Foreign Policy*, no. 15 (summer 1974), pp. 59–60; Marvin Kalb and Bernard Kalb, *Kissinger* (Boston: Little, Brown, 1974), p. 395.

26. Hoang Tung stated flatly, "In November, they [the US delegation] once more put forward the demand for a partial withdrawal." Interview, Hanoi, January 7, 1975.

27. Xerox copy of a four-page letter from Nixon to Thieu, dated November 14, 1972, released by Dr. Nguyen Tien Hung, former Minister of Planning in the Thieu government, at a press conference in Washington, D.C., April 30, 1975. The White House confirmed the authenticity of the documents released by Dr. Hung. *New York Times*, May 1, 1975.

28. Xuan Thuy, interviewed on ABC's "Issues and Answers," December 24, 1972. This was confirmed by US and Saigon government sources. See *The Guardian* (London), December 22, 1972, and *Boston Globe*, December 8, 1972.

29. See Kissinger's January 24 press conference, *New York Times*, January 25, 1973.

30. *New York Times*, November 30, 1972.

31. Address to the press by Xuan Thuy, Paris, December 19, 1972 (mimeographed).

32. James A. Wechsler, *New York Post*, December 28, 1972. Wechsler quotes a statement from the interview with Xuan Thuy on "Issues and Answers" which was not in the printed transcript because the program had actually ended.

33. Louis Wiznitzer, "Peace: What Went Wrong?" *American Report*, January 1–15, 1973, p. 7.

34. Kalb and Kalb, p. 400.

35. Agence France-Presse, Hanoi, November 29, 1972. This important dispatch, which was not published in either the *New York Times* or the *Washington Post*, was carried in the *Detroit News*, November 30, 1972, but *without* the crucial paragraphs quoted above.

36. Wiznitzer, p. 7. This would later be cited by Kissinger and Sullivan in a background news briefing as evidence of a North Vietnamese intention to "stall" the talks. See *New York Times*, December 21, 1972.

37. Agence France-Presse, Paris, December 8, 1972, published in part in *Boston Globe*, December 9, 1972.

38. The Pathet Lao had already taken a major step toward a peace settlement on September 22, 1972, when they offered immediate negotiations, without preconditions, dropping their previous insistence on an end to all US bombing in Laos before they would negotiate. MacAlister Brown and Joseph J. Zasloff, "The Pathet Lao and the Politics of Reconciliation in Laos," paper delivered at SEADAG Conference on Communist Movements and Regimes in Indochina, New York, September 30–October 2, 1974, p. 6.

39. Wiznitzer, p. 7.

40. Rear Admiral Brian McCauley, "Operation End Sweep," *U.S. Naval Institute Proceedings*, March 1974, p. 22.

41. Xuan Thuy, "Issues and Answers," December 24, 1972.

42. *The Guardian* (London), December 22, 1972.

43. Kalb and Kalb, p. 412.

44. *The Guardian* (London), December 22, 1972; Associated Press dispatch, Saigon, *Washington Star-News*, December 21, 1972.

45. Wilfred Burchett, "The Laws of Negotiation—U.S. Style," unpublished paper (mimeographed), 1974, p. 4.

46. Murray Marder, "North Vietnam: Pride in Taking Punishment," *Washington Post*, February 4, 1973, p. C4.

47. See *New York Times*, December 17, 1972, for the full transcript.

48. Xerox copy of the document entitled "Plan of General Uprising When a Political Solution Is Reached," translated by the US Information Service in Saigon. The document's contents were reported in detail in the *Washington Post*, November 6, 1972. For further discussion and quotation from this document, see D. Gareth Porter, "Does Thieu Continue the War to Avoid Political Defeat?," *The Christian Century*, April 25, 1973, p. 474.

49. A fairly complete picture emerges by comparing the coverage in the *New York Times*, *Washington Post*, *Washington Star-News*, and *Baltimore Sun* for December 21, 1972. Sullivan is named as the second official in the briefing in *The Guardian* (London), December 22, 1972.

50. Quoted in Thomas L. Hughes, "Foreign Policy: Men or Measures?" *Atlantic*, October 1974, p. 56.

51. *Washington Star-News*, December 20, 1972.

52. *Los Angeles Times*, July 22, 1973.

53. Associated Press dispatch, *Baltimore Sun*, December 30, 1972.

54. "Bach Mai Witness: Dr. Yvonne Capdeville," Paris Chapter, Committee of Concerned Asian Scholars, Information Packet No. 9 (January 1973), p. 2; *Washington Post*, December 30, 1972.

55. *Baltimore Sun*, December 28, 1972.

56. *New York Times*, December 22, 1972.

57. Agence France-Presse dispatch, *Le Monde*, December 30, 1972.

58. Marder, *Washington Post*, February 4, 1973.

59. *New York Times*, December 31, 1972.

60. "Bach Mai Witness," p. 1.

61. *Baltimore Sun*, December 28, 1972.

62. *Washington Post*, December 30, 1972.

63. Marder, *Washington Post*, February 4, 1973.

64. Ibid.

65. *U.S. News and World Report*, February 5, 1973, p. 18.

66. *Le Monde*, November 25, 1966.

67. Interview with Marge Tabankin, former president of the US National Student Association, on a visit to the DRV in June 1972, in *Off Our Backs*, September 1972, p. 26.

68. Marder, *Washington Post*, February 4, 1973.

69. Hanson Baldwin, *Boston Globe*, January 22, 1974.

70. Marder, *Washington Post*, February 4, 1973.

71. *Department of Defense Appropriations*, Hearings before Subcommittee of the Committee on Appropriations, House of Representatives, 93rd Congress, 1st Session, 1973, p. 18.

72. *Manchester Guardian Weekly*, January 6, 1973, p. 10; also Jack Anderson, *Washington Post*, January 3, 1973.

73. *U.S. News and World Report*, January 8, 1973, p. 17; ABC Evening News, December 22, 1972.

74. *Department of Defense Appropriations*, p. 14.

75. *Manchester Guardian Weekly*, January 6, 1973, p. 10.

76. *Washington Post*, December 21, 30, 1972; *New York Times*, December 21, 24, 1972; on Japan's reaction, see *Christian Science Monitor*, December 26, 1972. Reactions from foreign governments were reported to be far worse than anticipated. See Jack Anderson, *Syracuse Post-Standard*, January 9, 1973.

77. *Washington Post*, December 21, 1972.

78. *New York Times*, December 19, 1972.

79. *Washington Post*, December 22, 1972; also see *Baltimore Sun*, December 30, 1972.

80. *Baltimore Sun*, January 29, 1973.

81. *Baltimore Sun*, December 21, 1972; *U.S. News and World Report*, January 22, 1973, p. 8.

82. *U.S. News and World Report*, January 22, 1973, p. 8.

83. *Baltimore Sun*, December 30, 1972.

84. Quoted in *Time*, January 8, 1973, p. 14.

85. "The Vietnam Bombing: Senate Opposition Grows," *Congressional Quarterly Weekly Reports*, December 23, 1972, p. 3171.

86. *Baltimore Sun*, December 30, 1972.

87. *Washington Post*, December 30, 1972.

88. White House press secretary Ron Ziegler, quoted in *New York Times*, December 19, 1972.

89. *New York Times*, December 23, 1972.

90. *Boston Globe*, December 31, 1972.

91. Interview with Hoang Tung, Hanoi, January 7, 1975.

92. Richard Dudman, "The Lesson of Vietnam," *Congressional Record*, February 26, 1973, p. S3275.

93. *Baltimore Sun*, January 7, 1973.

94. Hong Ha, "Paris Ngay Nay Nam Ngoai," (Paris One Year Ago Today), *Nhan Dan*, Special Spring Issue, January 27, 1974.

95. Major Alfred K. Richeson, "The Four-Party Joint Military Commission," *Military Review*, August 1973, p. 19.

96. Unpublished Department of State Briefing Paper, "Interpretation of the Agreement on Ending the War and Restoring the Peace in Vietnam," (n.d., February 1973?), p. 5.

97. Ibid.

98. Hong Ha, "Paris Ngay. . . ."

6. *Implementing the Paris Agreement: I*

1. Nguyen Khanh Toan, "President Ho and International Solidarity," *Hoc Tap*, no. 11, November 1972.

2. Hoang Tung, "Our Very Great Victory and Our New Task," *Hoc Tap*, no. 4, April 1973.

3. "COSVN's Directive 02/73 'On Policies Related to the Political Settlement and Cease-Fire'," Vietnam Documents and Research Notes, no. 113, June 1973, p. 4.

4. Ibid.

5. Hoang Tung, "Our Very Great Victory"; speech by Major General Le Quang Dao, *Quan Doi Nhan Dan*, May 15, 1973. For public expressions of the post-Geneva line, see, for example, "Appeal of the Lao Dong Party," Vietnam News Agency, August 5, 1954, and speech by Vo Nguyen Giap, Vietnam News Agency, July 11, 1956, *Nhan Dan*, July 12, 1956.

6. Hoang Tung, "Our Very Great Victory."

7. "COSVN Directive 3," Vietnam Documents and Research Notes, no. 115, September 1973, p. 5.

8. "On Policies Related to the Political Settlement," pp. 9–12.

9. Ibid., p. 7.

10. Ibid., p. 13.

11. "Plan of General Uprising When a Political Solution Is Reached," translation of a captured document, made available by US Information Service in Saigon, p. 13. See also, Porter, "Does Thieu Continue the War . . . ," p. 475.

12. "On Policies Related to the Political Settlement," p. 14.

13. "Phai Quan Triet Chinh Sach Hoa Hoc Dan Toc" (We Must Thoroughly Understand the National Concord Policy), p. 1. Xerox copy of a document obtained by American Friends Service Committee personnel in Quang Ngai province in 1974. A similar statement is found in "On Policies Related to the Political Settlement," p. 11.

14. Nguyen Van Hieu, "Stability and Peace Can Be Achieved in Vietnam," *Le Monde Diplomatique,* June 1973.

15. "We Must Thoroughly Understand," p. 3.

16. *New York Times,* January 23, 1973. Similar orders had been reported to be in effect when the Party expected a cease-fire agreement in late October 1972. See *New York Times,* November 23, 1972.

17. *Christian Science Monitor,* November 4, 1972.

18. *Washington Post,* December 6, 1972; *Wall Street Journal,* December 21, 1972.

19. *Washington Post,* November 12, 1972.

20. *Tin Song,* December 7, 1972. Also see *Christian Science Monitor,* December 14, 1972.

21. *Washington Star-News,* December 8, 1972.

22. Excerpt from a letter from Nixon to Thieu, dated January 17, 1973, quoted in a statement by Dr. Nguyen Tien Hung at his press conference April 30, 1975, p. 10 (see note 27, Chap. 5).

23. Quoted in statement by Nguyen Tien Hung at his press conference April 30, 1975, p. 10 (see note 27, Chap. 5).

24. "Tong Thong Viet Nam Cong Hoa noi chuyen voi dong bao ve Ngung Ban va Hoa Binh" (President of the Republic of Viet Nam speaks with the compatriots about the cease-fire and peace), press release from the Information Office, RVN Embassy in Washington, D. C., no date.

25. Reuters dispatch, *Boston Globe,* January 25, 1973.

26. Associated Press dispatch, *Boston Globe,* January 24, 1973.

27. *Boston Globe,* January 30, 1973. The *Globe's* reporter found the chief of a Saigon-controlled village right on Route 1 in the Mekong Delta unfamiliar with the terms of the agreement.

28. *Christian Science Monitor,* March 16, 1973.

29. Interview with Richard Critchfield, *Washington Evening Star,* June 25, 1967.

30. Quoted in Milton Osborne, "A Base of Scepticism," *Quadrant,* June 1970, p. 27.

31. *Christian Science Monitor,* November 4, 1972.

32. "Pres. Thieu Assesses Present Situation," *Vietnam Bulletin,* vol. VII, no. 16 (August 31, 1972), p. 3.

33. Thieu quoted in Jack Langguth, "Thieu and Ky Think about the Unthinkable," *New York Times Magazine,* April 14, 1968, p. 72.

34. *Christian Science Monitor,* December 9, 1972.

35. *New York Times,* September 25, 1972.

36. *New York Times,* October 13, 1972.

37. *Washington Star-News,* January 25, 1973.

38. Ibid.

39. *Tin Song*, January 22, 1973.

40. This was a fear shared by "military experts" who were reported to feel that a "major danger to South Vietnam is that many veterans may desert the Army after a cease-fire in the belief their duty is over." *U.S. News and World Report*, January 29, 1973, p. 14.

41. François Debré, "Les Cartes de Thieu," *Le Nouvel Observateur*, November 20, 1972, p. 51.

42. *New York Times*, January 24, 1973.

43. See the comments by Pentagon spokesman Jerry Freidheim quoted in *Aerospace Daily*, November 6, 1972.

44. *Washington Post*, December 9, 11, 1972.

45. Jack Anderson, *Washington Post*, March 20, 1973; *Le Monde*, February 22, 1973, *Baltimore Sun*, November 28, 1973.

46. Xerox copies of letters from Nixon to Thieu, dated November 14, 1972 and January 5, 1973, distributed by Dr. Nguyen Tien Hung at a press conference in Washington, D.C., April 30, 1975.

47. *Boston Globe*, December 8, 1972.

48. *U.S. News and World Report*, April 23, 1973, p. 19.

49. "Plan of General Uprising," p. 16.

50. Ibid., pp. 16–17.

51. *Washington Star-News*, January 28, 1973.

52. *Washington Post*, March 29, 1973.

53. For typical reports on the immediate post-ceasefire fighting, see *Washington Post*, January 30, 1973; *New York Times*, January 30, 1973; Robert Shaplen, "Letter from Vietnam," *The New Yorker*, February 24, 1973, p. 106; *Baltimore Sun*, January 31, 1973; *New York Times*, January 29, 1973; *Washington Post*, January 29, 1973.

54. *Christian Science Monitor*, February 8, 1973.

55. *Baltimore Sun*, February 18, 1973.

56. *Christian Science Monitor*, February 12, 1973.

57. Associated Press dispatch, *Syracuse Post Standard*, January 29, 1973.

58. Communist forces were reported holding sections of Routes 1 and 13 north of Saigon at the time of the deadline. UPI dispatch, *Boston Globe*, January 28, 1973.

59. *Los Angeles Times*, January 29, 1973. Also see *Christian Science Monitor*, February 8, 1973.

60. *Thailand, Laos, Cambodia and Vietnam: April 1973*, Staff Report, Subcommittee on US Security Agreements, Committee on Foreign Relations, US Senate, 93rd Congress, 1st Session, 1973, p. 33.

61. CBS Evening News, January 30, 1973. The official ARVN spokesman claimed the Marines captured the camp ten minutes before the cease-fire. *Boston Globe*, January 30, 1973.

62. Le Ngoc, "The Ceasefire Refugee," *Vietnam Magazine*, vol. VI, no. 5, 1973, p. 12.

63. *New York Times*, January 31, 1973 and February 23, 1973. The PRG capture of Sa Huynh the night before the cease-fire was later confirmed by a defector from the Communists, Warrant Officer Nguyen Thanh Son, in an interview with Associated Press. *Baltimore Sun*, June 9, 1973.

64. A semiofficial Saigon account gave the figures of one killed, two wounded, and 289 missing in action at the Regional Forces post. Le Ngoc, p. 13.

65. *New York Times*, January 31, 1973.

66. Frances L. Starner, "Report from Central Vietnam," unpublished report, 1973, p. 7. An account published by the Saigon government in April claimed that the PLAF attack on Sa Huynh came precisely at the hour of the cease-fire. "Sa Huynh Tu Ngay 'Ngung Ban' " (Sa Huynh from the "Cease-fire" day), *Tin Que Huong* (News of the Fatherland), Washington, D.C., no. 212, April 14, 1973, p. 2.

67. *Boston Globe*, January 29, 1973.

68. *Newsweek*, February 19, 1973; London *Times*, February 7, 1973; *Washington Post*, February 8, 1973.

69. Reuters dispatch, *New York Times*, February 9, 1973.

70. *Washington Post*, February 1, 1973.

71. Note by General Tran Van Tra to ICCS, Liberation Radio, February 21, 1973; ARVN Brigadier General Tran Van Nhut said he used seven battalions to reconquer Sa Huynh. *Toronto Globe and Mail*, February 26, 1973.

72. Ibid.

73. *New York Times*, February 28, 1973.

74. *New York Times*, February 17, 1973.

75. *New York Times*, February 18, 22, 1973; *Washington Post*, March 1, 1973.

76. According to a Canadian ICCS source, an investigation by the Region 3 ICCS Headquarters team, conducted on the basis of physical evidence and interviews with five witnesses, showed that RVN aircraft had bombed Duc Co on February 19, killing and wounding PRG personnel.

77. Interview on NBC News, "Today," February 25, 1973.

78. *Washington Post*, March 29, 1973.

79. *Situation in Indochina*, Hearings before the Committee on Foreign Affairs, House of Representatives, 93rd Congress, 1st Session, 1973, p. 59.

80. *Thailand, Laos, Cambodia and Vietnam: April 1973*, p. 33.

81. *Baltimore Sun*, May 14, 1973.

82. *Christian Science Monitor*, March 20, 1973.

83. Letter from Earl and Pat Martin, Mennonite Central Committee, Quang Ngai province, to Senator Edward M. Kennedy, May 29, 1974.

84. *Thailand, Laos, Cambodia and Vietnam: April 1973*, p. 33.

85. "COSVN Directive 3," p. 9.

86. *Thailand, Laos, Cambodia and Vietnam: April 1973*, p. 33.

87. *Chinh Luan*, April 7, 1973; *Christian Science Monitor*, April 7, 1973.

88. Statement of Major General Hoang Anh Tuan, Deputy Chief, PRG Delegation, to the Two-Party JMC Meeting, March 31, 1973. Liberation Press Agency, Hanoi Radio, April 2, 1973.

89. Hoang Tung, "Our Very Great Victory."

90. "COSVN Directive 3," pp. 12–13.

91. Ibid., p. 13.

92. *New York Times*, February 28, 1973.

93. *Baltimore Sun*, March 11, 1973.

94. *Washington Post*, March 13, 1973.

95. *The Guardian* (London), February 23, 1973.

96. *Washington Post*, March 13, 1973; *New York Times*, March 20, 1973.

97. *New York Times*, March 14, 1973.

98. Unpublished Department of State Briefing Paper, "Interpretation of the Agreement on Ending the War and Restoring Peace in Viet-Nam" (n.d., February 1973?), p. 10.

99. See *New York Times*, March 17, 1973.

100. *Washington Post*, March 12, 1973.

101. *Washington Star-News*, March 14, 1973.

102. *New York Times*, March 16, 1973.

103. *New York Times*, April 8, 1973.

104. *Los Angeles Times*, April 1, 1973.

105. *Situation in Indochina*, p. 10. The State Department's own briefing paper makes the same point. "Interpretation of the Agreement," p. 6.

106. See D. Gareth Porter and Laura Summers, "Cambodia: Was There an Understanding?," in *Foreign Military Sales and Assistance Act*, Hearings before the Committee on Foreign Relations, US Senate, 93rd Congress, 1st Session, 1973, pp. 459–460.

107. CBS Evening News, April 9, 1973.

108. Reuters dispatch from Peking, *Los Angeles Times*, January 22, 1973.

109. Porter and Summers, p. 458.

110. This is the paraphrase of Kissinger's statement given by Secretary Rogers in testimony to the Senate Foreign Relations Committee. *Washington Post*, May 1, 1973.

111. *Washington Post*, April 12, 1973.

112. *Thailand, Laos, Cambodia and Vietnam: April 1973*, p. 36.

113. Ibid. In fact, the CIA estimate of Communist post-agreement casualties as of April 15 was 11,400, which would have meant that replacements did not even make up for battlefield losses.

114. *Washington Star-News*, April 19, 1973; *New York Times*, April 20, 1973; UPI dispatch from Saigon, *Chicago Tribune*, April 23, 1973.

115. *Thailand, Laos, Cambodia and Vietnam: April 1973*, p. 37.

116. *New York Times*, April 12, 1973.

117. *New York Times*, April 20, 1973.

118. *New York Times*, April 21, 1973.

119. *New York Times*, April 25, 1973.

120. *Washington Post*, April 26, 1973.

121. *Washington Post*, May 10, 1973.

7. *Implementing the Paris Agreement: II*

1. *Boston Globe*, February 5, 1973. "The Faceless Viet Cong" was the title of a derogatory article on the NLF by CIA analyst George Carver in *Foreign Affairs*, April 1966, pp. 357–372.

2. *Boston Globe*, January 30, 1973; *Los Angeles Times*, January 29, 1973.

3. Alfred K. Richeson, "The Four Party Joint Military Commission," *Military Review*, 57 (August 1973), p. 19.

4. "About U.S.-Saigon Observance of the Paris Agreement," *Viet-Nam Courier*, no. 11 (April 1973), p. 19.

5. Richeson, pp. 21–22.

6. "About U.S.-Saigon Observance of the Paris Agreement," p. 19.

7. *Baltimore Sun*, February 16, 1973.

8. Richeson, pp. 21–22.

9. *New York Times*, February 17, 1973.

10. *Newsday*, February 10, 1973.

11. *New York Times*, February 9, 1973.

12. *New York Times*, February 18, 1973.

13. *Washington Post*, February 9, 1973; "About U.S.-Saigon Observance of the Paris Agreement," p. 20.

14. *Washington Post*, February 9, 11, 1973.

15. Frances Starner, "Report from Central Vietnam," unpublished report, 1973, p. 8.

16. *New York Times*, February 26, 1973.

17. *New York Times*, February 29, 1973.

18. *New York Times*, February 15, 1973.

19. *New York Times*, February 29, 1973.

20. Richeson, p. 21. In the upper Mekong Delta the ICCS also offered to send teams to pickup sites before the PRG personnel arrived. *Christian Science Monitor*, March 23, 1973.

21. *Washington Post*, March 4, 1973; *Baltimore Sun*, March 4, 1973.

22. Full text of the agreement on privileges and immunities by the Four-Party Joint Military Commission issued to the press March 19, 1973.

23. Richeson, p. 21.

24. *Washington Star-News*, February 19, 1973.

25. *New York Times*, February 23, 1973.

26. "About U.S.-Saigon Observance of the Paris Agreement," p. 20.

27. PRG Commission for the Application of the Paris Agreement, "Rapport de la Délégation Sud Vietnamienne," International Conference for the Implementation of the Paris Agreement on Vietnam, Stockholm, March 29–31, 1974 (mimeographed), p. 6.

28. Associated Press dispatch, *Washington Star-News*, February 17, 1973.

29. An ARVN first lieutenant was arrested in February for having talked with his PLAF counterpart for an hour and a half, which discouraged other officers from doing the same thing. *Los Angeles Times*, February 27, 1973.

30. "Recapitulation of Event [sic] After the 45 Day Limit as Stipulated in the Joint Communiqué of June 13 1973, as presented by Nguyen Luu Vien," (Paris: RVN Delegation to the Conference between the two South Vietnamese Parties, 1973), p. 11.

31. For the RVN argument about the PRG's lack of territorial control, see "Note of the Embassy of Republic of Viet-Nam in Dakar to the Ministry of Foreign Affairs of the Republic of Senegal relating to the recognition of the so-called P. R. G. by Senegal, Dakar, August 15, 1973," *Foreign Affairs Review* (Saigon), vol. 1, no. 1 (November 1973), p. 55. The argument is repeated in

Thieu's message to the Secretary General of the Non-Aligned Countries Conference in Algiers, ibid., p. 19.

32. Telephone conversation with Robert T. Walkinshaw, December 14, 1974. This position was explicitly presented by both Foreign Minister Tran Van Lam and deputy chief of the RVN delegation in Paris Nguyen Xuan Phong in press conferences following the June 13 agreement. *New York Times*, June 14, 1973. Also see *The Economist*, February 16, 1974.

33. RVN Foreign Ministry communiqué, January 19, 1974.

34. For the full text of the June 13 communiqué, see *New York Times*, June 14, 1973.

35. See *Baltimore Sun*, June 8, 9, 12, 1973.

36. *New York Times*, June 16, 1973; *Baltimore Sun*, June 19, 1973.

37. *Boston Globe*, January 26, 1973.

38. See the report from a PRG village by Jacques Leslie, *Los Angeles Times*, February 4, 1973.

39. See John S. Hannon, Jr., "The International Control Commission Experience and the Role of an Improved International Supervisory Body in the Vietnamese Settlement," in Richard A. Falk, ed., *The Vietnam War and International Law*, vol. 3, sponsored by the American Society of International Law (Princeton, N.J.: Princeton University Press, 1972), pp. 772–795.

40. Charles Taylor, *Snow Job: Canada, The United States and Vietnam (1954 to 1973)* (Toronto: Anansi, 1974), p. 148; *Washington Post*, March 26, 1973.

41. See Paul Bridle, *Canada and the International Control Commissions in Indochina, 1954–1972* (Toronto: Canadian Institute of International Affairs, 1973), p. 26.

42. For the clearest exposition of the official Canadian view of the conflict, see the testimony of Hon. Paul Martin, Secretary of State for External Affairs, Main Estimates of the Department of External Affairs (1965–66), Minutes of Proceedings and Evidence, no. 1, House of Commons, 3rd Session, 26th Parliament, June 10, 1965, pp. 15–24; and Paul Martin, "Canada's Approach to the Vietnam Conflict," *External Affairs, Monthly Bulletin*, June 1967, pp. 221–234.

43. Martin, "Canada's Approach," pp. 231–232.

44. See, for example, Gauvin's interview with Associated Press, *Toronto Globe and Mail*, May 28, 1973.

45. For the official PRG explanation of the incident, see the statement issued by the Quang Tri Provincial People's Revolutionary Committee, Liberation Radio, April 8, 1973.

46. *New York Times*, April 10, 1973.

47. *New York Times*, April 13, 1973.

48. *Toronto Globe and Mail*, April 27, 1973.

49. *New York Times*, April 15, 1973; *Toronto Globe and Mail*, April 17, 1973.

50. *Toronto Globe and Mail*, May 5, 1973.

51. *Toronto Globe and Mail*, May 10, 1973.

52. *Toronto Globe and Mail*, May 25, 1973.

53. Ibid.

54. Taylor, pp. 171–172.

55. George LeBel, who attended the press conference, quoted the Indonesian

delegate in "South Viet Nam, The Paris Accords, Canada's Participation in the I.C.C.S. and the Political Prisoners," Report to the International Committee to Free South Vietnamese Political Prisoners from Detention, Torture and Death, May 15, 1973 (mimeographed), p. 6.

56. *New York Times*, February 26, 1973.

57. Canadian Press dispatch, *Montreal Star*, March 10, 1973; telegram from the Canadian Delegation to the ICCS to the Ministry of External Affairs, Ottawa, March 21, 1973, Annex I, Mitchell Sharp, *Viet-Nam: Canada's Approach to Participation in the International Commission of Control and Supervision* (Ottawa: Informational Canada, 1973), p. 34.

58. *U.S. News and World Report*, May 22, 1972, p. 18. Also see *Los Angeles Times*, April 9, 1972; *New York Times*, April 6, 1972; Associated Press dispatch, *Washington Star-News*, April 6, 1972.

59. *Washington Post*, March 15, 1973.

60. *Toronto Globe and Mail*, May 8, 17, 1973.

61. *Toronto Globe and Mail*, March 21, 1973.

62. *Toronto Globe and Mail*, May 8, 17, 1973. A later report, also written by the Canadian delegation in Can Tho, and called "Investigation Report R7/106," was circulated to newsmen in July. A copy was made available to the author by the Canadian Embassy in December 1973. It was based on interviews with four North Vietnamese prisoners, all of whom crossed into South Vietnam in June 1973 in the same unit and were captured together.

63. *Toronto Globe and Mail*, May 26, 29, 1973.

64. *Baltimore Sun*, June 1, 1968.

65. "Indonesia Sticks on Paris Agreement on Vietnam," *News, Views and Features from Indonesia* (published by the Embassy of Indonesia, Ottawa), June 18, 1973, p. 12.

66. "Statement of Views of Head of Canadian Delegation, Region VI," presented at the 35th ICCS Commissioners' Meeting, March 26, 1973, in Republic of Viet Nam, Ministry of Foreign Affairs, *Communist Violations of the Paris Agreement of January 27, 1973* (Saigon: June 1973), pp. 115–119.

67. Ibid.

68. Information provided by Polish ICCS delegation to Fred Branfman, Co-Director of the Indochina Resource Center, Saigon, July 25, 1973.

69. Ibid.

70. *Baltimore Sun*, March 10, 1973.

71. *Washington Star-News*, July 5, 1973.

72. Ibid.

73. Fred Branfman, "Vietnam: The Story of Complaint No. 103," *Last Post* (Toronto), November 1973.

74. *Toronto Globe and Mail*, February 26, 1973.

75. Ibid., March 12, 1973. The Canadian delegation, in a later report to Ottawa, attacked the Hungarian and Polish delegations' insistence on commenting on the absence of evidence from the other side, as reflecting their "partiality towards the PRG/DRVN." (Telegram from Canadian Delegation, March 21, 1973, Sharp, *Viet-Nam: Canada's Approach*, p. 34.)

76. *Toronto Globe and Mail*, May 24, 1973.

77. Letter from Mr. L. A. K. James, East Asia Division, Department of External Affairs, Ottawa, to Mrs. C. McEwen, Ottawa, October 5, 1973.

78. Report from Saigon by Robert Goralski, NBC Evening News, June 2, 1973, and interview with Goralski, Washington, D.C., October 28, 1974.

79. *Toronto Globe and Mail*, May 24, 1973.

80. Ambassador Michel Gauvin, "The Dismal Record of ICCS," *Viet-Nam Bulletin*, vol. VIII, no. 5, 6, May 1973, p. 16 (reprinted from *Vietnam Report*, vol. II, no. 9, May 1, 1973); telegram from Canadian Delegation, March 21, 1973.

81. *Toronto Star*, August 1, 1973.

82. *Washington Post*, March 4, 1973.

83. Telegram from the Canadian Delegation, March 21, 1973, p. 36.

84. Ibid.

85. Ibid.

86. Except where otherwise noted, the information contained in the following paragraphs on the mine deactivation operation in North Vietnam is drawn from Rear Admiral Brian McCauley, "Operation End Sweep," *U.S. Naval Institute Proceedings*, March 1974, pp. 19–25, and from an interview with one of the members of Admiral McCauley's staff.

87. "About U.S.-Saigon Observance of the Paris Agreement," p. 20.

88. Ibid.

89. Tad Szulc, "Behind the Vietnam Cease-Fire Agreement," *Foreign Policy*, no. 15, Summer 1974.

90. *Washington Post*, August 3, 1973.

8. Political Stalemate and the Shifting Military Balance

1. *New York Times*, June 14, 1973.

2. Address to the National Assembly, Saigon Radio, Domestic Service, December 12, 1972.

3. *Washington Star-News*, January 25, 1973.

4. *Washington Post*, January 31, 1973.

5. Embassy of the Republic of Viet-Nam, Information Office, "One Year of Fruitless Negotiations," Fact Sheet no. 06/74, March 19, 1974, p. 2.

6. Ibid., p. 3.

7. *Washington Star-News*, April 20, 1973.

8. This argument was made publicly by Hoang Duc Nha, then Commissioner General for Public Information, at a press conference in July. Saigon Radio, Domestic Service, July 30, 1973.

9. See *Christian Science Monitor*, April 13, 1973. Thieu also tried to implement a total economic blockade of the PRG zone. See his speech to the civil defense forces, August 5, 1973, Saigon Radio, Domestic Service, August 5, 1973.

10. Interview with Charles Benoit, New York City, March 27, 1974. Benoit visited the PRG zone along with *New York Times* correspondent James Markham in February 1974.

11. Thieu interview with *Dan Chu*, reprinted in *Vietnam Report*, July 15, 1973, p. 5.

12. Ibid.

13. "Preliminary Accord on Principles between the Two South Vietnamese Parties to the La Celle-St. Cloud Conference," in Ministry of Foreign Affairs, Republic of Vietnam, *One Year of Communist Violations of the Paris Agreement* (Saigon, February 1974), pp. 17–19.

14. Text of statement by Minister Nguyen Van Hieu, April 25, 1973, in *Vietnam News and Reports* (Montreal), no. 16–17 (April-May 1973), p. 9.

15. Embassy of the Republic of Viet-Nam Information Office, "The Republic of Viet-Nam's Position on General Elections," Fact Sheet no. 3/4, January 31, 1974, p. 4.

16. "Statement by the Provisional Revolutionary Government of the Republic of South Viet Nam on Achieving Peace and National Concord in South Vietnam," March 22, 1974, unofficial translation (mimeographed), p. 7.

17. Embassy of Viet-Nam, Information Section, "The Issue of Civilian Prisoners in South Viet-Nam," no. 06/73, May 29, 1973.

18. *Que Deviennent les 200,000 Prisonniers Politiques au Sud Vietnam?* (Paris: Communauté Vietnamienne, Bureau de Coordination de la Conférence International pour la Libération des Prisonniers Politiques au Sud-Vietnam, 1974), p. 5; also see Huynh Tan Mam, "Saigon's Civilian Political Prisoners," *NSA Magazine*, issues 7 and 8 (May-June 1974), p. 31. Mam, former Chairman of the Vietnam National Student Association, wrote this article in the form of a letter smuggled out of Chi Hoa prison in January 1974.

19. Undated memorandum by Alex Shimkin of *Newsweek* magazine, based on an interview with Colonel Ly Trong Song, RVN National Police, November 1971 (original typescript). The breakdown of those "sentenced to prison" by year, as given by Colonel Song, is as follows:

July–Dec.	1968	12,747
	1969	17,310
	1970	8,518
Jan.–Oct.	1971	4,432
	Total	43,007

20. In an interview with the author on May 20, 1971 in Saigon, Mr. McCann and Mr. Secor of the US Public Safety Division said that by 1968 there was "tremendous overcrowding" in the RVN prison system.

21. US Mission in Vietnam, "Handbook on Legal Processing of National Security Offenders," undated (1971), Xerox copy, pp. 10–12.

22. According to figures provided to the House Government Information Subcommittee in 1971, during the first six months of 1971, 5,619 An Tri cases were reviewed, of which 3,606 resulted in the release of the detainee. *U.S. Assistance Programs in Vietnam*, Hearings before a Subcommittee of the Committee on Government Operations, House of Representatives, 92nd Congress, 1st Session, p. 196.

23. Release data are given in Viet-Nam Information Office, *The Civilian Prisoner Question in South Viet Nam* (Washington, D. C., 1973), p. 35. The total number of sentences imposed from the beginning of 1970 through October 1971 was 12,950. Memorandum by Alex Shimkin, cited above.

24. Hoang Duc Nha told reporters in November 1972 that 40,000 "Communist agents" had been arrested in the previous few weeks (*Washington Post*, November 10, 1972). The figure of 14,000 prisoners sent to prison is given in *Relief and Rehabilitation of War Victims in Indochina: One Year After the Ceasefire*, A Study Mission Report, Subcommittee to Investigate Problems Connected with Refugees and Escapees, Committee on the Judiciary, US Senate, 93rd Congress, 2nd Session, 1974, p. 28.

25. US Study Team on Religious and Political Freedom in Vietnam, "Findings on Trip to Vietnam," June 1969 (mimeographed), p. 11; interview with McCann and Secor, cited above.

26. *New York Times*, December 11, 1972.

27. Conradin Pernier, "Rehabilitation Camps in the Province of Phong Dinh (Delta)," April 7, 1973. Given to Fred Branfman, Co-Director of the Indochina Resource Center, by Pernier, Saigon, 1973.

28. Telegram from US Embassy, Saigon, December 26, 1973, "Father Chan Tin's View of 'Political Prisoners': A Case Study of Militancy Overriding Objectivity" (declassified, January 16, 1974), p. 6.

29. Interview with McCann and Secor, cited.

30. US Study Team, "Findings on Trip to Vietnam," p. 11.

31. Embassy of Viet-Nam, "The Issue of Civilian Prisoners in South Viet-Nam," p. 5.

32. Robert Shaplen, "Letter from Saigon," *The New Yorker*, January 13, 1973, p. 79.

33. *Daily Telegraph*, April 18, 1973. Cited in *Political Prisoners in South Vietnam* (London: Amnesty International Publications, 1973), p. 6.

34. Letter from Ray Meyer, Second Secretary, US Embassy, Saigon, to Jerry M. Tinker, Staff Consultant, Senate Subcommittee on Refugees, in *Relief and Rehabilitation*, p. 137.

35. Republic of Viet-Nam, Office of the President, Commission-General of Civilian Proselytizing, "Van De Trao Tra Nhan Vien Dan Su" (The Problem of Exchange of Civilian Personnel), Document no. 11/73, April 1973.

36. Declaration of a former prisoner at Con Son, May 5, 1973, cited in *Que Deviennent*, p. 14.

37. Huynh Tan Mam, p. 31.

38. Letter from Prisoners at Con Son, February 17, 1973, cited in *Que Deviennent*, p. 14.

39. Republic of Viet-Nam, "Van De Trao Tra Nhan Vien Dan Su," p. 2.

40. *The Civilian Prisoner Question in South Vietnam*, p. 35; letter from Meyer, in *Relief and Rehabilitation*, p. 137.

41. Huynh Tan Mam, p. 31. "Statement by Fred Branfman," *Congressional Record*, September 18, 1973, p. S16790. Branfman had just returned from a seven-week visit to South Vietnam, primarily to investigate the problem of political prisoners. The statement was originally given in testimony before the Subcommittee on Far East and Pacific, House Committee on Foreign Affairs, in September 1973.

42. Republic of Viet-Nam, Commission-General of Civilian Proselytizing List

of Civil Servants, *Cadres and Civilians of the Republic of Viet-Nam Abducted by the Communists Since 1954* (Saigon, 1973).

43. On February 17, 1968 *Nhan Dan* reported that hundreds of Hue policemen, having rallied to the revolutionary government, had been formed into a brigade under the command of a former district chief of the right bank in Hue. Agence France-Presse dispatch, February 17, 1968.

44. US Mission Reports of Assassinations and Abductions, 1966–1969, in Stephen T. Hosmer, *Viet Cong Repression and Its Implications for the Future* (Santa Monica, Calif.: RAND Corporation, 1970), p. 65. This figure does not include officials abducted during the month of February 1968, for which no RVN records exist.

45. Hosmer, *Viet Cong Repression*, p. 100.

46. Telegram from US Embassy, "Father Chan Tin's View . . . ," p. 6.

47. Ibid.

48. Jane and David Barton, "Report on Quang Ngai Province Since the January Ceasefire," July 18, 1973 (mimeographed), p. 1.

49. *Washington Post*, January 18, 1973.

50. Official telegram from Office of the Prime Minister (RVN), National Council, Operation Phoenix, Text No. 7167/N2/B, April 5, 1973.

51. *Washington Post*, January 25, 1973.

52. *Washington Star-News*, January 25, 1973.

53. *Washington Post*, January 25, 1973.

54. Barton, "Report on Quang Ngai," p. 5.

55. *Washington Post*, January 25, 1973.

56. Matthew J. Seiden, "Reality of Pacification," *The New Republic*, April 29, 1974, p. 9. According to Seiden, refugees in one camp south of Danang said more than 100 people had been arrested since they had been moved to the camp in 1969 for the unauthorized departure of a relative.

57. *Christian Science Monitor*, March 16, 1973.

58. Edward L. Block, "US Aid to Vietnamese Refugees," *Indochina Chronicle*, no. 35 (August–September 1974), p. 14.

59. *Christian Science Monitor*, March 16, 1973; Frances Fitzgerald, *Boston Globe*, May 8, 1973.

60. Statement of Wells Klein, *Relief and Rehabilitation of War Victims in Indochina, Part IV: South Vietnam and Regional Problems*, Hearing before the Subcommittee to Investigate Problems Connected with Refugees and Escapees, Committee on the Judiciary, US Senate, 93rd Congress, 1st Session, 1973, p. 33.

61. *Washington Post*, September 3, 1974.

62. *Christian Science Monitor*, January 29, 1973.

63. *Los Angeles Times*, February 10, 1973.

64. Response of Edward L. Block to Embassy cables replying to his testimony (typescript), p. 16.

65. *Relief and Rehabilitation . . . One Year After the Ceasefire*, p. 16.

66. Block, "US Aid to Vietnamese Refugees," p. 13.

67. Testimony of Diane Jones, *Second Supplemental Appropriations for Fiscal Year 1974*, Hearings before the Committee on Appropriations, US Senate, 93rd Congress, 2nd Session, part 2, p. 1539.

68. Block, p. 13.

69. *Dai Dan Toc*, November 1–20, 1973, summarized in *Thoi Bao Ga*, no. 43 (January 1974), pp. 4–5.

70. Testimony of Diane Jones, pp. 1536–1537.

71. Robert C. Ranson, "Bereavement and a Pilgrimage," *New York Times*, February 19, 1974.

72. Testimony of Diane Jones, p. 1537.

73. Letter from Earl and Pat Martin, Quang Ngai, to Senator Edward M. Kennedy, May 29, 1974. (Xerox copy).

74. Deputy Mai Ngoc Duoc, "Nhan Dinh Ve Van De Phan Phoi Gao va Nan Doi tai Tinh Quang Ngai" (Observations on the Problem of Distribution of Rice and Hunger in Quang Ngai Province) April 1, 1974 (mimeographed), p. 7.

75. *International Bulletin* (Berkeley, Calif.), May 20–June 2, 1974, pp. 1, 8, citing *Le Monde*, May 8–10, 1974.

76. Seiden, "Reality of Pacification," p. 9.

77. *Washington Post*, September 30, 1973.

78. "Dan Bieu Nhom Quoc Gia Du Du Luat 'Hoan' Bau Cu Thuong Vien" (Representatives of the Nationalist Bloc Propose a Bill to "Postpone" the Senate Election), *Ban Tin* (Newsletter), no. 6 (June 1973?), p. 13. This newsletter was published semicovertly by a group of opposition Senators and Representatives in Saigon.

79. "Hanoi's Current Strategy for South Vietnam Through President Nguyen Van Thieu's Eyes," *Vietnam Report*, July 15, 1973, p. 7.

80. Saigon Radio Domestic Service, October 1, 1973.

81. *New York Times*, October 21, 1973; *Christian Science Monitor*, October 29, 1973.

82. *New York Times*, October 1, 3, 1973; *London Times*, October 5, 1973.

83. Embassy of the Republic of Viet-Nam Information Office, "Communist Violations of the Paris Agreement," Fact Sheet 02/73, December 5, 1973, p. 2.

84. DRV Foreign Ministry Statement, Vietnam News Agency, Hanoi Radio, October 8, 1973. On the same day, a Reuters dispatch from Saigon quoted an RVN press release as saying that 100 of its jets bombed areas along the Cambodian border for four straight days. *Thoi Bao Ga*, no. 43 (January 1974), p. 4.

85. See Liberation Radio, October 24, 26, 29, 31, November 5, 1973 for a detailed chronology of Saigon's air raids in this region. The Associated Press referred to a "heavy bombing and shelling campaign against Viet Cong bases" during the latter part of October and the beginning of November. *Washington Star-News*, November 6, 1973.

86. This was confirmed to the author by a State Department source who had visited the area personally in October 1973.

87. Liberation Radio, October 24, 29, November 1, 2, 3, 1973. For additional details on Saigon's operations in the area, see Liberation Radio, November 5, 6, 1973. A note detailing Saigon's nibbling operations in Quang Duc and demanding an immediate ICCS investigation was sent to the ICCS chairman on November 6. Liberation Radio, November 8, 1973.

88. *New York Times*, October 21, 1973.

89. Liberation Radio, October 15, 1973.

90. Again, the RVN continued to accuse the PRG of a major truce violation for having forced its withdrawal from Bach Ma. See "Communist Violations of the Paris Agreement," p. 2.

91. "Uproot Illegally Established Military Posts, Recover the Liberated Areas and Restore the People's Right to Mastership," Liberation Radio, November 11, 1973.

92. *New York Times*, November 5, 7, 1973.

93. ". . . For more than a month the Administration has been quietly alerting members of Congress to what it has described as the likelihood of a new North Vietnamese attack." *New York Times*, November 30, 1973. For other public statements and background briefings conveying the warning of a "possible" or "probable" major North Vietnamese offensive, see *New York Times*, October 25, 1973; *Washington Post*, October 31, 1973; and *Washington Star-News*, November 2, 1973.

94. See D. Gareth Porter, "Comment Washington a trompé le Congrès et le Public," *Le Monde Diplomatique*, July 1974.

95. Ibid.

96. *Los Angeles Times*, November 8, 1973; *Boston Globe*, November 9, 1973. Saigon spokesmen denied that the market area was hit, but Saigon radio made the curious statement that among the targets of the bombing raid were "grain storage facilities." Saigon Radio Domestic Service, November 8, 1973.

97. Liberation Radio, November 12, 13, 1973; *Philadelphia Inquirer*, November 12, 1973; Liberation Radio, December 4, 12, 1973.

98. *U.S. News and World Report*, January 28, 1974.

99. Saigon Radio Domestic Service, November 8, 1973.

100. UPI dispatch, Saigon, November 8, 1973.

101. *Washington Post*, December 29, 1973.

102. *Washington Post*, January 5, 1974.

103. Letter from Earl and Pat Martin, Quang Ngai, to Senator Edward M. Kennedy, May 29, 1974; Report from American Friends Service Committee personnel in South Vietnam, March 1974.

104. Notes on the PRG Weekly Press Conference, Camp Davis, February 23, 1974, by John Spragens, Jr. (typescript), p. 4. *Manchester Guardian*, August 31, 1974; *Vietnam: May 1974*, Staff Report for the Committee on Foreign Relations, US Senate, 93rd Congress, 2nd Session, 1974, pp. 2-3; Liberation Press Agency, February 12, 1974.

105. *Vietnam: May 1974*, p. 4; *Vietnam—A Changing Crucible*, Report of a Study Mission to South Vietnam, House Report no. 93-1196, 93rd Congress, 2nd Session, 1974, p. 4.

106. *Washington Post*, April 4, 1974; *New York Times*, April 7, 1974.

107. *Vietnam: May 1974*, pp. 15-16.

108. Saigon Radio Domestic Service, April 13, 1974.

109. *New York Times*, April 17, 1974; *Washington Post*, April 24, 1974.

110. *Philadelphia Inquirer*, May 11, 1974.

111. *Washington Post*, May 19, 1974; *Manchester Guardian*, August 31, 1974; Liberation Radio, July 24, 1974; *New York Times*, July 30, 1974.

316 notes to pp. 267-275

112. Liberation Radio, July 21, 1974.

113. Liberation Radio, July 21, August 7, 1974.

114. Liberation Radio, August 8, 1974; *Washington Post*, August 8, 1974. For an account of Saigon's military operations in Quang Nam during 1973, see Liberation Press Agency, Hanoi Radio, July 30, 1974.

115. *Manchester Guardian*, August 31, 1974; *New York Times*, September 28, 1974.

116. *Washington Post*, September 1, 1974; Liberation Radio, August 7, 19, 1974.

117. *Christian Science Monitor*, September 4, 1974.

118. "COSVN Directive 08," translation by the US Embassy, Saigon. Released by the State Department, February 1975 (mimeographed), p. 13.

119. Ibid., p. 12.

120. The following analysis, based on the author's trip to Hanoi in December and January, 1974–75, was published in a slightly different form in "Report from Hanoi: Pressing Ford to Drop Thieu," *The New Republic*, February 8, 1975, pp. 19–21.

Epilogue

1. *Time*, March 24, 1975, p. 20.

2. William Goodfellow, Pacific News Service dispatch from Quang Ngai, March 3, 1975.

3. *Christian Science Monitor*, April 1, 1975.

4. Don Oberdorfer, *Washington Post*, April 7, 1975.

5. The report of FULRO troops leading the operation on Ban Me Thuot was reported by Agence France-Presse correspondent Paul Leandri in *Le Monde*, March 14, 1975. Leandri was summoned to the National Police station for questioning about his dispatch and was shot by police as he tried to leave his compound in his car. *New York Times*, March 16, 1975. Leandri's story was confirmed by Catholic leader Father Tran Huu Thanh on the basis of conversations with refugees and priests from Ban Me Thuot. *Le Figaro*, March 19, 1975.

6. Oberdorfer, *Washington Post*, April 7, 1975.

7. Ibid.

8. Agence France-Presse dispatch by George Herbouze, *Los Angeles Times*, March 31, 1975 (Herbouze interviewed a French schoolteacher who was in Danang when the PRG took over); Associated Press dispatch from aboard the freighter *Pioneer Contender*, *Washington Star*, March 31, 1975.

9. Agence France-Presse dispatch, *New York Times*, April 24, 1975.

10. *Christian Science Monitor*, April 3, 1975.

11. In his news conference of April 19, PRG spokesman Vo Dong Giang announced that the general order for the assault on Saigon had gone out on April 4. *Washington Post*, April 20, 1975.

12. *New York Times*, April 2 and 3, 1975.

13. *Washington Post*, April 10, 1975. In an interview with a group of Americans, including the author, on April 7, 1975, the PRG ambassador to the Political Talks in Paris, Dinh Ba Thi, went considerably further in indicating his government's willingness to return to the political formula of the Paris Agreement. "We aimed at

a higher goal during the negotiations," he said, "but Kissinger wouldn't accept it, so the power of the National Council was very limited. But since the agreement talked about the National Council we must implement that." He further confirmed that the PRG was still prepared to accept the existence of two administrations through the electoral process outlined in the agreement, and that they were ready to reconstitute the Joint Military Commission by negotiations with a new Saigon government.

14. *Los Angeles Times*, March 22, 1975.

15. *Time*, April 21, 1975, p. 19.

16. See the interview with Ky's personal assistant, Deputy Nguyen Van Cu, *Chicago Tribune*, April 24, 1975.

17. Kissinger's background briefing, including substantial quotations, is covered, without naming Kissinger, in the *Los Angeles Times*, April 12, 1975.

18. *Washington Post*, April 20, 1975.

19. *Washington Post*, April 26, 1975 and May 5, 1975.

20. *Time*, May 5, 1975.

21. A Liberation Radio broadcast on April 30 said the final drive on the city began at 5 P.M. April 26. The highways leading out of Saigon were immediately cut and the airport was rocketed by the following night. *Washington Post*, April 26, 1975.

22. *Washington Post*, April 18, 1975.

23. *Time*, May 12, 1975; *Washington Star*, April 29, 1975; *Chicago Tribune*, April 29, 1975.

24. For an eyewitness account of the Saigon army's surrender, see James Fenton, "How War's End Came to Saigon," *Washington Post*, May 11, 1975.

25. Interview with Hoang Tung by an American delegation in Hanoi, May 6, 1975 (*Indochina Peace Campaign Newsletter*, May 18, 1975).

APPENDIX

The Vietnam Agreement and Protocols, Signed January 27, 1973 [1]

AGREEMENT ON ENDING THE WAR AND RESTORING PEACE IN VIETNAM

The Parties participating in the Paris Conference on Vietnam,

With a view to ending the war and restoring peace in Vietnam on the basis of respect for the Vietnamese people's fundamental national rights and the South Vietnamese people's right to self-determination, and to contributing to the consolidation of peace in Asia and the world,

Have agreed on the following provisions and undertake to respect and to implement them :

Chapter I

THE VIETNAMESE PEOPLE'S FUNDAMENTAL NATIONAL RIGHTS

Article 1

The United States and all other countries respect the independence, sovereignty, unity, and territorial integrity of Vietnam as recognized by the 1954 Geneva Agreements on Vietnam.

---

[1] Weekly Compilation of Presidential Documents, Jan. 29, 1973, pp. 45–64.

Chapter II

CESSATION OF HOSTILITIES—WITHDRAWAL OF TROOPS

Article 2

A cease-fire shall be observed throughout South Vietnam as of 2400 hours G.M.T., on January 27, 1973.

At the same hour, the United States will stop all its military activities against the territory of the Democratic Republic of Vietnam by ground, air and naval forces, wherever they may be based, and end the mining of the territorial waters, ports, harbors, and waterways of the Democratic Republic of Vietnam. The United States will remove, permanently deactivate or destroy all the mines in the territorial waters, ports, harbors, and waterways of North Vietnam as soon as this Agreement goes into effect.

The complete cessation of hostilities mentioned in this Article shall be durable and without limit of time.

Article 3

The parties undertake to maintain the cease-fire and to ensure a lasting and stable peace.

As soon as the cease-fire goes into effect:

(a) The United States forces and those of the other foreign countries allied with the United States and the Republic of Vietnam shall remain in-place pending the implementation of the plan of troop withdrawal. The Four-Party Joint Military Commission described in Article 16 shall determine the modalities.

(b) The armed forces of the two South Vietnamese parties shall remain in-place. The Two-Party Joint Military Commission described in Article 17 shall determine the areas controlled by each party and the modalities of stationing.

(c) The regular forces of all services and arms and the irregular forces of the parties in South Vietnam shall stop all offensive activities against each other and shall strictly abide by the following stipulations:

All acts of force on the ground, in the air, and on the sea shall be prohibited;

All hostile acts, terrorism and reprisals by both sides will be banned.

Article 4

The United States will not continue its military involvement or intervene in the internal affairs of South Vietnam.

Article 5

Within sixty days of the signing of this Agreement, there will be a total withdrawal from South Vietnam of troops, military advisers, and military personnel, including technical military personnel and military personnel associated with the pacification program, armaments, munitions, and war material of the United States and those of the other foreign countries mentioned in Article 3 (a). Advisers from the above-mentioned countries to all paramilitary organizations and the police force will also be withdrawn within the same period of time.

Article 6

The dismantlement of all military bases in South Vietnam of the United States and of the other foreign countries mentioned in Article 3 (a) shall be completed within sixty days of the signing of this Agreement.

Article 7

From the enforcement of the cease-fire to the formation of the government provided for in Articles 9 (b) and 14 of this Agreement, the two South Vietnamese parties shall not accept the introduction of troops, military advisers, and military personnel including technical military personnel, armaments, munitions, and war material into South Vietnam.

The two South Vietnamese parties shall be permitted to make periodic replacement of armaments, munitions and war material which have beeen destroyed, damaged, worn out or used up after the cease-fire, on the basis of piece-for-piece, of the same characteristics and properties, under the supervision of the Joint Military Commission of the two South Vietnamese parties and of the International Commission of Control and Supervision.

Chapter III

THE RETURN OF CAPTURED MILITARY PERSONNEL AND FOREIGN CIVILIANS, AND CAPTURED AND DETAINED VIETNAMESE CIVILIAN PERSONNEL

Article 8

(a) The return of captured military personnel and foreign civilians of the parties shall be carried out simultaneously with and completed not later than the same day as the troop withdrawal mentioned in Article 5. The parties shall exchange complete lists of the above-mentioned captured military personnel and foreign civilians on the day of the signing of this Agreement.

(b) The parties shall help each other to get information about those military personnel and foreign civilians of the parties missing in action, to determine the location and take care of the graves of the dead so as to facilitate the exhumation and repatriation of the remains, and to take any such other measures as may be required to get information about those still considered missing in action.

(c) The question of the return of Vietnamese civilian personnel captured and detained in South Vietnam will be resolved by the two South Vietnamese parties on the basis of the principles of Article 21 (b) of the Agreement on the Cessation of Hostilities in Vietnam of July 20, 1954. The two South Vietnamese parties will do so in a spirit of national reconciliation and concord, with a view to ending hatred and enmity, in order to ease suffering and to reunite families. The two South Vietnamese parties will do their utmost to resolve this question within ninety days after the cease-fire comes into effect.

Chapter IV

THE EXERCISE OF THE SOUTH VIETNAMESE PEOPLE'S RIGHT TO SELF-DETERMINATION

Article 9

The Government of the United States of America and the Government of the Democratic Republic of Vietnam undertake to respect the following principles for the exercise of the South Vietnamese people's right to self-determination:

(a) The South Vietnamese people's right to self-determination is sacred, inalienable, and shall be respected by all countries.

(b) The South Vietnamese people shall decide themselves the political future of South Vietnam through genuinely free and democratic general elections under international supervision.

(c) Foreign countries shall not impose any political tendency or personality on the South Vietnamese people.

Article 10

The two South Vietnamese parties undertake to respect the cease-fire and maintain peace in South Vietnam, settle all matters of contention through negotiations, and avoid all armed conflict.

Article 11

Immediately after the cease-fire, the two South Vietnamese parties will:

Achieve national reconciliation and concord, end hatred and enmity, prohibit all acts of reprisal and discrimination against individuals or organizations that have collaborated with one side or the other;

Ensure the democratic liberties of the people: personal freedom, freedom of speech, freedom of the press, freedom of meeting, freedom of organization, freedom of political activities, freedom of belief, freedom of movement, freedom of residence, freedom of work, right to property ownership, and right to free enterprise.

Article 12

(a) Immediately after the cease-fire, the two South Vietnamese parties shall hold consultations in a spirit of national reconciliation and concord, mutual respect, and mutual non-elimination to set up a National Council of National Reconciliation and Concord of three equal segments. The Council shall operate on the principle of unanimity. After the National Council of National Reconciliation and Concord has assumed its functions, the two South Vietnamese parties will consult about the formation of councils at lower levels. The two South Vietnamese parties shall sign an agreement on the internal matters of South Vietnam as soon as possible and do their utmost to accomplish this within ninety days after the cease-fire comes into effect, in keeping with the South Vietnamese people's aspirations for peace, independence and democracy.

(b) The National Council of National Reconciliation and Concord shall have the task of promoting the two South Vietnamese parties' implementation of this Agreement, achievement of national reconciliation and concord and ensurance of democratic liberties. The National Council of National Reconciliation and Concord will organize the free and democratic general elections provided for in Article 9 (b) and decide the procedures and modalities of these general elections. The institutions for which the general elections are to be held will be agreed upon through consultations between the two South Vietnamese parties. The National Council of National Reconciliation and Concord will also decide the procedures and modalities of such local elections as the two South Vietnamese parties agree upon.

Article 13

The question of Vietnamese armed forces in South Vietnam shall be settled by the two South Vietnamese parties in a spirit of national reconciliation and concord, equality and mutual respect, without foreign interference, in accordance with the postwar situation. Among the questions to be discussed by the two South Vietnamese parties are steps to reduce their military effectives and to demobilize the troops being reduced. The two South Vietnamese parties will accomplish this as soon as possible.

Article 14

South Vietnam will pursue a foreign policy of peace and independence. It will be prepared to establish relations with all countries irrespective of their political and social systems on the basis of mutual respect for independence and sovereignty and accept economic and technical aid from any country with no political conditions attached. The acceptance of military aid by South Vietnam in the future shall come under the authority of the government set up after the general elections in South Vietnam provided for in Article 9(b).

Chapter V

THE REUNIFICATION OF VIETNAM AND THE RELATIONSHIP BETWEEN NORTH AND SOUTH VIETNAM

Article 15

The reunification of Vietnam shall be carried out step by step through peaceful means on the basis of discussions and agreements between North and South Vietnam, without coercion or annexation by either party, and without foreign interference. The time for reunification will be agreed upon by North and South Vietnam.

Pending reunification:

(a) The military demarcation line between the two zones at the 17th parallel is only provisional and not a political or territorial boundary, as provided for in paragraph 6 of the Final Declaration of the 1954 Geneva Conference.

(b) North and South Vietnam shall respect the Demilitarized Zone on either side of the Provisional Military Demarcation Line.

(c) North and South Vietnam shall promptly start negotiations with a view to reestablishing normal relations in various fields. Among the questions to be negotiated are the modalities of civilian movement across the Provisional Military Demarcation Line.

(d) North and South Vietnam shall not join any military alliance or military bloc and shall not allow foreign powers to maintain military bases, troops, military advisers, and military personnel on their respective territories, as stipulated in the 1954 Geneva Agreements on Vietnam.

Chapter VI

THE JOINT MILITARY COMMISSIONS, THE INTERNATIONAL COMMISSION OF CONTROL
AND SUPERVISION, THE INTERNATIONAL CONFERENCE

Article 16

(a) The Parties participating in the Paris Conference on Vietnam shall immediately designate representatives to form a Four-Party Joint Military Commission with the task of ensuring joint action by the parties in implementing the following provisions of this Agreement:

The first paragraph of Article 2, regarding the enforcement of the cease-fire throughout South Vietnam;

Article 3(a), regarding the cease-fire by U.S. forces and those of the other foreign countries referred to in that Article;

Article 3(c), regarding the cease-fire between all parties in South Vietnam;

Article 5, regarding the withdrawal from South Vietnam of U.S. troops and those of the other foreign countries mentioned in Article 3(a);

Article 6, regarding the dismantlement of military bases in South Vietnam of the United States and those of the other foreign countries mentioned in Article 8(a);

Article 8(a), regarding the return of captured military personnel and foreign civilians of the parties;

Article 8(b), regarding the mutual assistance of the parties in getting information about those military personnel and foreign civilians of the parties missing in action.

(b) The Four-Party Joint Military Commission shall operate in accordance with the principle of consultations and unanimity. Disagreements shall be referred to the International Commission of Control and Supervision.

(c) The Four-Party Joint Military Commission shall begin operating immediately after the signing of this Agreement and end its activities in sixty days, after the completion of the withdrawal of U.S. troops and those of the other foreign countries mentioned in Article 3(a) and the completion of the return of captured military personnel and foreign civilians of the parties.

(d) The four parties shall agree immediately on the organization, the working procedure, means of activity, and expenditures of the Four-Party Joint Military Commission.

Article 17

(a) The two South Vietnamese parties shall immediately designate representatives to form a Two-Party Joint Military Commission with the task of ensuring joint action by the two South Vietnamese parties in implementing the following provisions of this Agreement:

The first paragraph of Article 2, regarding the enforcement of the cease-fire throughout South Vietnam, when the Four-Party Joint Military Commission has ended its activities;

Article 3(b), regarding the cease-fire between the two South Vietnamese parties;

Article 3(c), regarding the cease-fire between all parties in South Vietnam, when the Four-Party Joint Military Commission has ended its activities;

Article 7, regarding the prohibition of the introduction of troops into South Vietnam and all other provisions of this article;

Article 8(c), regarding the question of the return of Vietnamese civilian personnel captured and detained in South Vietnam;

Article 13, regarding the reduction of the military effectives of the two South Vietnamese parties and the demobilization of the troops being reduced.

(b) Disagreements shall be referred to the International Commission of Control and Supervision.

(c) After the signing of this Agreement, the Two-Party Joint Military Commission shall agree immediately on the measures and organization aimed at enforcing the cease-fire and preserving peace in South Vietnam.

Article 18

(a) After the signing of this Agreement, an International Commission of Control and Supervision shall be established immediately.

(b) Until the International Conference provided for in Article 19 makes definitive arrangements, the International Commission of Control and Supervision will report to the four parties of matters concerning the control and supervision of the implementation of the following provisions of this Agreement:

The first paragraph of Article 2, regarding the enforcement of the cease-fire throughout South Vietnam;

Article 3(a), regarding the cease-fire by U.S. forces and those of other foreign countries referred to in that Article;

Article 3(c), regarding the cease-fire between all the parties in South Vietnam;

Article 5, regarding the withdrawal from Vietnam of U.S. troops and those of the other foreign countries mentioned in Article 3(a);

Article 6, regarding the dismantlement of military bases in South Vietnam of the United States and those of the other foreign countries mentioned in Article 3(a);

Article 8(a), regarding the return of captured military personnel and foreign civilians of the parties.

The International Commission of Control and Supervision shall form control teams for carrying out its task. The four parties shall agree immediately on the location and operation of these teams. The parties will facilitate their operation.

(c) Until the International Conference makes definitive arrangements, the International Commission of Control and Supervision will report to the two South Vietnamese parties on matters concerning the control and supervision of the implementation of the following provisions of this Agreement:

The first paragraph of Article 2, regarding the enforcement of the cease-fire throughout South Vietnam, when the Four-Party Joint Military Commission has ended its activities;

Article 3(b), regarding the cease-fire between the two South Vietnamese parties;

Article 3(c), regarding the cease-fire between all parties in South Vietnam, when the Four-Party Joint Military Commission has ended its activities;

Article 7, regarding the prohibition of the introduction of troops into South Vietnam and all other provisions of this Article;

Article 8(c), regarding the question of the return of Vietnamese civilian personnel captured and detained in South Vietnam;

Article 9(b), regarding the free and democratic general elections in South Vietnam;

Article 13, regarding the reduction of the military effectives of the two South Vietnamese parties and the demobilization of the troops being reduced.

The International Commission of Control and Supervision shall form control teams for carrying out its tasks. The two South Vietnamese parties shall agree immediately on the location and operation of these teams. The two South Vietnamese parties will facilitate their operation.

(d) The International Commission of Control and Supervision shall be composed of representatives of four countries: Canada, Hungary, Indonesia and Poland. The chairmanship of this Commission will rotate among the members for specific periods to be determined by the Commission.

(e) The International Commission of Control and Supervision shall carry out its tasks in accordance with the principle of respect for the sovereignty of South Vietnam.

(f) The International Commission of Control and Supervision shall operate in accordance with the principle of consultations and unanimity.

(g) The International Commission of Control and Supervision shall begin operating when a cease-fire comes into force in Vietnam. As regards the provisions in Article 18(b) concerning the four parties, the International Commission of Control and Supervision shall end its activities when the Commission's tasks of control and supervision regarding these provisions have been fulfilled. As regards the provisions in Article 18(c) concerning the two South Vietnamese parties, the International Commission of Control and Supervision shall end its activities on the request of the government formed after the general elections in South Vietnam provided for in Article 9(b).

(h) The four parties shall agree immediately on the organization, means of activity, and expenditures of the International Commission of Control and Supervision. The relationship between the International Commission and the International Conference will be agreed upon by the International Commission and the International Conference.

Article 19

The parties agree on the convening of an International Conference within thirty days of the signing of this Agreement to acknowledge the signed agreements; to guarantee the ending of the war, the maintenance of peace in Vietnam, the respect of the Vietnamese people's fundamental national rights, and the South Vietnamese people's rights to self-determination; and to contribute to and guarantee peace in Indochina.

The United States and the Democratic Republic of Vietnam, on behalf of the parties participating in the Paris Conference on Vietnam, will propose to the following parties that they participate in this International Conference; the People's Republic of China, the Republic of France, the Union of Soviet Socialist Republics, the United Kingdom, the four countries of the International Commission of Control and Supervision, and the Secretary General of the United Nations, together with the parties participating in the Paris Conference on Vietnam.

Chapter VII

REGARDING CAMBODIA AND LAOS

Article 20

(a) The parties participating in the Paris Conference on Vietnam shall strictly respect the 1954 Geneva Agreement on Cambodia and the 1962 Geneva Agreements on Laos, which recognized the Cambodian and the Lao peoples' fundamental national rights, i.e., the independence, sovereignty, unity, and territorial integrity of these countries. The parties shall respect the neutrality of Cambodia and Laos.

The parties participating in the Paris Conference on Vietnam undertake to refrain from using the territory of Cambodia and the territory of Laos to encroach on the sovereignty and security of one another and of other countries.

(b) Foreign countries shall put an end to, all military activities in Cambodia and Laos, totally withdraw from and refrain from reintroducing into these two countries troops, military advisers and military personnel, armaments, munitions and war material.

(c) The internal affairs of Cambodia and Laos shall be settled by the people of each of these countries without foreign interference.

(d) The problems existing between the Indochinese countries shall be settled by the Indochinese parties on the basis of respect for each other's independence, sovereignty, and territorial integrity, and non-interference in each other's internal affairs.

Chapter VIII

THE RELATIONSHIP BETWEEN THE UNITED STATES AND THE DEMOCRATIC REPUBLIC OF VIETNAM

Article 21

The United States anticipates that this Agreement will usher in an era of reconciliation with the Democratic Republic of Vietnam as with all the peoples of Indochina. In pursuance of its traditional policy, the United States will contribute to healing the wounds of war and to postwar reconstruction of the Democratic Republic of Vietnam and throughout Indochina.

Article 22

The ending of the war, the restoration of peace in Vietnam, and the strict implementation of this Agreement will create conditions for establishing a new, equal and mutually beneficial relationship between the United States and the Democratic Republic of Vietnam on the basis of respect for each other's independence and sovereignty, and non-interference in each other's internal affairs. At the same time this will ensure stable peace in Vietnam and contribute to the preservation of lasting peace in Indochina and Southeast Asia.

Chapter IX

OTHER PROVISIONS

Article 23

This Agreement shall enter into force upon signature by plenipotentiary representatives of the parties participating in the Paris Conference on Vietnam. All the parties concerned shall strictly implement this Agreement and its Protocols.

Done in Paris this twenty-seventh day of January, One Thousand-Nine Hundred and Seventy-Three, in Vietnamese and English. The Vietnamese and English texts are official and equally authentic.

[Separate Numbered Page]

For the Government of the United States of America :

WILLIAM P. ROGERS,
Secretary of State.

For the Government of the Republic of Vietnam :

TRAN VAN LAM,
Minister for Foreign Affairs.

[Separate Numbered Page]

For the Government of the Democratic Republic of Vietnam :

NGUYEN DUY TRINH,
Minister for Foreign Affairs.

For the Provisional Revolutionary Government of the Republic of South Vietnam :

NGUYEN THI BINH,
Minister for Foreign Affairs.

AGREEMENT ON ENDING THE WAR AND RESTORING PEACE IN VIETNAM

The Government of the United States of America, with the concurrence of the Government of the Republic of Vietnam,

The Government of the Democratic Republic of Vietnam, with the concurrence of the Provisional Revolutionary Government of the Republic of South Vietnam,

With a view to ending the war and restoring peace in Vietnam on the basis of respect for the Vietnamese people's fundamental national rights and the South Vietnamese people's right to self-determination, and to contributing to the consolidation of peace in Asia and the world,

Have agreed on the following provisions and undertake to respect and to implement them :

[Text of Agreement Chapters I–VIII Same As Above]

Chapter IX

OTHER PROVISIONS

Article 23

The Paris Agreement on Ending the War and Restoring Peace in Vietnam shall enter into force upon signature of this document by the Secretary of State of the Government of the United States of America and the Minister for Foreign Affairs of the Government of the Democratic Republic of Vietnam, and upon signature of a document in the same terms by the Secretary of State of the Government of the United States of America, the Minister for Foreign Affairs of the Government of the Republic of Vietnam, the Minister for Foreign Affairs of the Government of the Democratic Republic of Vietnam, and the Minister for Foreign Affairs of the Provisional Revolutionary Government of the Republic of South Vietnam. The Agreement and the protocols to it shall be strictly implemented by all the parties concerned.

Done in Paris this twenty-seventh day of January, One Thousand Nine Hundred and Seventy Three, in Vietnamese and English. The Vietnamese and English texts are official and equally authentic.

For the Government of the United States of America :

WILLIAM P. ROGERS,
Secretary of State.

For the Government of the Democratic Republic of Vietnam :

NGUYEN DUY TRINH,
Minister for Foreign Affairs.

Protocol on Prisoners and Detainees

[White House press release dated January 24]

PROTOCOL TO THE AGREEMENT ON ENDING THE WAR AND RESTORING PEACE IN VIETNAM CONCERNING THE RETURN OF CAPTURED MILITARY PERSONNEL AND FOREIGN CIVILIANS AND CAPTURED AND DETAINED VIETNAMESE CIVILIAN PERSONNEL

The Parties participating in the Paris Conference on Vietnam.

In implementation of Article 8 of the Agreement on Ending the War and Restoring Peace in Vietnam signed on this date providing for the return of captured military personnel and foreign civilians, and captured and detained Vietnamese civilian personnel,

Have agreed as follows:

THE RETURN OF CAPTURED MILITARY PERSONNEL AND FOREIGN CIVILIANS

Article 1

The parties signatory to the Agreement shall return the captured military personnel of the parties mentioned in Article 8(a) of the Agreement as follows:

All captured military personnel of the United States and those of the other foreign countries mentioned in Article 3(a) of the Agreement shall be returned to United States authorities;

All captured Vietnamese military personnel, whether belonging to regular or irregular armed forces, shall be returned to the two South Vietnamese parties; they shall be returned to that South Vietnamese party under whose command they served.

Article 2

All captured civilians who are nationals of the United States or of any other foreign countries mentioned in Article 3(a) of the Agreement shall be returned to United States authorities. All other captured foreign civilians shall be returned to the authorities of their country of nationality by any one of the parties willing and able to do so.

Article 3

The parties shall today exchange complete lists of captured persons mentioned in Articles 1 and 2 of this Protocol.

Article 4

(a) The return of all captured persons mentioned in Articles 1 and 2 of this Protocol shall be completed within sixty days of the signing of the Agreement at a rate no slower than the rate of withdrawal from South Vietnam of United States forces and those of the other foreign countries mentioned in Article 5 of the Agreement.

(b) Persons who are seriously ill, wounded or maimed, old persons and women shall be returned first. The remainder shall be returned either by returning all from one detention place after another or in order of their dates of capture, beginning with those who have been held the longest.

Article 5

The return and reception of the persons mentioned in Articles 1 and 2 of this Protocol shall be carried out at places convenient to the concerned parties. Places of return shall be agreed upon by the Four-Party Joint Military Commission. The parties shall ensure the safety of personnel engaged in the return and reception of those persons.

Article 6

Each party shall return all captured persons mentioned in Articles 1 and 2 of this Protocol without delay and shall facilitate their return and reception. The detaining parties shall not deny or delay their return for any reason, including the fact that captured persons may, on any grounds, have been prosecuted or sentenced.

THE RETURN OF CAPTURED AND DETAINED VIETNAMESE CIVILIAN PERSONNEL

Article 7

(a) The question of the return of Vietnamese civilian personnel captured and detained in South Vietnam will be resolved by the two South Vietnamese parties on the basis of the principles of Article 21 (b) of the Agreement on the Cessation of Hostilities in Vietnam of July 20, 1954, which reads as follows:

"The term 'civilian internees' is understood to mean all persons who, having in any way contributed to the political and armed struggle between the two parties, have been arrested for that reason and have been kept in detention by either party during the period of hostilities."

(b) The two South Vietnamese parties will do so in a spirit of national reconciliation and concord with a view to ending hatred and enmity in order to ease suffering and to reunite families. The two South Vietnamese parties will do their utmost to resolve this question within ninety days after the cease-fire comes into effect.

(c) Within fifteen days after the cease-fire comes into effect, the two South Vietnamese parties shall exchange lists of the Vietnamese civilian personnel captured and detained by each party and lists of the places at which they are held.

TREATMENT OF CAPTURED PERSONS DURING DETENTION

Article 8

(a) All captured military personnel of the parties and captured foreign civilians of the parties shall be treated humanely at all times, and in accordance with international practice.

They shall be protected against all violence to life and person, in particular against murder in any form, mutilation, torture and cruel treatment, and outrages upon personal dignity. These persons shall not be forced to join the armed forces of the detaining party.

They shall be given adequate food, clothing, shelter, and the medical attention required for their state of health. They shall be allowed to exchange post cards and letters with their families and receive parcels.

(b) All Vietnamese civilian personnel captured and detained in South Vietnam shall be treated humanely at all times, and in accordance with international practice.

They shall be protected against all violence to life and person, in particular against murder in any form, mutilation, torture and cruel treatment, and outrages against personal dignity. The detaining parties shall not deny or delay their return for any reason, including the fact that captured persons may, on any grounds, have been prosecuted or sentenced. These persons shall not be forced to join the armed forces of the detaining party.

They shall be given adequate food, clothing, shelter, and the medical attention required for their state of health. They shall be allowed to exchange post cards and letters with their families and receive parcels.

Article 9

(a) To contribute to improving the living conditions of the captured military personnel of the parties and foreign civilians of the parties, the parties shall, within fifteen days after the cease-fire comes into effect, agree upon the designation of two or more national Red Cross societies to visit all places where captured military personnel and foreign civilians are held.

(b) To contribute to improving the living conditions of the captured and detained Vietnamese civilian personnel, the two South Vietnamese parties shall, within fifteen days after the cease-fire comes into effect, agree upon the designation of two or more national Red Cross societies to visit all places where the captured and detained Vietnamese civilian personnel are held.

WITH REGARD TO DEAD AND MISSING PERSONS

Article 10

(a) The Four-Party Joint Military Commission shall ensure joint action by the parties in implementing Article 8 (b) of the Agreement. When the Four-

Party Joint Military Commission has ended its activities, a Four-Party Joint Military team shall be maintained to carry on this task.

(b) With regard to Vietnamese civilian personnel dead or missing in South Vietnam, the two South Vietnamese parties shall help each other to obtain information about missing persons, determine the location and take care of the graves of the dead, in a spirit of national reconciliation and concord, in keeping with the people's aspirations.

OTHER PROVISIONS

Article 11

(a) The Four-Party and Two-Party Joint Military Commissions will have the responsibility of determining immediately the modalities of implementing the provisions of this Protocol consistent with their respective responsibilities under Articles 16 (a) and 17 (a) of the Agreement. In case the Joint Military Commissions, when carrying out their tasks, cannot reach agreement on a matter pertaining to the return of captured personnel they shall refer to the International Commission for its assistance.

(b) The Four-Party Joint Military Commission shall form, in addition to the teams established by the Protocol concerning the cease-fire in South Vietnam and the Joint Military Commissions, a subcommission on captured persons and, as required, joint military teams on captured persons to assist the Commission in its tasks.

(c) From the time the cease-fire comes into force to the time when the Two-Party Joint Military Commission becomes operational, the two South Vietnamese parties' delegations to the Four-Party Joint Military Commission shall form a provisional sub-commission and provisional joint military teams to carry out its tasks concerning captured and detained Vietnamese civilian personnel.

(d) The Four-Party Joint Military Commission shall send joint military teams to observe the return of the persons mentioned in Articles 1 and 2 of this Protocol at each place in Vietnam where such persons are being returned, and at the last detention places from which these persons will be taken to the places of return. The Two-Party Joint Military Commission shall send joint military teams to observe the return of Vietnamese civilian personnel captured and detained at each place in South Vietnam where such persons are being returned, and at the last detention places from which these persons will be taken to the places of return.

Article 12

In implementation of Articles 18 (b) and 18 (c) of the Agreement, the International Commission of Control and Supervision shall have the responsibility to control and supervise the observance of Articles 1 through 7 of this Protocol through observation of the return of captured military personnel, foreign civilians and captured and detained Vietnamese civilian personnel at each place in Vietnam where these persons are being returned, and at the last detention places from which these persons will be taken to the places of return, the examination of lists, and the investigation of violations of the provisions of the above-mentioned Articles.

Article 13

Within five days after signature of this Protocol, each party shall publish the text of the Protocol and communicate it to all the captured persons covered by the Protocol and being detained by that party.

Article 14

This Protocol shall come into force upon signature by plenipotentiary representatives of all the parties participating in the Paris Conference on Vietnam. It shall be strictly implemented by all the parties concerned.

Done in Paris this twenty-seventh day of January, One Thousand Nine Hundred and Seventy-Three, in Vietnamese and English. The Vietnamese and English texts are official and equally authentic.

[Separate Numbered Page]

For the Government of the United States of America:

WILLIAM P. ROGERS,
Secretary of State.

For the Government of the Republic of Vietnam:

TRAN VAN LAM,
Minister for Foreign Affairs.

For the Government of the Democratic Republic of Vietnam:

NGUYEN DUY TRINH,
Minister for Foreign Affairs.

For the Provisional Revolutionary Government of the Republic of South Vietnam:

NGUYEN THI BINH,
Minister for Foreign Affairs.

PROTOCOL TO THE AGREEMENT ON ENDING THE WAR AND RESTORING PEACE IN VIETNAM CONCERNING THE RETURN OF CAPTURED MILITARY PERSONNEL AND FOREIGN CIVILIANS AND CAPTURED AND DETAINED VIETNAMESE CIVILIAN PERSONNEL

The Government of the United States of America, with the concurrence of the Government of the Republic of Vietnam,

The Government of the Democratic Republic of Vietnam, with the concurrence of the Provisional Revolutionary Government of the Republic of South Vietnam,

In implementation of Article 8 of the Agreement on Ending the War and Restoring Peace in Vietnam signed on this date providing for the return of captured military personnel and foreign civilians, and captured and detained Vietnamese civilian personnel,

Have agreed as follows:

[Text of Protocol Articles 1–13 same as above]

Article 14

The Protocol to the Paris Agreement on Ending the War and Restoring Peace in Vietnam concerning the Return of Captured Military Personnel and Foreign Civilians and Captured and Detained Vietnamese Civilian Personnel shall enter into force upon signature of this document by the Secretary of State of the Government of the United States of America and the Minister for Foreign Affairs of the Government of the Democratic Republic of Vietnam, and upon signature of a document in the same terms by the Secretary of State of the Government of the United States of America, the Minister for Foreign Affairs of the Government of the Republic of Vietnam, the Minister for Foreign Affairs of the Government of the Democratic Republic of Vietnam, and the Minister for Foreign Affairs of the Provisional Revolutionary Government of the Republic of South Vietnam. The Protocol shall be strictly implemented by all the parties concerned.

Done in Paris this twenty-seventh day of January, One Thousand Nine Hundred and Seventy-Three, in Vietnamese and English. The Vietnamese and English texts are official and equally authentic.

For the Government of the United States of America:

WILLIAM P. ROGERS,
Secretary of State.

For the Government of the Democratic Republic of Vietnam:

TRAN VAN LAM,
Minister for Foreign Affairs.

Protocol on the International Commission of Control and Supervision

[White House press release dated January 24]

PROTOCOL TO THE AGREEMENT ON ENDING THE WAR AND RESTORING PEACE IN VIETNAM CONCERNING THE INTERNATIONAL COMMISSION OF CONTROL AND SUPERVISION

The parties participating in the Paris Conference on Vietnam,

In implementation of Article 18 of the Agreement signed on this date providing for the formulation of the International Commission of Control and Supervision,

Have agreed as follows:

Article 1

The implementation of the Agreement is the responsibility of the parties signatory to the Agreement.

The functions of the International Commission are to control and supervise the implementation of the provisions mentioned in Article 18 of the Agreement. In carrying out these functions, the International Commission shall:

(a) Follow the implementation of the above-mentioned provisions of the Agreement through communication with the parties and on-the-spot observation at the places where this is required;

(c) When necessary, cooperate with the Joint Military Commissions in deterring and detecting violations of the above-mentioned provisions.

Article 2

The International Commission shall investigate violations of the provisions described on Article 18 of the Agreement on the request of the Four-Party Joint Military Commission, or of the Two-Party Joint Military Commission, or of any party, or, with respect to Article 9(b) of the Agreement on general elections, of the National Council on National Reconciliation and Concord, or in any case where the International Commission has other adequate grounds for considering that there has been a violation of those provisions. It is understood that, in carrying out this task, the International Commission shall function with the concerned parties' assistance and cooperation as required.

Article 3

(a) When the International Commission finds that there is a serious violation in the implementation of the Agreement or a threat to peace against which the Commission can find no appropriate measure, the Commission shall report this to the four parties to the Agreement so that they can hold consultations to find a solution.

(b) In accordance with Article 18 (f) of the Agreement, the International Commission's reports shall be made with the unanimous agreement of the representatives of all the four members. In case no unanimity is reached, the Commission shall forward the different views to the four parties in accordance with Article 18 (b) of the Agreement, or to the two South Vietnamese parties in accordance with Article 18 (c) of the Agreement, but these shall not be considered as reports of the Commission.

Article 4

(a) The headquarters of the International Commission shall be at Saigon.

(b) There shall be seven regional teams located in the regions shown on the annexed map* and based at the following places:

Region I, Hue; Region II, Danang; Region III, Pleiku; Region IV, Phan Thiet; Region V, Bien Hoa; Region VI, My Tho; and Region VII, Can Tho.

The International Commission shall designate three teams for the region of Saigon-Gia Dinh.

*See map on p. 333

(c) There shall be twenty-six teams operating in the areas shown on the annexed map and based at the following places in South Vietnam :

Region I. Quang Tri, Phu Bai.
Region II. Hoi An, Tam Ky, Chu Lai.
Region III. Kontum, Hau Bon, Phu Cat, Tuy An, Ninh Hoa, Ban Me Thuot.
Region IV. Da Lat, Bao Loc, Phan Rang.
Region V. An Loc, Xuan Loc, Ben Cat, Cu Chi, Tan An.
Region VI. Moc Hoa, Giong Trom.
Region VII. Tri Ton, Vinh Long, Vi Thanh, Khanh Hung, Quan Long.

(d) There shall be twelve teams located as shown on the annexed map and based at the following places: Gio Linh (to cover the area south of the Provisional Military Demarcation Line), Lao Bao, Ben Het, Duc Co, Chu Lai, Qui Nhon, Nha Trang, Vung Tau, Xa Mat, Bien Hoa Airfield, Hong Ngu, and Can Tho.

(e) There shall be seven teams, six of which shall be available for assignment to the points of entry which are not listed in paragraph (d) above and which the two South Vietnamese parties choose as points for legitimate entry to South Vietnam for replacement of armaments, munitions, and war material permitted by Article 7 of the Agreement. Any team or teams not needed for the above-mentioned assignment shall be available for other tasks, in keeping with the Commission's responsibility for control and supervision.

(f) There shall be seven teams to control and supervise the return of captured and detained personnel of the parties.

Article 5

(a) To carry out its tasks concerning the return of the captured military personnel and foreign civilians of the parties as stipulated by Article 8(a) of the Agreement, the International Commission shall, during the time of such return, send one control and supervision team to each place in Vietnam where the captured persons are being returned, and to the last detention places from which these persons will be taken to the places of return.

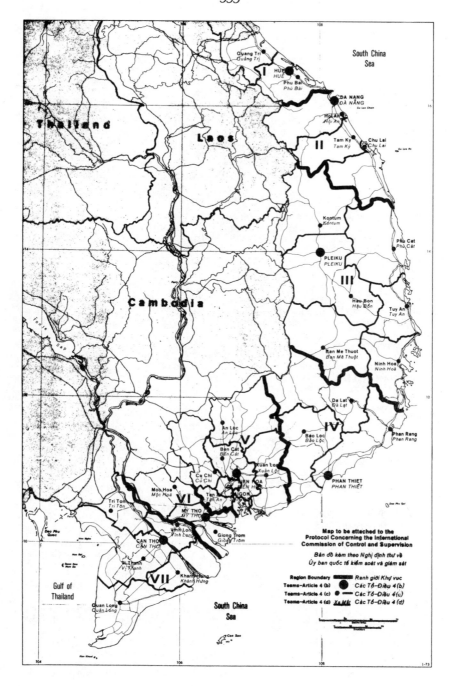

South China
Sea

Quang Tri
Quảng Trị

I

HUÉ
HUÉ

Phu Bai
Phú Bài

DA NANG
ĐÀ NẴNG

Cu Lao Cham

Hoi An
Hội An

Thailand

Laos

Tam Ky
Tam Kỳ

Chu Lai
Chu Lai

II

Cu Lao Re

Kontum
Kontum

Phu Cat
Phú Cát

PLEIKU
PLEIKU

III

Hau Bon
Hậu Bồn

Tuy An
Tuy An

Cambodia

Ban Me Thuot
Ban Mê Thuột

Ninh Hoa
Ninh Hoà

Tonle Sap

Da Lat
Đà Lạt

An Loc
An Lộc

Bao Loc
Bảo Lộc

IV

Phan Rang
Phan Rang

Ben Cat
Bến Cát

V

Cu Chi
Củ Chi

Xuan Loc
Xuân Lộc

BIEN HOA

Mob.Hoa
Mộc Hoá

Tan An
Tân An

SAIGON

PHAN THIET
PHAN THIET

Tri Ton
Tri Tôn

VI

MY THO
MỸ THO

Dao Phu Qui

Dao Phu Quoc

Hon Nghe

Vinh Long
Vĩnh Long

Giong Trom
Giồng Trôm

CAN THO
CẦN THƠ

Hon Rai

Map to be attached to the
Protocol Concerning the International
Commission of Control and Supervision

*Bản đồ kèm theo Nghị định thư và
Ủy ban quốc tế kiểm soát và giám sát*

Quan Son
Hon Da

Vi Thanh
Vị Thanh

Khanh Hung
Khánh Hưng

VII

Region Boundary	Ranh giới Khu vực
Teams–Article 4 (b)	Các Tổ–Điều 4 (b)
Teams–Article 4 (c)	Các Tổ–Điều 4 (c)
Teams–Article 4 (d)	Các Tổ–Điều 4 (d)

Gulf of
Thailand

Quan Long
Quản Long

South China
Sea

Con Son

Hon Khoai

(b) To carry out its tasks concerning the return of the Vietnamese civilian personnel captured and detained in South Vietnam mentioned in Article 8 (c) of the Agreement, the International Commission shall, during the time of such return, send one control and supervision team to each place in South Vietnam where the above-mentioned captured and detained persons are being returned, and to the last detention places from which these persons shall be taken to the places of return.

Article 6

To carry out its tasks regarding Article 9 (b) of the Agreement on the free and democratic general elections in South Vietnam, the International Commission shall organize additional teams, when necessary. The International Commission shall discuss this question in advance with the National Council of National Reconciliation and Concord. If additional teams are necessary for this purpose, they shall be formed thirty days before the general elections.

Article 7

The International Commission shall continually keep under review its size, and shall reduce the number of its teams, its representatives or other personnel, or both, when those teams, representatives or personnel have accomplished the tasks assigned to them and are not required for other tasks. At the same time, the expenditures of the International Commission shall be reduced correspondingly.

Article 8

Each member of the International Commission shall make available at all times the following numbers of qualified personnel :
(a) One senior representative and twenty-six others for the headquarters staff.
(b) Five for each of the seven regional teams.
(c) Two for each of the other international control teams, except for the teams at Gio Linh and Vung Tau, each of which shall have three.
(d) One hundred sixteen for the purpose of providing support to the Commission Headquarters and its teams.

Article 9

(a) The International Commission, and each of its teams, shall act as a single body comprising representatives of all four members.
(b) Each member has the responsibility to ensure the presence of its representatives at all levels of the International Commission. In case a representative is absent, the member concerned shall immediately designate a replacement.

Article 10

(a) The parties shall afford full cooperation, assistance, and protection to the International Commission.
(b) The parties shall at all times maintain regular and continuous liaison with the International Commission. During the existence of the Four-Party Joint Military Commission, the delegations of the parties to that Commission shall also perform liaison functions with the International Commission. After the Four-Party Joint Military Commission has ended its activities, such liaison shall be maintained through the Two-Party Joint Military Commission, liaison missions, or other adequate means.
(c) The International Commission and the Joint Military Commissions shall closely cooperate with and assist each other in carrying out their respective functions.
(d) Wherever a team is stationed or operating, the concerned party shall designate a liaison officer to the team to cooperate with and assist it in carrying out without hindrance its task of control and supervision. When a team is carrying out an investigation, a liaison officer from each concerned party shall have the opportunity to accompany it, provided the investigation is not thereby delayed.
(e) Each party shall give the International Commission reasonable advance notice of all proposed actions concerning those provisions of the Agreement that are to be controlled and supervised by the International Commission.

(f) The International Commission, including its teams, is allowed such movement for observation as is reasonably required for the proper exercise of its functions as stipulated in the Agreement. In carrying out these functions, the International Commission, including its teams, shall enjoy all necessary assistance and cooperation from the parties concerned.

Article 11

In supervising the holding of the free and democratic general elections described in Articles 9 (b) and 12 (b) of the Agreement in accordance with modalities to be agreed upon between the National Council of National Reconciliation and Concord and the International Commission, the latter shall receive full cooperation and assistance from the National Council.

Article 12

The International Commission and its personnel who have the nationality of a member state shall, while carrying out their tasks, enjoy privileges and immunities equivalent to those accorded diplomatic missions and diplomatic agents.

Article 13

The International Commission may use the means of communication and transport necessary to perform its functions. Each South Vietnamese party shall make available for rent to the International Commission appropriate office and accommodation facilities and shall assist it in obtaining such facilities. The International Commission may receive from the parties, on mutually agreeable terms, the necessary means of communication and transport and may purchase from any source necessary equipment and services not obtained from the parties. The International Commission shall possess these means.

Article 14

The expenses for the activities of the International Commission shall be borne by the parties and the members of the International Commission in accordance with the provisions of this Article:
(a) Each member country of the International Commission shall pay the salaries and allowances of its personnel.
(b) All other expenses incurred by the International Commission shall be met from a fund to which each of the four parties shall contribute twenty-three percent (23%) and to which each member of the International Commission shall contribute two percent (2%).
(c) Within thirty days of the date of entry into force of this Protocol, each of the four parties shall provide the International Commission with an initial sum equivalent to four million, five hundred thousand (4,500,000) French francs in convertible currency, which sum shall be credited against the amounts due from that party under the first budget.
(d) The International Commission shall prepare its own budgets. After the International Commission approves a budget, it shall transmit it to all parties signatory to the Agreement for their approval. Only after the budgets have been approved by the four parties to the Agreement shall they be obliged to make their contributions. However, in case the parties to the Agreement do not agree on a new budget, the International Commission shall temporarily base its expenditures on the previous budget, except for the extraordinary, one-time expenditures for installation or for the acquisition of equipment, and the parties shall continue to make their contributions on that basis until a new budget is approved.

Article 15

(a) The headquarters shall be operational and in place within twenty-four hours after the cease-fire.
(b) The regional teams shall be operational and in place, and three teams for supervision and control of the return of the captured and detained personnel shall be operational and ready for dispatch within forty-eight hours after the cease-fire.
(c) Other teams shall be operational and in place within fifteen to thirty days after the cease-fire.

Article 16

Meetings shall be convened at the call of the Chairman. The International Commission shall adopt other working procedures appropriate for the effective discharge of its functions and consistent with respect for the sovereignty of South Vietnam.

Article 17

The Members of the International Commission may accept the obligations of this Protocol by sending notes of acceptance to the four parties signatory to the Agreement. Should a member of the International Commission decide to withdraw from the International Commission, it may do so by giving three months notice by means of notes to the four parties to the Agreement, in which case those four parties shall consult among themselves for the purpose of agreeing upon a replacement member.

Article 18

This Protocol shall enter into force upon signature by plenipotentiary representatives of all the parties participating in the Paris Conference on Vietnam. It shall be strictly implemented by all the parties concerned.

DONE in Paris this twenty-seventh day of January, One Thousand Nine Hundred and Seventy-Three, in Vietnamese and English. The Vietnamese and English texts are official and equally authentic.

[Separate Numbered Page]

For the Government of the United States of America:

WILLIAM P. ROGERS,
Secretary of State.

For the Government of the Republic of Vietnam:

TRAN VAN LAM,
Minister for Foreign Affairs.

[Separate Numbered Page]

For the Government of the Democratic Republic of Vietnam:

NGUYEN DUY TRINH,
Minister for Foreign Affairs.

For the Provisional Revolutionary Government of the Republic of South Vietnam:

NGUYEN THI BINH,
Minister for Foreign Affairs.

PROTOCOL TO THE AGREEMENT ON ENDING THE WAR AND RESTORING PEACE IN VIETNAM CONCERNING THE INTERNATIONAL COMMISSION OF CONTROL AND SUPERVISION

The Government of the United States of America, with the concurrence of the Government of the Republic of Vietnam,

The Government of the Democratic Republic of Vietnam, with the concurrence of the Provisional Revolutionary Government of the Republic of South Vietnam,

In implementation of Article 18 of the Agreement on Ending the War and Restoring Peace in Vietnam signed on this date providing for the formation of the International Commission of Control and Supervision,

Have agreed as follows:

[Text of Protocol Articles 1–17 same as above]

Article 18

The Protocol to the Paris Agreement on Ending the War and Restoring Peace in Vietnam concerning the International Commission of Control and Supervision shall enter into force upon signature of this document by the Secretary of State of the Government of the United States of America and the Minister for Foreign Affairs of the Government of the Democratic Republic of Vietnam, and upon signature of a document in the same terms by the Secretary of State of the Government of the United States of America, the Minister for Foreign Affairs of the Government of the Republic of Vietnam, the Minister for Foreign Affairs of the Government of the Democratic Republic of Vietnam, and the Minister for Foreign Affairs of the Provisional Revolutionary Government of the Republic of South Vietnam. The Protocol shall be strictly implemented by all the parties concerned.

DONE in Paris this twenty-seventh day of January, One Thousand Nine Hundred and Seventy-Three, in Vietnamese and English. The Vietnamese and English texts are official and equally authentic.

For the Government of the United States of America:

WILLIAM P. ROGERS,
Secretary of State.

For the Government of the Democratic Republic of Vietnam:

NGUYEN DUY TRINH,
Minister for Foreign Affairs.

Protocol on the Cease-Fire in South Viet-Nam and the Joint Military Commissions

[White House press release dated January 24]

PROTOCOL TO THE AGREEMENT ON ENDING THE WAR AND RESTORING PEACE IN VIETNAM CONCERNING THE CEASE-FIRE IN SOUTH VIETNAM AND THE JOINT MILITARY COMMISSIONS

The parties participating in the Paris Conference on Vietnam,

In implementation of the first paragraph of Article 2, Article 3, Article 5, Article 6, Article 16 and Article 17 of the Agreement on Ending the War and Restoring Peace in Vietnam signed on this date which provide for the cease-fire in South Vietnam and the establishment of a Four-Party Joint Military Commission and a Two-Party Joint Military Commission,

Have agreed as follows:

CEASE-FIRE IN SOUTH VIETNAM

Article 1

The High Commands of the parties in South Vietnam shall issue prompt and timely orders to all regular and irregular armed forces and the armed police under their command to completely end hostilities throughout South Vietnam, at the exact time stipulated in Article 2 of the Agreement and ensure that these armed forces and armed police comply with these orders and respect the cease-fire.

Article 2

(a) As soon as the cease-fire comes into force and until regulations are issued by the Joint Military Commissions, all ground, river, sea and air combat forces of the parties in South Vietnam shall remain in place; that is, in order to ensure a stable cease-fire, there shall be no major redeployments or movements that would extend each party's area of control or would result in contact between opposing armed forces and clashes which might take place.

(b) All regular and irregular armed forces and the armed police of the parties in South Vietnam shall observe the prohibition of the following acts:

(1) Armed patrols into areas controlled by opposing armed forces and flights by bomber and fighter aircraft of all types, except for unarmed flights for proficiency training and maintenance;

(2) Armed attacks against any person, either military or civilian, by any means whatsoever, including the use of small arms, mortars, artillery, bombing and strafing by airplanes and any other type of weapon or explosive device;

(3) All combat operations on the ground, on rivers, on the sea and in the air;

(4) All hostile acts, terrorism or reprisals; and

(5) All acts endangering lives or public or private property.

Article 3

(a) The above-mentioned prohibitions shall not hamper or restrict:

(1) Civilian supply, freedom of movement, freedom to work, and freedom of the people to engage in trade, and civilian communication and transportation between and among all areas in South Vietnam;

(2) The use by each party in areas under its control of military support elements, such as engineer and transportation units, in repair and construction of public facilities and the transportation and supplying of the population;

(3) Normal military proficiency training conducted by the parties in the areas under their respective control with due regard for public safety.

(b) The Joint Military Commissions shall immediately agree on corridors, routes, and other regulations governing the movement of military transport aircraft, military transport vehicles, and military transport vessels of all types of one party going through areas under the control of other parties.

Article 4

In order to avert conflict and ensure normal conditions for those armed forces which are in direct contact, and pending regulation by the Joint Military Commissions, the commanders of the opposing armed forces at those places of direct contact shall meet as soon as the cease-fire comes into force with a view to reaching an agreement on temporary measures to avert conflict and to ensure supply and medical care for these armed forces.

Article 5

(a) Within fifteen days after the cease-fire comes into effect, each party shall do its utmost to complete the removal or deactivation of all demolition objects, mine-fields, traps, obstacles or other dangerous objects placed previously, so as not to hamper the population's movement and work, in the first place on waterways, roads and railroads in South Vietnam. Those mines which cannot be removed or deactivated within that time shall be clearly marked and must be removed or deactivated as soon as possible.

(b) Emplacement of mines is prohibited, except as a defensive measure around the edges of military installations in places where they do not hamper the population's movement and work, and movement on waterways, roads and railroads. Mines and other obstacles already in place at the edges of military installations may remain in place if they are in places where they do not hamper the population's movement and work, and movement on waterways, roads and railroads.

Article 6

Civilian police and civilian security personnel of the parties in South Vietnam, who are responsible for the maintenance of law and order, shall strictly respect the prohibitions set forth in Article 2 of this Protocol. As required by their responsibilities, normally they shall be authorized to carry pistols, but when required by unusual circumstances, they shall be allowed to carry other small individual arms.

Article 7

(a) The entry into South Vietnam of replacement armaments, munitions, and war material permitted under Article 7 of the Agreement shall take place under the supervision and control of the Two-Party Joint Military Commission and of the International Commission of Control and Supervision and through such points of entry only as are designated by the two South Vietnamese parties. The two South Vietnamese parties shall agree on these points of entry within fifteen days after the entry into force of the cease-fire. The two South Vietnamese parties may select as many as six points of entry which are not included in the list of places where teams of the International Commission of Control and Supervision are to be based contained in Article 4(d) of the Protocol concerning the International Commission. At the same time, the two South Vietnamese parties may also select points of entry from the list of places set forth in Article 4(d) of that Protocol.

(b) Each of the designated points of entry shall be available only for that South Vietnamese party which is in control of that point. The two South Vietnamese parties shall have an equal number of points of entry.

Article 8

(a) In implementation of Article 5 of the Agreement, the United States and the other foreign countries referred to in Article 5 of the Agreement shall take with them all their armaments, munitions, and war material. Transfers of such items which would leave them in South Vietnam shall not be made subsequent to the entry into force of the Agreement except for transfers of communications, transport, and other non-combat material to the Four-Party Joint Military Commission or the International Commission of Control and Supervision.

(b) Within five days after the entry into force of the cease-fire, the United States shall inform the Four-Party Joint Military Commission and the International Commission of Control and Supervision of the general plans for timing of complete troop withdrawals which shall take place in four phases of fifteen days each. It is anticipated that the numbers of troops withdrawn in each phase are not likely to be widely different, although it is not feasible to ensure equal numbers. The approximate numbers to be withdrawn in each phase shall be given to the Four-Party Joint Military Commission and the International Commission of Control and Supervision sufficiently in advance of actual withdrawals so that they can properly carry out their tasks in relation thereto.

Article 9

(a) In implementation of Article 6 of the Agreement, the United States and the other foreign countries referred to in that Article shall dismantle and remove from South Vietnam or destroy all military bases in South Vietnam of the United States and of the other foreign countries referred to in that Article, including weapons, mines, and other military equipment at these bases, for the purpose of making them unusable for military purposes.

(b) The United States shall supply the Four-Party Joint Military Commission and the International Commission of Control and Supervision with necessary information on plans for base dismantlement so that those Commissions can properly carry out their tasks in relation thereto.

THE JOINT MILITARY COMMISSIONS

Article 10

(a) The implementation of the Agreement is the responsibility of the parties signatory to the Agreement.

The Four-Party Joint Military Commission has the task of ensuring joint action by the parties in implementing the Agreement by serving as a channel of communication among the parties, by drawing up plans and fixing the modalities to carry out, coordinate, follow and inspect the implementation of the provisions mentioned in Article 16 of the Agreement, and by negotiating and settling all matters concerning the implementation of those provisions.

(b) The concrete tasks of the Four-Party Joint Military Commission are:

(1) To coordinate, follow and inspect the implementation of the above-mentioned provisions of the Agreement by the four parties;

(2) to deter and detect violations, to deal with cases of violation, and to settle conflicts and matters of contention between the parties relating to the above-mentioned provisions;

(3) To dispatch without delay one or more joint teams, as required by specific cases, to any part of South Vietnam, to investigate alleged violations of the Agreement and to assist the parties in finding measures to prevent recurrence of similar cases;

(4) To engage in observation at the places where this is necessary in the exercise of its functions;

(5) To perform such additional tasks as it may, by unanimous decision, determine.

Article 11

(a) There shall be a Central Joint Military Commission located in Saigon. Each party shall designate immediately a military delegation of fifty-nine persons to represent it on the Central Commission. The senior officer designated by each party shall be a general officer, or equivalent.

(b) There shall be seven Regional Joint Military Commissions located in the regions shown on the annexed map and based at the following places:

Regions:	Places	Regions:	Places
I	Hué	V	Bien Hoa
II	Danang	VI	My Tho
III	Pleiku	VII	Can Tho
IV	Phan Thiet		

Each party shall designate a military delegation of sixteen persons to represent it on each Regional Commission. The senior officer designated by each party shall be an officer from the rank of Lieutenant Colonel to Colonel or equivalent.

(c) There shall be a joint military team operating in each of the areas shown on the annexed map and based at each of the following places in South Vietnam:

Region I
Quang Tri
Phu Bai

Region II
Hoi An
Tam Ky
Chu Lai

Region III
Kontum
Hau Bon
Phu Cat
Tuy An
Ninh Hoa
Ban Me Thuot

Region IV
Da Lat
Bao Loc

Phan Rang

Region V
An Loc
Xuan Loc
Ben Cat
Cu Chi
Tan An

Region VI
Moc Hoa
Giong Trom

Region VII
Tri Ton
Vinh Long
Vi Thanh
Khanh Hung
Quan Long

Each party shall provide four qualified persons for each joint military team. The senior person designated by each party shall be an officer from the rank of Major to Lieutenant Colonel, or equivalent.

(d) The Regional Joint Military Commissions shall assist the Central Joint Military Commission in performing its tasks and shall supervise the operations of the joint military teams. The region of Saigon-Gia Dinh is placed under the responsibility of the Central Commission which shall designate joint military teams to operate in this region.

(e) Each party shall be authorized to provide support and guard personnel for its delegations to the Central Joint Military Commission and Regional Joint Military Commissions, and for its members of the joint military teams. The total number of support and guard personnel for each party shall not exceed five hundred and fifty.

(f) The Central Joint Military Commission may establish such joint sub-commissions, joint staffs and joint military teams as circumstances may require. The Central Commission shall determine the numbers of personnel required for any additional sub-commissions, staffs or teams it establishes, provided that each party shall designate one-fourth of the number of personnel required and that the total number of personnel for the Four-Party Joint Military Commission, to include its staffs, teams, and support personnel, shall not exceed three thousand three hundred.

(g) The delegations of the two South Vietnamese parties may, by agreement, establish provisional sub-commissions and joint military teams to carry out the tasks specifically assigned to them by Article 17 of the Agreement. With respect to Article 7 of the Agreement, the two South Vietnamese parties' delegations to the Four-Party Joint Military Commission shall establish joint military teams at the points of entry into South Vietnam used for replacement of armaments, munitions and war material which are designated in accordance with Article 7 of this Protocol. From the time the cease-fire comes into force to the time when the Two-Party Joint Military Commission becomes operational, the two South Vietnamese parties' delegations to the Four-Party Joint Military Commission shall form a provisional sub-commission and provisional joint military teams to carry out its tasks concerning captured and detained Vietnamese civilian personnel. Where necessary for the above purposes, the two South Vietnamese parties may agree to assign personnel additional to those assigned to the two South Vietnamese delegations to the Four-Party Joint Military Commission.

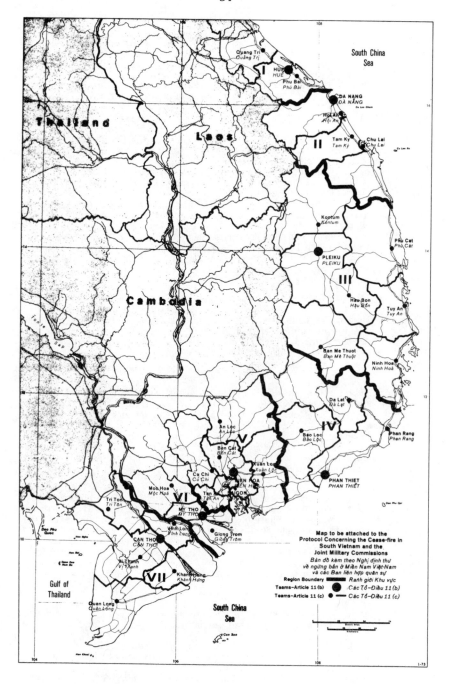

Map to be attached to the
Protocol Concerning the Cease-fire in
South Vietnam and the
Joint Military Commissions

Bản đồ kèm theo Nghị định thư
về ngừng bắn ở Miền Nam Việt-Nam
và các Ban liên hợp quân sự

Region Boundary — *Ranh giới Khu vực*
Teams—Article 11 (b) ● *Các Tổ—Điều 11 (b)*
Teams—Article 11 (c) ● *Các Tổ—Điều 11 (c)*

Article 12

(a) In accordance with Article 17 of the Agreement which stipulates that the two South Vietnamese parties shall immediately designate their respective representatives to form the Two-Party Joint Military Commission, twenty-four hours after the cease-fire comes into force, the two designated South Vietnamese parties' delegations to the Two-Party Joint Military Commission shall meet in Saigon so as to reach an agreement as soon as possible on organization and operation of the Two-Party Joint Military Commission, as well as the measures and organization aimed at enforcing the cease-fire and preserving peace in South Vietnam.

(b) From the time the cease-fire comes into force to the time when the Two-Party Joint Military Commission becomes operational, the two South Vietnamese parties' delegations to the Four-Party Joint Military Commission at all levels shall simultaneously assume the tasks of the Two-Party Joint Military Commission at all levels, in addition to their functions as delegations to the Four-Party Joint Military Commission.

(c) If, at the time the Four-Party Joint Military Commission ceases its operation in accordance with Article 16 of the Agreement, agreement has not been reached on organization of the Two-Party Joint Military Commission, the delegations of the two South Vietnamese parties serving with the Four-Party Joint Military Commission at all levels shall continue temporarily to work together as a provisional two-party joint military commission and to assume the tasks of the Two-Party Joint Military Commission at all levels until the Two-Party Joint Military Commission becomes operational.

Article 13

In application of the principle of unanimity, the Joint Military Commissions shall have no chairman, and meetings shall be convened at the request of any representative. The Joint Military Commissions shall adopt working procedures appropriate for the effective discharge of their functions and responsibilities.

Article 14

The Joint Military Commissions and the International Commission of Control and Supervision shall closely cooperate with and assist each other in carrying out their respective functions. Each Joint Military Commission shall inform the International Commission about the implementation of those provisions of the Agreement for which that Joint Military Commission has responsibility and which are within the competence of the International Commission. Each Joint Military Commission may request the International Commission to carry out specific observation activities.

Article 15

The Central Four-Party Joint Military Commission shall begin operating twenty-four hours after the cease-fire comes into force. The Regional Four-Party Joint Military Commissions shall begin operating forty-eight hours after the cease-fire comes into force. The joint military teams based at the places listed in Article 11 (c) of this Protocol shall begin operating no later than fifteen days after the cease-fire comes into force. The delegations of the two South Vietnamese parties shall simultaneously begin to assume the tasks of the Two-Party Joint Military Commission as provided in Article 12 of this Protocol.

Article 16

(a) The parties shall provide full protection and all necessary assistance and cooperation to the Joint Military Commissions at all levels, in the discharge of their tasks.

(b) The Joint Military Commissions and their personnel, while carrying out their tasks, shall enjoy privileges and immunities equivalent to those accorded diplomatic missions and diplomatic agents.

(c) The personnel of the Joint Military Commissions may carry pistols and wear special insignia decided upon by each Central Joint Military Commission. The personnel of each party while guarding Commission installations or equipment may be authorized to carry other individual small arms, as determined by each Central Joint Military Commission.

Article 17

(a) The delegation of each party to the Four-Party Joint Military Commission and the Two-Party Joint Military Commission shall have its own offices, communications, logistics and transportation means, including aircraft when necessary.

(b) Each party, in its areas of control shall provide appropriate office and accommodation facilities to the Four-Party Joint Military Commission and the Two-Party Joint Military Commission at all levels.

(c) The parties shall endeavor to provide to the Four-Party Joint Military Commission and the Two-Party Joint Military Commission, by means of loan, lease, or gift, the common means of operation, including equipment for communication, supply, and transport, including aircraft when necessary. The Joint Military Commissions may purchase from any source necessary facilities, equipment, and services which are not supplied by the parties. The Joint Military Commissions shall possess and use these facilities and this equipment.

(d) The facilities and the equipment for common use mentioned above shall be returned to the parties when the Joint Military Commissions have ended their activities.

Article 18

The common expenses of the Four-Party Joint Military Commission shall be borne equally by the four parties, and the common expenses of the Two-Party Joint Military Commission in South Vietnam shall be borne equally by these two parties.

Article 19

This Protocol shall enter into force upon signature by plenipotentiary representatives of all the parties participating in the Paris Conference on Vietnam. It shall be strictly implemented by all the parties concerned.

DONE in Paris this twenty-seventh day of January, One Thousand Nine Hundred and Seventy-Three, in Vietnamese and English. The Vietnamese and English texts are official and equally authentic.

[Separate Numbered Page]

For the Government of the United States of America :

WILLIAM P. ROGERS,
Secretary of State.

For the Government of the Republic of Vietnam :

TRAN VAN LAM,
Minister for Foreign Affairs.

[Separate Numbered Page]

For the Government of the Democratic Republic of Vietnam :

NGUYEN DUY TRINH,
Minister for Foreign Affairs.

For the Provisional Revolutionary Government of the Republic of South Vietnam :

NGUYEN THI BINH,
Minister for Foreign Affairs.

PROTOCOL TO THE AGREEMENT ON ENDING THE WAR AND RESTORING PEACE IN VIETNAM CONCERNING THE CEASE-FIRE IN SOUTH VIETNAM AND THE JOINT MILITARY COMMISSIONS

The Government of the United States of America, with the concurrence of the Government of the Republic of Vietnam,

The Government of the Democratic Republic of Vietnam, with the concurrence of the Provisional Revolutionary Government of the Republic of South Vietnam,

In implementation of the first paragraph of Article 2, Article 3, Article 5, Article 6, Article 16 and Article 17 of the Agreement on Ending the War and

Restoring Peace in Vietnam signed on this date which provide for the cease-fire in South Vietnam and the establishment of a Four-Party Joint Military Commission and a Two-Party Joint Military Commission,

Have agreed as follows:

[Text of Protocol Articles 1–18 same as above]

Article 19

The Protocol to the Paris Agreement on Ending the War and Restoring Peace in Vietnam concerning the Cease-fire in South Vietnam and the Joint Military Commissions shall enter into force upon signature of this document by the Secretary of State of the Government of the United States of America and the Minister for Foreign Affairs of the Government of the Democratic Republic of Vietnam, and upon signature of a document in the same terms by the Secretary of State of the Government of the United States of America, the Minister for Foreign Affairs of the Government of the Republic of Vietnam, the Minister for Foreign Affairs of the Government of the Democratic Republic of Vietnam, and the Minister for Foreign Affairs of the Provisional Revolutionary Government of the Republic of South Vietnam. The Protocol shall be strictly implemented by all the parties concerned.

DONE in Paris this twenty-seventh day of January, One Thousand Nine Hundred and Seventy-Three, in Vietnamese and English. The Vietnamese and English texts are official and equally authentic.

For the Government of the United States of America:

WILLIAM P. ROGERS,
Secretary of State.

For the Government of the Republic of Vietnam:

NGUYEN DUY TRINH,
Minister for Foreign Affairs.

Protocol on Mine Clearing in North Vietnam

[White House press release dated January 24]

PROTOCOL TO THE AGREEMENT ON ENDING THE WAR AND RESTORING PEACE IN VIETNAM CONCERNING THE REMOVAL, PERMANENT DEACTIVATION, OR DESTRUCTION OF MINES IN THE TERRITORIAL WATERS, PORTS, HARBORS, AND WATERWAYS OF THE DEMOCRATIC REPUBLIC OF VIETNAM

The Government of the United States of America,

The Government of the Democratic Republic of Vietnam,

In implementation of the second paragraph of Article 2 of the Agreement on Ending the War and Restoring Peace in Vietnam signed on this date,

Have agreed as follows:

Article 1

The United States shall clear all the mines it has placed in the territorial waters, ports, harbors, and waterways of the Democratic Republic of Vietnam. This mine clearing operation shall be accomplished by rendering the mines harmless through removal, permanent deactivation, or destruction.

Article 2

With a view to ensuring lasting safety for the movement of people and watercraft and the protection of important installations, mines shall, on the request of the Democratic Republic of Vietnam, be removed or destroyed in the indicated areas; and whenever their removal or destruction is impossible, mines shall be permanently deactivated and their emplacement clearly marked.

Article 3

The mine clearing operation shall begin at twenty-four hundred (2400) hours GMT on January 27, 1973. The representatives of the two parties shall consult immediately on relevant factors and agree upon the earliest possible target date for the completion of the work.

Article 4

The mine clearing operation shall be conducted in accordance with priorities and timing agreed upon by the two parties. For this purpose, representatives of the two parties shall meet at an early date to reach agreement on a program and a plan of implementation. To this end :

(a) The United States shall provide its plan for mine clearing operations, including maps of the minefields and information concerning the types, numbers and properties of the mines ;

(b) The Democratic Republic of Vietnam shall provide all available maps and hydrographic charts and indicate the mined places and all other potential hazards to the mine clearing operations that the Democratic Republic of Vietnam is aware of ;

(c) The two parties shall agree on the timing of implementation of each segment of the plan and provide timely notice to the public at least forty-eight hours in advance of the beginning of mine clearing operations for that segment.

Article 5

The United States shall be responsible for the mine clearance on inland waterways of the Democratic Republic of Vietnam. The Democratic Republic of Vietnam shall, to the full extent of its capabilities, actively participate in the mine clearance with the means of surveying, removal and destruction and technical advice supplied by the United States.

Article 6

With a view to ensuring the safe movement of people and watercraft on waterways and at sea, the United States shall in the mine clearing process supply timely information about the progress of mine clearing in each area, and about the remaining mines to be destroyed. The United States shall issue a communique when the operations have been concluded.

Article 7

In conducting mine clearing operations, the U.S. personnel engaged in these operations shall respect the sovereignty of the Democratic Republic of Vietnam and shall engage in no activities inconsistent with the Agreement on Ending the War and Restoring Peace in Vietnam and this Protocol. The U.S. personnel engaged in the mine clearing operations shall be immune from the jurisdiction of the Democratic Republic of Vietnam for the duration of the mine clearing operations.

The Democratic Republic of Vietnam shall ensure the safety of the U.S. personnel for the duration of their mine clearing activities on the territory of the Democratic Republic of Vietnam, and shall provide this personnel with all possible assistance and the means needed in the Democratic Republic of Vietnam that have been agreed upon by the two parties.

Article 8

This Protocol to the Paris Agreement on Ending the War and Restoring Peace in Vietnam shall enter into force upon signature by the Secretary of State of the Government of the United States of America and the Minister for Foreign Affairs of the Government of the Democratic Republic of Vietnam. It shall be strictly implemented by the two parties.

Done in Paris this twenty-seventh day of January, One Thousand Nine Hundred and Seventy-Three, in Vietnamese and English. The Vietnamese and English texts are official and equally authentic.

For the Government of the United States of America :

WILLIAM P. ROGERS,
Secretary of State.

For the Government of the Democratic Republic of Vietnam :

NGUYEN DUY TRINH,
Minister for Foreign Affairs.

UNITED STATES–NORTH VIETNAM COMMUNIQUE, FEBRUARY 14, 1973 [1]

Dr. Henry A. Kissinger, Assistant to the President of the United States, arrived in Hanoi on February 10, 1973, and left Hanoi on February 13, 1973. He was accompanied by Mr. Herbert G. Klein, Director of Communications for the Executive Branch, Ambassador William H. Sullivan, Deputy Assistant Secretary of State, and other American officials.

During his stay in Hanoi, Dr. Henry A. Kissinger was received by Premier Pham Van Dong, Special Advisor Le Duc Tho, and Vice Premier Nguyen Duy Trinh. The DRVN side and the U.S. side had frank, serious, and constructive exchanges of views on the implementation of the agreement on ending the war and restoring peace in Vietnam which was signed in Paris on January 27, 1973, as well as post-war relations between the Democratic Republic of Vietnam and the United States, and other subjects of mutual concern. Special Advisor Le Duc Tho and Dr. Kissinger also held discussions in a continuation of their meetings which took place in Paris during the past four years. In addition to these working sessions, Dr. Kissinger and his party visited a number of points of interest in Hanoi.

The two sides carefully reviewed the implementation of the Paris Agreement on Vietnam in the recent period. They discussed various imperative measures which should be taken to improve and expedite the implementation of the agreement, and also agreed that they would continue to have periodic exchanges of views in order to ensure that the agreement and its protocols are strictly and scrupulously implemented, as the signatories have undertaken.

The two sides welcomed the discussions between the two South Vietnamese parties for the purpose of carrying out the provisions concerning self-determination in South Vietnam, in accordance with the stipulations of the Paris Agreement on Vietnam.

The Democratic Republic of Vietnam and the United States declared that the full and scrupulous implementation of the Paris Agreement on Vietnam would positively contribute to the cause of peace in Indochina and Southeast Asia on the basis of strict respect for the independence and neutrality of the countries in this region.

The two sides reaffirmed that the problems existing between the Indochinese countries should be settled by the Indochinese parties on the basis of respect for each other's independence, sovereignty, and territorial integrity, and non-interference in each other's internal affairs. They welcomed the negotiations between the parties in Laos, which are intended to produce a peaceful settlement in that country.

The two sides exchanged views on the manner in which the United States will contribute to healing the wounds of war and to post-war economic reconstruction in North Vietnam. They agreed to establish a DRVN–U.S. Joint Economic Commission. This Commission, which will be composed of an equal number of representatives from each side, will be charged with the task of developing the economic relations between the Democratic Republic of Vietnam and the United States.

The two sides also exchanged views on the convening of International Conference on Vietnam, as provided for in Article 19 of the Paris Agreement on Vietnam. They will continue their consultations with the other participants in the conference so as to prepare the ground for a successful meeting.

The two sides considered the post-war relationship between the Democratic Republic of Vietnam and the United States, and examined concrete steps which can be taken to normalize the relations between the two countries. They agreed on certain general principles which should govern their mutual relations.

—All provisions of the Paris Agreement on Vietnam and its protocols should be fully and scrupulously implemented.

—The Democratic Republic of Vietnam and the United States should strive for a new relationship based on respect for each other's independence and sovereignty, non-interference in each other's internal affairs, equality and mutual benefit.

—The normalization of the relations between the Democratic Republic of Vietnam and the United States will help to ensure stable peace in Vietnam and contribute to the cause of peace in Indochina and Southeast Asia.

Dr. Kissinger and his party expressed warm appreciation for the hospitality extended by the Democratic Republic of Vietnam. Both sides hope that this visit will mark the beginning of new bilateral relations.

---

[1] Department of State Bulletin, Mar. 5, 1973, pp. 262–263.

97. DECLARATION OF THE INTERNATIONAL CONFERENCE ON VIET-NAM [1]

The Government of the United States of America;
The Government of the French Republic;
The Provisional Revolutionary Government of the Republic of South Viet-Nam;
The Government of the Hungarian People's Republic;
The Government of the Republic of Indonesia;
The Government of the Polish People's Republic;
The Government of the Democratic Republic of Viet-Nam;
The Government of the United Kingdom of Great Britain and Northern Ireland;
The Government of the Republic of Viet-Nam;
The Government of the Union of Soviet Socialist Republics;
The Government of Canada; and
The Government of the People's Republic of China;
In the presence of the Secretary-General of the United Nations;

With a view to acknowledging the signed Agreements; guaranteeing the end-ing of the war, the maintenance of peace in Viet-Nam, the respect of the Viet-namese people's fundamental national rights, and the South Vietnamese people's right to self-determination; and contributing to and guaranteeing peace in Indochina;

Have agreed on the following provisions, and undertake to respect and imple-ment them;

Article 1

The Parties to this Act solemnly acknowledge, express their approval of, and support the Paris Agreement on Ending the War and Restoring Peace in Viet-Nam signed in Paris on January 27, 1973, and the four Protocols to the Agree-ment signed on the same date (hereinafter referred to respectively as the Agreement and the Protocols).

Article 2

The Agreement responds to the aspirations and fundamental national rights of the Vietnamese people, *i.e.*, the independence, sovereignty, unity, and terri-torial integrity of Viet-Nam, to the right of the South Vietnamese people to self-determination, and to the earnest desire for peace shared by all countries in the world. The Agreement constitutes a major contribution to peace, self-determination, national independence, and the improvement of relations among countries. The Agreement and the Protocols should be strictly respected and scrupulously implemented.

Article 3

The Parties to this Act solemnly acknowledge the commitments by the parties to the Agreement and the Protocols to strictly respect and scrupulously imple-men the Agreement and the Protocols.

Article 4

The Parties to this Act solemnly recognize and strictly respect the funda-mental national rights of the Vietnamese people, *i.e.*, the independence, sover-eignty, unity, and territorial integrity of Viet-Nam, as well as the right of the South Vietnamese people to self-determination. The Parties to this Act shall strictly respect the Agreement and the Protocols by refraining from any action at variance with their provisions.

Article 5

For the sake of a durable peace in Viet-Nam, the Parties to this Act call on all countries to strictly respect the fundamental national rights of the Viet-namese people, *i.e.*, the independence, sovereignty, unity, and territorial integrity of Viet-Nam and the right of the South Vietnamese people to self-determination and to strictly respect the Agreement and the Protocols by refraining from any action at variance with their provisions.

Article 6

(a) The four parties to the Agreement or the two South Vietnamese parties may, either individually or through joint action, inform the other Parties to

[1] Department of State Press Release, Mar. 5, 1973.

this Act about the implementation of the Agreement and the Protocols. Since the reports and views submitted by the International Commission of Control and Supervision concerning the control and supervision of the implementation of those provisions of the Agreement and the Protocols which are within the tasks of the Commission will be sent to either the four parties signatory to the Agreement or to the two South Vietnamese parties, those parties shall be responsible, either individually or through joint action, for forwarding them promptly to the other Parties to this Act.

(b) The four parties to the Agreement or the two South Vietnamese parties shall also, either individually or through joint action, forward this information and these reports and views to the other participant in the International Conference on Viet-Nam for his information.

Article 7

(a) In the event of a violation of the Agreement or the Protocols which threatens the peace, the independence, sovereignty, unity, or territorial integrity of Viet-Nam, or the right of the South Vietnamese people to self-determination, the parties signatory to the Agreement and the Protocols shall, either individually or jointly, consult with the other Parties to this Act with a view to determining necessary remedial measures.

(b) The International Conference on Viet-Nam shall be reconvened upon a joint request by the Government of the United States of America and the Government of the Democratic Republic of Viet-Nam on behalf of the parties signatory to the Agreement or upon a request by six or more of the Parties to this Act.

Article 8

With a view to contributing to and guaranteeing peace in Indochina, the Parties to this Act acknowledge the commitment of the parties to the Agreement to respect the independence, sovereignty, unity, territorial integrity, and neutrality of Cambodia and Laos as stipulated in the Agreement, agree also to respect them and to refrain from any action at variance with them, and call on other countries to do the same.

Article 9

This Act shall enter into force upon signature by plenipotentiary representatives of all twelve Parties and shall be strictly implemented by all the Parties. Signature of this Act does not constitute recognition of any Party in any case in which it has not previously been accorded.

Done in twelve copies in Paris this second day of March, One Thousand Nine Hundred and Seventy-Three, in English, French, Russian, Vietnamese, and Chinese. All texts are equally authentic.

For the Government of the United States of America:
WILLIAM P. ROGERS,
The Secretary of State.

For the Government of the French Republic:
MAURICE SCHUMANN,
The Minister for Foreign Affairs.

For the Provisional Revolutionary Government of the Republic of South Viet–Nam:
NGUYEN THI BINH,
The Minister for Foreign Affairs.

For the Government of the Hungarian People's Republic:
JANOS PETER,
The Minister for Foreign Affairs.

For the Government of the Republic of Indonesia:
ADAM MALIK,
The Minister for Foreign Affairs.

For the Government of the Polish People's Republic:
STEFAN OLSZOWSKI,
The Minister for Foreign Affairs.

For the Government of the Democratic Republic of Viet-Nam:

NGUYEN DUY TRINH,
The Minister for Foreign Affairs.

For the Government of the United Kingdom of Great Britain and Northern Ireland:

ALEC DOUGLAS-HOME,
The Secretary of State for Foreign and Commonwealth Affairs.

For the Government of the Republic of Viet-Nam:

TRAN VAN LAM,
The Minister for Foreign Affairs.

For the Government of the Union of Soviet Socialist Republics:

ANDREI A. GROMYKO,
The Minister for Foreign Affairs.

For the Government of Canada:

MITCHELL SHARP,
The Secretary of State for External Affairs.

For the Government of the People's Republic of China:

CHI PENG-FEI,
The Minister for Foreign Affairs.

INDEX